Writing Research Papers

A Complete Guide

Eighth Edition

James D. Lester

Austin Peay State University

lishers

3/99

ACKNOWLEDGMENTS **Pages 15, 16** From *Out of the Storm* by Noah André Trudeau. Copyright © 1994 by Noah André Trudeau. Reprinted by permission of Little Brown and Company. **P.17** "Civil War" by Richard N. Current, *Collier's Encyclopedia*, Vol. 6, page 548. Copyright © 1994 by P. F. Collier, L. P. Reprinted by permission. **P.18** "Dyslexia" and "Television Advertising" from *Social Sciences Index*, June 1994, Vol. 21, No. 1. Reprinted by permission of the H. W. Wilson Company. **P.32** Index citation, "What is reality? The thin and blurring line" by Steve McClellan from The Business CollectionTM. Copyright © 1994 Information Access Company. Reprinted by permission. **P.34** "Dyslexia" and "Television Advertising" from *Social Sciences Index*, June 1994, Vol. 21, No. 1. Reprinted by permission of the H. W. Wilson Company. **P.37** Index citation, "United States Civil War" from Expanded Academic IndexTM. Copyright © 1994 Information Access Company. Reprinted by permission. **P.43** Printout from UNCOVER. Reprinted by permission. **P.45** From *Bibliographic Index: A Cumulative Bibliography of Bibliographies*, April 1994, page 205. Reprinted by permission of the H. W. Wilson Company. **P.47** Excerpt from "Television in Politics." Reprinted with permission of R. R. Bowker, a Reed Reference Publishing Company, from *Books in Print Subject Guide 1993-1994*, Vol. 4. Copyright © 1993 by Reed Elsevier Inc. **P.49** Reprinted from *Magill's Bibliography of Literary Criticism*, Vol. 2, page 709. By permission of the publisher, Salem Press, Inc. Copyright © 1979 by Frank Magill. **P.50** "Frost, Robert (1874-1963)." Reprinted by permission of the Modern Language Association of America from *1983 MLA International Bibliography of Books and Articles on the Modern Languages and Literatures*. Copyright © 1983 by the Modern Language Association of America. **P.51** From *Encyclopedia of Psychology*, 2nd ed., Vol.1 edited by Raymond J. Corsini. Reprinted by permission of John Wiley & Sons, Inc. **P.51** From *Out of the Storm* by Noah André Trudeau. Copyright © 1994 by Noah André Trudeau. Reprinted by permission of Little, Brown and Company. **P.52** From The *Reader's Guide to Periodical Literature (Unabridged)*, Vol. 94, No. 5, July 1994, page 242. Reprinted by permission of The H. W. Wilson Company. **P.54** From *Psychological Abstracts*, December 1994, Vol. 81, No. 12. Copyright © 1994 by the American Psychological Association, Inc. Reprinted by permission of the American Psychological Association, Inc. **P.55, 56** "Children" entries from *Dissertation Abstracts International*. The dissertation titles and abstracts contained here are published with permission of University Microfilms, Inc., publishers of *Dissertation Abstracts International* (copyright © 1991 by University Microfilms, Inc.) and may not be reproduced without their prior permission. **P.57** "Faulkner, William," "Fawcett, Farrah," and "Feiffer, Jules" from *Biography Index*, May 1991. Reprinted by permission of the H. W. Wilson Company. **P.58** From "Anne Sexton" by Susan Resnick Parr from *American Writers*, Supplement II, Part 2, by A. Walton Litz, editor in chief, pages 669-700. Copyright © 1981 Charles Scribner's Sons. Reprinted with permission of Simon & Schuster Macmillan. **P.59** "Water" and "Water Pollution" from *The Wall Street Journal Index*, April-June 1994. Reprinted by permission of the Wall Street Journal Index. Copyright © 1994 by Dow Jones & Company, Inc. All rights reserved worldwide. **P.61** The *CQ Researcher*, April 29, 1994. Reprinted by permission of Congressional Quarterly. **P.62** *Monthly Catalog of United States Government Publications*, May 1991, No. 1171. Cataloging Branch, Library Division, Library Programs Service, Superintendent of Documents, U.S. Government Printing Office, Washington, DC, 1991. **P.63** From *PAIS International in Print*, January-April 1994, Vol. 4, No. 4, page 75. Reprinted by permission. **P.64** "King, Martin Luther, 1929-1968," "Religion and the life of the nation," "University of Illinois Press" from *Essay and General Literature Index*, June 1991. Reprinted by permission of the H. W. Wilson Company. **P.69** Reproduced from Edition 20 of the *Dewey Decimal Classification*, published in 1989, by permission of Forest Press, a division of OCLC Online Computer Library Center, owner of copyright. **P.100, 101** From *Child Development*, April 1994. Copyright © 1994 by The Society for Research in Child Development, Inc. Reprinted by permission. **P.103** From *The Book Review Digest*, Vol. 90, No. 3, May 1994, page 163. Reprinted by permission of The H. W. Wilson Company. **P.104, 105** "The Suffocating Politics of Pollution" by Betsy Carpenter in *U.S. News & World Report*, June 20, 1994. Copyright © 1994 by U.S. News & World Report. Reprinted by permission. **P.107** From B. N. Raina, "Dickinson's 'Because I Could Not Stop for Death.' " *The Explicator*, Vol. 43, No. 4, pages 11-12, 1985. Reprinted with permission of the Helen Dwight Reid Educational Foundation. Published by Heldref Publications, 1319 Eighteenth Street N.W., Washington, DC 20036-1802. Copyright © 1985. **P.109** "AIDS Education May Breed Intolerance" by Philip Yam, from *Scientific American*, September 1991. Reprinted with permission. Copyright © by Scientific American, Inc. All rights reserved. **P.125** From "The Love Song of J. Alfred Prufrock" by T. S. Eliot. Reprinted by permission of Faber & Faber, Ltd. **P.186** "Parenthood" from *USA Today*, September 1990. Copyright © 1990 USA Today. Reprinted with permission. **P.187** "The Skaters" by John Gould Fletcher. **P.227** From "Cognitive Aspects of Psychomotor Performance" by Edwin A. Locke and Judith F. Bryan in *Journal of Applied Psychology*, Vol. 50, 1966. Copyright © 1966 by the American Psychological Association. Reprinted by permission of the author. **P.228** Chart from Carmen J. Finley, Jack M. Thompson, and Alberta Cognata, "Stability of the California Short Form Test of Mental Maturity: Grades 3, 5, and 7" *California Journal of Educational Research* 17 September(1966):165. Reprinted by permission of the *Educational Research Quarterly*. **P.229** From "Toxicity of Clostridium Histolyticum" by Nishida and Imaizumi, *Journal of Bacteriology*, February 1966. Reprinted by permission of the American Society for Microbiology. **P.324** Figure, "Psychiatrists' Attitudes Toward Etiological Theories of Infantile Autism" from "A National Survey of Mental Health Professionals Concerning the Causes of Early Infantile Autism" by B. J. Gallagher, B. J. Jones, and Meoghan Byrne in *Journal of Clinical Psychology* 46, 1990, page 936. Reprinted by permission of Clinical Psychology Publishing Company, Inc., and the author. **P.332** Figure from "Early Recognition of Autism" by Julie Osterling and Geraldine Dawson in *Journal of Autism and Developmental Disorders*, Vol. 24, No. 3, June 1994. Reprinted by permission of Plenum Publishing Corporation and the author.

Writing Research Papers: A Complete Guide, Eighth Edition

Copyright © 1996 by HarperCollins College Publishers

HarperCollins® and ® are registered trademarks of HarperCollins Publishers Inc.

ISBN (Student Edition) 0-673-99449-X, (Instructor's Edition) 0-673-99450-3

97 98 9 8 7 6 5

Contents

Preface vi
Introduction 1

1 *Finding a Topic* 5

1a Generating Ideas for a Research Paper 6
1b Using a Computer Search to Discover a Good Topic 11
1c Using Printed Materials to Discover and Evaluate a Topic 15
1d Drafting a Research Proposal 18
1e Narrowing the General Subject to a Specific Topic 24

2 *Gathering Data* 27

2a Learning the Organization of Your Library 29
2b Developing a Working Bibliography 31
2c The Electronic Library: Using a Computer Search 35
2d Searching the Printed Bibliographies 45
2e Searching the Printed Indexes 51
2f Searching the Indexes to Federal Government Documents 61
2g Searching For Essays Within Books 64
2h Using the Microforms 65
2i Using the Printed Catalog Cards 65
2j Collecting Data Outside the Library 71

3 *Organizing Ideas and Setting Goals* 81

3a Charting a Direction and Setting Goals 81
3b Using General Models (Paradigms) to Stimulate Your Note Taking 87
3c Writing a Formal Outline 90

4   *Finding and Reading the Best Sources* 97

4a Finding the Best Source Materials 97
4b Deciding Whether to Read All or Part of a Source 013
4c Responding to the Sources 106
4d Selecting a Mix of Both Primary and Secondary Sources 110
4e Preparing an Annotated Bibliography 112
4f Preparing a Review of the Literature on a Topic 114

5   *Writing Notes* 119

5a Creating Effective Notes 120
5b Writing Direct Quotation Notes 123
5c Writing Summary Notes 128
5d Writing Précis Notes 129
5e Writing Paraphrased Notes 134
5f Writing Personal Notes 136
5g Avoiding Plagiarism 138

6   *Writing the Paper* 145

6a Writing a Final Thesis Sentence 146
6b Writing a Title 148
6c Understanding Your Purpose and Role as a Writer 149
6d Writing with a Computer 150
6e Drafting Your Paper 154
6f Writing the Introduction of the Paper 158
6g Writing the Body of the Research Paper 163
6h Writing the Conclusion of the Research Paper 169
6i Revising the Rough Draft 172
6j Editing Before You Type the Final Manuscript 174
6k Proofreading Before the Final Computer Printout 179

7   *Blending Reference Material into Your Writing* 181

7a Blending a Reference into Your Text 182
7b Citing a Source When No Author Is Listed 184
7c Identifying Nonprint Sources That Have No Page Number 185
7d Using a Double Reference to Cite Somebody Who Has Been Quoted in a Book or Article 185
7e Citing Frequent Page References to the Same Work 187
7f Citing Material from Textbooks and Large Anthologies 187
7g Adding Extra Information to In-Text Citations 189
7h Punctuating Citations Properly and with Consistency 191
7i Indenting Long Quotations of Prose and Poetry 193
7j Altering Initial Capitals in Some Quoted Matter 195
7k Using Ellipsis Points to Omit Portions of Quoted Matter 196
7l Using Brackets to Insert Your Words Inside Quoted Matter 198

8 *Handling Format* 201

   8a Preparing the Final Manuscript in MLA Style 201
   8b Glossary: Techniques for Preparing the Manuscript in MLA Style 205
   8c Sample Paper: A Short Essay with Documentation 240
   8d Sample Paper: A Formal Research Paper 246

9 *Works Cited: MLA Style* 265

   9a Format for the Works Cited Page 266
   9b Bibliographic Form: Books 268
   9c Bibliographic Form: Periodicals 282
   9d Bibliographic Form: Newspapers 287
   9e Bibliographic Form: Government Documents 289
   9f Electronic Sources (CD-ROM, Internet, E-Mail, Databases 291
   9g Bibliographic Form: Other Sources 298

10 *Using APA Style* 307

   10a Writing in the Proper Tense for an APA-Styled Paper 307
   10b Using In-Text Citations in APA Style 309
   10c Preparing a Working Draft or Publishing the Manuscript 312
   10d Preparing the List of References 313
   10e Writing the Abstract 318
   10f Sample Paper in APA Style 318

11 *Form and Style for Other Disciplines* 333

   11a Using the Name and Year System 334
   11b Using the Number System 345
   11c Using the Footnote System 358

   Appendix Reference Sources 365
   Index 398

Preface

Several factors have influenced the development of the eighth edition of *Writing Research Papers: A Complete Guide*. In particular, I have adjusted the recommendations on form and style to meet the demands of three newly revised style guides, one by the Modern Language Association, one by the American Psychological Association, and one by the Council of Biology Editors. In addition, I have changed the text's prevailing assumptions about the work habits of students who write research papers in this age of the computer.

New Standards for the MLA Style

The Modern Language Association has published the fourth edition (1995) of its *MLA Handbook for Writers of Research Papers*, edited by Joseph Gibaldi. Because we have always conformed to the guidelines set forth by the Modern Language Association, an update to the new standards has been necessary. First, the new MLA handbook has added extensively to the rules for citing electronic sources. The difficulty in this area, of course, is that electronic sources do not remain stable. Thus a source cited by a student on one day may be altered within days or weeks. Nevertheless, we can only cite the source used and note the electronic address where the document might be available—with no guarantees to future researchers. Perhaps a minimal standard in the future will be the dating of electronic documents so that the same document, though altered in some fashion, will appear in two or three forms.

Second, although the basic works cited form for books, journal articles, and magazine articles remains unchanged, the new MLA style has altered the form of most other bibliographic citations in many subtle ways. Finally, in another major change, MLA style now requires single spacing after periods throughout research papers.

New Standards for the APA Style

The *Publication Manual of the American Psychological Association* has also appeared in a new fourth edition (1994) and its new rules are adopted here. The new APA style presents a different sort of challenge because it advocates two types of manuscripts. One is a "copy or working draft" manuscript written by professionals that will eventually become a typeset article. The other is a "final" manuscript written by authors of student papers, theses, and dissertations. To distinguish between the two, examples of both forms are given in Chapter 10, and the copy or working draft form is provided in the sample APA paper. In order to avoid confusion, instructors should specify what sort of manuscript is expected: either the copy draft or the final polished manuscript.

New Standards for the CBE Style

The Council of Biology Editors has issued a new edition (1994) of its style manual, *Scientific Style and Format: The CBE Manual for Authors, Editors, and Publishers*. This guide advocates two citation and reference styles:

1. The name and year system for general biological studies (see "Using the Name and Year System for Papers in the Biological and Earth Sciences," 338–44).
2. The number system for biomedical papers (see "Using the Number System for Papers in the Medical Sciences," 351–52, especially the list of references on 356–57).

A New Emphasis on Researching and Writing with Computers

Throughout this edition, you will see a stronger emphasis on both the student's use of electronic sources and the use of the computer to write the research paper. In past editions, my assumption has been that most students write bibliography cards, develop handwritten notes, and then type the paper. Today, with the arrival of the Information Superhighway, most students now access Infotrac, the Internet, or SilverPlatter, use the computerized Public Access Catalog, and then keyboard on a computer their bibliography list, their notes, and the various drafts of the paper. Although I have not abandoned the traditional methods, I have addressed the new technical methods for researching and writing first in each case.

As a result, almost every chapter presents the electronic method first and the traditional method second.

Plagiarism

The text devotes a full section in Chapter 5 to the problems of plagiarism. This section of the book has been reproduced in other publications because of its insightful help to the student. It explains the role of the researcher, who must cite sources honestly and accurately in order to share with the reader the fundamental scholarship of a narrow topic. Rather than taking a negative approach and merely warning students against plagiarism, the text encourages critical thinking so that students learn to assimilate ideas in their notes and to incorporate them in the manuscript in a clear, well-documented progression. It displays methods for achieving correct citations, it explains the rules, and it condemns blatant disregard for scholarly conventions. The text also explains the gray area of "common knowledge" facts.

Sample Papers

The text includes many sample papers so that students can see how to write and format their own manuscripts:

- Research proposals
- An annotated bibliography
- A review of the literature on a topic
- Abstracts in MLA and APA style

- A short essay with documentation of a few sources
- Two research papers in MLA style
- A research paper in APA style
- A research paper in the number style
- A portion of a paper in footnote style

Additional sample papers appear in the Instructor's Manual.

Collecting Data Outside the Library

Many instructors now require students to search for material outside the library. Therefore, the text features a comprehensive section on citing and documenting information from various types of sources: interviews, letters, questionnaires, local government documents, television programs, and original tests and experiments.

Supplements

The author has written an extensive *Instructor's Manual* which includes chapter-by-chapter ideas for classroom activities in addition to some forty worksheets which can be copied and used in your classroom. The Manual also includes four easily reproduced sample research papers in each of the most common styles (MLA, APA, Number, and Chicago.)

Acknowledgments

Students by the millions and instructors by the thousands have used this text in its previous seven editions. Many students and faculty members have made contributions to the quality of the book. For that I am grateful. In particular, I need to thank Patti Bracy, Marcia Thompson, Stefan Hall, and Jay Wickham for their contributions of sample research papers.

Special thanks goes to Anne May Berwind, head of Library Information Services at Austin Peay State University. She revised the list of references in the appendix and added a few annotations for selected works on the list.

Professional reviewers for the eighth edition offered many helpful ideas; they include the following: Peggy Brent, Hinds Community College; Lynn Bryce, Saint Cloud State University; Sister Elizabeth Bryson, Salve Regina University; Judith L. Burken, Kellogg Community College; Adele M. Carpenter, Lewis and Clark Community College; Mary A. Fortner, Lincoln Land Community College; Margaret Gwathmey, Skyline College; Kim Brian Lovejoy, Indiana University—Purdue University at Indianapolis; Faye J. Maclaga, Wilson Technical Community College; Alice Maclin, Dekalb College; Elizabeth R. Nelson, St. Peter's College; Grace Powell, Wenatchee Valley College; Kathleen G. Rousseau, West Virginia University; Michael W. Shurgot, South Puget Sound Community College; James Stokes, University of Wisconsin—Stevens Point; Judith Barton Williamson, Sauk Valley Community College; and Roger V. Zimmerman, Lewis and Clark Community College.

I appreciate also the support of my family, and so I thank Martha, Jim, Mark, Debbie, Caleb, and Sarah for their unending enthusiasm and encouragement.

James D. Lester

Introduction

RATIONALE FOR RESEARCH WRITING

This writing manual provides a step-by-step explanation of the process of research writing. It will encourage you to approach the assignment one step at a time—from selecting a significant and appropriate topic to producing a polished manuscript. You will develop confidence as you complete each stage of the process and begin the next one. You will become adept at several skills:

1. Narrowing your focus to a manageable topic
2. Locating source materials and taking notes
3. Analyzing, evaluating, and interpreting materials
4. Arranging and classifying materials
5. Writing the paper with a sense of purpose as well as with clarity and accuracy
6. Handling problems of quoting and properly documenting your sources

In time, you will come to understand that knowledge is not always something conveyed by experts in books and articles for you to copy onto the pages of your research papers. You must also generate new ideas about the issues related to your topic and defend your position with the weight of your argument as well as the strength of your evidence. You will want to cite certain sources because they support *your* ideas, not merely because they relate to your subject.

The creation of a long, scholarly paper seldom develops in a neat, logical progression. The work, spread over several weeks, often demands that you work both forward and backward in various starts and stops. One way to succeed is to follow the order of this text—choose a topic, gather data,

1

plan and write a draft, revise and polish the manuscript, and develop a final bibliography. Word processing makes each of these tasks easier, and this manual explains computer technology as appropriate to the task.

Chapter 1 will help you find a topic that has merit as a scholarly issue or research question. The chapter shows how to search library sources for a topic, and it helps you to:

Examine your own experience.
Reconsider your cultural background.
Evaluate issues within your favorite academic disciplines.

Chapter 2, "Gathering Data," offers you three distinct sources of research: (1) the electronic library; (2) the printed resources; and (3) information found outside the library, such as interviews, letters, lectures, or questionnaires. The arrival of the information highway has required libraries to speed up their chase along such networks as Internet and others. Therefore, a major portion of Chapter 2 serves as a nonprofessional's introduction to researching by computer.

Chapters 3, 4, and 5 will help you organize a plan, practice critical reading, and write notes. Included is a discussion of how to avoid *plagiarism,* an error of scholarship that afflicts many students who think proper scholarly credit is unnecessary or who become confused about proper placement of references.

Chapters 6 and 7 provide details about writing the paper—from title and outline to introduction, body, and conclusion. In particular, Chapter 6 will help you frame the thesis in the introduction, develop it in the body, and discuss it in the conclusion. You will also be reminded of three vital phases—revising, editing, and proofreading. Chapter 6 also includes a section on adapting your writing to the demands and the rewards of word processing. Chapter 7 explains the value of in-text citations to help you distinguish your own comments from paraphrases and quotations borrowed from the source materials.

Chapter 8 explains matters of formatting and mechanics. It shows you how to design the paper, from the title page to the Works Cited page and from underlining to proper numbering. Sample papers in MLA (Modern Language Association) style are provided on pages 240–63.

Chapter 9 explains how to write the individual bibliographic entries so that you can fully document all your sources on the Works Cited page.

Chapter 10 explains APA (American Psychological Association) style and correlates its features with MLA style. You will need to use APA style for papers in several disciplines outside the English class, such as psychology, education, political science, and sociology.

Chapter 11 explains the documentation style for disciplines other than English and psychology. It explains in detail how to document with the *name-and-year system* for papers in the social sciences, business, and the physical or biological sciences. It explains the *number system* for use with papers in the applied sciences and medical sciences. It explains the *footnote* and *endnote* systems for use with some papers in the liberal arts. Writing samples of each of these systems are provided in Chapter 11.

Finally, the Appendix contains a thorough list of reference works and journals shown alphabetically by field of study. For every discipline included, a list of study guides, the important databases, the appropriate printed bibliographies, and the most useful indexes to literature in the journals are provided. Consult it as you begin research in a specific discipline, such as drama, home economics, geology, or women's studies.

1 *Finding a Topic*

Choosing a topic for a research paper can be easy (any topic will serve) yet very complicated (an informed choice is crucial). Select a person, a person's work, or a specific thing to study—for example, President Bill Clinton, John Steinbeck's *Of Mice and Men,* or Nintendo games. Select from any area that interests you:

Current events (handguns in schools)
Education (electronic classrooms)
Social issues (the high cost of health-care services)
Science (poisonous drugs from the monkshood, or aconite, flower)

Whatever the topic, the subject for a research paper must meet three demands:

1. It must have a serious purpose, one that demands analysis of the issues, argues from a position, and explains complex details.
2. It must address the academic community, both your follow students and the faculty.
3. The thesis (or hypothesis) must be one that you can prove within the confines of the paper.

> *Note:* **Choose a topic with a built-in issue so that you can interpret the issue and cite the opinions of outside sources.**

You need not abandon a favorite topic, such as fishing at Lake Cumberland. Just be certain to give it a serious, scholarly perspective. For example:

```
The Effects of Toxic Chemicals on the Fish in Lake
Cumberland
```

Instead of a paper entitled, "The Cartoon Strip *Calvin and Hobbes*," a better topic would be:

```
The Role of Fantasy in Calvin and Hobbes
    or
Gender Issues in Calvin and Hobbes
```

The next topic suggests a built-in issue:

```
The Addiction of Some People to Video Games
```

Two questions arise from this last topic: Do certain children and adults get addicted to video games? If so, what are the results?

Another controversial issue is whether talk shows are objective in their presentation of news and other factual data. An appropriate title for a paper on this topic might be:

```
Television Talk Shows and Objectivity
```

When your topic addresses a problem or raises an issue, you have a reason to:

Examine specific sources in the library.
Share your point of view with the reader.
Write a meaningful conclusion.

Start by personally reflecting on your interests (see Section 1a, which follows). If that doesn't produce a good topic, use a computer search at the library (see Section 1b). If computers are unavailable, use the library's printed sources to search out a topic (see Section 1c).

1a   GENERATING IDEAS FOR A RESEARCH PAPER

Three techniques will help you with topic selection before you enter the library:

1. Reflect on your personal experiences to find a topic that touches your lifestyle or career ambitions.
2. Talk with other people because collaborative learning can broaden your vision of the issues.
3. Speculate about the subject, and discover ideas by listing issues, asking questions, engaging in freewriting, and utilizing other techniques.

These three steps will not only help you find a primary topic but also help you produce a secondary list of issues, terms, questions, and a few written notes.

Using Personal Experience for Topic Discovery

Most people have special interests as demonstrated by their selections for television viewing, their choice of magazines, and their clubs and activities. One of these three techniques can serve you in selecting a topic:

1. Combine a personal topic with some aspect of your academic studies. For example:
   a. A personal interest in skiing combined with an academic study of sports medicine might yield a topic entitled "Therapy for Torn Ligaments."
   b. An interest in children combined with a study of childhood psychology might lead to a topic entitled "Children Know More Than We Think."
   c. Concern about your personal checkbook combined with a study of government economic policies might generate a paper entitled "Deficit Spending: The Ultimate Payment."
   d. The contaminated well water on your family's farm combined with a study of chemical toxins might yield a topic entitled "The Poisoning of Underground Water Tables."

2. Use your career interests to narrow a general subject to a specific topic. For instance, assume that three writers all select the same general subject—latchkey children:
   a. Student 1, who plans a career in law enforcement, focuses on the criminal dangers for latchkey children, who must return from school to empty houses and apartments.
   b. Student 2, who plans a career in communication, investigates television programming during after-school hours for the lonely child.
   c. Student 3, who is majoring in economics, conducts a cost-benefit analysis of different child-care options for school children.

The three writers have a personal stake in the issues addressed, and each may arrive at different conclusions about the general topic of latchkey children.

3. Let your cultural background prompt you toward detailed research into your roots, your culture, and the mythology and history of your ethnic background. For example, four students might develop these topics:
   a. The Indian Wars from the Native American's point of view
   b. Chinese theories on the roles of women
   c. Bicultural experiences of Hispanic students
   d. Pride as a motivator for the behavior of young Afro-Americans

Caution: Do not become too emotional about your personal response to your heritage; research writing must maintain its objectivity.

Talking with Others to Find a Subject

As some researchers do, you may need to start your research sitting on a park bench with a friend or across the coffee table from a colleague or relative. Ask people in your school and community for ideas and topics that need investigation, and allow them to respond to your questions. Listen to what they say.

Interviews

One writer wanted to write a paper that argued for more liberal arts courses in high-school curriculums. Before spending hours reading sources, however, she talked by phone with her former high school teachers. She discovered that a liberal arts curriculum was in place; the problem was something different—how to motivate students toward liberal arts courses in a marketplace that demands utilitarian skills, such as typing, auto mechanics, and computer programming. In the end, the writer developed a different sort of paper, all because she took time to consult with others.

Collaborative Learning

Listen to the advice of your peers in group learning sessions.

1. Consult with three or four students about your topic.
2. Listen to the concerns of others.
3. Take careful notes.
4. Adjust your research accordingly.

Your peers may suggest additional explanations and definitions, or they may argue for stronger, more detailed arguments.

Speculating About Your Subject to Discover Ideas

At some point you may need to sit back, relax, and use your imagination to contemplate the issues. Out of meditation may come topics and subtopics worthy of investigation. Ideas can be generated in these ways:

Keeping a Research Journal

Unlike a diary of personal thoughts about your daily activities or a journal of creative ideas (poems, stories, or scenarios), the research journal is a collection of ideas and materials on specific issues. You can maintain the journal on your computer or in a notebook. In it should be listed issues, questions, notes, bits of freewriting (see the following paragraph), and photocopied materials. In effect, you can keep all your initial ideas and materials in one notebook rather than on cards or individual sheets. If you buy a notebook that has pockets on the inside covers, you will have a place to store any miscellaneous items. If you know the computer procedures, you can scan source materials and incorporate them directly into your files.

Freewriting

To free write, merely focus on a topic and write whatever comes to mind. Continue writing with your mind on the topic. Do not worry about grammar, style, or penmanship. The result? You have started writing. Once your brain is engaged, ideas will flow forth. The exercise requires nonstop writing for a page or so to develop valuable phrases, comparisons, episodes, and specific thoughts that help focus issues of concern. Note this brief example:

```
     Global communication networks seem to be changing
the world order and the attitudes of the common people
who now have a better grasp of events at home and
abroad. News networks were able to respond instantly
when armed forces attacked Baghdad in the gulf war, when
the voting booths opened in South Africa, and when
Haiti's military junta refused to recognize the results
of a free election. International communication networks
like CNN now link us into a global community. Dictators
cannot perform brazen acts of violence and oppression
without the focus of television cameras and instant
transmission world-wide. Immediate response by the world
to an act of violence can usually end it before the
power structure can get entrenched.—Emmie Alexander
```

This freewriting has set the path for this writer's investigation into world politics and the glare of the television cameras.

Listing Key Words

During your search for a subject, keep a sharp eye out for fundamental terms and concepts that might focus the direction of your research. One student, while considering a topic for his Native American studies course, listed several terms and phrases about oral traditions of the Blackfoot tribe:

boasting	invoking spirits	singing
making medicine	storytelling	reciting history
war chants	jokes and humor	

The key words set the stage for writing the rough outline for a paper, as explained in the next paragraph.

Arranging Key Words into a Rough Outline

As you develop ideas and begin listing key terms and subtopics, you should recognize the hierarchy of major and minor issues.

```
                Native American Oral Traditions
Chanting                  Narrating          Singing
    for war                   history            hymns
    for good health           stories            folk songs
    for religion              jokes
                              boasts
```

This arrangement shows an initial ranking of ideas, one that can and should change during the research process.

Clustering

Another method for discovering the hierarchy of your primary topics and subtopics is to cluster ideas around a central subject. The cluster of related topics can generate a multitude of ideas, which are all joined and interconnected, as shown in the illustration shown here:

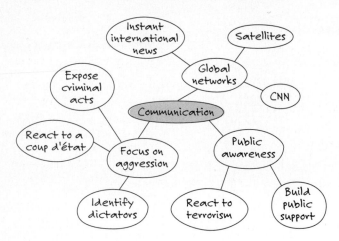

Asking Questions

Stretch your imagination with questions. They can focus your attention on primary issues and help you frame a workable topic. Having read Henry Thoreau's essay "Civil Disobedience," one writer asked:

```
What is civil disobedience?

Is dissent legal? Is it moral? Is it patriotic?

Is dissent a liberal or a conservative activity?

Should the government encourage or stifle dissent?

Is passive resistance effective?
```

Answering the questions can lead the writer to a central issue and even produce a thesis statement to drive the entire project.

Another student framed questions by using the rhetorical modes, as shown here:

COMPARISON   How does a state lottery compare with
             horse racing?

DEFINITION   What is a lottery in legal terms? in
             religious terms?

CAUSE AND EFFECT   What are the consequences of a state
                   lottery on funding for education,
                   highways, prisons, and social programs?

PROCESS   How are winnings distributed?

CLASSIFICATION   What types of lotteries exist, and which
                 are available in this state?

EVALUATION   What is the value of a lottery to the
             average citizen? What are the
             disadvantages?

Any one of these questions can identify a key issue worthy of research.

A third student framed questions for a study across the curriculum on the subject of sports gambling:

ECONOMICS   Does sports gambling benefit a college's
             athletic budget? the national economy?

PSYCHOLOGY   What is the effect of gambling on the mental
             attitude of the college athlete who knows
             huge sums of money hang in the balance on
             his or her performance?

HISTORY   Does gambling on sporting events have an
             identifiable tradition?

SOCIOLOGY   What compulsion in human nature prompts
             people to gamble on athletic prowess?

Such questions help to identify a working topic.

1b   USING A COMPUTER SEARCH TO DISCOVER A GOOD TOPIC

The new computer technology can list and classify topics quickly, as explained in this section.

Using the Public Access Catalog (PAC)

Most college libraries now have a *Public Access Catalog* (PAC), which is a computer version of the card catalog files. Used properly early in your work, it can guide you quickly from general subjects to subtopics and finally to specific books. To use the PAC, follow these five steps:

1. Select a general subject. Enter a general subject at the keyboard of the PAC. For example:

    WOMEN

2. View the subtopics. Examine the various subtopics displayed on the screen:

    ```
    1 WOMEN
    2—WOMEN AND ART
    3—WOMEN AND CHRISTIANITY
    4—WOMEN AND INDUSTRY
    5—WOMEN AND MEDICINE
    6—WOMEN AND POLITICS
    ```

3. Select one topic. Scan the list to look for an interesting topic. Each topic has additional subdivisions. For example, Item 6, WOMEN AND POLITICS, has the following breakdown:

    ```
    WOMEN AND POLITICS
      —ABSTRACTS
      —ADDRESSES ESSAYS LECTURES
      —BIBLIOGRAPHY
      —CONGRESSES
      —CROSS-CULTURAL STUDIES
    ```

4. View specific references. If you keyboard "ADDRESSES ESSAYS LECTURES," for example, the program will display a specific list of book titles as follows:

    ```
    WOMEN AND POLITICS—ADDRESSES ESSAYS LECTURES
    ```

    ```
    1. Electoral systems in comparative perspective: Their
       impact on women and minorities (1994)
    2. Women in power: the secrets of leadership (1992)
    3. Women, politics, and change (1990)
    4. The warrior queens (1989)
    5. Toward a feminist theory of the state (1989)
    ```

    In addition to specific titles of books, PAC has, in essence, led you to a listing of contemporary issues.

5. Print. If one book looks interesting, you can enter the number, display a complete description of the book, and print it. For example:

```
BIBLIOGRAPHIC RECORD—

Rule, Wilma, and Zimmerman, Joseph F., eds.
  Electoral systems in comparative perspective: Their im-
pact on women and minorities / 1st ed. / Westport, Conn.:
Greenwood Press, 1994. xi, 259 p. :ill. ; 25cm.
  Bibliography: p. 247-250.
LOCATION; Political science stacks
CALL NUMBER: JF/1057/E43/1994
12/7/94 Not charged to a user.
```

In effect, the PAC has rapidly identified a specific issue about a broad topic and provided information on a book for your preliminary reading.

Note: **Use this computer search to control the size of the project. If the computer lists 50 or 60 books and 200 or more articles, the topic is too broad. Narrow it. If it provides one book and only two or three articles, you must broaden the topic.**

Using CD-ROM Files

In addition to a PAC, most college libraries now have **CD-ROM** facilities, which means that database files, such as *Readers' Guide to Periodical Literature* or *Psychological Abstracts,* are located on a compact disc (CD) stored as *read-only memory* (ROM) in the computer. *ROM* means the computer can read the files for you, but nobody can write into the files to change them.

CD-ROM systems have different names (for example, *InfoTrac, UMI-ProQuest,* or *SilverPlatter*), but their function is the same: to help you work from a general subject to specific topics and, finally, to the reading materials. They send you to appropriate magazine and journal articles by subject or to microfiche files that you can read and copy. Libraries vary in their CD-ROM holdings, so it is important for you to develop a working relationship with the reference librarians. To use CD-ROM files, follow these steps:

1. Select a database. The computers in a library reference room feature a variety of databases. For example, the ACADEMIC INDEX is general; PSYCINFO (psychological sources) and ERIC (educational sources) are specific.
2. List a general subject. Keyboard in a general subject to launch the search. For example:

   WOMEN

3. Scan the subtopics. Read the list of subtopics provided on the screen, and narrow your search to one.

```
WOMEN AND POPULAR CULTURE
WOMEN AND POLITICS
WOMEN AND PRISON
WOMEN AND PUBLIC LIFE
```

4. Select one topic. Enter a choice, such as WOMEN AND POLI-
   TICS, to get a printout of articles.

   ```
   Hillary the pol. (Profile of Hillary Rodham Clinton) Con-
   nie Bruck The New Yorker, May 30, 1994 v70 n15 p58(39)
   —Abstract Available—
   ```

   ```
   Golden State warriors. (1994 California gubernatorial
   candidates) Jordan Bonfante. Time, May 9, 1994 v143 n19
   p54(1).
   —Abstract Available—
   ```

   ```
   Women and democratization: conceptualizing gender rela-
   tions in transition politics. Georgina Waylen. World Pol-
   itics, April 1994 v46 n3 p327(28)
   ```

   ```
   Why suffrage for American women was not enough. Elisabeth
   Perry. History Today, Sept 1993 v43 p36(6)
        Abstract: The efforts of women political activists
        were crucial in winning the right to vote, but after
        the success of the suffrage movement, relatively few
        women sought elective office. The reasons underlying
        the slow progress U.S. women have made toward
        achieving political parity with men are examined.
   ```

5. Read the abstract. If an article seems appropriate to your work,
   read any available abstract, such as the one just shown. Use abstracts to familiarize yourself with issues and new terminology.

6. Print a copy of the source. While you have the reference on the
   screen, you may also print it. You can then carry it into the
   stacks and search for the journal or magazine for some preliminary reading. However, wait until you have framed a thesis sentence before you start note taking. If the article looks relevant to
   your interests, make a photocopy of it while you have it in hand.
   Remember to photocopy front matter for the title, author, date,
   and volume number in case you do use the article.

7. Search several topics at once. Use CD-ROM as well as the PAC to
   begin research with two or three topics at once. For example:

   ```
   TELEVISION and NEWS and OBJECTIVITY
   ```

   ```
   BASKETBALL and VIOLENCE
   ```

   ```
   ANCONITE and DRUGS and POISON
   ```

   The computer will search and list only those articles that match
   the terms, thereby narrowing the search considerably.

8. Use individual diskettes. Individual CD-ROM diskettes make available the entire volumes of major works. To get ideas for your research, you might use a diskette, for example, to search the Bible, to examine the complete works of Shakespeare, to browse through a 21-volume encyclopedia, or to trace a topic through the full text of 107 different books on U.S. history. New diskettes are being produced every day, such as those that contain the *Oxford English Dictionary,* the *Oxford Textbook of Medicine,* and *Countries of the World.* CD-ROM technology is changing the way scholars conduct their research.

1c USING PRINTED MATERIALS TO DISCOVER AND EVALUATE A TOPIC

After a computer search and your personal listing, freewriting, and clustering, research further for exploratory reading in reference books, biographies, and periodicals. Look to see how your topic is being talked about in the literature. Carefully read the titles of articles, and make a record of key terminology. Look for tips on how to focus the topic, be it medical trauma centers, the role of women in Robert Browning's poetry, or automobile emissions control.

Figure 1
Table of contents from
Out of the Storm:
The End of the Civil
War, April–June
1865 *by Noah A. Trudeau, 1994*

Contents

List of Maps	ix
Preface	xi
Author's Note	xv
PART I: *World on the Edge*	1
1. "We may expect weighty news any minute"	3
2. Breakthrough in the East	14
3. CAPTURED!!	49
PART II: *An End to Valor*	87
4. The Death of an Army	89
5. "After four years of arduous service"	117
6. "For God's sake, cease firing! We have the fort!"	153
7. Heads of State	188
Interlude: Oldham's Odyssey (Part One)	206
8. Slow Dance in North Carolina	208
9. "My God—the President's shot!"	220
10. The Bennett Farmhouse	237
11. Potter's Raid	245
12. "The whole country seemed to be alive with demons"	252
13. "My husband and baby are gone!"	263

How did this place affect the peace accord?

Inspecting a Book's Table of Contents to Find and Evaluate a Subject

A book's table of contents subdivides all major subjects, so scan one for a topic of interest. As shown in Figure 1, the student has found a challenging topic, one that provokes a question and might launch an exploratory investigation.

Examining a Book's Index to Discover a Subject

Most books contain an index, which lists the book's contents alphabetically. Such listings have investigative possibilities, as with the multiple entries for *Appomattox* shown in Figure 2.

Figure 2

Index from Out of the Storm: The End of The Civil War, April–June 1865 *by Noah A. Trudeau, 1994*

Why did Appomattox become so important as a site for a peace accord?

Index

Abbeville, Georgia, 292–295
Abbeville, South Carolina, 206, 288, 289
Adams, Charles F., 80–81
Adams, Daniel W., 186
Alabama, C.S.S., 365
Alabama River, 167, 170, 172, 173, 179
Alabama troops: infantry (Alabama Reserves, 181, 183) (54th Regiment, 243)
Albany, Georgia, 263
Albany, New York, 280
Alexander, Andrew J., 156, 180
Alexander, E. Porter, 78, 97–98, 119, 121, 134
Alexandria, Louisiana, 336
Alexandria, Virginia, 316
Allen, Charles J., 179
Allen, Henry, 373
Allen, Vanderbilt, 412
Alvord, Henry E., 412
Amelia Court House, Virginia, 56, 58, 89–93, 95–102, 128, 192, 214, 356
Amelia Springs, Virginia, 98, 107, 357
Ames, Adelbert, 396
Anderson, Nelson, 396–397
Anderson, Richard H., 46, 59, 74, 91, 107, 109–113, 127
Anderson, Robert, 60, 220–222, 250, 350
Andersonville Prison, 262, 263–264, 375–377
André, Leo, 340
Andrews, Christopher C., 6, 182, 327–328

Andrews, Eliza, 353
Andrews, Julius A., 177
Andrews, Sidney, 380–382
Anthony, Susan B., 347–348
Apple Tree (at Appomattox), 147
Appomattox Court House, Virginia, 130–135, 137–139, 141, 146, 149–150, 216, 356, 357
Appomattox River, 50, 51, 56, 59, 70, 90–92, 110, 118, 122, 125, 129, 133
Appomattox Station, 119, 122, 126–130, 133
Armstrong, Frank C., 155–156
Arnold, Samuel, 360
Arthur, Chester A., 417
Ascension Island, 366–367
Atlanta, Georgia, 10, 207, 296
Atlantic Monthly, 381
Atzerodt, George, 225, 231, 360, 374–375
Augur, Christopher C., 410
Augusta, Georgia, 296
Austin, Texas, 359
Ayres, Romeyn B., 21, 24, 29, 32–36, 407
Babcock, Orville E., 25, 28, 141–142
Badeau, Adam, 16, 72–73, 128–129
Barlow, Francis, 120
Barnum, P. T., 298
Barrett, Theodore H., 301–310
Barringer, Rufus, 43, 74, 195
Bartlett, Joseph, 35, 38, 44
Barton, Seth, 115

The logical follow-up to this discovery involves reading the designated pages to consider issues and to find a general subject. Feel free to shift topics during this stage; for example, the student's investigation of the episode at the Bennett Farmhouse might shift the focus to Susan B. Anthony's role at the close of the Civil War.

Scanning an Encyclopedia Article

An encyclopedia contains not only an alphabetic list of topics but also in-depth discussions that can trigger your own ideas. Keep in mind that encyclopedias present a rising degree of complexity. The most accessible is *World Book,* then *Collier's Encyclopedia* and *Encyclopedia Americana,* then *Encyclopaedia Britannica,* followed by subject-specific encyclopedias, such as *Encyclopedia of World Literature in the 20th Century.* In addition, you can consult encyclopedias on CD-ROM diskettes or find an encyclopedia on-line, if you have the equipment and the expertise to access the information. Note how one student made critical comments on the photocopied article shown in Figure 3 in order to evaluate a possible topic.

This student's marginal note could become the central focus of research.

Figure 3
Encyclopedia article from Collier's Encyclopedia, *1993 edition, under the topic,* "Civil War, U.S."

Peace Terms. Peace rumors and more or less irregular peace overtures preceded, accompanied, and followed the election. Lincoln stated his peace terms thus (Dec. 6, 1864): 1) a complete cessation of hostilities, with no armistice; 2) reunion, and; 3) "no receding" from the stand he had previously taken on the question of slavery. He and Seward met with Stephens and two other Confederate peace commissioners on shipboard in Hampton Roads (Feb. 3, 1865), but reached no agreement, Stephens and his colleagues having been authorized to discuss peace only on the basis of Confederate independence. Lincoln expressed the general spirit of his peacemaking—"with malice toward none; with charity for all"—in his second inaugural address (Mar. 4, 1865). In Richmond, after Lee's evacuation, he was willing to recognize "rebel" state governments, at least temporarily. He approved Grant's terms to Lee.

Lincoln and the peace accords at Appomattox and other places

Later, however, Lincoln appeared to yield somewhat to the clamor of the Radicals. He withdrew his permission for the Confederate legislature of Virginia to assemble. At his final cabinet meeting (April 14) he seemed to approve in principle the military occupation of the postwar South. What his course in Reconstruction would have been, if he had lived, can only be guessed. This much is probable: he would have disapproved of the Sherman-Johnston convention under which Johnston surrendered (April 18), which amounted practically to a treaty of peace, and a very generous one, just as his successor, President Johnson, disapproved of it.

Searching the Headings in Reference Books

Any index found in the reference room of a library, such as the *Readers' Guide to Periodical Literature, the Bibliographic Index,* or the *Humanities Index,* categorizes and subdivides topics in alphabetic order. A key word or phrase will often enable you to find an issue about the general subject in which you are interested. A fragment of the *Social Sciences Index* is shown in Figure 4 with a student's notation in the margin.

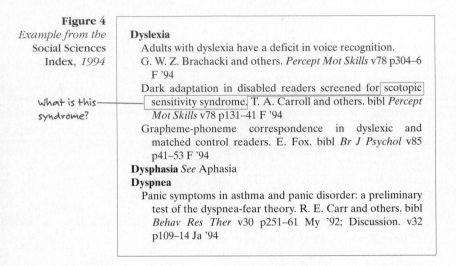

Figure 4
Example from the
Social Sciences
Index, *1994*

Dyslexia
     Adults with dyslexia have a deficit in voice recognition.
     G. W. Z. Brachacki and others. *Percept Mot Skills* v78 p304–6
       F '94

What is this —
syndrome?

     Dark adaptation in disabled readers screened for scotopic
     sensitivity syndrome. T. A. Carroll and others. bibl *Percept*
       Mot Skills v78 p131–41 F '94
     Grapheme-phoneme correspondence in dyslexic and
       matched control readers. E. Fox. bibl *Br J Psychol* v85
       p41–53 F '94
Dysphasia *See* Aphasia
Dyspnea
     Panic symptoms in asthma and panic disorder: a preliminary
       test of the dyspnea-fear theory. R. E. Carr and others. bibl
       Behav Res Ther v30 p251–61 My '92; Discussion. v32
       p109–14 Ja '94

This student can now connect the broad topic dyslexia with one of several subtopics: voice recognition, scotopic sensitivity syndrome, and grapheme-phoneme correspondence.

Topic selection goes beyond choosing a general category (*athletics* or *dyslexia*); it includes finding a research-provoking issue (Dyslexia in adults affects not only sight but also hearing).

1d   DRAFTING A RESEARCH PROPOSAL

A research proposal is a short paragraph that identifies four essential ingredients of your work:

1. The purpose of the paper (explain, analyze, argue).
2. The intended audience (general or specialized).
3. Your voice as the writer (informer or advocate).
4. The preliminary thesis sentence or opening hypothesis.

One writer, sitting at the computer, developed this research proposal and sent it on-line to the instructor:

This paper will examine objectivity
on television talk shows, which
promote their news value but seem
more concerned about titillating the
audience to build their ratings and
advertising dollars. Objectivity is an
ideal, and viewers should understand
that television gives us symbolic
reality like a novel or a staged drama.
The talk show host, the guests, the
studio audience, and even the viewer at
home are all participants in a staged
show that has little to do with
reality.—Stefan Hall

Having identified an issue, the next step for this writer is to search for evidence to defend his argument. See also "Understanding Your Purpose and Role as a Writer," Section 6c, 149–50.

Explaining Your Purpose in the Research Proposal

Research papers accomplish different tasks:

1. They explain and define the topic.
2. They analyze the specific issues.
3. They persuade the reader with the weight of evidence.

Usually, one of these purposes will dominate the paper, but you will probably employ all the purposes in one way or another. For example, the writer of the research proposal on talk shows must explain the structure of the shows, analyze the role of the various participants, and persuade readers that talk shows are not objective.

Use the *explanatory purpose* to review and itemize factual data. One writer defined *cocaine* and explained how it came from the coca shrub of South America. Another writer explained how advertisers have gained entrance into classrooms by providing free educational materials. The explanatory purpose is also used when you summarize a book or article to explain its contribution to a particular field of knowledge. (See Section 4e, pages 112–14, for a sample annotated bibliography and Section 4f, pages 114–18, for a sample literature review paper.)

Use the *analytic purpose* to classify various parts of the subject and to investigate each one in depth. One writer examined the effects of cocaine on the brain, the eyes, the lungs, the heart, and so on. Another writer classified and examined the methods used by advertisers to reach school children with their messages. One writer examined the role of the trickster in Native American mythology, while another explored the image of women in Shakespeare's sonnets. Still another analyzed the effects of television on the language development of children. Use analysis for discovery, examination, deliberation, and speculation.

Use the *persuasive purpose* to defend your argument convincingly. One writer argued that advertisers have not enticed children into bad habits such as eating improperly, smoking cigarettes, drinking alcohol, and behaving violently. She insisted, instead, that advertising merely reflected the life style found in the average home. Persuasion enables you to reject the general attitudes about a problem and affirm new theories, advance a solution, recommend a course of action, or (at the least) invite the reader into an intellectual dialogue. For example, condemning violence on television may be a worthy argument, but it is a weak topic for a research paper because most people will agree with you. A stronger argument to make is that television, like the movies, should govern itself with ratings (e.g., G, PG, PG-13, R) and use late-night time slots for R-rated programs.

In summary, you need to explain the subject, classify and analyze the issues, anticipate the reader's objections and questions, and reach a conclusion. Be aware that bias and prejudice are your enemies, not your allies, because the scholarly research paper, unlike a position paper, should be reasonable, not strident; cautious in assertions, not rash; and well defended by your use of sources.

Identifying Your Audience for the Research Proposal

You will want to design your research paper for an audience of interested readers who expect a depth of understanding on your part and evidence of your background reading on whatever special topic you have chosen. A discourse community is a body of readers with special needs. For example, Stefan Hall, in writing about television talk shows (see pages 247–63 for the complete paper), must go beyond the surface elements. As he says, "The scholarly issue at work here is the construction of reality." With the help of his sources, he develops an in-depth analysis.

Readers of a paper on social issues (working mothers, latchkey children, overcrowded prisons) expect analysis that points toward a social theory or answer. Readers of an academic interpretation of a novel expect to read literary theories on the novel's symbolism, narrative structure, or characterization. Readers of a business report on outdoor advertising expect statistical evidence that will defend a general proposition, especially as it reflects the demographics of the targeted consumers and the cost of reaching them.

Therefore, the nature of the audience affects a thesis proposal, an interpretation, or a report of investigative research. The audience determines whether you will give an analysis, present an explanation, or provide special charts and tables on your findings. As you look to identify your audience, keep in mind three essential steps:

1. Identify your audience and respond accordingly. Audience identification will affect your topic, its development, your voice and style, and even your choice of words.
2. Meet the needs of your readers. Are you telling them everything they need to know without insulting their intelligence? Are you saying something worthwhile or new? Do not bore them or insult their intelligence by retelling known facts from an encyclopedia. (This latter danger is the reason many instructors discourage the use of an encyclopedia as a source.)
3. Invite your readers into the discussion by approaching the topic from an interesting and different point of view. For example, you might address literature students with an economic interpretation of a novel, present marketing students with a biological study of human behavior in the marketplace, or approach history students with a geographic study of a nation's destiny.

Identifying Your Role as a Researcher in the Proposal

Your voice should reflect the investigative nature of your work, so try to display your knowledge. Refer to authorities you have consulted; do not hide them. Offer quotations. Provide charts or graphs that you have created or copied from source documents. Your instructors will give you credit for using such sources in your paper. Just be certain that you give in-text citations to the sources to reflect your academic honesty. To fulfill your role, you must simultaneously investigate, explain, defend, and argue the issue at hand, all the while using proper citations.

Speak from your specialized point of view. You must appear to be at ease with the subject, writing from knowledge that is well grounded and citing the source material only to augment and highlight the discourse. In short, make it *your* discourse, not a collection of quotations from experts in the books and journals you have used.

Expressing Your Thesis Sentence in the Research Proposal

A thesis sentence expands your topic into a scholarly proposal, one that you will try to prove and defend in your paper. It does not state the obvious. For example, the statement that too much television is harmful to children will not provoke an academic discussion because your readers already know that an excess of anything is harmful. The writer must narrow and isolate one issue by finding a critical focus. The following is a much improved thesis sentence:

```
Violence in children's programming echoes an
adolescent's fascination with brutality.
```

This sentence advances an idea that the writer can develop fully and defend with the evidence. The writer has made a connection between television violence and the focusing agent, adolescent psychology. Look at three more examples:

THESIS   The elasticity of children's eyes makes it perfectly safe for them to sit close to the television screen.

THESIS   Television cartoons can affect a child's attitude toward violence.

THESIS   Objectivity can never be perfectly presented by any television broadcast or perceived by any viewer.

In the first example, the writer uses expertise in physical development to provide a critical focus. In the second, the writer combines television viewing with psychological development. In the third, the writer advances a comparison of reality with the creative arts of television.

Accordingly, a writer's critical approach to the subject affects the thesis. One writer's social concern for battered wives will generate a different thesis than another's psychological interest and a third's biological approach:

SOCIAL APPROACH   Public support of safe houses for battered wives seems to be public endorsement of divorce.

PSYCHOLOGICAL APPROACH   The masochism of some women traps them in a marriage of painful love.

BIOLOGICAL APPROACH   Battered wives may be the victims of their own biological conditioning.

Each thesis statement will provoke a response from the reader, who will demand a carefully structured defense in the body of the paper.

Your thesis is not your conclusion or your answer to a problem. Rather, the thesis anticipates your conclusion and sets in motion the examination of facts so that you can reach, in the conclusion, the special idea of your paper.

Note below how four writers developed different thesis sentences even though all their papers were entitled: Santiago in Hemingway's *The Old Man and the Sea*.

Note: This novel narrates the toils of an old Cuban fisherman named Santiago who has not caught a fish for many days. He desperately needs the money to be gained by returning with a good catch of fish. On this day he catches a marlin, which pulls him far out to sea. Finally, Santiago ties the huge marlin to the side of his small boat. However, during the return in the darkness, sharks attack the marlin so that he arrives home with only a skeleton of the fish. He removes his mast and carries it, like a cross, up the hill to his home.

THESIS   Poverty forced Santiago to venture too far and struggle beyond reason in his attempt to land the marlin.

The writer of this first thesis will examine the economic conditions of Santiago's trade.

THESIS   The giant marlin is a symbol for all of life's obstacles and hurdles, and Santiago is a symbol for all suffering humans.

The writer of this second thesis will examine the religious and social symbolism of the novel.

THESIS   Santiago represents a dying breed, the person who confronts alone the natural elements without modern technology.

The writer of this third thesis will explore the history of fishing equipment and explain both Santiago's grandeur and his failure in that light.

THESIS   Hemingway's portrayal of Santiago demonstrates the author's deep respect for Cuba and its stoic heroes.

The writer of this fourth thesis will take a social approach in order to examine Cuban culture and its influence on Hemingway.

Each of these preliminary thesis sentences serves a writer who knows the specific nature of the paper and what types of sources to consult. Later, each writer can frame a final thesis sentence, one to serve the reader (see Section 6a, pages 146–48.

Make the preliminary thesis sentence a part of your research proposal. For example:

> This paper on The Old Man and the Sea, by Ernest Hemingway, will examine for fellow literature students the social conditions of the old Cuban who seems to be struggling for survival. I suspect that poverty forced Santiago to venture too far and struggle beyond reason in his attempt to land the marlin.—Ramon Lopez

This writer and his instructor now have an understanding of the paper's purpose, its audience, the role of the student as a literary interpreter, and the paper's narrow focus on Santiago's economic status.

The following research proposal demonstrates one student's plan for interviewing and charting the social attitudes of a target audience.

```
The NIMBY syndrome (Not In My Backyard) now prevails

across the nation in rural as well as urban neighborhoods.

People know that we must build prisons, store toxic

wastes, and give health care to AIDS victims, but they

cry, "Not in my backyard." This paper will examine the

social attitudes of the people as based on interviews

of 20 people in two neighborhoods. The report will

examine responses in three areas: social responsibility,

self-reliance, and self-protection.—Virginia Forte
```

1e   NARROWING THE GENERAL SUBJECT TO A SPECIFIC TOPIC

As explained above, you should narrow your focus to a specific issue, such as: The Role of the Narrator in "The Raven" or The Symbolic Blackness of Poe's "The Raven." Research requires accurate facts and evidence in support of a specific proposition. Drafting a research proposal (see Section 1c) will narrow the topic, but you may also need to use the following techniques to focus your subject even further.

Narrowing and Focusing with Comparison Topics

Historians compare Robert E. Lee and Ulysses S. Grant. Political scientists compare Bill Clinton and George Bush. Literary scholars compare the poets John Keats and Thomas Hardy. Any two works, any two persons, any two groups may serve as the basis for a comparative study. However, the study should focus on issues. Note how one writer uses a rough outline to set up the differences between Alexander Hamilton and Thomas Jefferson on fiscal issues:

National Bank	Currency	Tariffs
Jefferson	Jefferson	Jefferson
Hamilton	Hamilton	Hamilton

Rather than discuss Jefferson's policies and then Hamilton's, this writer will focus on the issues—the national bank, the currency, and tariffs. The plan limits the discussion to specific issues.

Restricting and Narrowing with Disciplinary Interests

Every discipline, whether it be sociology, geology, or literature, has its analytic categories, which are those areas requiring detailed study, such as *behavior* of mice (psychology), the *demographics* of a target audience (marketing), and the *function* of loops and arrays (computer science). Literature students, for example, soon learn the importance of these terms:

```
imagery              symbolism              theme

setting              irony                  character

plot                 structure              genre
```

Those who write about literature-related topics must learn to compose symbolic studies, image studies, or thematic studies. In contrast, a researcher in psychology must proceed with *observation* of subjects, conduct *tests* on rats, or make a *cognitive approach* to the data. Of course, you don't want to overuse the language of the discipline to the point of writing unclearly, but you do want to use the terms of the field to help narrow your subject. (See also "Identifying Your Audience for the Research Proposal" in Section 1d, pages 20–21.)

Narrowing the Topic to Match Source Materials

Library sources often determine the fate of research. Your preliminary work should include a brief search for available sources. Will you have enough books and articles on the topic? Are they up-to-date? On what topics have other writers focused? For example, one writer started with the general subject *Texas* and narrowed it to *political figures*. She found several catalog cards on *Sam Houston*—books written primarily in the 1930s and 1960s—and she found only one article at the CD-ROM terminal. Although Sam Houston is a good subject, the sources were out-of-date. The student wanted a topic of contemporary interest. Economic factors in Texas seemed more important in the literature. Accordingly, she began to shift her focus to the financial condition of the state. She saw numerous articles about the cost of health care, which raised this question: Can the economy of Texas support the spiraling health-care costs without affecting other programs, such as the state's support of education?

In this way, the writer matched her topic with a ready supply of literature in newspapers, magazines, and journals. Then she was ready to turn her attention to gathering the data she needed for her paper.

2 *Gathering Data*

For most writing projects you must research a specific subject, for example, politically correct language, world banking networks, or DNA fingerprinting. The search for sources has become easier, thanks to modern technology—book catalogs on computers, database information available by telephone transmission, and compact discs within computers that can search thousands of journal articles for you and print out a bibliography.

Printed catalogs and indexes are becoming rare, and you may even see the demise within this decade of the printed versions of *Social Sciences Index, Psychological Abstracts, Business Periodicals Index,* and many other reference sources.

For that reason, researchers need to learn how to use the new electronic library. Therefore, this chapter is divided into five distinct parts:

The layout of the library
Format for bibliographic entries
Electronic sources
Printed bibliographies, indexes, and catalogs
Sources outside the library

After a brief tour of library organization and an overview of how to develop bibliographies, this chapter sends you down the electronic highway to help you access printouts of sources found in the Public Access Catalog (PAC), CD-ROM, and other computer-generated data. Then the chapter explains how to search the printed catalogs and indexes. After all, the computer searches only go back five years or less, so you will need to supplement your electronic search with a look at some of the printed indexes.

In addition, the chapter discusses how to go beyond the library to collect information from a television program, an interview, a questionnaire, and other sources (see Section 2j).

The search for sources is a serious task. Some leads will turn out to be dead ends; others will provide only trivial information. Some research will be duplicated, and a recursive pattern will develop; that is, you will go back and forth from reading, to searching indexes, and back again to reading. One idea modifies another, you discover connections, and eventually a fresh perspective emerges.

Your research strategy might conform to the following list, with adjustments for individual needs:

Searching available sources: Access electronic sources as well as the printed indexes, abstracts, bibliographies, and reference books.

Refining the topic and evaluating the sources: Spend time browsing, reading abstracts, skimming articles, comparing sources, making citation searches, and skimming through pertinent sections of books.

Reading and note taking: Examine books, articles, essays, reviews, computer printouts, and government documents.

This preliminary work serves several purposes:

1. It gives you an overview of the subject.
2. It provides a beginning set of reference citations.
3. It defines and restricts the subject.
4. It suggests the availability of sufficient source materials with diverse opinions and real disagreements.

In your search for sources and data, there are two shortcuts you can use. First, you can use computer searches. Some universities are now wired campuswide, making it possible for you to conduct research on a personal computer in your dormitory room, in a classroom, or in a laboratory. At your work station, you can save time by accessing the public-access catalog (PAC), Internet, the CD-ROM services, and other electronic sources. Once tapped into these resources, you can develop a working bibliography, scan abstracts and some entire articles, and in general make substantive advances before you ever even enter the library. (See Section 2c, "The Electronic Library: Using a Computer Search," pages 35–45.)

Second, you can also use the Appendix of this book. The "List of Reference Sources, by Discipline" (pages 365–97) advises you about the best sources in psychology, art, black literature, myth and folklore, and many other disciplines. For example, it tells writers researching the field of physical education to search ERIC and the *Current Index to Journals in Education,* but it sends computer science students to INSPEC and the *Computer Literature Index.* It highlights the best CD-ROM and database sources as well as the best printed indexes. (See pages 35–65 for additional details.)

2a LEARNING THE ORGANIZATION OF YOUR LIBRARY

Because of the sheer number of books and magazines and because of the vast array of retrieval systems, it is to your advantage to tour the library and learn its layout—the circulation desk, the reference room, and the stacks. Use the following as your guide to explore personally the library.

Circulation Desk

The circulation desk is usually located at the front of the library where personnel can point you in the right direction and later check out the books you wish to borrow. Many libraries now have computerized machines for book checkout and electronic security devices to prevent theft. Whenever you cannot find a book on your own, check with the circulation desk or the computer terminals to determine whether it is checked out, on reserve, or lost. If the book is checked out, you may be able to place a hold order so that the librarians can contact you when the book is returned. The circulation desk also handles most general business, such as renewals, collection of fines, handling of keys, and making change for video and photocopying machines.

Reference Room

The reference room is where you will find general and specialized encyclopedias, biographic dictionaries, and other general works to help refine your topic. Reference librarians know the best resources for most topics, so take advantage of their expertise. After your subject is determined, the reference room provides the bibliographies and indexes for your search of the sources. (See Section 2d, "Searching the Printed Bibliographies," pages 45–51, and 2e, "Searching the Printed Indexes," pages 51–61.) While working in the reference room, you should develop a set of bibliographic entries (see pages 31–35) that will direct your reading in books and articles. New technology, such as the InfoTrac system (see pages 37–39), will help you narrow the topic and will provide a printed list of sources.

Public-Access Catalog (PAC)

Most libraries have computerized their card catalog files. The PAC will locate all books, listing them by author, title, and subject—all interfiled in one alphabetic catalog. For examples, see Section 1b, pages 12–13. If your library still uses the card catalog system, see Section 2i, pages 65–68.

CD-ROM and On-line Database Facilities

A new type of library has emerged, one with access to sources by local computer and also by national networks that dispatch information on almost any topic—bibliographies, abstracts, and even the full text of some articles. (See Section 2c, "The Electronic Library: Using a Computer Search.")

Reserve Desk

Instructors often place books and articles on reserve with short loan periods (two hours or one day) so that large numbers of students will have access to them. This system prevents one student from keeping an important, even crucial, book for two weeks while others suffer from its absence. Your library may also place on reserve other valuable items that might otherwise be subject to theft. These include recordings, statistical information, unbound pamphlets and papers, and videotapes.

Stacks

The numerous shelves (stacks) of the library hold books organized by call number. If a library has open stacks, it is here that you can locate specific books and browse for others that interest you. However, if a library has closed stacks, you are not permitted into the stacks at all. To gain access, you must provide the call numbers of the books you want to an attendant who will retrieve them for you.

Interlibrary Loans

One library may borrow from another. The interlibrary loan service thereby supplements a library's resources by making additional materials available from other libraries. However, receiving a book or article by interlibrary loan may take seven to ten days. Ask your librarian about interlibrary loans available at your library. Some libraries are networking with others by facsimile (fax) machine. You may also use a document delivery service, but the cost is high.

Photocopiers

Photocopying services provide a real convenience, enabling you to carry home articles from journals and reserve books that cannot be taken from the library. However, copyright laws protect authors and place certain restrictions on the library. You may only use the copying machines and duplicating services for your own individual purposes. Be sure that you give proper credit to the sources. (See Section 5g, "Avoiding Plagiarism," pages 138–44, and also Section 8b, "Copyright Law," page 222.)

Nonprint Materials

Libraries serve as a storehouse for recordings, videotapes, film, microfilm, and many other nonprint items. Such materials are usually listed in the general catalog or in a special catalog. By searching these overlooked holdings, you may uncover a valuable lecture on cassette tape or a significant microfiche collection of manuscripts. Ask your librarian about vertical files, which contain articles clipped from magazines and newspapers. These are usually kept in alphabetic order by topic, not by title.

> **Note: Microfilm is a roll of film on which images (such as the pages of a newspaper) are reproduced in greatly reduced size; microfiche is a single sheet of microfilm that preserves a considerable number of pages.**

Archives and Special Collections

You might select a topic that requires use of a special collection at your library. Many libraries are government depository libraries and house special collections and archives. Others, through donations and purchases, house collections of special import, for example, the Robert Browning collection at Baylor University, the James Joyce holdings at Tulsa University, and so forth.

2b   DEVELOPING A WORKING BIBLIOGRAPHY

A working bibliography is a list of the sources that you plan to read before drafting your paper. Too few sources indicate that your topic is too narrow or obscure. Too many sources indicate that you need a tighter focus. A working bibliography has three purposes:

1. It locates articles and books for note-taking purposes.
2. It provides information for the in-text citations, as in the following example written in MLA style: "The numerous instances of child abuse among stepfathers has been noted by Stephens (31–32) and by McCormick (419)."
3. It provides information for the final Works Cited page (see Chapter 9, pages 265–306), so you should preserve all computer printouts and handwritten notes.

Handwritten cards have been traditional tools for researchers, but these are gradually giving way to the new technology. Computer printouts easily substitute for handwritten cards. A typical printout is shown in Figure 5.

Figure 5
InfoTrac printout

```
Database: Expanded Academic Index

Key Words: television news objectivity

What is reality? The thin and blurring
lines. (Special report: Reality TV)

Broadcasting & Cable, April 12, 1993 v123
n15 p27(2)

Author: Steve McClellan

Subjects:    Docudrama television programs—
             Moral and ethical aspects
             Television broadcasting of
             news—Moral and ethical aspects
             Journalism—Objectivity

Bus. Collection: 70Y2893          AN: 13665608
```

Make printouts of relevant sources, such as the one shown in Figure 5, so that later, at your computer, you can create a file entitled Works Cited (see Figure 6). Type in new sources on a daily basis. *Note:* At some work stations, you can import the bibliographic data into your file and rearrange it to whatever format you are using.

Figure 6
*Keyboarded
bibliographic entry
for student's
Works Cited file*

```
McClellan, Steve. "What Is Reality?
    The Thin and Blurring Line."
    Broadcasting and Cable 12 Apr.
    1993: 27-28. InfoTrac Expanded
    Academic Index. CD-ROM.
    Information Access. 2 Feb. 1995.
```

In contrast, the card system requires you to record each source by hand on an individual card, as shown on page 33.

An advantage of handwritten cards is that it is easy to collate them into alphabetic order; however, many computers have a SORT command that can alphabetize the bibliography automatically. The disadvantage of handwritten cards is that you must keyboard the same data at a later time.

McClellan, Steve. "What is Reality?
The Thin and Blurring Line."
Broadcasting and Cable 12 Apr.
1993: 27-28. InfoTrac Expanded
Academic Index. CD-ROM.
Information Access. 2 Feb. 1995.

Regardless of which method you use to keep track of your sources, you must convert the bibliographic material into MLA style (or some other academic form, such as APA style). Each working bibliographic entry should contain the following information, with variations, of course, for books, periodicals, and government documents.

1. Author's name
2. Title of the work
3. Publication information
4. Library call number, database, or Internet identification code
5. *Optional:* A personal note about the contents of the source

The bibliographic forms displayed in Figures 7–9 and elsewhere in this chapter show correct MLA style for basic entries as entered into a computer file. *Note:* This working file should contain call numbers and special notations. Handwritten bibliographic cards should follow the same format as these keyboarded forms.

```
E477.6
T78
1994
      Trudeau, Noah Andre
      Out of the Storm: The End of the Civ-
      il War, April-June 1865
      Boston: Little, Brown, 1994
            1st ed., 470p.
            Bibliography: p. 437-457
      ISBN 0-316-85328-3
```

Figure 7
A book cited in the PAC, followed by a keyboarded bibliographic entry, in MLA style, for a student's Works Cited file

For special sources (e.g., lecture, letter, or map), consult the Index, which will direct you to appropriate pages in Chapter 9 for examples of almost every imaginable type of bibliographic entry. If needed, consult Chapters 10 and 11 for citation forms in fields of study other than literature and language.

Figure 7
(cont'd)
A book cited in
the PAC, followed
by a keyboarded
bibliographic entry,
in MLA style, for a
student's
Works Cited file

```
E477.6/T78/1994
Trudeau, Noah Andre. Out of the Storm:
     The End of the Civil War, April-
     June 1865. Boston: Little, Brown,
     1994.
               Bibliography on 437-57.
```

Figure 8
A journal article
cited in Social
Sciences Index,
followed by a
keyboarded
bibliographic entry,
in MLA style,
for a student's
Works Cited file

```
Television advertising
The frequency and nature of alcohol and
     tobacco advertising in televised
     sports: 1990 through 1992. P. A. Madden
     and J. W. Grube. Am J Public Health v84
     p297-9 F '94
Gender stereotypes in MTV commercials:
     the beat goes on. N. Signorielli and
     others. bibl J Broadcast Electron
     Media v38 p91-101 Wint '94
```

```
Madden, P. A., and J. W. Grube. "The
     Frequency and Nature of Alcohol
     and Tobacco Advertising in
     Televised Sports: 1990 through
     1992." American Journal of Public
     Health 84 (1994): 297-99.
```

Teen-agers *See* Youth
Television
    Birkerts, S. Television: the medium in the
mass age. (*In* Birkerts, S. An artificial wilderness
p369–81)
Telling of stories *See* Storytelling
Telotte, J. P.
    Through a pumpkin's eye; the reflexive na-
ture of horror. (*In* American horrors: ed. by G.
A. Waller p114–28)

Figure 9
*An essay from
within a book,
cited in* Essay and
General Literature
Index, *followed by
a keyboarded
bibliographic entry,
in MLA style, for a
student's Works Cited
file (Note: Publisher's
city is not listed; add
it when you have the
book in hand.)*

Birkerts, Sven. An artificial wilderness; essays on 20th-century literature. Morrow 1987 430p ISBN 0-688-07113-9 LC 87-12383

```
Birkerts, Sven. "Television: The Medium
    in the Mass Age." An Artificial
    Wilderness: Essays on 20th Century
    Literature. Ed. Sven Birkerts.
    N.p.: Morrow, 1987. 369-81.
```

2c   THE ELECTRONIC LIBRARY: USING A COMPUTER SEARCH

During the 1990s, you are witnessing a major revolution in library reference materials. Card catalogs have been put in the garbage. The bulky
printed indexes have begun to disappear. Microfilm and microfiche have
replaced printed versions of magazines and newspapers. Newly created

software programs now create files and perform retrospective searches on microcomputers.

It is important that you not be intimidated by the new technology; you will catch on fast and surprise yourself at how much more quickly research can be performed. For instance, rather than search the printed volumes of *Readers' Guide to Periodical Literature, Humanities Index,* and *Social Sciences Index,* you can now scan computer screens and get a bibliographic printout on any source that looks promising. You can learn to use the Public Access Catalog (PAC) and the CD-ROM facilities by yourself; use DIALOG and Internet only after special training.

With the help of fiber-optic technology, universities are moving rapidly to multipurpose information machines that will give you access to all electronic sources—PAC, CD-ROM, the DIALOG database, and the computer network Internet. After a brief training period, you will get an account number and can enter any of several systems on the server network. These systems, described in the following paragraphs, may be accessed from the work station or from individual, discrete systems.

PAC

(See Section 1b, pages 12–13, for discussion and examples). The computer will provide a printout similar to that shown in Figure 10.

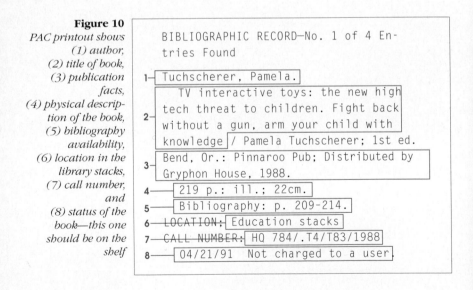

Figure 10
PAC printout shows
(1) author,
(2) title of book,
(3) publication facts,
(4) physical description of the book,
(5) bibliography availability,
(6) location in the library stacks,
(7) call number, and
(8) status of the book—this one should be on the shelf

```
     BIBLIOGRAPHIC RECORD—No. 1 of 4 En-
     tries Found

1—┤Tuchscherer, Pamela.│
         TV interactive toys: the new high
2—┤ tech threat to children. Fight back
    without a gun, arm your child with
    knowledge│/ Pamela Tuchscherer; 1st ed.
3—┤ Bend, Or.: Pinnaroo Pub; Distributed by
    Gryphon House, 1988.
4——┤ 219 p.: ill.; 22cm.│
5——┤ Bibliography: p. 209-214.│
6——LOCATION:│Education stacks│
7——CALL NUMBER:│HQ 784/.T4/T83/1988│
8——┤04/21/91  Not charged to a user│
```

You can then transfer the information to your computer file, as shown in Figure 11.

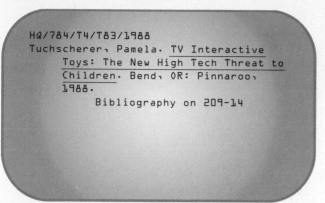

Figure 11
*A keyboarded
bibliographic entry,
in MLA style, from
PAC for a student's
Works Cited file*

CD-ROM

(See Section 1b, pages 13–15, for discussion and examples). Use the new technology to narrow your area of interest by entering your subject, such as *computers, desktop publishing, graphics, Robert Frost, women,* or *dramatic monologue.* The computer will find material that matches the descriptive words. You can then make a printout similar to the one shown in Figure 12.

Figure 12
*CD-ROM printout
shows (1) subject,
(2) title of the
article,
(3) description,
(4) author,
(5) title of the
periodical,
(6) date,
(7) volume number,
(8) issue number,
(9) page number,
and
(10) total number of
pages of the article*

1— UNITED STATES CIVIL WAR

   1. Prevaricating through Georgia: Sherman's 'Memoirs' as a source on the Atlanta campaign. (William T. Sherman and the 1864 Civil War campaign) Albert Castel. Civil War History, March 1994 v40 n1 p48(24)—Abstract Available—

2— 2. Sherman called it the way he saw it.
3— (accuracy of Sherman's 'Memoirs') (response to Albert Castel in this issue, p.
4— 48) John F. Marszalek. Civil War History —5
6— March 1994 v40 n1 p 72(7).—Abstract
   Available— 7 8 9 10

   3. Barksdale's Mississippi bridgade at Fredericksburg. (William Barksdale and the Battle of Fredericksburg, December 1862) Steve C. Hawley. Civil War History, March 1994 v40 n1 p5(20).

   4. Women in battle in the Civil War. Richard Hall. Social Education, Feb 1994 v58 n2 p80(3).

Figure 13
*Keyboarded
bibliographic entry
for a periodical
source found on*
ProQuest, Silver-
Platter, *or* InfoTrac

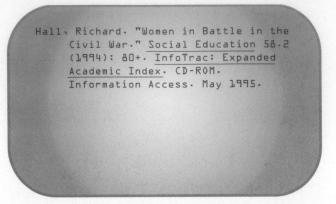

```
Hall, Richard. "Women in Battle in the
    Civil War." Social Education 58.2
    (1994): 80+. InfoTrac: Expanded
    Academic Index. CD-ROM.
    Information Access. May 1995.
```

As shown in Figure 13, list the issue number when you cannot be certain, without looking, that the journal is paged continuously. Also, use a format such as *80+* rather than *80–82* when you cannot be certain that the pages of the article are continuous.

Keep in mind that electronic publishing by means of CD-ROM extends beyond indexes. It can provide abstracts and even the full text of many kinds of materials. Following is a brief sample of the hundreds of files now available on CD-ROM. (Your library may have these particular diskettes and others.)

U.S. History (The full text of 107 history books with 1,000 images,
    tables, and maps)
Grolier's Encyclopedia
Shakespeare (complete works)
The Bible
Oxford English Dictionary (more than 250,000 key words)
McGraw-Hill Science and Technical Reference Set (100,000 terms;
    7,300 articles)
Redshift (explores outer space)
Franklin Roosevelt: History Maker
Mastering Math

When using such CD-ROM diskettes, you can actually read information from the diskettes and get printouts of material. Be sure to mention CD-ROM (see Figure 14) or InfoTrac abstracts in your bibliography (see pages 294–95).

> **Warning:** The InfoTrac and ProQuest abstracts are written by employees of the InfoTrac and ProQuest companies, not by the original authors. Therefore, try not to quote from these abstracts. If you must, use them with discretion. (See pages 13–15 for more details.)

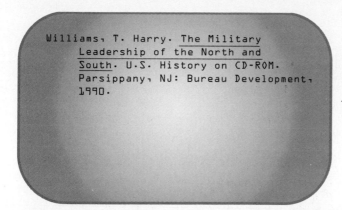

Figure 14
A keyboarded bibliographic entry to a book, in MLA style, from a CD-ROM diskette for a student's Works Cited file

DIALOG (and Other National Vendors)

DIALOG is an online database using a telephone modem to connect a library with a national vendor. In brief, you or a librarian can connect your library's computer by phone to a national database vendor, such as DIA-LOG, which will transmit by telephone hookup various files, such as:

SCISEARCH (articles on scientific topics)
GEOBASE (articles on geology and earth sciences)
ERIC (articles on education and related topics)

(See the Appendix, pages 365–97, for the database sources in your field of research.)

Database searches for source materials are available at most libraries, but use this search only if you have the experience or the librarian has time to work with you. There may be a waiting list for users. Generally, librarians discourage undergraduate use of computer searches for small research papers of eight pages or less for one reason: the computer is only cost-effective for large retrospective searches, not for narrow searches that most research papers require. After all, the database vendors charge the library about $75 per hour when logged on. If you use DIALOG or some other national vendor, you may be required to pay a fee from $1 up to $60 or more. Fee schedules vary from university to university because some libraries absorb the cost while others charge for computer time. Determine these charges *in advance.*

An on-line database search involves several steps. First, you must answer a few questions and provide some information about your search request:

1. What title would best describe your paper's content?
2. Using scientific, technical, and common names, list specific topics, synonyms, closely related phrases, and alternate spellings of your subject.

3. List related topics to exclude in order to narrow the search.
4. Do you desire any foreign language entries? If so, which language(s)?
5. Do you wish to limit citations to a specific publication year(s)?

Second, the librarian assisting you will use your answers to identify three key terms, called descriptors. (*Note:* To find descriptors, refer if necessary to a computer thesaurus, such as *Thesaurus of ERIC Descriptors* or *Thesaurus of Psychological Index Terms.*) Your chosen key terms, such as the three shown here, will control a search of citations:

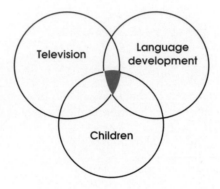

Third, you or the librarian must select an appropriate file, such as ERIC; log on by telephone modem; enter the subject profile; and begin the computer search.

```
File ERIC

Set       Items        Description
S1       101810        CHILDREN
S2         1038        TODDLERS
S3         6022        INFANTS
S4        16123        TELEVISION
S5         8339        LANGUAGE ACQUISITION
S6         7176        LANGUAGE RESEARCH
S7           13        (CHILDREN OR TODDLERS OR INFANTS) AND
                         TELEVISION AND LANGUAGE ACQUISITION
                         AND LANGUAGE RESEARCH
```

Fourth, the computer will browse through records to select only those that match the subject profile, that is, articles that include all three descriptors—in our example, television, children, and language development. Then the computer will provide its report. (See Figure 15 for a portion of the report.) You may then decide to order a copy of the abstract or, in some cases, the full text if the printed version is not available in your library. (See Section 9f, pages 294–95, for instructions about using an abstract as one of your sources.)

```
7/5/1

EJ338919 FL517179

     Television as a Talking Picture Book: A
     Prop for Language Acquisition. Lemish,
     Dafna; Rice, Mabel L. Journal of Child
     Language, v13 n2 p251-74 Jun 1986
     Language: English Document Type: JOURNAL
     ARTICLE (080); RESEARCH REPORT (143)

     Provides longitudinal observations of
young children's behaviors while viewing
television in their own homes when the
children were actively involved in the
process of language acquisition. The
observations show an overwhelming and
consistent occurrence of language-related
behaviors among children and parents in the
viewing situation.

7/5/2

EJ3009869 CS730477

     The Verbal Language of Public
     Television. Stevens, Kathleen C. Reading
     Horizons, v25 n2 p83-86 Win 1985
     Language: English Document Type: JOURNAL
     ARTICLE (080); RESEARCH REPORT (143)

     Analyzes the language of five popular
children's shows on public television.
Suggests that the public television shows
provide a superior language model than that
of commercial televison.
```

Figure 15
*Two entries of
13 from a DIALOG
search of the
ERIC database*

At the end of the database printout, you will find a summary for the esti-mated cost for the search, as shown here:

```
07jun91 13:36:59 User0118 Session B1155.1
        $1.98 0.066 Hrs
        $1.30 13 Type(s) in Format 5
$3.28 Estimated cost File1
$0.79 Tymnet
        $4.07 Estimated cost this search
Logoff: level 26.04.03 B 13:37:00
```

Remember, you still need to convert the citations to MLA style, as shown in Figure 16.

Figure 16
*A keyboarded
bibliographic entry,
in MLA style, from
DIALOG for a
student's
Works Cited file*

```
Lemish, Dafna, and Mabel L. Rice.
   "Television as a Talking Picture
   Book: A Prop for Language
   Acquisition." Journal of Child
   Language 13 (1986): 251-74. 8 pp.
   Online. DIALOG. 3 May 1995.
```

Internet

The information highway is in place, and you may need to travel it sooner than you think. Internet is a worldwide computer network for the exchange of information in several domains—education, commerce, government, military, and others. Internet holds all the domains together; it is a network of thousands of smaller networks, such as BIALIK (Brandeis University), a poetry network; BIOSERVE (University of Maryland), a data and software network in biotechnology; COMSERVE (Rensselaer Polytechnic Institute), a network for the study of human communication; and MAC-SERVE (Princeton University), a repository of utilities, games, notes, and graphic items. On these networks, e-mail (electronic mail) flashes back and forth from state to state and nation to nation.

The Internet links your school's computer with those across the United States and in most foreign countries. In most instances, you need training to use the Internet, after which you will receive an academic account number and access to your university's mainframe, such as VAX.

After the brief training session, you can use such Internet navigators as GOPHER, VERONICA, or CARL UNCOVER to find information. CARL UN-COVER, for example, responds to your key term request as follows:

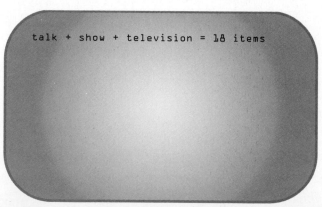

```
talk + show + television = 18 items
```

It will list the 18 sources and give you specific details about each one. One such source is shown in Figure 17.

Figure 17
Computer printout from UNCOVER, an Internet navigator

```
AUTHOR(S):    Nelson, E. D.
              Robinson, B. W.
TITLE(S)      "Reality Talk" or "Telling
              Tales"? The Social
              Construction of Sexual
              and Gender Deviance on a
              Television Talk Show.
       In:    Journal of contemporary
              ethnography.
              APR 01 1994 v23 n 1
     Page:    51
SICI CODE:    0891-
              2416(19940401)23:1L.51:R⁻0";1-
ISSUE STATUS: Published
```

This article may be available in your library, at no cost to you. To have it faxed from CARL UNCOVER, the following charges apply:

```
Service chg.   $8.50
Copyright fee  $3.00
Total Cost:    $11.50
```

As discussed earlier, carry the printout to the stacks to see whether the article is available. Otherwise, a faxed copy will cost you $11.50. If you read and use the article, make a bibliographic entry; as shown in Figure 18.

Figure 18
Keyboarded bibliographic entry for a source found on the Internet

```
Nelson, E. D., and B. W. Robinson.
   "'Reality Talk' or 'Telling
   Tales'? The Social Construction of
   Sexual and Gender Deviance on a
   Television Talk Show." Journal of
   Contemporary Ethnography 23.1
   (1994): 51. 17 pp. Online.
   Internet. 22 Mar. 1995.
```

E-Mail

E-mail (electronic mail) moves across the various computer networks, as described earlier. Let's look briefly at one system: BITNET (Because It's Time Network). BITNET extends electronic mail to anyone on the network, so you could collaborate on a research project with somebody at another college, passing information back and forth. After a display of special codes and descriptors, a message on BITNET will look similar to the example shown in Figure 19.

Figure 19
Example of E-Mail

From: Glover@PennState.Bitnet 5-Jun-1994
To: Tom Mitchell <Mitchell@UTAustin.BITNET>

Subj: Steroids and skeletal damage

Since our last correspondence I have interviewed 15 athletes, 12 male and 3 female, who have used steroids extensively during the past four to six years. The subjects all attend a small college nearby, so I will conduct follow-up interviews both here and on site. Only two have refused my request for additional information. Six have agreed to magnetic resonance imaging so that we can search for damage to the soft tissues in the bones. With these subjects at hand, we can launch our investigation in earnest.

Pete Glover
Penn State University

If you expect to use a network file in your paper, you will need to keyboard a Works Cited entry, as shown in Figure 20. *Note:* E-mail is usually not a retrievable item, so providing a path is not necessary (see also 298).

Figure 20
A keyboarded bibliographic entry, in MLA style, from E-mail for a student's Works Cited file

Glover, Peter. "Steroids and Skeletal
    Damage." E-mail to the author.
    5 June 1994.

Facsimile (FAX) Machines

Some libraries now use fax machines by which they transmit a facsimile (a copy or an image of printed matter) by electronic means. This service speeds interlibrary loans (see page 30), so the waiting period may be only a day or two. You may even get the document you need the same day.

2d   SEARCHING THE PRINTED BIBLIOGRAPHIES

The traditional library of printed reference works now appears side by side with the new computer workstations because you may need to supplement your computer printouts with the traditional method of searching through various bibliographies and indexes.

Printed Bibliographies

In the reference section of your library, you will find many types of printed bibliographies. Some are general guides to a wide range of subjects; some are bibliographic guides to other bibliographies, listed by subject; and some are specialized for narrow fields. You must decide how to begin the research process.

If you have a clearly defined topic, skip to page 48, "Using a Shortcut: Searching the Specialized Bibliographies." However, if you are still trying to formulate a clear focus, begin with general guides and gradually narrow to discipline-specific bibliographies, as discussed next.

Starting the Search with General Bibliographies

Computer searches only reach back for five years or less, so begin with a recent issue or two of this source:

Bibliographic Index: A Cumulative Bibliography of Bibliographies.
    New York: Wilson, 1938–date.

This work, updated annually, provides page numbers to many different books and journals that contain bibliographies on numerous subjects. Although *Bibliographic Index* originally covered only the years 1937–1942, it is kept current by supplements. Figure 21 provides an example from *Bibliographic Index* of 1994.

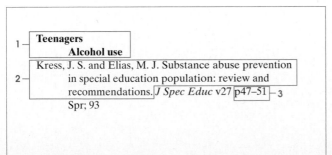

Figure 21
Example from Bibliographic Index, *1994, shows (1) subject heading, (2) entry of a book that contains a bibliography on teenagers, and (3) specific pages on which bibliography is located*

```
Kress, J.S, and M.J. Elias. "Substance
   Abuse Prevention in Special Edu-
   cation Population: Review and
   Recommendations." Journal of
   Special Education 27 (1993): 47-
   51.
        Features a Bibliography on
   these five pages.
```

If the displayed source seems to fit your research, you would probably want to write a bibliographic note for it (as shown in Figure 22) and then go in search of it.

If you want to conduct a thorough, comprehensive search, one that reaches back in time, consult one or two of the following general reference works, which contain bibliographies that direct you to sources on a wide range of subjects.

Besterman, Theodore. *A World Bibliography of Bibliographies.* 4th ed. 5 vols. Lausanne: Societas Bibliographica, 1965.

Hillard, James. *Where to Find What: A Handbook to Reference Service.* 3rd ed. Metuchen, NJ: Scarecrow, 1991.

McCormick, Mona. *The New York Times Guide to Reference Materials.* Rev. ed. New York: Times Books, 1986.

Sheehy, Eugene P., ed. *Guide to Reference Books.* 10th ed. Chicago: ALA, 1986.

Using the Trade Bibliographies

Trade bibliographies, intended primarily for use by booksellers and librarians, can help you in three ways. They can help you to (1) discover sources not listed in other bibliographies or in the card catalog; (2) locate facts of publication, such as place and date; and (3) learn whether a book is in print. Start with this work:

Subject Guide to Books in Print. New York: Bowker, 1957–date.

It supplies excellent subject indexes. Figure 23 shows a sample from the 1994 issue.

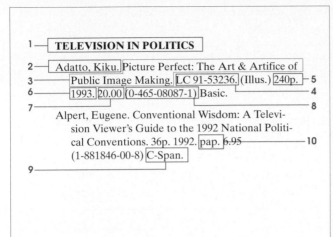

Figure 23
Example from Subject Guide to Books in Print, *1994,*
shows (1) subject,
(2) author, (3) title,
(4) Library of Congress number,
(5) number of
pages, (6) date of
publication,
(7) price, (8) International Standard
Book Number (used
when ordering),
(9) publisher, and
(10) paperback
book

Make a note of any promising source, as shown in Figure 24.

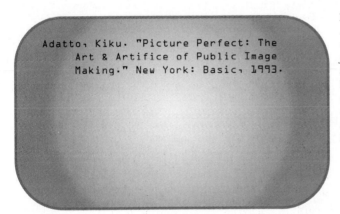

Figure 24
Keyboarded
bibliographic entry
for source found in
Subject Guide to
Books in Print
(The publisher's city
will be listed in a
separate section of
Books in Print.*)*

You may also use the following trade bibliographies:

Books in Print. New York: Bowker, 1948–date.
   This work provides an author-title index to the *Publisher's Trade List Annual* (New York: Bowker, 1874–date), which lists all books currently in print.
Publishers' Weekly. New York: Bowker, 1872–date.
   This journal offers the most current publication data on new books and new editions.
Paperbound Books in Print. New York: Bowker, 1955–date.
   This work is useful in locating paperback books on one topic, especially books available at local bookstores rather than the library.

Cumulative Book Index. New York: H. W. Wilson, 1900–date.
This work is useful in finding complete publication data on one
book or locating *all* material in English on a particular subject.

The National Union Catalog: A Cumulative Author List. Ann Arbor:
Edwards, 1953–date.
Basically, this work is the card catalog in book form, but use it to
find titles reported by other libraries.

Library of Congress Catalog: Books, Subjects. Washington, D. C.: Library of Congress, 1950–date.
This work is useful for its subject classification, which provides a
ready-made bibliography to books on hundreds of subjects. Separate volumes are available for the years 1950–1954, 1955–1959,
1960–1964, and annually thereafter.

Union List of Serials in Libraries of the United States and Canada.
3rd ed. New York: H. W. Wilson, 1965.
Supplements, *New Serial Titles,* Washington, D.C.: Library of Congress, 1953–date. This work can be consulted to determine
whether a nearby library has a magazine or journal that is unavailable in your library.

Ulrich's International Periodicals Directory. Ed. Merle Rohinsky.
15th ed. New York: Bowker, 1973.
This work is useful in locating current periodicals, both domestic
and foreign, and in ordering photocopied reprints of articles.

Using a Shortcut: Searching the Specialized Bibliographies

If you have a well-developed research proposal (see Section 1d), you
can go directly to reference guides, bibliographies, and indexes for your
discipline as listed in the appendix of this book, pages 365–97. For example, one student entitled his highly focused paper "The Role of Female Talk
Show Hosts on Network Television." He looked under "Women's Studies"
on pages 396–97 of the Appendix and found 20 sources, 4 of which were:

Women in Popular Culture: A Reference Guide
Womanhood Media: Current Resources About Women
Women in America: A Guide to Information Sources
Women's Studies Abstracts

You can use the Appendix in the same manner. It is a shortcut to essential
information for disciplinary studies in almost any field, from black literature to folklore to geology and many others. It not only lists but also anno-
tates the most important sources.

In another instance, a student had narrowed his study to Robert Frost's
poetry. The Appendix, under "Language and Literature," directed him to
Magill's Bibliography of Literary Criticism, an index to literary interpretations, an excerpt of which is shown in Figure 25.

Figure 25
Example from Magill's Bibliography of Literary Criticism *shows (1) author and dates, (2) title of work, and (3) citation of a critical work on the poem*

1 ——————— **ROBERT FROST**
(1874–1963)

2 —| **"After Apple Picking"**

Brooks, Cleanth. *Modern Poetry and the Tradition.* Chapel Hill: University of North Carolina Press, 1939, pp. 114–116. Reprinted in *Robert Frost: An Introduction.* Edited by Robert A. Greenberg and James G. Hepburn, New York: Holt, Rinehart, 1961, pp. 3–5.

Brooks, Cleanth and Robert Penn Warren. *Understanding Poetry.* New York: Holt, 1950, pp. 389–397.

3 —| **Brower, Reuben A.** *The Poetry of Robert Frost: Constellations of Intention.* New York: Oxford University Press, 1963, pp. 23–27.

Conder, John J. "'After Apple Picking': Frost's Troubled Sleep," in *Frost: Centennial Essays.* Edited by the Committee on the Frost Centennial of the University of Southern Mississippi. Jackson: University Press of Mississippi, 1974, pp. 171–181.

The resulting bibliographic note is shown in Figure 26.

Figure 26
Keyboarded bibliographic entry for source found in Magill's Bibliography of Literary Criticism

```
Brower, Reuben A. The Poetry of Robert
     Frost: Constellations of
     Intention. New York: Oxford UP,
     1963.
          see esp. pp. 23-27
```

Works similar to Magill's bibliography are *Poetry Explication* and *Twentieth Century Short Story Explicator.* Language and literature students should also examine the *MLA International Bibliography,* which indexes literary interpretations annually. An extract is shown in Figure 27.

Another shortcut is searching out encyclopedias for your field, such as *Encyclopedia of Social Work, Encyclopedia of Psychology,* or *Encyclopedia of Geographic Information.* Look especially for bibliographic lists at the end of encyclopedia articles, such as the one shown in Figure 28 from *Encyclopedia of Psychology.*

Figure 27

*Example from
MLA International
Bibliography shows
(1) author and
dates, (2) general
articles about Frost's
poetry, and (3) an
article about a spe-
cific poem*

1 — | **FROST, ROBERT (1874–1963)**

[8762] Iwayama, Tajiro. "Robert Frost." 439–475 in Ogata, Toshihiko, ed. *America Bungaku no Jikotenkai: 20-seiki no America Bungaku II.* Kyoto: Yamaguchi; 1982. ii, 638 pp.

[8763] Monteiro, George. "'A Way *Out* of Something': Robert Frost's Emily Dickinson." *CentR.* 1983 Summer; 27(3): 192–203. [†Relationship to Dickinson, Emily; includes comment on Bogan, Louise; MacLeish, Archibald; Wilbur, Richard.]

Poetry

[8764] Daniel, Charles L. "Tonal Contrasts in the Imagery of Robert Frost." *WGCR.* 1982 May; 14:12–15. [†Light imagery; dark imagery.]

[8765] Gage, John T. "Humour en Garde: Comic Saying in Robert Frost's Poetic." *Thalia.* 1981 Spring-Summer; 4(1): 54–61. [†Role of humor.]

[8766] Gonzàlez Martín, Jerónimo P. "Approximación a la poesía de Robert Frost." *CHA.* 1983 Apr.; 394: 101–153. [†Includes biographical information.]

[8767] Greenhut, D. S. "Colder Pastoral: Keats, Frost, and the Transformation of Lyric." *MHLS.* 1983; 6: 49–55. [†Lyric poetry. Use of pastoral. Treatment of landscape compared to Keats, John.]

2 — **[8768]** Marks, Herbert. "The Counter-Intelligence of Robert Frost." *YR.* 1982 Summer; 72(4): 554–578. [†Treatment of revelation, concealment. Sources in Bible; Milton, John: *Paradise Lost.*]

[8769] Slights, William W. E. "The Sense of Frost's Humor." *CP.* 1983 Spring; 16(1): 29–42. [†Humor; comedy; relationship to reader.]

[8770] Sutton, William A. "Some Robert Frost 'Fooling'." *MTJ.* 1983 Spring; 21(3): 61–62. [†Relationship to Clemens, Samuel.]

[8771] Trikha, Manoramma B. *Robert Frost: Poetry of Clarifications.* Atlantic Highlands, NJ: Humanities; 1983. 259 pp. [†Use of metaphor; symbolism. Sources in Emerson, Ralph Waldo; James, William.]

Poetry/"Away"

3 — **[8772]** Kau, Joseph. "Frost's 'Away!': Illusions and Allusions." *NMAL.* 1983 Winter; 7(3): Item 17.

Poetry/"Beech"

[8773] Will, Norman P. "Robert Frost's 'Beech': Faith Regained." *NMAL.* 1982 Spring-Summer; 6(1): Item 2.

Poetry/A Boy's Will (1913)

[8774] Wordell, Charles B. "Robert Frost from *A Boy's Will* to *North of Boston.*" *SALit.* 1983 June; 19:1–13. [†*North of Boston.*]

FURTHER REFERENCES

Clarke, E., & Dewhurst, K. *An illustrated history of brain function.*

Clarke, E., & O'Malley, C. D. *The human brain and spinal cord.*

Ferrier, D. *The functions of the brain.*

Finger, S., & Stein, D. G. *Brain damage and recovery: Research and clinical perspectives.*

McHenry, L. C., Jr. *Garrison's history of neurology.*

Figure 28
Sample bibliography from the end of an article in Encyclopedia of Psychology, *2nd ed., 1994.*

When you get into the stacks, look for bibliographies at the end of the books. An example of one is shown in Figure 29.

SECONDARY SOURCES

Abbott, Edith. "The Civil War and the Crime Wave of 1865–70." Social Service Review, 1977.

Amis, Moscws N. *Historical Raleigh,* 1913.

Andrews, Marietta M. *Scraps of Paper.* 1929.

Badeau, Adam. *Military History of U. S. Grant.* 1885.

Bailey, Mrs. Hugh. "Mobile's Tragedy: The Great Magazine Explosion of 1865." *Alabama Review,* 1968.

Bakeless, John. "The Mystery of Appomattox." *Civil War Times Illustrated,* 1970.

Figure 29
A portion of a bibliography list at the end of N. A. Trudeau's book, Out of the Storm

Bibliographies also appear in most scholarly journals at the end of the articles. For example, students of history depend upon the bibliographies within various issues of *English Historical Review,* and students of literature find bibliographies in *Studies in Short Fiction.* In addition, the journals themselves provide subject indexes to their own contents. For example, if your subject is *adoption,* you will discover that a majority of your sources are located in a few key journals. In such an instance, going straight to the index of one of these journals will be a shortcut.

2e   SEARCHING THE PRINTED INDEXES

An index furnishes the exact page number(s) to specific sections of books and to individual articles in magazines, journals, and newspapers. By tradition, a bibliography is a list of works on a single subject, but even a bibliography often has specific page numbers. Note that *Bibliographic Index* features both functions in its title: it *indexes* the page numbers of *bibliographies* to be found in various sources.

Fundamentally, there are five types of indexes: (1) indexes to literature in periodicals, (2) indexes to materials in books and collections, (3) indexes to materials in newspapers, (4) indexes to abstracts, and (5) indexes to pamphlets.

Of course, you can shortcut the process by going directly to the specialized indexes of your discipline, such as *Music Index* or *Philosopher's Index* (see pages 48–51).

Searching the Printed Indexes to Periodicals

For contemporary views in trade magazines, you can begin with a printed index to general magazines. Use the CD-ROM facilities if they are available (see pages 37–39).

Readers' Guide to Periodical Literature. New York: H. W. Wilson, 1900–date.

Although it indexes many nonscholarly publications, such as *Teen, Needle and Craft,* and *Southern Living,* the *Readers' Guide* also indexes important reading for the early stages of research in magazines such as:

Aging	*Foreign Affairs*	*Psychology Today*
American Scholar	*Foreign Policy*	*Scientific Review*
Astronomy	*Health*	*Science Digest*
Bioscience	*Negro History Bulletin*	*Science*
Business Week	*Oceans*	*SciQuest*
Earth Science	*Physics Today*	*Technology Review*

An entry from *Readers' Guide to Periodical Literature* is shown in Figure 30.

Figure 30 *Example from* Readers' Guide to Periodical Literature *shows (1) subject, (2) title of article, (3) author, (4) illustrated with portraits, and (5) name of periodical and publication data.*

1 — **TELEVISION BROADCASTING**
News
Courage, fear and the television newsroom [address, September 1993] D. Rather. *Television Quarterly* v 27 No1 p87–94 '94
2 — Frank Stanton: born to indispensability [cover story; interview] A. Unger. il pors *Television Quarterly* v 27
3 —
4 — No1 p2–17 '94
Is everything okay? [anchorman D. Rather] C. Pierce. il pors *Gentleman's Quarterly* v64 p196–203 + Ap '94
News, ethics, and split-personality journalism. E. E. Dennis.
5 — *Television Quarterly* v27 n1 p29–35

Bibliographic entries should be made for any sources that look promising. See Figure 22, page 46, for an example.

If your study involves a social science, consult the following index:

Social Sciences Index. Vols. 1—. New York: H. W. Wilson, 1974–
  date.

This work indexes journal articles for 263 periodicals in these fields:

anthropology   geography   political science
economics   law and criminology psychology
environmental science medical science   sociology

Researchers in the humanities should consult:

Humanities Index. New York: H. W. Wilson, 1974–date.

This work catalogs 260 publications in these fields:

archaelogy   language and literature   philosophy
classical studies   area studies   political criticism
folklore   literary   religion
history   performing arts   theology

For sources prior to 1974, consult two works that preceded *Humanities Index* and *Social Sciences Index:*

International Index. Vols. 1–18. New York: H. W. Wilson,
  1907–1965.
Social Sciences and Humanities Index. Vols. 19–61. New York: H.
  W. Wilson, 1965–1974.

Other general indexes of importance are the following:

Applied Science and Technology Index. New York: Wilson,
  1958–date.
  An index for chemistry, computer science, electronics, engineer-
  ing, geology, mathematics, photography, physics, and other relat-
  ed fields.
Biological and Agricultural Index. New York: Wilson, 1947–date.
  An index for agriculture, biology, botany, zoology, and related
  fields.
Business Periodicals Index. New York: Wilson, 1958–date.
  An index to many important journal articles for accounting, ad-
  vertising, business, marketing, and related fields.
Education Index. New York: Wilson, 1929–date.
  An index for education, physical education, and related fields.
Recently Published Articles. Washington, D.C.: American Historical
  Association, 1976–date.
  An index to journal articles in history and related fields.

In addition to these major indexes, you should examine especially the indexes for your discipline as listed in the Appendix of this book on pages
365–97.

Searching an Index to Abstracts

An index to abstracts, although it requires an extra step in the process, will actually accelerate your work. You can read an abstract in the reference room and only if the article appears promising will you need to pursue the search.

The Appendix to this book (pages 365–97) lists by discipline the important indexes to abstracts, such as these:

Abstracts of English Studies
Biological Abstracts
Chemical Abstracts
Psychological Abstracts
Sociological Abstracts

For example, a student with the topic *suicide* searched the Appendix under "Indexes to Journal Articles in Psychology"; she then searched the appropriate issue of *Psychological Abstracts* for abstract number 45492, as shown in Figure 31.

If the source appears useful, this writer should make an appropriate bibliographic card and then quote from the original journal, which in Fig-

Figure 31
Example from
Psychological
Abstracts, *1994,*
shows
(1) abstract
number,
(2) author,
(3) affiliation,
(4) title of
the article,
(5) citation that tells
you where to find
the full article, and
(6) abstract of the
article

Suicide—Serials: 44592, 45312, 45313, 45343, 45489, 45491, 45492, 45494, 45497, 45501, 45516, 45522, 45831, 46048, 46233, 46295, 46387, 46414 46662, 46852, 47426 **Books:** 45528, 45530

1 — 45492. **Komisin, Lola Kelly.** (St Elizabeth Hosp Medical Ctr, Youngstown, OH) **Personality type and suicidal behaviors in college students.** *Journal of Psychological Type,* 1992, Vol 24, 24–32. Investigated the relationship between psychological type and various categories of suicidal behavior in college students. In addition, the relationship between type and the individual's perception of the problem or situation causing the most unhappiness was examined for each of the suicidal behavior categories. The Myers-Briggs Type Indicator and a shortened version of the Suicidal Behavior Questionnaire were administered to 367 college students. Results indicate that Ss fitting the INFP psychological type were more likely to engage in suicidal behaviors, while Ss fitting the ESTJ psychological type were least likely to engage in suicidal behaviors. The findings also suggest that the problems commonly identified as contributing to suicidal behavior are interpersonal in nature and may be moderated by personality.

ure 31 is *Journal of Psychological Type.* If the journal is not available, the researcher may quote from the abstract and note that fact in the text and in the bibliographic entry (see 294–95). That is, let your readers know that you are citing from an abstract, not from the entire article. *Note:* the original authors usually write the abstracts that appear in printed indexes. You may quote from these abstracts. The same is not true with InfoTrac and ProQuest abstracts (see page 38).

You may wish to read the abstracts to the dissertations of graduate students, as listed in this reference source:

> *Dissertation Abstracts International.* (Ann Arbor: Univ. Microfilms, 1970–date.

Look for issue Number 12, Part II, of each volume; it contains the cumulative subject and author indexes for Issues 1–12 of the volume's two sections—*A: Humanities and Social Sciences* and *B: Sciences and Engineering.* For example, the index of *Dissertation Abstracts International A* of May 1991 (see Figure 32) lists the following entries under the heading *Children:*

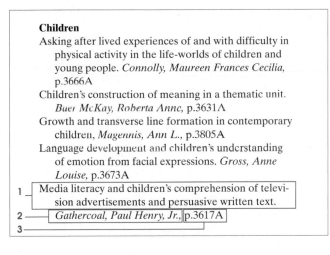

Children
Asking after lived experiences of and with difficulty in physical activity in the life-worlds of children and young people. *Connolly, Maureen Frances Cecilia,* p.3666A
Children's construction of meaning in a thematic unit. *Buer McKay, Roberta Anne,* p.3631A
Growth and transverse line formation in contemporary children, *Magennis, Ann L.,* p.3805A
Language development and children's understanding of emotion from facial expressions. *Gross, Anne Louise,* p.3673A
1 — Media literacy and children's comprehension of television advertisements and persuasive written text.
2 — *Gathercoal, Paul Henry, Jr.,* p.3617A
3 —

Figure 32
Example from the index to Vol. 46, Dissertation Abstracts International, *1991, shows (1) title of dissertation, (2) author, and (3) page number where abstract can be found*

The abstract of Paul Gathercoal's dissertation is found on page 3617A. It appears as shown in Figure 33.

An abstract, of course, only briefly summarizes the entire work. As has already been explained, you may cite the abstract in your paper if you include the words *dissertation abstract* in the text and in your Works Cited entry (see pages 300–01). If you need the full dissertation and have time, order a copy of the complete work from University Microfilms, Inc., Ann Arbor, MI 48106.

Figure 33

Example from
Dissertation
Abstracts
International, *1991,*
shows
(1) title of
dissertation;
(2) author, degree
earned, school, and
date;
(3) total number
of pages of the
dissertation;
(4) faculty chair of
the dissertation
committee;
(5) order number if
you desire to order a
copy of the complete
work, and
(6) the abstract

1— **Media literacy and children's comprehension of television advertisements and persuasive written text.** Gather-
2— coal, Paul Henry, Jr. Ph.D. *University of Oregon,* 1990.
3— 258 pp. Adviser: Edna P. DeHaven **Order Number**
5— **DA9111111**
4—

6— The purpose of this study was to measure the effect a media literacy course of instruction had on children's comprehension of television advertisements and persuasive written text. This study differed from previous research inasmuch as a *process* approach to teaching and learning media literacy was implemented and measured for a significant effect on children's comprehension of television advertisements and their comprehension of persuasive written text.

A nonequivalent control group design was used. Fifth grade students and teachers in two elementary schools within one public school district in Oregon participated in the study. One elementary school housed the treatment group and the other housed the control group. There were three separate classes of fifth grade students in each school. All students were pretested for comprehension of television advertisements and persuasive written text. The treatment and control groups' pretest and posttest mean scores were statistically tested for significant differences.

A t-test for independent groups, with alpha set at 0.05, was employed to measure statistical significance. Testing indicated that there was no discernible bias between the treatment and control groups' pretest mean scores for comprehension of television advertisements $[t(119) = .11, \ p = .915]$ and persuasive written text $[t(113) = 1.18, \ p = .241]$. However the treatment group's posttest mean scores were significantly higher than the control group's mean scores for comprehension of television advertisements $[t(112) = 3.15, \ p = .001]$ and persuasive written text $[t(111) = 2.54, \ p = .0065]$. The findings suggest that a *process* oriented media literacy course of instruction can significantly improve children's comprehension of television advertisements and persuasive written text.

Searching the Biographical Indexes for Authors and Personalities

When writing about a specific person, the reference section provides multiple sources, some specific to a field, such as *American Men and Women of Science: The Physical and Biological Sciences* and *Who's Who in Hard Money Economics*. The Appendix of this book, pages 365–97 , lists biographical studies by discipline. Several general indexes have value.

Biography Index: A Quarterly Index to Biographical Material in Books and Magazines. New York: H. W. Wilson, 1946/47–date.

Biography Index is a starting point for studies of famous persons. It gives clues to biographical information for people of all lands. Note the short excerpt from *Biography Index,* as shown in Figure 34.

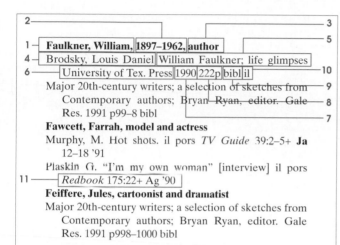

Figure 34
Example from
Biography Index,
*1991, (1) subject,
(2) dates of subject's
birth and death, (3)
subject's profession,
(4) author of the
biography, (5) title
of the biography,
(6) publisher,
(7) date of publica-
tion, (8) number of
pages, (9) contains a
bibliography,
(10) illustrated, and
(11) publication
data for a periodical*

Current Biography Yearbook. New York: Wilson, annually.

This work provides a biographical sketch of important people. Most articles are three to four pages in length and, most importantly, they include a short bibliography at the end.

Contemporary Authors. Detroit: Gale, annually.

Use this biographical guide for current writers in the fields of drama, fiction, journalism, motion pictures, nonfiction, poetry, television, among others. It provides a thorough overview of most contemporary writers, giving a list of writings; biographic facts (including a current address and agent); a list of writings; sidelights; and, in many cases, an interview by *Contemporary Authors (CA)* with the author. Most entries include a bibliography of additional sources to the writer.

Dictionary of Literary Biography. Detroit: Gale, 1978–date.

In more than 100 volumes, this work provides a profile of thousands of writers under such titles as these:

American Humorists, 1800–1950
Victorian Novelists After 1885
American Newspaper Journalists, 1926–1950

A comprehensive index will help you locate the article on your author. Use the *Dictionary of Literary Biography* not only for the profile of the author but also for the bibliography that ends each essay. Figure 35 shows a portion of the bibliography on poet Anne Sexton.

Figure 35
Sample excerpt from
Dictionary of
Literary Biography

WORKS OF ANNE SEXTON

POEMS

To Bedlam and Part Way Back. Boston: Houghton Mifflin, 1960.
All My Pretty Ones. Boston: Houghton Mifflin, 1962.
Selected Poems. London: Oxford University Press, 1964.
Live or Die. Boston: Houghton Mifflin, 1966; London: Oxford University Press, 1967.
Poems. London: Oxford University Press, 1968. With Thomas Kinsella and Douglas Livingstone.
Love Poems. Boston: Houghton Mifflin, 1969; London: Oxford University Press, 1969.
Transformations. Boston: Houghton Mifflin, 1971; London: Oxford University Press, 1972.
The Book of Folly. Boston: Houghton Mifflin, 1972; London: Chatto and Windus, 1974.
The Death Notebooks. Boston: Houghton Mifflin, 1974; London: Chatto and Windus, 1975.
The Awful Rowing Toward God. Boston: Houghton Mifflin, 1975; London: Chatto and Windus, 1977.
45 Mercy Street, edited by Linda Gray Sexton. Boston: Houghton Mifflin, 1976; London: Martin Secker and Warburg, 1977.
Words for Dr. Y, edited by Linda Gray Sexton. Boston: Houghton Mifflin, 1978.

CHILDREN'S BOOKS (with Maxine Kumin)

Eggs of Things. New York: Putnam, 1963.
More Eggs of Things. New York: Putnam, 1964.
Joey and the Birthday Present. New York: McGraw-Hill, 1971.
The Wizard's Tears. New York: McGraw-Hill, 1975.

BIBLIOGRAPHY

Northouse, Cameron, and Thomas P. Walsh. *Sylvia Plath and Anne Sexton: A Reference Guide.* Boston: G. K. Hall and Co., 1974

CRITICISM AND REVIEWS

Alvarez, A. *Beyond All This Fiddle: Essays, 1955–57.* New York: Random House, 1969.
Boyers, Robert. "*Live or Die:* The Achievement of Anne Sexton." *Salmagundi,* 2, no. 1:41–71 (Spring 1967). Reprinted in *Anne Sexton, The Artist and Her Critics,* edited by J. D. McClatchy. Bloomington and London: Indiana University Press, 1978 (hereafter referred to as McClatchy).
Dickey, James. "Five First Books." *Poetry,* 97, no. 5:318–19 (February 1961). Reprinted in his *Babel to Byzantium.* New York: Farrar, Straus and Giroux, 1968. Also in McClatchy.
Fields, Beverly. "The Poetry of Anne Sexton." In *Poets in Progress,* edited by Edward Hungerford. Evanston Ill.: Northwestern University Press, 1967. Pp. 251–85.
Gullans, Charles. "Poetry and Subject Matter: From Hart Crane to Turner Cassidy." *The Southern Review,* 7, no. 2:497–98 (Spring 1970). Reprinted in McClatchy.
Howard, Richard. "Anne Sexton: 'Some Tribal Female Who Is Known but Forbidden.'" In his *Alone with America: Essays on the Art of Poetry in the United States Since 1950.* New York: Atheneum, 1971. Pp. 442–50

Of course, you need to make bibliographic cards for any sources that show promise for your research.

Searching the Newspaper Indexes

Newspapers provide contemporary information. Each of these indexes is helpful:

> *Bell and Howell's Index to the Christian Science Monitor.* Christian Science Publishing Society, annually.
> *The New York Times Index.* New York: New York Times, 1913–date.
> *Official Index* [to *The London Times*]. London: *Times,* 1907–date.
> *The Wall Street Journal Index.* New York: Dow Jones, annually.

By indexing the individual newspapers, each of these works indirectly indexes most newspapers by revealing the date on which the same news probably appeared in other newspapers. Many libraries have the *New York Times* and the *Wall Street Journal* on microfilm (see "Using the Microforms," page 65). One student, writing about water pollution, found the list of sources shown in Figure 36.

Figure 36
Example from Wall Street Journal Index, *1994, shows*
(1) subject;
(2) description of the article;
(3) length of the article —(S) short, (M) medium length,(L) long; and
(4) date, section number, page number, and column (April 18, Section B, page 5, column 1)

1 — WATER

The EPA, concerned about potentially hazardous concentrations of lead in well water, plans to make an unusual

2 — announcement that amounts to a public health warning about the possible dangers of lead contamination from certain types of underground pumps widely used in private wells. (M) Ap 18 - B, 5:1 — 4

3 — The Philadelphia Suburban Water Co unit of Philadelphia Suburban Corp will invest $2 million to install over four miles of 16-inch pipe to bring surface water to Chester County PA. (S)Je 6 - A, 71:3

WATER POLLUTION
see also Oil Spills

The EPA, which has heretofore been vague about how cities should deal with the problem of sewage overflow that happens after heavy rains, unveiled new procedures aimed at expediting treatment of sewage. Under the new procedures, cities must immediately adopt certain controls, such as maximizing sewage flow into treatment plants and prohibiting combined sewer overflows during dry weather. (M)Ap 12 - B, 5:1

The cleanup efforts that have transformed the Boise River over the past 24 years are examined. For various reasons, however, both environmentalists and industry have been slow to acknowledge the extent to which the nation's filthiest urban rivers have been cleaned up. (L)Ap 22 - A, 1:4

Note: Because the year is not given in the entries, you have to get it from the front of the volume you use, in this case 1994. The title is not listed; you must record it when you read the article. For sample bibliographic entries, see pages 287–89.

Searching the Pamphlet Files and Pamphlet Indexes

Librarians scan newspapers, bulletins, pamphlets, and miscellaneous materials for items of interest. They clip these and file them alphabetically by subject. You should make the pamphlet file, sometimes called the vertical file, a regular stop during preliminary investigation. It will have clippings on many topics, such as "Asbestos in the Home," "Carpel Tunnel Syndrome," "Everything Doesn't Cause Cancer," and "Medicare and Coordinated Care Plans."

The principal index to published pamphlets is:

Vertical File Index: A Subject and Title Index to Selected Pamphlet Material. New York: H. W. Wilson, 1932/35–date.

Your library may not own many of the items listed by this index, but it gives a description of each entry, the price, and the information for ordering the pamphlet. Remember, too, that the federal government publishes many pamphlets and booklets on a vast array of topics. (See Section 2f immediately following.)

National publications, such as the *Social Issues Resources Series* (*SIRS*), collect articles on special topics and reprint them as one unit on a special subject, such as abortion, AIDS, prayer in public schools, and pollution. With *SIRS* you will have 10 or 12 articles readily available on any listed topic.

The *CQ Researcher* provides one pamphlet devoted to one topic, such as "Talk Show Democracy." The text of the pamphlet examines the issues, gives background information, shows a chronology of important talk show events, expresses an outlook, and provides an annotated bibliography. It even has quotable and paraphrasable material as well as a list of additional sources, as shown by the example in Figure 37.

See the sample research paper by Stefan Hall, pages 247–63, for the way in which one researcher provided a Works Cited entry to the *CQ Researcher*.

Figure 37
A portion of a bibliographic list from the CQ Researcher *4.16 (1994)*

Books

Chester, Edward W., *Radio, Television and American Politics,* **Sheed & Ward, 1969.**

This book by an American historian was described as the first complete history of the role of radio and television in American politics. The 19-page bibliography includes a host of books and articles about the early decades of radio and television.

King, Larry, with Mark Stencel, *On the Line: The New Road to the White House,* **Harcourt Brace, 1993.**

The noted radio and television talk show host chronicles candidates' increased use of call-in programs during the 1992 presidential campaign. He concludes call-in programs help "empower" the public but says the traditional press has a continuing role to play in covering politics.

Levin, Murray B., *Talk Radio and the American Dream,* **Lexington Books, 1987.**

Levin, a professor of political science at Boston University, studied hundreds of hours of talk radio tapes from two programs—one with a liberal host, the other a conservative—from 1977 and 1982. He says that "[n]o medium is more available to the disenchanted as talk radio" and "none is so prone to undermine the legitimacy" of government, business and other institutions.

2f SEARCHING THE INDEXES TO FEDERAL GOVERNMENT DOCUMENTS

All branches of the federal government publish massive amounts of material. Many documents have great value for researchers, but locating the material can be difficult and frustrating. Look especially for the following:

> U.S. Superintendent of Documents. *Monthly Catalog of United States Government Publications.* Washington, D.C.: Government Printing Office, 1895–present. Monthly.

It has an index called "Title Keyword" that provides the catalog number for all entries. A sample from the index is shown in Figure 38.

When writing your bibliographic entry (see Figure 39), include the ordering number because your library may not have the bulletin. If time permits, you can order it from the Superintendent of Documents, Government Printing Office, Washington, D.C. 20402.

Figure 38

Example from index to Monthly Catalog of United States Government Publications *shows (1) subject, (2) partial title, (3) item number, (4) author, (5) title, (6) publication facts, (7) description, and (8) subject classifications*

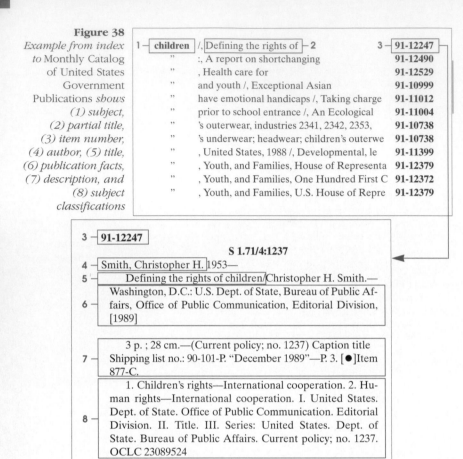

```
1 – children    /, Defining the rights of – 2              3 – 91-12247
         "        :, A report on shortchanging          91-12490
         "        , Health care for                     91-12529
         "        and youth /, Exceptional Asian         91-10999
         "        have emotional handicaps /, Taking charge  91-11012
         "        prior to school entrance /, An Ecological  91-11004
         "        's outerwear, industries 2341, 2342, 2353,  91-10738
         "        's underwear; headwear; children's outerwe  91-10738
         "        , United States, 1988 /, Developmental, le  91-11399
         "        , Youth, and Families, House of Representa  91-12379
         "        , Youth, and Families, One Hundred First C  91-12372
         "        , Youth, and Families, U.S. House of Repre  91-12379
```

```
3 – 91-12247
                        S 1.71/4:1237
4 – Smith, Christopher H. 1953—
5 –    Defining the rights of children/Christopher H. Smith.—
       Washington, D.C.: U.S. Dept. of State, Bureau of Public Af-
6 –    fairs, Office of Public Communication, Editorial Division,
       [1989]

       3 p. ; 28 cm.—(Current policy; no. 1237) Caption title
7 –    Shipping list no.: 90-101-P. "December 1989"—P. 3. [●]Item
       877-C.

       1. Children's rights—International cooperation. 2. Hu-
       man rights—International cooperation. I. United States.
8 –    Dept. of State. Office of Public Communication. Editorial
       Division. II. Title. III. Series: United States. Dept. of
       State. Bureau of Public Affairs. Current policy; no. 1237.
       OCLC 23089524
```

Note: Most federal publications are published by the Government Printing Office (GPO) in Washington, DC, regardless of the branch of government that issues them.

Figure 39

Keyboarded bibliographic entry, in MLA style, to a government document

```
S 1.71/4:1237
Smith, Christopher H. Defining the
     Rights of Children. Washington:
     GPO, 1989.
```

A second place to look for government publications is *Public Affairs Information Service Bulletin* (New York: P.A.I.S., semimonthly). A sample entry from this work, known as *PAIS,* is shown in Figure 40.

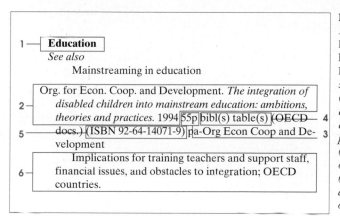

Figure 40
Example from Public Affairs Information Service Bulletin, *1994, shows (1) subject; (2) citation to the author, title, and date; (3) number of pages in the booklet; (4) contains a bibliography and tables; (5) order number; and (6) description of the article*

If this 55-page booklet looks promising for a paper you are writing, record it on a card. If your library does not house that special bulletin, you can write your request to:

Superintendent of Documents
Government Printing Office
Washington, D.C. 20402

Most documents are free and will be shipped immediately.

Search out other indexes in the government documents section of your local library and learn their resources. In many libraries a separate card catalog lists governmental holdings. The Government Printing Office, like other publishers, is converting to CD-ROM, so look for government documents on a computer if one is available.

The *Congressional Record* is the key publication of the legislative branch. Senate and House bills, documents, and committee reports are published daily with regular indexes. The *Congressional Record* should be available at your library. If not, write either the Senate Documents Room or the House Documents Room for free copies of specific legislation.

Senate Documents Room   House Documents Room
SH-BO4 Capitol Building   B-18 Ford Building
Washington, D.C. 20510   Washington, D.C. 20515

Public Papers of the Presidents of the United States is the publication of the executive branch. All members of the president's cabinet publish enormous amounts of vital information. Again, your best source for information and documents is the Superintendent of Documents.

The U.S. Code and the Constitution are the primary publications of the judicial branch. The Supreme Court regularly publishes decisions, codes, and other rulings, as do appellate and district courts. State courts also publish rulings and court results on a regular basis.

See pages 289–91 for correct methods of writing bibliographic citations to government documents of all three branches.

2g   SEARCHING FOR ESSAYS WITHIN BOOKS

Some essays get lost within collections and anthologies. You can find these essays listed by subject in the following reference work:

> *Essay and General Literature Index, 1900–1933.* New York: H. W. Wilson, 1934. Supplements, 1934–date.

This reference work indexes material within books and collections of both a biographic and a critical nature. This index enables you to find essays *within* books that you might otherwise overlook. For example, as shown in Figure 41, A. J. Raboteau's article, "Martin Luther King, Jr., and the Tradition of Black Religious Protest," appears on pages 46–65 of a book entitled *Religion and the Life of the Nation,* edited by R. A. Sherrill.

Figure 41
Example from
Essay and General
Literature Index,
June 1994, shows
(1) subject,
(2) author of article,
(3) title of article or
chapter in the book,
(4) title of the book
in which the article
appears,
(5) editor of the book,
(6) page numbers to
the article,
(7) separate entry
for Sherrill's book,
and
(8) separate entry
for the publisher

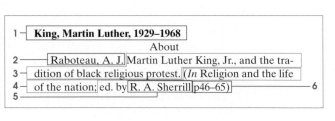

```
1─ King, Martin Luther, 1929–1968
                        About
2────────Raboteau, A. J. Martin Luther King, Jr., and the tra-
3─ dition of black religious protest. (In Religion and the life
4─ of the nation; ed. by R. A. Sherrill p46–65)────────── 6
5─
```

```
   Religion and the life of the nation; American recoveries;
      edited by Rowland A. Sherrill. University of Ill.
7─    Press 1990 268p ISBN 0-252-01693-9; 0-252-06111-X
      (pa) LC 89-35983
```

```
   University of Ill. Press, 54 E. Gregory Dr., Champaign,
      Ill. 61820 Tel 217-333-0950; refer orders to C.U.P.
8─    Services, P.O. Box 6525, Ithaca, N.Y. 14851 Tel 607-
      277-2211; 800-666-2211
```

You will need all three citations from *Essay and General Literature Index* in order to write the bibliographic entry for the Works Cited page (see Chapter 9, page 276).

2h USING THE MICROFORMS

When ordering periodicals, libraries can either buy expensive printed volumes or purchase inexpensive microform versions of the same material. Most libraries have a mixture of the two. Your library will specify in the cardex files (the list of periodicals) how journals and magazines are housed.

In particular, most libraries now store national newspapers, weekly magazines, and dissertation abstracts on microforms. This information takes the form of reels of filmed information (microfilm) or flat sheets of filmed information (microfiche). To access the microforms:

Determine if the material sought is kept on microfilm or microfiche.
Locate the microfilm or microfiche files.
Use a microfilm or microfiche reader (they differ).
Read the article.

Should you need a hard copy of a microfilmed article, the library will either supply coin-operated machines for that purpose or copy it for you.

Your library may also house guides to special microform holdings, which carry such titles as *American Culture 1493–1806: A Guide to the Microfilm Collection* or perhaps *American Periodicals 1800–1850: A Guide to the Microfilm Collection.*

Every library has its own peculiar holdings of microfilm and microfiche materials, and you must understand the particular system in use in order to take advantage of it.

2i USING THE PRINTED CATALOG CARDS

Your library's card catalog may exist as a traditional card bank in file cabinets rather than as a PAC computer file. In theory, the printed card catalog includes every book in the library, filed by subject, author, and title. In truth, the catalog is not always kept current with the latest holdings, so check with a librarian if you need a recently published work.

Begin your research at the catalog by searching a subject. Theoretically, every book available in the library is filed under one or more common headings, which are printed at the top of the card. Thus, for example, searching under the heading "Television and Children" (see Figure 42) would produce a number of books on the same subject.

The next procedure is to record call numbers and relevant information onto appropriate cards so you can keyboard the information later, as shown in Figure 43.

Figure 42
Subject cards

TELEVISION AND CHILDREN.

HQ
784   Durkin, Kevin.
T4   Television, sex roles, and
D88   children:a developmental social
1985   psychological account / Kevin
          Durkin-Milton Keynes; Philadelphia;
          Open University Press, c1985

TELEVISION AND CHILDREN.
HQ
799.2   Howe, Michael J. A., 1940-
T4   Television and children / Michael
H68   J. A. Howe—London: New University
1977b   Education, 1977.
            157 p.; 23 cm.

TELEVISION AND CHILDREN.
HQ
784   Cullingford, Cedric.
T4   Children and television/ Cedric
C84   Cullingford.—New York: St. Martin's
1984   Press, 1984.
            x, 239 p.; 23 cm.
            Includes index.
            ISBN 0-312-13235-2

TELEVISION AND CHILDREN.
HQ
784   Buckingham, David, 1954—
T4   Children talking television:
B83   the making of television literacy /
1993   by David Buckingham.—London;
          Washington, D.C.: Falmer Press,
          1993. xiv, 321 p.; 25 cm.— (Critic-
          al perspectives on literary [i.e.
          literacy] and education)
            Includes bibliographical refer-
          ences (p. 298-314) and index.

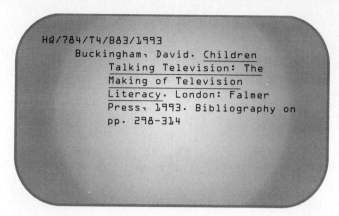

Figure 43
Sample keyboarded bibliographic entry with call number

HQ/784/T4/B83/1993
Buckingham, David. <u>Children</u>
Talking Television: The
Making of Television
Literacy. London: Falmer
Press, 1993. Bibliography on
pp. 298-314

Record the *complete* call number—in this case, HQ/784/T4/B83/1993. When you find this book in the stacks, you will discover other books on the subject nearby. Also, watch especially for bibliographic notations, which will signal an additional list of sources on the subject.

You can also search the catalog by an author's name, using the author card (see Figure 44), or by the book's title, using the title card (see Figure 45).

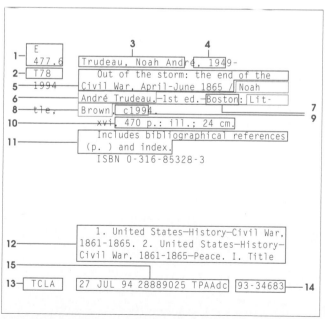

Figure 44
Example of author card shows (1) classification number, (2) author number, (3) author, (4) life span of author, (5) title, (6) editor, (7) place of publication, (8) publisher, (9) date of publication, (10) technical description, (11) note on contents of the book, (12) separate card filed under two subject headings and the title, (13) publisher of this card, (14) order number, and (15) Library of Congress call number

Figure 45
*Example of title
card shows (1) title,
usually typed in
black ink; (2) main
entry card filed un-
der "Trudeau, Noah
André"; and
(3) subject headings
under which you
will find this same
card*

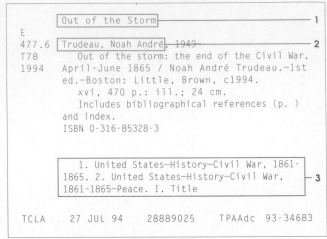

Distinguishing the Dewey Decimal System from the Library of Congress System

Your library will classify its books by one of two systems, the Dewey Decimal system or the Library of Congress (LC) system. Understanding the system your library uses is necessary it you want to use it fully as a resource. The Dewey system, for example, lists Trudeau's *Out of the Storm: The End of the Civil War, April–June 1865* (see Figure 45) with the number 973.7 T78o, and the LC system uses the number E477.6T78 1994.

Dewey Decimal System

The Dewey system has 100 divisions as shown in Figure 46. The 900 category, labeled "Geography & history," lists this subdivision: 970 General history of North America. The Trudeau book (see Figure 45) belongs to this category and is designated 973.7. in the Dewey system.

Immediately below the Dewey classification numbers are a second line of letters and numerals based on the Cutter Three-Figure Author Table. For example, T78o is the author number for Trudeau's *Out of the Storm*. The letter *T* is the initial of the author's last name. Next the Cutter table subclassifies with the Arabic numerals 78 and with the lowercase o to designate the first important letter in the title in order to distinguish this entry from similar books by Trudeau. Thus, the complete call number for Trudeau's book is 973.7/T78o. You must use the entire set to locate the book.

Figure 46
From the
Dewey Decimal
Classification and
Re73
lative Index

Second Summary*
The Hundred Divisions

000	**Generalities**	**500**	**Natural sciences & mathematics**
010	Bibliography	510	Mathematics
020	Library & information sciences	520	Astronomy & allied sciences
030	General encyclopedic works	530	Physics
040		540	Chemistry & allied sciences
050	General serials & their indexes	550	Earth sciences
060	General organizations & museology	560	Paleontology Paleozoology
070	News media, journalism, publishing	570	Life sciences
080	General collections	580	Botanical sciences
090	Manuscripts & rare books	590	Zoological sciences
100	**Philosophy & psychology**	**600**	**Technology (Applied sciences)**
110	Metaphysics	610	Medical sciences Medicine
120	Epistemology, causation, humankind	620	Engineering & allied operations
130	Paranormal phenomena	630	Agriculture
140	Specific philosophical schools	640	Home economics & family living
150	Psychology	650	Management & auxiliary services
160	Logic	660	Chemical engineering
170	Ethics (Moral philosophy)	670	Manufacturing
180	Ancient, medieval, Oriental philosophy	680	Manufacture for specific uses
190	Modern Western philosophy	690	Buildings
200	**Religion**	**700**	**The arts**
210	Natural theology	710	Civic & landscape art
220	Bible	720	Architecture
230	Christian theology	730	Plastic arts Sculpture
240	Christian moral & devotional theology	740	Drawing & decorative arts
250	Christian orders & local church	750	Painting & paintings
260	Christian social theology	760	Graphic arts Printmaking & prints
270	Christian church history	770	Photography & photographs
280	Christian denominations & sects	780	Music
290	Other & comparative religions	790	Recreational & performing arts
300	**Social sciences**	**800**	**Literature & rhetoric**
310	General statistics	810	American literature in English
320	Political science	820	English & Old English literatures
330	Economics	830	Literatures of Germanic languages
340	Law	840	Literatures of Romance languages
350	Public administration	850	Italian, Romanian, Rhaeto-Romanic
360	Social services; association	860	Spanish & Portuguese literatures
370	Education	870	Italic literatures Latin
380	Commerce, communications, transport	880	Hellenic literatures Classical Greek
390	Customs, etiquette, folklore	890	Literatures of other languages
400	**Language**	**900**	**Geography & history**
410	Linguistics	910	Geography & travel
420	English & Old English	920	Biography, genealogy, insignia
430	Germanic languages German	930	History of ancient world
440	Romance languages French	940	General history of Europe
450	Italian, Romanian, Rhaeto-Romanic	950	General history of Asia Far East
460	Spanish & Portuguese languages	960	General history of Africa
470	Italic languages Latin	970	General history of North America
480	Hellenic languages Classical Greek	980	General history of South America
490	Other languages	990	General history of other areas

*Consult schedules for complete and exact headings

Library of Congress Classification System

The LC system also uses a combination of letters and numerals for its divisions, as shown in Figure 47. Note that *E–F* designates "History: America (Western Hemisphere)." Accordingly, Trudeau's book is assigned *E–F* with the subentries 477.6. Then, as with the Cutter system, LC uses the first letter of the author's name and a number, *T*78.

Figure 47
*From the Library
of Congress
system*

**LIBRARY OF CONGRESS CLASSIFICATION
SCHEDULES**

For sale by the Cataloging Distribution Service, Library of Congress, Building 159, Navy Yard Annex, Washington, D.C. 20541, to which inquiries on current availability and price should be addressed.

A	General Works
B–BJ	Philosophy, Psychology
BL–BX	Religion
C	Auxiliary Sciences of History
D	History: General and Old World (Eastern Hemisphere)
E–F	History: America (Western Hemisphere)
G	Geography. Maps. Anthropology. Recreation
H	Social Science
J	Political Science
K	Law (General)
KD	Law of the United Kingdom and Ireland
KE	Law of Canada
KF	Law of the United States
L	Education
M	Music
N	Fine Arts
P–PA	General Philology and Linguistics.
	Classical Languages and Literatures
PA Supplement	Byzantine and Modern Greek Literature.
	Medieval and Modern Latin Literature
PB–PH	Modern European Languages
PG	Russian Literature
PJ–PM	Languages and Literatures of Asia, Africa, Oceania, American Indian Languages, Artificial Languages
P–PM Supplement	Index to Languages and Dialects
PN, PR, PS, PZ	General Literature, English and American Literature, Fiction in English.
	Juvenile Belles Lettres
PQ Part 1	French Literature
PQ Part 2	Italian, Spanish, and Portuguese Literatures
PT Part 1	German Literature
PT Part 2	Dutch and Scandinavian Literatures
Q	Science
R	Medicine
S	Agriculture
T	Technology
U	Military Science
V	Naval Science
Z	Bibliography, Library Science

Another example of these systems follows:

Library of Congress:	***Dewey Decimal***
TD [Environmental Technology]	628.53 [Engineering & allied operations]
833 [Air Pollution]	
.H48 [Author Number]	H461u [Author Number]

By using either set of numbers, depending upon your library, you would find this book:

Hesketh, Howard E. *Understanding and Controlling Air Pollution.* 2nd ed. Ann Arbor: Ann Arbor Science, 1974.

2j   COLLECTING DATA OUTSIDE THE LIBRARY

Conduct primary research in the laboratory and in the field whenever your topic permits. Without doubt, the library is an invaluable source of information when writing a research paper, but materials also exist in other places. Converse with other people in person or by letter, and if time permits conduct in-depth interviews or use a questionnaire. Watch for television specials, visit the court house archives, and perhaps do some empirical research under the guidance of an instructor (see pages 78–79).

Interviewing Knowledgeable People

Talk to persons who have experience with your subject. Personal interviews are time-consuming, but they can elicit valuable in-depth information. It will be information that few others will have.

If necessary, post a notice, such as the following, soliciting help: "I am writing a study of local folklore. Wanted: people who have a knowledge of regional tales." Look to organizations for experienced persons. For example, the writer on folklore might contact the county historian, a senior citizens's organization, or a local historical society.

Prepare in advance several pertinent, focused questions. For accuracy, use a tape recorder (with permission of the person interviewed, of course). Conduct telephone interviews only if you find them necessary; they will not be as thorough as interviews conducted face-to-face.

Do not base your conclusions on the evidence of one person; consult with several people and weigh their opinions in the same way in which you consider the evidence from various written sources.

Keep in mind three criteria for the interview:

Consult with experienced persons.
Be courteous and on time for interviews.
Be prepared with a set of questions for initiating the interview.

When you are finished gathering information, keyboard the bibliographic entry as shown in Figure 48.

Figure 48
Keyboarded bibliographic entry for an interview

```
Thornbright, Mattie Sue. Personal
       interview. 15 Jan. 1994.
```

For a published interview see Chapter 9, page 302.

Writing Letters

Correspondence provides a written record for research. Ask pointed questions so that correspondents will respond directly to your central issues. As a courtesy, provide a self-addressed, stamped envelope. Note this example:

```
April 5, 1994

Mrs. M. W. Beach
512 Meadowlark
Clarksville, TN 37040

Dear Mrs. Beach:

I am a college student conducting research into folklore
of Montgomery County. In particular, I need specifics on
tales of ghosts. Are any ghosts said to haunt homes in
this region? Which homes? Do the ghosts have names?

I have enclosed a self-addressed stamped envelope, but
you may telephone me with the information if that method
would be more convenient for you.

Sincerely yours,

Peggy Thompson
560 Thompson Hall
APSU Station
Clarksville, TN 37044
(615) 555-4657
```

If you receive information for your research paper by letter, keyboard it properly for your bibliography, as shown in Figure 49.

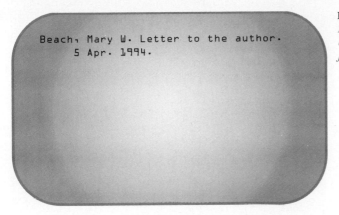

Figure 49
Keyboarded bibliographic entry for a letter

Examining Audiovisual Materials

Important data can be found in audiovisual materials—audio cassettes, films, filmstrips, music, phonograph recordings, slides, and videocassettes. You will find these sources both on and off campus. Consult such guides as *Educational Film & Video Locator* (film, filmstrips, and tapes), *Media Review Digest* (nonprint materials), *Video Source Book* (video catalog), *The Film File,* or *International Index to Recorded Poetry.*

If you use any audiovisual material in your research, record it in the correct style as shown in Figure 50. (See also 9g, 301–306.)

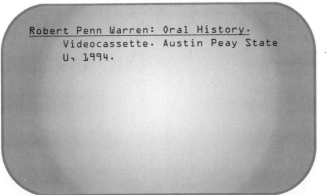

Figure 50
Keyboarded bibliographic entry for a video

Watching Television and Listening to Radio Programs

Numerous quality programs are available on television and radio if you watch the schedules carefully. In particular, check the programming of the Public Broadcasting System. In addition, national and local talk shows often discuss important issues. Remember to keep accurate notes relating to names, statements, and program title. If you find something worthwhile, you will need to cite these sources as bibliographic entries, as shown in Figure 51.

Figure 51
Keyboarded bibliographic entry for a television program

```
"Newsmakers Sunday." CNN News. CNN.
       Atlanta. 12 Jan. 1994.
```

Attending Lectures and Public Addresses

Watch bulletin boards and the newspaper for a featured speaker who might visit your campus. Take careful notes and, if it is made available, retain a copy of the lecture or speech. Remember, too, that many lectures, reproduced on video, are available in the library or in departmental files. A properly styled citation for a lecture is shown in Figure 52.

Figure 52
Keyboarded bibliographic entry for a lecture

```
Petty-Rathbone, Virginia. "Edgar Allan
       Poe and the Image of Ulalume."
       Lecture. Brown Hall, U of
       Kentucky. 3 May 1994.
```

Investigating Local Government Documents

Search the files on three levels of government—city, county, and state. As a constituent, you are entitled to the services of local, state, and federal officials. If your topic demands it:

Consult with the personnel at the mayor's office by phone or in person

Attend a city council meeting

Search out printed documents

The latter is available from three different sources.

First, visit the county clerk's office where you can find facts on each election, census, marriage, birth, and death. These archives include wills, tax rolls, military assignments, deeds to property, and much more. Therefore, a trip to the local courthouse can be rewarding, helping you trace the history of the area and its people.

Second, contact by phone a state office that relates to your research, such as Consumer Affairs (general information), Public Service Commission (which regulates public utilities such as the phone companies), Department of Human Services (which administers social and welfare services). The agencies may vary by name in your state. Remember, too, that the state has an archival storehouse for its records. As with the county records, these are available for public review. At this statehouse, you might investigate certain legislative documents that have affected your legislative district. Keep in mind that you will need diligence, will need to query strangers, and will need to travel off campus.

Third, a U.S. senator or representative can send booklets printed by the Government Printing Office. A list of these materials, many of which are free, appears in a monthly catalog issued by the Superintendent of Documents, *Monthly Catalog of United States Government Publications* (Washington, D.C.: Government Printing Office, 1895–date). Most college libraries house this catalog. In addition, you can visit personally the National Archives Building in Washington, D.C., or visit one of the regional branches in Atlanta, Boston, Chicago, Denver, Fort Worth, Kansas City, Los Angeles, New York, Philadelphia, or Seattle. Their archives contain court records and government documents, which you can review in two books: *Guide to the National Archives of the United States* and *Select List of Publications of the National Archives and Record Service.* You can borrow some documents on microfilm if you consult *Catalog of National Archives Microfilm Publications,* which can be found in most college libraries.

One researcher, for example, found the table shown in Figure 53 while looking for information on shifts in population.

The researcher also made a bibliographic entry, as shown in Figure 54, to record the source of this table.

Figure 53

Table on population from Courtenay M. Slater and George E. Hall, eds., 1993 County and City Extra. Reproduced by permission of Slater-Hall Information Products, from Bernan Press, Lanbam, MD, 1993 (copyright).

Population change, 1980-1990

Cities with the most rapid population growth

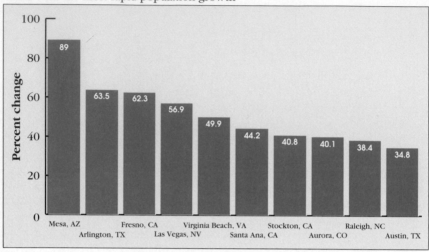

Figure 54
Keyboarded bibliographic entry to 1993 County and City Extra

```
REF/HA/202/A37
"Population Change, 1980-1990." 1993
     County and City Extra: Annual
     Metro, City and County Data Book.
     Ed. Courtnenay M. Slater and
     George E. Hall. Lanham, MD: Bernan
     Press, 1993.
```

Reading Personal Papers

Search out letters, diaries, manuscripts, family histories, and other personal materials that contribute to your study. In particular, college libraries often house private collections. The city librarian may help you to contact the county historian and private citizens who collect local documents; thereby, librarians can help access this rich source of eyewitness accounts. Figure 55 shows a bibliographic entry to record a personal paper.

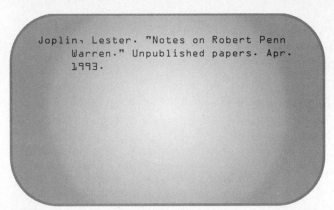

Figure 55
*Keyboarded
bibliographic entry
for personal papers*

```
Joplin, Lester. "Notes on Robert Penn
    Warren." Unpublished papers. Apr.
    1993.
```

See also "Unpublished Paper," Chapter 9, page 306.

Conducting a Survey with a Questionnaire

Questionnaires often produce accurate data that you can tabulate and analyze quickly. However, various degrees of bias can creep into a questionnaire unless the questions are worded very carefully and you remain objective. If necessary, let somebody else proofread the questions. Be on guard against your own prejudices, for the danger is that the results of your questionnaire may prove only what you want them to. Using a loaded question is a common error when writing a questionnaire. For example:

```
Do you believe in supporting the morality of America by
protesting against abortion clinics?
```

This question assumes that a *no* answer will come only from those who have no respect for the morality of America.

Be on guard against questions that are too personal (Do you ever smoke marijuana? How often?). Change them to open-ended questions (Do your acquaintances ever smoke marijuana in your presence? If yes, how often?).

Figure 56
*Keyboarded
bibliographic entry
for a questionnaire*

```
Mason, Valerie, and Sarah Mossman.
    "Child Care Arrangements of
    Parents Who Attend College."
    Questionnaire. Knoxville: U of
    Tennessee. Jan. 1994.
```

In general, a random sampling will survey every part of a selected population by age, sex, race, education, income, residence, and other factors. Use the formal survey as an information-obtaining device only when you are experienced with tests and measurements as well as statistical analysis.

A bibliographic entry for a questionnaire is shown in Figure 56. See also "Miscellaneous Materials," Chapter 9, 302–03.

Writing a Case Study

A case study is a formal report based upon your examination of a pre-arranged subject. For example, it might require you to examine patterns of behavior in order to build a profile of a person that is based on biographic data, interviews, tests, and observations. Once completed, the case study becomes evidence for your research paper. Such work should only be conducted under the guidance of your instructor or supervisor.

If you do have the opportunity to write and use a case study for a research paper, Figure 57 illustrates the format for a bibliographic entry.

Figure 57
*Keyboarded
bibliographic entry
for a case study*

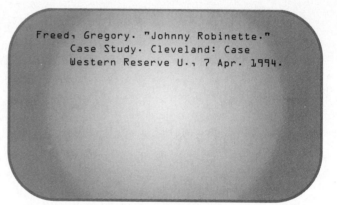

Freed, Gregory. "Johnny Robinette."
    Case Study. Cleveland: Case
    Western Reserve U., 7 Apr. 1994.

Conducting Experiments, Tests, and Measurements

Empirical research, usually performed in a laboratory, can determine why and how things exist, function, or interact with one another. If you use such research in your paper, you need to explain your methods and findings in pursuit of the hypothesis (your thesis). Such an experiment thereby becomes primary evidence for your paper.

For example, if you experimented with a species of reptiles at a test site near Cherokee Lake, you would have to write a report that provided four distinct parts:

1. *Introduction* to explain the design of your experiment:

a. Present the purpose of the study.

b. State the hypothesis and how it relates to the problem.

c. Provide the theoretical implications of the study.

d. Explain the manner in which the study relates to previously published work.

2. *Method* to describe what you did and how you conducted the study:

a. Name the specific subjects who participated, whether human or animal (e.g., 15 third-grade students)

b. Describe the apparatus to explain your equipment and how you used it.

c. Summarize the procedure(s) used in the execution of each stage of your work.

3. *Results* to report your findings:

a. Summarize the data that you collected.

b. Provide the necessary statistical treatment of the findings with tables, graphs, and charts.

c. Include findings that conflict with your hypothesis.

4. *Discussion* to explain the implications of your work:

a. Evaluate the data and its relevance to the hypothesis.

b. Interpret the findings as necessary.

c. Discuss the implications of the findings.

d. Qualify the results and limit them to your specific study.

e. Make inferences from the results.

Your experiment and the writing of the report will probably require the assistance of your instructor. Seek his or her advice often.

If used, empirical research should be entered in the works cited in the style shown in Figure 58.

Figure 58
Keyboarded bibliographic entry for test results

```
King, Ralph. Frequency Graph. New
    Brunswick, NJ: Rutgers U. 15 Dec.
    1994.
```

3 *Organizing Ideas and Setting Goals*

After the initial search of library sources, you need to organize your ideas so that reading and note taking will relate directly to your specific needs. Your notes must grow from carefully drawn plans, which may include a research proposal, a list of ideas or questions that establish your key terminology, or a rough outline. In addition, the design of your study should match an appropriate academic model, called a *paradigm*. Possible paradigms are discussed in Section 3b. This chapter also includes instructions for crafting a final outline to keep your manuscript well ordered.

3a CHARTING A DIRECTION AND SETTING GOALS

Do not plunge too quickly into note taking. You need to know *what* to look for and *why* you need it; therefore, frame your key ideas in a chart or outline. To do this, you need the necessary terminology for labeling your notes.

Using Your Research Proposal to Direct Your Note Taking

Your research proposal (see pages 18–24) may introduce issues. For example, the last sentence of this research proposal names four topics worthy of research.

```
I want to address young people who think they need a tan
in order to be beautiful. Preliminary investigation
indicates that ultraviolet radiation causes severe skin
damage that is cumulative; that is, it builds adverse
effects with each exposure. My role is to investigate
```

```
the facts and explore options for those who desire a
good tan. I need information on skin types, sun expo-
sure, tanning beds, and types of skin damage.
```

Another writer sketched the following research proposal, which lists a couple of key terms (objectivity, symbolic reality) and names four classes of people that need investigation—host, guest, studio audience, and the viewer at home. This writer will know what to search for in articles and books.

```
This paper will examine objectivity on television talk
shows, which promote their news value but seem more
concerned about titillating the audience to build their
ratings and advertising dollars. Objectivity is an
ideal, and viewers should understand that television
gives us symbolic reality like a novel or a staged
drama. The talk show host, the guests, the studio
audience, and even the viewer at home are all
participants in a staged show that has little to do with
reality.—Stefan Hall
```

(See pages 247–63 for Hall's complete paper.)

Listing Key Ideas to Set Directions for Note Taking

To develop your key terminology, follow two fairly simple steps: (1) jot down ideas or words in a rough list, and (2) expand the list to show a hierarchy of major and minor ideas. One researcher started with this set of key words:

```
Natural sun
Tanning beds
Sunscreens
Time in the sun or under the screen
Ultraviolet radiation
Skin damage
```

The writer could begin note taking with this list and write one of the entries at the top of each note card.

Ranking Your Major Headings and Their Subheadings

As early as possible, arrange the topics into a rough outline, which should show the hierarchy of the issues and their importance:

```
The tanning process
    Natural sun
    Artificial light at tanning salons
    Time in the sun or under the screen
```

```
Effects of radiation on the skin
    Immediate skin damage
    Long-term skin damage
Protection
    Oils
    Sunscreens
    Time control
```

This outline, although sketchy, provides the terminology for scanning sources, checking alphabetic indexes, and conducting interviews or questionnaires (see Section 2j).

Using Questions to Identify Issues

You might also find it useful to list questions about your topic. The questions will invite you to develop answers in your notes.

```
Is there such a thing as a healthy tan?
How does a tan differ from sunburn?
What causes skin damage?
How prevalent is skin damage?
What are short-term consequences of a sunburn?
What are long-term consequences of a sunburn?
```

You should try to answer every question with at least one note card. One question might lead to others, and your answer to a question might produce a topic sentence for a paragraph, as shown by the note that one student keyboarded into the computer:

```
Skin damage              Rennick 63

One source argues that no tan is
healthy. "Anything that damages the
skin—and burning certainly does that—
cannot be considered safe" (Rennick
63).
```

Setting Goals by Using the Modes of Development

Try to anticipate the kinds of development you will need, and build notes that *define, compare, or explain a process*. These are modes of development that build effective paragraphs. For example, one writer developed this list:

<u>Define</u> child abuse.

<u>Contrast</u> child abuse with discipline of a child.

<u>Illustrate</u> abuse with several examples.

Use <u>statistics</u> and <u>scientific data</u>.

Search out <u>causes</u> with a focus on the parents.

Determine the <u>consequences</u> of abuse with a focus on the children.

Read and use a <u>case study</u>.

Explore the step-by-step stages of the <u>process</u>.

<u>Classify</u> the types and <u>analyze</u> the problem.

Give <u>narrative</u> examples.

With this list in hand, a writer can search for material to develop as *contrast, process, definition,* and so forth. One student keyboarded this note:

> Define <u>television</u>
>
> Most television shows are nothing more than a presentation, an easily accessible and understandable entertainment for the masses. What we must accept is that television is like a novel, a history text, a play, or a newspaper.

Another writer keyboarded the note shown below, which *contrasts* discipline with child abuse.

> Contrast child abuse with discipline
>
> Discipline is training that develops self-control and orderliness in children. It may include forms of punishment, but it has the best interests of the child in mind. In contrast, says Magnuson, "abuse violates the child for the gratification of the adult" (25).

Using Approaches Across the Curriculum to Chart Your Major Ideas

Each scholarly discipline can provide valuable insight into any given topic. Suppose, for example, that you wish to examine an event from U.S. history, such as the Battle of Little Big Horn. The following five academic disciplines would approach the topic in different ways:

POLITICAL SCIENCE   The political ambitions of General Custer may have propelled him into hasty action.

ECONOMICS   The push to conquer the Native Americans was, in part, a push to open the country to development that would enrich the nation.

MILITARY SCIENCE   The mathematical numbers were not correct for success; Custer's troops were divided at the wrong time and place.

PSYCHOLOGY   General Custer's ego may have precipitated the massacre, an event that deeply affected the thinking of most Americans, many of whom responded with hostility toward Native Americans.

GEOGRAPHY   The juncture of the Little Big Horn and the Big Horn rivers was strategically important to migrating Native Americans.

Your consideration of topics across the curriculum might produce valuable paragraphs, such as this one:

The year 1876 stands as a monument to the western policies of Congress and the President, but Sitting Bull and Custer seized their share of glory. Custer's egotism and political ambitions overpowered his military savvy (Lemming 6). Also, Sitting Bull's military tactics (he told his braves to kill rather than show off their bravery) proved devastating for Custer and his troops who no longer had easy shots at "prancing, dancing Indians" (Potter 65).

Using Your Thesis to Chart the Direction of Your Research

If you have a thesis sentence, you can frame a rough outline by listing concepts that will expand upon the thesis, as shown next:

THESIS Objectivity can never be perfectly presented by
any television broadcast nor perceived by any
viewer.

A. Real sensory data and facts provide objectivity.

B. Television provides a type of symbolic reality.

C. Viewers develop their own subjective reality.

The outline gives the writer, Stefan Hall, three categories that require detailed research in support of his thesis (see Hall's complete paper on pages 247–63). The next writer uses the same technique to list four areas worthy of investigation.

THESIS Television can have positive effects on a child's
language development.

A. Television introduces new words.

B. Television reinforces word usage and proper
syntax.

C. Literary classics come alive verbally on
television.

D. Television provides the subtle rhythms and
musical effects of accomplished speakers.

Revising Your Goals During Research

Your preliminary plans are not a binding contract, so revise the direction of your work periodically to reflect changes in your thinking and your response to the source material. Allow the paper to develop and grow; add new topics, discard others, rearrange the order, identify and develop new key words, and subordinate minor elements.

Writing a research paper is a recursive process, which means that you will examine your goals several times, rechart your direction, and move forward again. Parts of your general plan will expand or shrink in importance as you gather data and write the drafts.

These questions are helpful in evaluating your overall plan:

1. What is my role as researcher? Am I reviewing, discovering, interpreting, or theorizing?
2. What is my thesis? Will my notes and records defend and illustrate my proposition? Is the evidence convincing?
3. How specialized is my audience? Do I need to write in nontechnical language, or may I assume that the audience is knowledgeable in this field and expects in-depth discussion of substantive issues?

Your answers will determine, in part, the research notes you will need. (See also Section 3c, "Writing a Formal Outline.")

3b   USING GENERAL MODELS (PARADIGMS) TO STIMULATE YOUR NOTE TAKING

A paradigm is a universal outline, one that governs most papers of a given type. It is not content specific but provides a general model or formula. For example, this next paradigm governs reports of original research in the various scientific disciplines. (See also 2j, pages 78–79.)

INTRODUCTION	The problem
	The background
	The purpose and rationale
METHOD	Subjects
	Apparatus
	Procedure
RESULTS	
DISCUSSION	

A *paradigm,* like the one above, is a broad scaffold and a basic platform of reasoning for all papers of a certain nature. In contrast, a traditional outline, with its specific detail on various levels of subdivision, is useful for only one paper. To phrase it another way, the paradigm is an ideal pattern for the paper and the outline is a specific, content-oriented plan. They intermingle to form a unified whole.

Paradigm for Advancing Your Ideas and Theories

If you want to advance a theory in your paper, use this next design, but adjust it to fit your needs. Eliminate some items, and add new elements as necessary.

INTRODUCTION	Establishment of the problem or question
	Discussion of its significance
	Necessary background information
	Introduction of experts who have addressed the problem
	Thesis sentence that addresses the problem from a perspective not yet advanced by others
BODY	Issues involved in the problem
	Examination of the problem from past to present
	Comparison and analysis of the details and minor issues
	Citations of experts who have addressed the same problem
CONCLUSION	Advancement and defense of your theory as it grows out of evidence in the body
	Directives or a plan of action
	Additional work and research that is needed

Paradigm for the Analysis of Creative Works

If you plan a literary analysis of poetry, fiction, or drama, use this next paradigm and adjust it to your subject and purposes:

INTRODUCTION   Identification of the work
                Brief summary in one sentence
                Background information that relates to the thesis
                Biographical facts about the author that relate to the
                   specific issues
                Quotations and paraphrases of authorities that
                   establish the scholarly traditions
                Thesis sentence that establishes your particular views
                   of the literary work

BODY   Analysis divided according to such elements as
                   imagery, theme, character development, structure,
                   symbolism, narration, language, and so forth

CONCLUSION   Fundamental focus on the author of the work, not just
                   the elements of analysis as explained in the body
                In particular, a conclusion that explores the
                   contributions of the writer in concord with your
                   thesis sentence

Use this same pattern, with appropriate modifications, for a study of music, art, nonfiction, and other artistic works.

Paradigm for Position Papers

If you are writing a position paper for philosophy, religion, political science, or some other field, your paper should conform in general to this next paradigm:

INTRODUCTION   Statement that establishes the problem or controversial
                   issue that your paper will examine
                Summary of the issues
                Definition of key terminology
                Quotations and paraphrasing of sources to build the
                   controversial nature of the subject
                Background to establish the relationship between past
                   and present
                Thesis sentence to establish your position

BODY   Arguments in defense of one side
                Analysis of the issues, both pro and con
                Evidence from your reading, including quotations
                   as appropriate

CONCLUSION   Reestablishment of your thesis to make clear your
                   position, which should be one that grows logically
                   from your analysis and discussion of the issues

Paradigm for Analysis of History

If you are writing a historical or political science paper that analyzes events and their causes and consequences, your paper should conform in general to the following plan:

INTRODUCTION   Identification of the event
                 The background leading up to the event
                 Quotations and paraphrases of experts
                 A thesis sentence

BODY   Thorough analysis of the background events leading
                    up to the event
                 Tracing one historic episode to another
                 Chronological sequence that explains how one event
                    relates directly to the next
                 Citation of authorities who have also investigated this
                    event in history

CONCLUSION   Consequences of this event on the course of history
                 Reaffirmation of your thesis and, if possible, an
                    explanation on how the course of history was
                    altered by this one event

Paradigm for a Comparative Study

Writing a comparative study requires you to examine two schools of thought, two issues, or the positions taken by two persons. The paper compares and contrasts the issues, as outlined in the following general plan that offers three choices for the arrangement of the body of the paper:

INTRODUCTION   Establishment of A
                 Establishment of B
                 Brief comparison of the two
                 Introduction of the central issues
                 Citation of source materials on the subjects
                 Presentation of your thesis sentence

BODY (CHOOSE ONE)

Examination of A	Similarities of A and B	Issue 1
		Discussion of A and B
Examination of B	Differences of A and B	Issue 2
		Discussion of A and B
Comparison and contrast of A and B	Discussion of central issues	Issue 3
		Discussion of A and B

CONCLUSION   Discussion of significant issues
Conclusion that ranks one over the other
or
Conclusion that rates the respective genius of each
side

Remember that the formulas provided above are general guidelines, not ironclad rules. Use them in that spirit, and adjust each as necessary to meet your special needs.

3c   WRITING A FORMAL OUTLINE

Charting a general direction and using an appropriate paradigm will help with your note taking and with drafting a few paragraphs. However, you may need a more detailed outline for writing the complete paper and for self-evaluation of the rough draft.

A formal outline classifies the issues of your study into clear, logical categories with main heads and one or more levels of subheads.

Note: **A formal outline is not rigid and inflexible; you may, and should, modify it while writing and revising.**

Not all papers require the formal outline, and not all researchers need one. For example, a short research paper can be created from key words or a list of issues. After all, the rough outline and a first draft are preliminary steps to discovering what needs expression. However, most writers benefit by developing a formal outline that classifies the investigation into clear, logical divisions. The formal outline, which can be written before or after the first draft, keeps the final manuscript on track. The outline gives unity and coherence (see pages 157–58) to your miscellaneous handwritten notes, computer drafts, and photocopied materials. It helps to change rough ideas into polished ones.

Using Standard Outline Symbols

List your major categories and subtopics in this form:

I. _____   First major heading
  A. _____   Subheading of first degree
    1. _____   Subheadings of second degree
    2. _____
      a. _____   Subheadings of third degree
      b. _____

(1) _____		Subheadings of fourth degree
(2) _____		
(a) _____		Subheadings of fifth degree
(b) _____		
B. _____		Subheading of first degree

The degree to which you continue the subheads will depend, in part, upon the complexity of the subject. Subheads in a research paper seldom carry beyond the first series of small letters.

An alternative form, especially for papers in business and the sciences, is the *decimal outline,* which divides material by numerical divisions, as follows:

1. ——
  1.1. ——
      1.1.1. ——
      1.1.2. ——
      1.1.3. ——
  1.2. ——
      1.2.1. ——
      1.2.2. ——
2. ——

Writing a Formal Topic Outline

The topic outline is built with balanced phrases. The advantage of the topic outline is the speed with which you can develop it. Note this example that uses noun phrases:

```
II.   Television's effects on children

      A. Vocabulary development

      B. Reading ability

      C. Visual arts appreciation

      D. Writing efficiency

      E. Discovery of technology
```

The topic outline may also use gerund phrases ("Learning a vocabulary" and "Learning to read") or infinitive phrases ("To develop a vocabulary" or "To learn to read"). Shown next is one section of an outline in three different forms. The first uses noun phrases:

```
III.   The senses

       A. Receptors to detect light

          1. Rods of the retina

          2. Cones of the retina
```

The second uses gerund phrases:

```
III.   Sensing the environment
       A. Detecting light
          1. Sensing dim light with retina rods
          2. Sensing bright light with retina cones
```

The third uses infinitive phrases:

```
III.   To use the senses
       A. To detect light
          1. To sense dim light
          2. To sense bright light
```

The following is a portion of Stefan Hall's topic outline, which was written after he had sketched a rough draft. It helped him organize and classify his ideas, showing him, in particular, where to place some of his expert testimony.

```
I.   Distorting the truth with television news and talk
     shows
     A. Skewing and distorting objectivity
        1. Recognizing television as a presentation,
           like a drama
        2. Contriving an illusion (Schiller quote)
        3. Falsifying the line between fact and fiction
           (Keller quote)
     B. Perceiving objectivity in television broadcasts.
II.  Finding the scholarly issues in the way we
     construct reality
     A. Identifying three categories (Cohen, Adoni, and
        Bantz quote)
        1. Recognizing the objective social reality
        2. Accepting a symbolic social reality
        3. Building our own subjective social reality
     B. The producers: dressing television as "real" or
        "objective"
        1. Presenting both sides of a controversy
           (Kuklinski quote)
        2. Squeezing out reality to conform to a format
        3. Rehearsing and editing to compromise
           objectivity
```

Writing a Formal Sentence Outline

The sentence outline requires full sentences for each heading and subheading. It has two advantages over the topic outline:

1. Many entries in a sentence outline can serve as topic sentences for paragraphs, thereby accelerating the writing process.
2. The pattern of subjects and verbs establishes the logical direction of your thinking. (For example, "Vocabulary development" becomes "Television viewing can improve a child's vocabulary.")

Consequently, the sentence outline brings into the open any possible organizational problems rather than hiding them as a topic outline might do. The time devoted to writing a complete sentence outline, like writing complete, polished notes (see pages 120–21), will serve you well when you write the rough draft and revise it.

This next example of a sentence outline includes page citations so that sentences of the outline can be transferred easily into the text.

I. Television affects children in key areas of
    learning.
    A. Television viewing can improve the vocabulary of
       children.
       1. Negative comments by Powell and Winkeljohann
          note the simplistic nature of TV language and
          the more important role of the home
          environment.
          a. Powell fears children will lose the
             ability to express verbally their deep
             thoughts and feelings (42).
          b. Winkeljohann tested TV viewing of sets of
             children with both good and poor vocabularies,
             but she claims TV was not the "variable"
             influencing their language levels (100).
       2. A study by Rice and Woodsmall and one by
          Singer et al. tested children and found
          improved vocabulary.
          a. Rice and Woodsmall tested 3- and 5-year-
             olds who learned "novel" words on the basis
             of a short television exposure (425).
          b. Singer et al. demonstrate how children
             retain specialized vocabularies after TV
             viewing (88).
       3. Postman says children gain enormous factual
          knowledge by TV viewing (35).
       4. Surely they accumulate words in the process
          so that television offers a foundation for
          vocabulary development.

Using Notes from a Research Journal to Enrich an Outline

If you have kept a research journal, you have probably developed a number of paragraphs on your chosen topic. Review the journal, and assign each paragraph to a section of your paper. Do this by making a note, such as "put in the conclusion," or by assigning an outline number, "use in II.A.1," for example. Note this next example from Stefan Hall's computer notes. (To see how he used the material, see page 255.)

```
Put this paragraph under II.D.1
      People compromise their objectivity in
several ways. A couple of critics, Good & Hetter
(49-52) tell about an orphan who was searching for
his sister in Mexico. An  agent grabbed at the
chance to peddle the boy s story to a book agent,
a television show, and two movie producers. And we
all know about the witnesses in the O.J. Simpson
trial who compromised their testimony by talking
with publicity agents before talking with police
detectives. When Hard Copy features a quotation
from an  eyewitness, must we assume that it is
reality? Some people have what I call the
"gullible" factor; they believe any darn thing.
```

Using Basic, Dynamic Order to Chart the Course of Your Work

The finished paper should trace the issues, defend and support a thesis, and provide a dynamic progression of issues and concepts that point toward the conclusion. Each section of the paper should move your writing from identification of a problem, to analysis of the issues supported with evidence, and finally to your interpretation and discussion of the findings. For every research paper, no matter what the topic, the dynamics are generated by building anticipation in the introduction, investigating the issues in the body, and providing a final judgment.

If you have any hesitation about the design of your paper, start with this bare-bones model and expand it with your material:

```
          Title
    I.  Identify the subject
        A. Explain the problem
        B. Provide background information
        C. Frame a thesis statement
```

II.   Analyze the subject
    A. Examine the first major issue
    B. Examine the second major issue
    C. Examine the third major issue
III. Discuss your findings
    A. Restate your thesis and point beyond it
    B. Interpret the findings
    C. Provide answers, solutions, and a final opinion

Readers, including your instructor, are accustomed to this sequence for research papers. It offers plenty of leeway.

To the introduction you can add a quotation, an anecdote, a definition, statistics, and other material discussed more specifically in Section 6f. Within the body you can compare, analyze, give evidence, trace historical events, and many other matters as explained in Section 6g. In the conclusion you can challenge an assumption, take exception to a prevailing point of view, and reaffirm your thesis, as explained in Section 6h. Flesh out each section, adding subheadings as necessary. This next model adds specific content to an introduction:

Advertising in the Schools

I.   The quest for a child's money
    A. The past and a new view about children and their money
      1. Children with money
        a. Allowances and spending money
        b. Effects on the marketplace
      2. Commercial advertising in the schools
        a. Channel One
        b. Educational material from McDonald's
        c. Student clubs that sell merchandise
    B. Problems with advertising in the schools
      1. Advertisers in the classroom
        a. Quotation by Carol Herman
        b. Buying classroom time
      2. Money as the target, not the mind of the child
    C. The thesis statement: The student ought to have school as a safe zone away from the commercials.

As shown above, you should write the thesis sentence into the outline where it will appear in the paper, usually at the end of the introduction, as shown in Item C above. The thesis is the main idea of the entire paper, so do not label it as Item I in the outline. Otherwise, you may search fruitlessly for parallel ideas to put in Items II, III, and IV. (See also pages 158–59 on using the thesis in the opening.)

In every case, treat an outline or organizational chart as a tool. Like an architect's blueprint, it should contribute to, not inhibit, the construction of a finished product.

4 Finding and Reading the Best Sources

The research paper assignment tests your scholarship, especially your ability to find and cite appropriate and relevant sources. Some student researchers photocopy entire journal articles and carry armfuls of books from the library. Such diligence is misplaced. The quality of your citations far outweighs the quantity of your source materials.

This chapter offers tips about selecting and using the sources. It cuts to the heart of the matter: How do I find the best sources? Should I read all or just part of a source? How do I respond to it? The chapter also demonstrates how to write both an annotated bibliography and a review of the literature on a limited topic.

4a FINDING THE BEST SOURCE MATERIALS

Electronic sources and printed indexes can display books and articles for you, but they cannot guarantee the quality of what you find. You must do that yourself. Be skeptical about accepting every printed word as absolute. Constantly review, verify, and double-check the words of your sources. Techniques for finding the most reliable sources do exist, as explained in the following paragraphs.

Consulting with Your Instructor and the Librarians

Do not hesitate to ask your instructor or the librarians for help in finding sources. Instructors know the field, know the best writers, and can provide a brief list to get you started. Sometimes instructors will even pull books from their office shelves to give you a starting point.

Librarians know the resources of the library. Their job is to serve your research needs. They help find the appropriate reference book or the most relevant journal article.

Using Recent Sources

A book may look valuable, but if its copyright date is 1938, its content is suspect: time and new developments have probably passed it by (unless, of course, the work is a classic in its field). Scientific and technical topics always require up-to-date sources. Learn to depend upon monthly and quarterly journals as well as books. (See appropriate indexes for your field in the Appendix, pages 365–97.)

Using Journals and Magazines

In general, scholarly journals offer more reliable evidence than popular magazines. Objectivity may not be the magazine writer's purpose in writing articles, while usually, academic articles for journals are objectively documented. In addition, journal writers publish through university presses and academic organizations that require every article to pass the scrutiny of a jury of critics before its publication. Therefore, try to find a journal article or two to supplement your research in magazines. For example, in his research paper (247–63) Stefan Hall used both magazines (*U.S. News and World Report, Broadcasting and Cable,* and *The New Yorker*) and journals (*Journal of Popular Culture, Journal of Politics,* and *Columbia Journalism Review*).

Using Scholarly Books, Trade Books, and Encyclopedias

Scholarly books, like journal articles, are subjected to careful review before publication. Scholarly books treat academic topics with in-depth discussions and careful documentation of the evidence. A college library is a repository for scholarly publications—technical and scientific works, doctoral dissertations, publications of the university presses, reference books, and many textbooks.

Trade books, in general, do not explore scholarly subjects, and they seldom provide documentation. You will find trade books (for example, *How to Launch a Small Business* or *The Life of a Texas Ranger*) in public book stores and public libraries.

Stefan Hall used both types in his research paper (247–63), the trade book *News from Nowhere* and the scholarly books, *Social Conflict and Television News* and *Objectivity and the News: The Public and the Rise of Commercial Journalism.*

Encyclopedias, by design, contain brief surveys of every well-known person, event, place, and accomplishment. They will serve you well during preliminary investigation, but most instructors prefer that you go beyond encyclopedias in order to cite from scholarly books and journal articles.

Finally, be aware that many organizations publish slanted, biased articles to promote their views. There's nothing wrong with the practice, but you should be aware of such editorial policies. For example, the *New Republic* presents a liberal view of society, while the *National Review* remains staunchly conservative. A report on health care may seem reasonable on the surface, but if the publication is sponsored by a health-care insurance company, you must exercise caution. Seek the advice of your instructor if you suspect biased reporting in one of your sources.

Reading About the Author

You may need to search out information about an author for several reasons:

1. To provide biographical details in your introduction. For example, the primary topic may be Carl Jung's psychological theories of the unconscious, but some information about Jung's career might be appropriate in the paper.
2. To discuss a creative writer's life in relationship to his or her work. For instance, Joyce Carol Oates's personal life may shed some light on your reading of her stories or novels.
3. To verify the standing and reputation of somebody that you want to paraphrase or quote in your paper.

You can learn about a writer and his or her work in a biography. The librarian can help you find appropriate works, such as these:

Contemporary Authors, a set of biographies on contemporary writers
Dictionary of American Negro Biography, a review of writers and important figures in the black movement
Who's Who in Philosophy, a list and discussion of the best writers and scholars in the field

You can find reference works similar to these three books for almost every field. The Appendix, pages 365–97, lists many of them.

Conducting a Citation Search

A citation search is the discovery of authors whose works have been cited repeatedly in the literature. For example, one writer located the list of references shown in Figures 59 and 60 at the end of two articles on child abuse, and she looked for authors who appeared more than once.

The researcher marked those authors that have more than one article (Baydar, Bradley et al., and Brooks-Gunn). They deserve consideration as authorities.

Figure 59
Example from Child Development, *1994, shows authors who appear twice or more on the list with different essays*

References

Achenbach, T. M., & Edelbrock, C. S. (1984). Psychopathology of childhood. *Annual Review of Psychology, 35,* 227–256.

Bakeman, R., & Brown, J. V. (1980). Early interaction: Consequences for social and mental development at three years. *Child Development, 51,* 437–447.

Baydar, N., & Brooks-Gunn, J. (1991). Effects of maternal employment and child-care arrangements in infancy on preschoolers' cognitive and behavioral outcomes: Evidence from the Children of the NLSY. *Development Psychology, 27*(6), 932–945.

Baydar, N., Brooks-Gunn, J., & Furstenberg, F. F., Jr. (1993). Antecedents of literacy in disadvantaged youth. *Child Development, 64,* 815–829.

Benasich, A. A., Brooks-Gunn, J., & McCormick, M. C. (in press). Behavior problems in the two-to-five-year-old: Measurement and prognostic ability. *Journal of Developmental and Behavioral Pediatrics, 13.*

Bradley, R. H., & Caldwell, B. M. (1980). The relation of the home environment, cognitive competence, and IQ among males and females. *Child Development, 51,* 1140–1148.

Bradley, R. H., Caldwell, B. M., Rock, S. L., Ramey, C. T., Barnard, K. E., Gray, C., Hammond, M. A., Mitchell, S., Gottfried, A. W., Sigel, L., & Johnson, D. L. (1989). Home environment and cognitive development in the first three years of life: A collaborative study including six sites and three ethnic groups in North America. *Developmental Psychology, 25,* 217–235.

Brooks-Gunn, J., Guo, G., Furstenberg, F. F., & Baydar, N. (in press). Who drops out of and who continues beyond high school? A 20-year study of Black youth. *Journal of Youth and Adolescence.*

Brooks-Gunn, J., Klebanov, P. K., Liaw, F., & Spiker, D. (1993). Enhancing the development of low birthweight, premature infants: Changes in cognition and behavior over the first three years. *Child Development, 64,* 736–753.

The name *Bradley, R. H.* with others occurs in both Figures 59 and 60, which suggests that (1) this person and his associates are authorities in this field and (2) the student should examine these works in detail.

References

Ballard, J. L., Novak, K. K., & Driver, M. (1979). A simplified score for assessment of fetal maturation of newly born infants. *Journal of Pediatrics,* **95,** 769–774.

Bandura, A. (1977). *Social learning theory.* Englewood Cliffs, NJ: Prentice-Hall.

Bates, J. E., Freeland, C. A., & Lounsbury, M. L. (1979). Measurement of infant difficultness. *Child Development,* **50,** 794–803.

Belsky, J. (1984). The determinants of parenting: A process model. *Child Development,* **55,** 83–96.

Bloom, B. S. (1964). *Stability and change in human characteristics.* New York: Wiley.

Boyce, W. T., & Jemerin, J. M. (1990). Psychobiological differences in childhood stress response: I. Patterns of illness and susceptibility. *Developmental and Behavioral Pediatrics,* **11,** 86–93.

Bradley, R. H., & Caldwell, B. M. (1984). The HOME Inventory and family demographics. *Developmental Psychology,* **20,** 315–320.

Bradley, R. H., & Caldwell, B. M. (1988). Using the HOME Inventory to assess the family environment. *Pediatric Nursing,* **14,** 97–102.

Bradley, R. H., Caldwell, B. M., & Rock, S. L. (1990). Home environment classification system: A model for assessing the home environments of developing children. *Early Education and Development,* **1,** 238–265.

Bradley, R. H., Caldwell, B. M., Rock, S. L., Ramey, C. T., Barnard, K. E., Gray, C., Hammond, M. A., Mitchell, S., Gottfried, A. W., Siegel, L., & Johnson, D. L. (1989). Home environment and cognitive development in the first 3 years of life: A collaborative study involving six sites and three ethnic groups in North America. *Developmental Psychology,* **25,** 217–235.

Bradley, R. H., & Casey, P. H. (1992). Family environment and behavioral development of low-birthweight children, annotations. *Developmental Medicine and Child Neurology,* **34,** 822–826.

Bradley, R. H., Rock, S. L., Whiteside, L., Caldwell, B. M., & Brisby, J. A. (1991). Dimensions of parenting in families having children with disabilities. *Exceptionality,* **2,** 41–61.

Bretherton, I., & Waters, E. (1985). Growing points of attachment theory and research. *Monographs of the Society for Research in Child Development,* **50,** (1–2, Serial No. 209).

Figure 60
Example from Child Development, *1994, shows name of author who participated in writing three articles on the subject*

You should search several bibliographies and mark your bibliographic cards with stars or circles each time a source is cited more than once. Two or more stars would suggest *must* reading. In this way, the sources themselves suggest additional important books and articles. There are three citation indexes that can do some of this work for you:

> *Arts and Humanities Citation Index (AHCI)* 1977–date.
> *Science Citation Index (SCI)* 1961–date.
> *Social Sciences Citation Index (SSCI)* 1966–date

Examining the Book Reviews

Whenever one book serves as the cornerstone for your research, you can test its critical reputation by reading a review or two. Two works provide summaries and critical points of view:

> *The Booklist.* Chicago: American Library Association, 1905–date.
>> A monthly magazine that reviews new books for librarians.
>> This work includes brief summaries and recommendations.
> *Book Review Digest.* New York: H. W. Wilson, 1905–date.
>> Arranged alphabetically by author, this work provides an evaluation of several thousand books each year. It features summaries and brief quotations from the reviews to uncover the critical reception of the work.

Other reviews are hidden here and there in magazines and journals. To find them, use one of the following indexes:

> *Book Review Index.* Detroit: Gale, bimonthly.
>> This work indexes reviews in 225 magazines and journals.
> *Current Book Review Citations.* New York: H. W. Wilson, annually.
>> This work gives an author-title index to book reviews published in more than 1000 periodicals.
> *Index to Book Reviews in the Humanities.* Williamston, Michigan: Phillip Thompson Publishing, annually.
>> This index to reviews in various periodicals has entries listed by author, title, and reviewer.
> *Index to Book Reviews in the Social Sciences.* Williamston, Michigan: Phillip Thompson Publishing, annually.
>> This index to reviews in social science periodicals has entries listed by author, title, and then reviewer.

A sample page of *Book Review Digest,* shown in Figure 61, illustrates the type of information available in a review of books. After bibliographic details, it summarizes the book and then provides the reviews, one from the *Booklist* and another from the *Library Journal.* If both reviewers give a positive response to a book, as is the case in Figure 61, a researcher can feel good about using it as a source.

Figure 61

*Example from
Book Review
Digest, 1994, shows
(1) author, title,
and facts of
publication,
(2) Dewey call
number and
subject entries for
card catalog,
(3) Library of
Congress call
number,
(4) summary
description of the
work,
(5) Booklist's
evaluation of the
book, and
(6) Library
Journal's evaluation
of the book*

1 — **KERNS, LAWRENCE L.** Helping your depressed child; a reassuring guide to the causes and treatments of childhood and adolescent depression; [by] Lawrence L. Kerns, with Adrienne B. Lieberman. 284p pa $12.95 1993 Prima Pub.; for sale by St. Martin's Press

2 — 618.92 1. Children—Diseases 2. Depression, Mental 3. Child psychiatry

3 — ISBN 1-55958-275-8 (pa)   LC 92-32926

4 — SUMMARY: This work is intended to help parents "in recognizing the warning signs of clinical depression. Possible causes of depression and its potential effects—including academic failure, delinquency, eating disorders, and self-destructive behavior—are considered, . . . and strategies are suggested for working with depressed youths to open communication and build self-esteem." (Libr J) Index.

5 — REVIEW: *Booklist* v89 p1483 Ap 15 '93. Denise Perry Donavin (110w)
"The subtitle sums the book up perfectly. there is reassurance and information throughout this essential guide. . . . The focus here is on counseling, more than medication, and little attention is given to how depression interacts with other common problems such as anxiety or ADD [attention deficit disorder]. Suicide prevention and substance abuse problems are discussed. The authors are quite attentive to parental responses and touch as well upon the reverberations felt throughout the family. Only recently has the issue of children and depression been given due attention, so this book provides necessary coverage of a little-addressed topic."

6 — REVIEW: *Libr J* v118 p104 My 1 '93. Linda Cullum (190w)
"More than six million young persons in the United States suffer from serious depression. Kerns (psychology, Univ. of Illinois), a national lecturer on the subject of childhood depression, collaborates with medical writer Liebman to present a highly practical and accessible study of this [condition]. . . . An excellent section on therapeutic methods, including the often overlooked subject of hospitalization, is featured. Illustrative examples, tables, and checklists are used throughout. Recommended for parenting collections."

4b   DECIDING WHETHER TO READ ALL OR PART OF A SOURCE

Many writers have trouble determining the value of a particular article or book. However, such a determination will help you decide whether to read all or part of it as a source for your paper.

Evaluating an Article

1. The *title*. Look for key words that have relevance to your topic before you start reading an article. For example, *Children and Parents* may look ideal for a research paper on child abuse until you read the entire title, including the subtitle: *Children and Parents: Growing Up in New Guinea.*

2. An *abstract*. If an abstract is available on CD-ROM or in an abstracting publication (e.g., *Psychological Abstracts*), read it before searching for the printed article. If a printed article is preceded by an abstract, read it first. Reading an abstract is the best way to ascertain whether an essay or a book will serve your specific needs.

3. The *opening paragraphs*. If the opening of an article shows no relevance to your study, abandon it.

4. Each *topic sentence* of paragraphs in the body. These sentences will give you a digest of the author's main points.

5. The *closing paragraphs*. If the opening of an article seems promising, skim the closing for relevance. Read the entire article only if this survey encourages you.

Figure 62 shows an article that has been evaluated according to the guidelines just presented.

Figure 62
Article highlighting the opening paragraph, the topic sentences, and the closing paragraph
(Source: *U.S. News & World Report*, June 20, 1994)

The Suffocating politics of pollution

Digging trenches in the nation's clean-air war

Carrol Toledo, age 26, is in good health, a regular jogger who logs 20 miles a week. Yet at this time of year; she cuts back on her running or moves her workout indoors. As summer arrives, a brown haze often settles over Crystal City, Va., and even this physically fit accountant finds herself sucking for a breath of air.

Four years after Congress passed the Clean Air Act Amendments of 1990, 1 out of 4 Americans is still gasping for breath when lung-crippling smog reaches its summer peak. Although no one disputes the worthy public goal of clear blue skies, states are struggling with the complexities of reaching that goal. Indeed, several states are embroiled in bitter battles with federal officials over how best to clean up their noxious air. Two weeks ago, for instance, Environmental Protection Agency officials threatened to withhold approval of all new major transportation projects in Northern Virginia, including those needed for the Walt Disney Co.'s proposed history theme park near Civil War battle sites. In a letter to Gov. George Allen, agency officials declared that the state was behind in submitting a plan for a tough new program to control vehicle emissions, a major contributor to polluted skies. "We figured this would get their attention," says Peter Kostmayer, the regional EPA administrator.

In a haze. Despite such regulatory power plays, even federal environmental officials concede that getting rid of smog is a much harder challenge than anyone ever anticipated. When law-makers wrote the Clean Air Act in 1970, they focused on cleaning up tailpipe emissions. Today, new cars emit 90 percent less of the hydrocarbons that contribute to smog than they did in the late 1960s, a remarkable improvement by any measure. Yet for several reasons, the American landscape remains shrouded in smog, says Margaret Walls of Resources for the Future, a non-profit research organization in Washington, D. C. People are keeping their cars longer, and older cars are generally dirtier; about 10 percent of cars spew out 30 percent of the hydrocarbons. Americans also drive twice as many miles today as they did in 1970.

Unlike the old law, which left much of the responsibility for meeting health standards up to states, the new clean-air legislation gives the federal EPA wide-ranging enforcement powers. The law orders any state that flunks federal standards to come up with a comprehensive cleanup plan, which must be submitted to the EPA in stages. A missed deadline automatically starts an EPA penalty clock. If after 18 months the state still has failed to produce the missing provisions, the EPA must restrict development in the region. Six months later, it will cut off the state's federal highway funds.

Still, it's clear that the federal stick has not yet forced states to meet deadlines.

Last November, about half the states failed to file smog reduction plans as required, and about 10 states still have not provided the agency with provisions due in November 1992. Clean-air activists doubt that states will do any better next November at hitting another crucial deadline.

The problem is that plans are subject to the same merciless lobbying that slowed reauthorization of the Clean Air Act four years ago. Some of the elements in a cleanup plan are mandatory: For example, among other pollution-cutting schemes, the nation's smoggiest cities must introduce some alternative-fuel fleets, and they must use gasoline that has been reformulated to reduce evaporation. But states can also use their discretion in deciding how to get clean air, and it's these elements of a plan that arouse special interests and tempers. In Virginia, for instance, the fight is over vehicle emissions inspections, which when done right can help chop a region's smog-producing emissions by up to 25 percent. The EPA and clean-air advocates argue for centralized testing stations; when service stations are given the responsibility for both testing and repair, they say, there are incentives to cheat and keep polluting vehicles on the road. The Allen administration, supported by the service station lobby, maintains that cheating is a minor problem that can be effectively policed.

It's in such trenches that the clean-air war is being fought nationwide: emissions testing here and fireplace restrictions and carpooling incentives there. But most environmentalists no longer believe that these measures will be enough over the long term. The only way to clean up the skies for good is to wean Americans from their cars, they contend, and that means community and regional planning. When it's possible to get to work, take the kids to the playground and pick up a bottle of wine without hopping in a car, Americans may all breathe a little easier.

Evaluating a Book

A book requires a more diligent investigation than does an article. Several additional items must be considered before a proper evaluation can be made.

1. A *table of contents*. A book's table of contents may reveal chapters that speak directly to your topic. Often, only one chapter is useful.

2. The *preface* or *introduction*. An author's preface serves as an overview of the entire book, pinpointing the primary subject of the text and the particular approach of the author. Read an author's preface to find a statement of purpose. For example, one folklore student's reading of a preface put a new perspective on *The Bell Witch of Tennessee* in which the author, Charles Bailey Bell, says:

   > The name "Bell Witch" has always been resented by the family. They are sensitive to such an appellation. . . . The Author shall relate in this book what was handed down to him by his father, Dr. J. T. Bell, he having the recollections of his father, John Bell, Jr.[1]
   >
   > From: *A Mysterious Spirit: The Bell Witch of Tennessee* (Nashville: Elder, 1972).

   The author, Charles Bell, reveals his built-in bias about the folklore. He is a descendent of one of the principals in the story, which will color his account of what happened. To counterbalance such bias, the student searched for other sources and found contrasting views in four other books on the Bell Witch by M. V. Ingram, Sharon Shebar, Gladys Barr, and Parks Miller.

3. The *index*. A book's index will list names and terminology with page numbers for all items mentioned within the text. One student, for example, planned to research Andrew Wyeth's 1961 painting *Christina's World*. She found Wanda Corn's book, *The Art of Andrew Wyeth,* but neither the preface nor table of contents mentioned her subject, so she turned to the index and found what she needed:

   Christina's World, 38, 39, 40, 55, 74, 78, 93, 95, 143, 144, 164.

   As a side benefit, she also found at the back of the book a bibliography to Wyeth's letters and interviews and two books and articles about him.

4c   RESPONDING TO THE SOURCES

When you find source material relevant to your subject, you must respond in several ways:

1. As you read, write notes that record key ideas.
2. Write notations in the margins of photocopied materials.
3. Outline the key ideas of the source.
4. Write a summary or précis to summarize the whole.

Selecting Key Ideas for Your Notes

In many instances you may borrow only one idea from a source, one that you can rephrase into your own words. Figure 63 shows B. N. Raina's original statement; note the two highlighted sentences in the middle of the essay.

Dickinson's BECAUSE I COULD NOT STOP FOR DEATH

It has been the general difficulty with critical exegeses of Emily Dickinson's "Because I could not stop for Death—" that (1) "Death" and "Immortality" in the first stanza seem unaccountably syncopated, and (2) that "I first surmised the Horses' Head/Were toward Eternity—" of the end of the poem remains equally enigmatically without derivation. I offer the following interpretive possibility.

The crux of the poem's meanings, I suggest, is in the first two lines, "Because I could not stop for Death—/He kindly stopped for me—". We have tended mechanically to read this to mean that since the narrative subject of the poem finds herself rather too involved in the humdrum of living, with no thought of death, Death like a civil gentleman-suitor stops by in his chaise and four to take the busy persona out for the final ride, paradoxically, to the accompaniment of "Immortality." I think the lines lead us into a simplistic literalness because of the deceptive surface. Read them as you would a prototypical "romantic" utterance and the problem begins to solve itself.

To wit, translate the persona's not stopping for death into an imaginative perception of the nonreality of death. Death is death only to those who live within the time-bound finite world outside of the imaginative infinity of consciousness. That being so, the "stopped" of the second line takes on a profoundly rich ambiguity. Whereas clearly the metaphor of Death stopping by is to be retained as one level of courtship, more essentially, since the persona's consciousness has negated death, Death in turn stops, that is, *ceases* to be (the full richness of the initial "because" should now be apparent). And, appropriately, from that dialectic of consciousness is *generated* "Immortality."

—Use this idea!

Figure 63
Passage of importance to the researcher.
(Source: B. N. Raina, "Dickinson's 'Because I Could Not Stop for Death,'" *The Explicator* 43.3 (1985): 11–12.)

Rather than photocopy the entire piece, the researcher read first, related the reading to her thesis and her own outline, and keyboarded the note shown in Figure 64.

Figure 64
*Sample note
keyboarded by the
researcher*

B. N. Raina observes that death for
this speaker is an "imaginative
perception of the nonreality of death"
(12) so that death is confronted as a
window to everlasting life.
    from Raina 11-12 on Dickinson's
    "Because I Could Not Stop for
    Death"

Writing Notations on Photocopied Materials

Avoid making marks on library books and magazines, but *do* make marginal notes in your own books and magazines or on photocopied materials. Underline sentences, circle key ideas, ask questions, and react with your own comments. Figure 66 shows how one student expressed his own response to a source he was reviewing.

Outlining the Key Ideas of a Source

Most books have a table of contents, which outlines the basic ingredients of the book. Consult it for issues that deserve your critical reading. In the case of an essay, you can frame your own outline to capture an author's primary themes. Specifically, list the main ideas and subtopics (1) to show the hierarchy of issues, (2) to identify parallel parts, and (3) to locate supporting ideas. The goal is to discover the author's primary and secondary ideas.

Figure 65 shows a rough outline of Philip Yam's essay (illustrated in Figure 66). It reveals the central ideas one researcher found in the essay.

Figure 65
*Sample handwritten
outline of an essay.*

AIDS education
    Education explains casual contact
    Short training sessions breed intolerance
    Long sessions promote tolerance
    Pamphlets mislead
    In-house speakers improve attitudes

AIDS education
is crucial.

AIDS education may
cause problems.

Short programs
and the pamphlets
themselves make
workers nervous
and wary.

The answer is
longer sessions by
in-house speakers.

AIDS Education May Breed Intolerance

Two thirds of Americans would be concerned about sharing a bathroom with someone who has AIDS. One third would not lend their tools to an infected co-worker. Proximity and casual contact, of course, are not considered to be vectors for the spread of the disease. So education about the modes of transmission and known risk factors should be the best weapon against such worries.

Not necessarily, say researchers at the Georgia Institute of Technology. David M. Herold and John M. Maslyn, who study organizational behavior, believe a little education may be worse than no education at all. They found that some AIDS education programs made workers less tolerant of those with the disease.

The main culprits were programs that provided only a brochure or a presentation from an outside expert that lasted less than 45 minutes. Unfortunately, such education makes up more than half of all types of AIDS schooling in the workplace, according to the study. In contrast, longer programs, those lasting more than two hours, improved the attitudes of employees.

The problem, the researchers say, stems from the educational materials published by public health organizations. These pamphlets emphasize behavioral changes that would reduce the risk of infection. "Most education materials just show little blood cells being attacked by little monsters," Herold observes. And short corporate education sessions never discuss "how to be supportive and deal with others." Employees come away with a "Now-that-I-know-how-you-get-it, why-should-I-help-you attitude," Herold says.

Credibility is also an issue. The study found that 45-minute presentations could improve attitudes, but only if they were given by in-house spokespersons. Insiders, Herold notes, are better able to address fears specific to that workplace.

Providing information about AIDS to workers is "crucially important," Herold asserts. Most problems do not come from those with AIDS but from other workers "who raise hell with their supervisor." Moreover, as improvements in treatment allow infected people to remain healthy longer, Herold notes that more businesses "are going to have to confront the issue of workers with AIDS."

—*Philip Yam*

Writing a Summary or a Précis

A *summary* condenses into a brief note the key ideas of a source. More than anything else, it serves to remind you later on about the source's relevance to your study. In some cases you will use the summary in your paper. For further details about writing a summary, see Section 5c, pages 128–129.

A *précis* is a highly polished summary, one that you can transfer to your paper or use in an annotated bibliography. Use the précis to review a piece of writing or to write a plot summary. For further details and examples, see Section 5d "Writing Précis Notes," pages 129–133.

Figure 67 presents a quick summary of Philip Yam's article:

Figure 67
Sample summary of an article keyboarded into a computer by one student

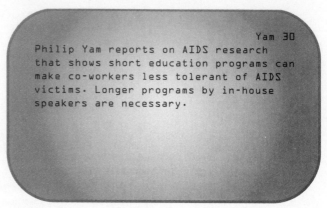

```
                                    Yam 30
Philip Yam reports on AIDS research
that shows short education programs can
make co-workers less tolerant of AIDS
victims. Longer programs by in-house
speakers are necessary.
```

4d SELECTING A MIX OF BOTH PRIMARY AND SECONDARY SOURCES

Primary sources are the original words of a writer, in the form of a novel, a speech, an eyewitness account, a letter, an autobiography, an interview, or the results of original research. Feel free to quote often from a primary source because it has direct relevance to your discussion. For example, if you examine a poem by Dylan Thomas, you must quote the poem. If you examine Bill Clinton's domestic policies on health care, you must quote from White House documents.

Secondary sources are works about somebody or about somebody's accomplishments. Secondary sources are writings about the primary sources and about the authors who produce them. Examples of secondary sources are reporters who respond to a presidential speech, reviewers who examine new scientific findings, and scholars who analyze the imagery of a poem. A biography provides a secondhand view of the life of a notable person, and a history book interprets events. These evaluations, analyses, and interpretations provide ways of looking at original, primary sources.

Do not quote liberally from secondary sources. Be selective. Use a well-worded sentence, not the entire paragraph. Work a key phrase into your text, not eight or nine lines. (See "Selecting Key Ideas for Your Notes" pages 107–08.)

The subject area of a research paper determines in part the nature of the source materials. Use the chart shown here as a guide:

	Primary Sources	***Secondary Sources***
Literature	Novels, poems, plays, short stories, letters, diaries, manuscripts, autobiographies, films, videos of live performances	Journal articles, reviews, biographies, critical books about writers and their works
Government, Political Science, History	Speeches, writings by presidents and others, the *Congressional Record*, reports of agencies and departments, documents written by historic figures	Newspaper reports, news magazines, political journals and newsletters, journal articles, history books
Social Sciences	Case studies; findings from surveys and questionnaires; reports of social workers, psychiatrists, and lab technicians	Commentary and evaluations in reports, documents, journal articles, and books
Sciences	Tools and methods, experiments, findings from tests and experiments, observations, discoveries, test patterns	Interpretations and discussions of test data as found in journals and books (scientific books, which are quickly dated, are less valuable than up-to-date journals)
Fine Arts	Films, paintings, music, sculptures as well as reproductions and synopses of these for research purposes	Evaluations in journal articles, critical reviews, biographies, and critical books about the artists and their works
Business	Market research and testing, technical studies and investigations, drawings, designs, models, memorandums and letters, computer data	Discussion of the business world in newspapers, business magazines, journals, government documents, and books
Education	Pilot studies, term projects, sampling results, tests and test data, surveys, interviews, observations, statistics, computer data	Analysis and evaluation of educational experimentation in journals, reports, pamphlets, and books

4e   PREPARING AN ANNOTATED BIBLIOGRAPHY

One way to evaluate a source is to write an annotated bibliography. An annotation notes quickly the contents of a book or article. If you write an annotated bibliography, you must read and evaluate each of your sources. The sample that follows examines several magazine articles that address issues surrounding the Children's Television Education Act of 1990. The work produces a clear picture of both the positive and the negative reactions to educational programming for children in the 1990s. For instructions on writing an annotation, see Section 5d, "Using the Précis to Write an Annotated Bibliography," pages 131–132. For instructions on writing the citation to a source, see Chapter 9 for MLA style, as shown below, or Chapter 10 for APA style.

Annotated Bibliography

Buckingham, David. "Boxing Clever: Children's
        Sophistication in Mass Media." <u>Times Educational</u>
        <u>Supplement</u> 23.4008 (Apr. 1993): vi. This author
        cites research to show that children make clever
        decisions about what they watch on television. He
        refutes the idea that children are passive prey
        for unscrupulous or uncaring programmers. Class,
        gender, and racial factors play a role, but in
        every case the child's critical perceptions are
        better than formerly estimated.

Forst, Graham. "Our Misspelt Youth." <u>World Press Review</u>
        Apr. 1992: 50. This writer condemns television's
        effect on the reading habits of children. He warns
        that children are "semi-illiterates" because they
        watch television rather than read. He endorses a
        return to reading as vital for children.

Freeman, Mike. "Kids Still Favor Big 'E' over Three
        R's." <u>Broadcasting and Cable</u> 17 Jan. 1994: 24+.
        Freeman argues that most stations present
        educational programs only because they are tied
        to license renewal. He cites a survey that shows
        children would rather watch live-action shows and
        fantasy. Thus, the Children's Television Education

Act of 1990 has not altered viewing habits of children.

Goodman, David. "These New Series Deliver Informative Messages in Entertaining Formats." <u>Broadcasting and Cable</u> 29 Mar. 1993: 62+. This writer praises the results caused by the Children's Television Education Act of 1990, saying that television stations now have incentives to produce and show educational programs. He argues that stations should benefit by many excellent programs now on the market.

Healy, Jane M. "10 Reasons 'Sesame Street' Is Bad News for Reading." <u>Education Digest</u> 56.2 (1991): 63-66. This writer examines the most popular educational/entertainment program for children, but she denies its value in educating children. She specifies ten ways in which it fails to accomplish reasonable academic goals.

Henderson, Zorika Petic. "Children's T.V. Still 'Wonder Bread' of the Mind." <u>Human Ecology Forum</u> 21 (1993): 25. This writer argues that, despite the CTEA of 1990, children's programs still lack sufficient educational substance. This judgment gives evidence that, despite incentives, major networks did not offer educational programs in 1991 and 1992.

Kosier, Richard T., and Candace A. Morgan. "A Show with Class." <u>English Journal</u> 83.1 (1994): 48-51. These writers report on a class project in Milford, Connecticut. Students produced a weekly television show that provided educational programming for local children. The incentives of the Children's Television Education Act of 1990 would appear to be working in this instance.

Zoglin, Richard. "If Not the Jetsons, What?" <u>Time</u> 22 Mar. 1993: 64+. Zoglin reports on the power structure between legislators and local television stations.

> Stations defend the educational value of such programs
> as <u>Super Mario Brothers</u> and <u>The Jetsons</u>, but
> legislators are demanding genuine educational shows.

4f   PREPARING A REVIEW OF THE LITERATURE ON A TOPIC

The review of literature presents a set of summaries in essay form for two purposes:

1. It helps you investigate the topic because it forces you to examine and then to show how each source addresses the problem.
2. It organizes and classifies the sources in some reasonable manner for the benefit of the reader. When preparing such a review, do not simply list summaries of the sources without relating each source to your thesis.

The essay shown here classifies two types of sources: critics who endorse the use of television in education and the critics who condemn its use.

To write summaries of your key sources, see Section 5c, pages 128–129.

To blend source material into your survey, see Section 7a, pages 182–184.

To write the bibliography entries, see Chapter 9, pages 265–306.

Marcia Thompson
English 1010
15 May 1994

Selected Review of Literature: Effects
of the Television Act of 1990 on Children's Programming

In the late 1940s, researchers began to study the effects of television viewing on children (see, for example, the 1951 book by Shayon and the 1980 text by Moody). Unfortunately, no definitive answer has surfaced on the central question: Does television have a place in a child's learning development?

The Children's Television Education Act of 1990 addressed the problem, but results are mixed. Several critics praise the act and its effects; others deny its effect and continue to belittle the networks for their failure to provide educational programming.

The purpose of this survey is to examine the negative and positive effects of television programming on children's language development. The literature is split on the issue.

Negative Positions

Several critics see little, if any value, in television's effect on language development of children. As recently as 1994, Mike Freeman argued that most stations present educational programs only because they are tied to license renewal. He cites a survey that determines that children would rather watch live-action shows and fantasy. Thus, the Children's Television Education Act of 1990, according to Freeman, has not altered viewing habits of children.

Zorika P. Henderson argues that, despite the CTEA of 1990, children's programs still lack sufficient educational substance. The judgment is based on evidence that major networks, ignoring incentives, did not offer educational programs in 1991 and 1992.

Graham Forst recently condemned television's effect on the reading habits of children. He warns that children are semi-illiterates because they watch television rather than read. He endorses a return to reading as vital for children.

Jane Healy in 1991 condemned Sesame Street, long a favorite of children as well as their parents. Healy considers briefly the virtues of this popular educational/entertainment program, but she denies its value in educating children. She lists ten ways in which it fails to accomplish academic goals.

Positive Positions

A number of critics praise the Children's Television Education Act of 1990 and note its positive effects. In 1993 David Buckingham cited research to show that children make clever decisions about what they watch

on television. He refutes the idea that children are
passive prey for unscrupulous or uncaring programmers.
Class, gender, and racial factors play a role, but in
every case the child's critical perceptions are better
than formerly estimated.

David Goodman praises the results caused by the
Children's Television Education Act of 1990, saying that
television stations now have incentives to produce and
show educational programs. He argues that stations
should benefit by many excellent programs now on the
market. In fact, the students themselves can get
involved, as reported in 1994 by Richard Kosier and
Candace Morgan. These writers report on a class project
in Milford, Connecticut, where students produce a weekly
television show that provides educational programming
for local children. The incentives of the CTEA of 1990
would appear to be working in this instance.

David Considine embraces the visual media as
vital to the education of new generations and argues
that teachers need to "integrate this technology" into
their classroom with "visual literacy training"
(639-640). Robert Abelman advocates television as "a
potentially useful and powerful tool" for classroom
teachers. The introduction of "television literacy" into
the curriculum will encourage critical thinking and
imaginative responses, especially by gifted children
(166).

Conclusion

Throughout their discussions, all critics find both
positives and negatives. Roger Fransecky reflects this
duality. He argues that "television is important,
universal, and subtle" (717). However, he insists that
television becomes "junk food" for children unless
teachers actively lead their students into paths of

inquiry and critical thinking about what they view on the tube.

Richard Zoglin reflects on this positive-negative conflict by examining the power structure between legislators and local television stations. Stations defend the educational value of such programs as <u>Super Mario Brothers</u> and <u>The Jetsons</u>, but legislators are demanding genuine educational shows.

Finally, as with any educational tool, the teachers and the parents will play the key roles in selecting a program, using it wisely, and--when necessary--turning off the television set.

Works Cited

Abelman, Robert. "Television Literacy for Gifted Children." <u>Roeper Review</u> 9 (1987): 166-69.

Buckingham, David. "Boxing Clever: Children's Sophistication in Mass Media." <u>Times Educational Supplement</u> 23 Apr. 1993: 6.

Considine, David M. "Visual Literacy and the Curriculum: More to It Than Meets the Eye." <u>Language Arts</u> 64 (1987): 634-40.

Forst, Graham. "Our Misspelt Youth." <u>World Press Review</u> Apr. 1992: 50.

Fransecky, Roger B. "Perspectives: Children, Television, and Language Education." <u>Language Arts</u> 58 (1981): 713-20.

Freeman, Mike. "Kids Still Favor Big 'E' over Three R's." <u>Broadcasting and Cable</u> 17 Jan. 1994: 24+.

Goodman, David. "These New Series Deliver Informative Messages in Entertaining Formats." <u>Broadcasting and Cable</u> 29 Mar. 1993: 62+.

Healy, Jane M. "10 Reasons 'Sesame Street' Is Bad News for Reading." <u>Education Digest</u> 56.2 (1991): 63-66.

Henderson, Zorika Petic. "Children's T.V. Still 'Wonder Bread' of the Mind." <u>Human Ecology Forum</u> 21.2 (1993): 25.

Kosier, Richard T., and Candace A. Morgan. "A Show with Class." <u>English Journal</u> 83.1 (1994): 48-51.

Moody, Kate. <u>Growing Up on Television: The TV Effect</u>. New York: Times Books, 1980.

Shayon, Robert. <u>Television and Our Children</u>. New York: Longmans, 1951.

Zoglin, Richard. "If Not the Jetsons, What?" <u>Time</u> 22 Mar. 1993: 64+.

5 *Writing Notes*

Note taking, the heart of research, must proceed with thoughtful decisions. Chapter 4 explained how to make appropriate selections from relevant sources. Now you must learn to take notes from your selections to fit your thesis. If you write notes of high quality, you will not need to rewrite them for the paper; they will fit the appropriate places in your outline. (See Chapter 3 for how to create an outline.)

You will need to write a variety of different types of notes. Remember, you cannot quote everything. Only about 10 to 15 percent of your paper should feature direct quotation of the secondary sources. Therefore, consider the following strategies for taking notes. Each is explained fully in this chapter.

Write a *quotation note* to share with your reader the wisdom and distinguished syntax of an authority.

Write a *summary note* to make a quick overview of factual data or opinion that has marginal value; you can return to the source later if necessary.

Write a *précis note* to capsulize the essence of one writer's ideas. This type of note includes the plot summary to explain briefly an entire story or novel, the review note, the abstract, and the annotation to a bibliographic entry.

Write a *paraphrase note* to explain in your own words the prevailing wisdom of a particular scholar. In this form of note taking, you interpret and restate what the authority has said.

Write a *personal note* for each of your own ideas to generate a substantial body of individual concepts, not merely a set of borrowed viewpoints.

5a CREATING EFFECTIVE NOTES

Whether you write your notes with a computer (see "Using a Computer for Note Taking" that follows) or by hand, you should keep in mind these guidelines:

1. *Write one item per note.* Put only one item of information in each note to facilitate shuffling and rearranging the data during all stages of organization.

2. *List the source.* Before writing the note, abbreviate the exact source (for example, "Thornton 431") to serve as a quick reference to the full bibliographic card. Some researchers use a system of key numbers by which they number the notes to match their numbered bibliographic entries. However, you need the author and page number for an in-text citation, not a key number, so placing the name and page on a note is better. Besides, you might lose your key to the sources!

3. *Label each note.* Write a brief line at the top of each note to describe the contents (for example, "objectivity on television"). An alternative is to put one of your outline headings on it (for example, "Television as a presentation"). Later, the headings will speed arrangement of the notes to fit the design of your paper.

4. *Write a full note.* When you have a source in your hands, write full, well-developed sentences. Full wording in the note will

Figure 68
Conventions of style for writing notes

Identifying sources, 7a, 182–84	Darrel Abel in his third volume of <u>American</u> <u>Literature</u> narrates the hardships of the Samuel Clemens family in Hannibal, yet Abel asserts **Under-scoring,** 8b, 238–40
Using lower case after *that,* **7j,** 195–96	that "despite such hardships, and domestic grief which included the deaths of a brother and sister, young Sam Clemens [Mark Twain] had a happy and reasonably carefree boyhood" **Interpolations,** 7l, 198–200
Page citations, 7a, 182–84	(11-12). Abel acknowledges the value of Clemens's "rambling reminiscences dictated as a **Single quotation marks,** 7h, 193
Punctuation with quotations, 7h, 191–93	'Autobiography' in his old age" (12). Of those days Clemens says, "In the small town . . . **Ellipsis points,** 7k, 196–98
Signaling your under-scoring of another's words, 7l, 199	<u>everybody</u> [my underlining] was poor, but didn't know it; and everybody was comfortable, and did know it" (qtd. in Abel 12). Clemens felt at home in Hannibal with everybody at the same level of poverty. **One source quotes another, 7d,** 185–90

speed the writing of your first draft (see page 108 for an example). Avoid the temptation to photocopy everything with the hope that materials will fall miraculously into place at a later time.

5. *Keep everything.* Try to save every card, sheet, scrap, and note in order to authenticate a date, age, page number, or full name.

6. *Label your personal notes.* Write notes to record your own thoughts, but mark them "PER" (personal note), "my idea," "mine," or "personal note." Later on, you will know that the note is your idea, not something borrowed.

7. *Conform to conventions of research style.* Write complete, well-structured notes the first time so that you can incorporate them easily and correctly into your manuscript. The example shown in Figure 68 demonstrates the correct style for citing sources, and your notes ought to conform to these conventions.

Using a Computer for Note Taking

The computer affects note-taking strategies in several ways:

1.   You can enter your notes into the word processing software using one of two methods:

a. Write each note as a separate temporary file under a common directory so that each can be moved later into the appropriate section of your TEXT file by a COPY, READ, or INSERT command. In other words, you should first create a directory, perhaps with the title *FAULKNER*. Second, build a set of files, each with its distinctive title, perhaps the name of a critic, *WATSON,* the name of a character, *SNOPES,* or the name of an issue, *GREED.* Periodically, you ought to print a hard copy of these notes, which should include the name of the file. You can then edit them on the printed sheets as well as on the computer monitor. *Note:* your instructor may also request a copy of these notes.

b. Write all notes into a single file, labeled with a short title, such as "NOTES." With this method, your notes will be gathered in *one* file, not numerous ones. It is advisable to give each new note a code word or phrase. When you begin the actual writing of the paper, merely open this same file of notes and begin writing at the top of the file, which will push the notes down as you write. When you need one of your notes, use the SEARCH command to look for the code word or phrase or scan down through the file to find the appropriate note. Again, printing a hard copy of the notes before beginning the actual writing will provide reference points for your work. With this method, you can move your notes easily within the one document by using the CUT and

PASTE commands or BLOCK and COPY commands, which will transfer them quickly into your text. Hopefully, you will finish the paper at the same time that you exhaust your notes.

2. During the drafting stage, as explained above, you can copy notes directly into your rough draft by moving blocks or by pasting files. However, keep original notes on file in case they are needed again in their original form. In this way, you can build and edit your TEXT file and still keep a copy of each note on the disk for proofreading against the finished pages of the TEXT file.

3. Computer notes often approximate the form of a rough draft, so write your computer notes in a complete, fluid writing style because that way the material will not need to be rekeyboarded. You need only move the note into your rough draft and then revise it to fit the context.

4. You can record the bibliographic information for each source you encounter by listing it in a BIBLIO file so that you build the necessary list of references in one alphabetic file. Chapter 9 shows the correct MLA forms (see Chapter 10 for APA forms).

5. Computers make it possible for you to download material into your computer files from a variety of sources and to print it out in hardcopy form. Many students across the country are now downloading files from the Internet, from E-mail, from CD-ROM files (such as an encyclopedia or the works of Shakespeare), and from database files. They also use Optical Scan Recognition (OCR) to scan and download text, graphics, and photography. If you use these types of sources, be certain—always—to record the source accurately so that you can cite it correctly on your Works Cited page.

The availability of word processing programs offers you these various alternatives for note taking. However, you should take advantage of the new technology only if you have the necessary expertise and only if a computer is available to you throughout the project.

Developing Handwritten Note Cards

Many researchers cannot or prefer not to use a computer for note taking. Developing a set of note cards has been for years a tried-and-true method for developing a long paper. In addition to the earlier guidelines (see pages 119–21), your handwritten cards should conform to these additional conventions:

1. *Use ink.* Write notes legibly in ink because penciled notes become blurred after repeated shuffling of the cards.
2. *Use index cards.* In general, use either 4- by 6-inch or the smaller 3- by 5-inch index cards for recording data. Unlike large sheets of paper, cards are easily shuffled and rearranged.

3. *Write only on one side of a card.* Material on the back of a card may be overlooked. Use the back side, if at all, for personal notes and observations. If you do write on the back, mark "OVER" on the front. Staple together two or more cards.

5b   WRITING DIRECT QUOTATION NOTES

Copying the words of another person is the easiest type of note to write. However, you must be careful to obey a few rules.

1. Do not copy the words of a source into your paper in such a way that readers will think *you* wrote the material.
2. Use the exact words of the source.
3. Provide an in-text citation to author and page number in this form: (Lester 34–35). If you use the author's name to introduce the paraphrase or quotation, do not give it again with the page number (see Figure 69).
4. Give the author's name often at the beginning of quotations, and use the parenthetical citation for page number only, as shown in the keyboarded note in Figure 69.

Figure 69
Keyboarded note card showing direct quotation

```
Construction of reality from Cohen et
al. 34
- - - - - - - - - - - - - - - - - - - - - - - -
The scholarly issue at work here is the
construction of reality by any viewer
of television. Cohen, Adoni, and Bantz
label the construction a social process
"in which human beings act both as the
creators and products of the social
world" (34).
```

5. Begin and end every quotation with a quotation mark, as shown in Figure 69.
6. Place the in-text citation *outside* the final quotation mark but *inside* the period.
7. Carefully choose the quoted material. It should be important and well phrased, not something trivial or something that is common knowledge. For example, you would *not* quote "John F. Kennedy was a democrat from Massachusetts" (Rupert 233). However, you would quote "John F. Kennedy's Peace Corp left a legacy of lasting compassion for the downtrodden" (Rupert 233).

8. Write notes from both primary sources (original words by a writer or speaker) and secondary sources (comments after the fact about original works). (See Section 4d, "Selecting a Mix of Both Primary and Secondary Sources.")

9. Try to quote key sentences and short passages, not entire paragraphs. Find the essential statement and feature it; do not force your reader to fumble through a long quoted passage in search of the relevant statement.

Look at the keyboarded note card shown in Figure 70. In it the writer concisely quotes two important passages.

Figure 70
Keyboarded note showing how to blend quotations into the text

```
Tabloid television
------------------
Tabloid television is not merely the
news as much as it is entertainment.
For example, Kuklinsky and Sigelman
argue that "the networks live by the
dictum 'keep it short and to the
point,'" so they make the news "lively"
(821). Another source warns that
"entertainment news now dominates the
networks, not hard news" (Henderson 74).
```

This note meets the following checklist of requirements:

☑ It uses authors' exact words.

☑ It cites authors and page.

☑ It uses quotation marks correctly.

☑ The page citation is outside the final quotation mark but inside the period.

☑ The material is well written and worthy of quotation.

Quoting the Primary Sources

Frequent quotation of *primary sources* is necessary because you should cite poetry, fiction, drama, letters, and interviews. In other cases, you may want to quote liberally from a presidential speech, quote a businessperson, or reproduce computer data.

When you quote a primary source, quote exactly, retain spacing and margins, and spell words as in the original. An example is shown in Figure 71.

```
Images of frustration in Eliot's "Prufrock," 5
---------------
"For I have known them all already,
    known them all:--
Have known the evenings, mornings,
    afternoons,
I have measured out my life with
    coffee spoons;
I know the voices dying with a
    dying fall
Beneath the music of a farther room.
    So how should I presume?"
```

Figure 71
Sample note on a student's computer that quotes a stanza of poetry as a primary source
(Source: T. S. Eliot, "The Love Song of J. Alfred Prufrock.")

The student has copied six lines of the poem even though she may use only a line or two. Having in your notes an entire sentence (or an entire paragraph of prose) assures accuracy in handling the quotation within the body of the research paper. With computer notes, you should double-space all material so that you can transfer it, without alteration, into your text.

Figure 72 illustrates a note that quotes from a novel:

```
Awakening like being born        Rosso 43
---------------
"There was the morning's penumbra, the
room, the wind, that beat its swollen
hands against the wall; and it was as
if he had just risen to the surface,
his eyes barely opened. Immersed in
something liquid. This was the
sensation he still had, as if he had
floated up from a deep abyss. Was it
an interrupted dream?"
```

Figure 72
Sample computer note that quotes a paragraph from a novel as a primary source
(Source: Renzo Rosso, *The Hard Thorn,* trans. William Weaver (London: Alan Ross, 1966) 43.)

Even though you know you are quoting, put in the quotation marks as a reminder. You will need them in your paper for run-in quotations but not block quotations (see pages 182–84 and 193–95).

Quoting the Secondary Sources

Quote from secondary sources for three specific reasons:

1. To display excellence in ideas *and* expression by the source
2. To explain complex material

3. To set up a statement of your own, especially if it spins off, adds to, or takes exception to the source as quoted

The overuse of direct quotations from secondary sources indicates either (1) that you did not have a clear focus and copied verbatim just about everything related to the subject, or (2) that you had inadequate evidence and used numerous quotations as padding. Therefore, limit quotations from secondary sources by using only a phrase or a sentence.

Incorporate a quoted phrase into your note by making it a grammatical part of your sentence; as shown in Figure 73.

Figure 73
*Keyboarded
note card that
incorporates short
phrases from two
sources*

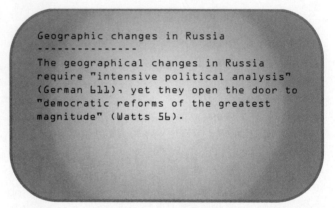

```
Geographic changes in Russia
----------------
The geographical changes in Russia
require "intensive political analysis"
(German 611), yet they open the door to
"democratic reforms of the greatest
magnitude" (Watts 56).
```

If you quote an entire sentence, make the quotation a direct object, as shown in Figure 74. It tells *what* the authority says.

Figure 74
*Keyboarded
note card that
quotes an entire
sentence*

```
Geographic changes in Russia
----------------
In response to the changes in Russia,
one critic notes, "The American
government must exercise caution and
conduct intensive political analysis"
(German 611).
```

Remember, the headings on your note cards will help you locate them within a computer file full of notes.

Figure 75 illustrates two computer notes that contain quotations from secondary sources.

Figure 75
Sample computer notes quoting secondary sources

```
TV as reality                Keller 202
---------------
"For shows that are often referred to as
'reality' shows, there's a lot of theatre
going on. 'Current Affair' and 'America's
Most Wanted' are the most extreme, but
others indulge in their share of
recreations. The problem is that the line
between news/entertainment, fact/fiction,
accuracy/effect is more than blurred--it's
intentionally trampled."
```

```
TV & objectivity              Schiller 2
---------------
"News reports repeatedly claim that, ideally
at least, they recount events without the
intrusion of value judgments or symbols. News
is a map, a veridical representation, a report
on reality, and hence not really a story at
all, but merely the facts--this is the claim.
But news--akin to any literary or cultural
form—must rely upon conventions. Formally
created and substantially embodied conventions
alone can be used to contrive the illusion of
objectivity. How else could we recognize news
as a form of knowledge?"
```

Observe next how the writer of the note shown in Figure 76 carefully worked the quotations into a meaningful paragraph that fits his style and MLA format.

```
    Don Schiller says that we accept
television news as reality because "news--
akin to any literary or cultural form--must
rely upon conventions . . . to contrive the
illusion of objectivity" (2), while Teresa
Keller proclaims that "the problem is that
the line between news/entertainment,
fact/fiction, accuracy/effect is more than
blurred--it's intentionally trampled"
(202).
```

Figure 76
A portion of a finished manuscript that shows how to combine key passages from two sources

Additional examples of handling quoted materials may be found in Chapter 7.

5c   WRITING SUMMARY NOTES

You may write two types of summary notes. The first is a quick sketch of material, as discussed in this section, and the second is the more carefully drawn *précis,* as explained in Section 5d.

The typical summary note represents borderline information for your study. It briefly profiles the material without great concern for style or expression. In fact, you can sometimes frame it as an outline. Your purpose when writing a summary note is quick, concise writing without careful wording. If its information is needed, you can rewrite it later in a clear, appropriate prose style and, if necessary, return to the source for revision. Use summary notes for several types of information:

1. Source material that appears to have marginal value
2. Facts that do not fit a code word or an outline heading
3. Statistics that have questionable value for your study
4. The interesting position of a source speaking on a closely related subject but not on your specific topic
5. A reference to several works that address the same issue

Figure 77 offers an example of the first type of summary note.

Figure 77
Keyboarded note that quickly summarizes the general content of several sources

```
Sources about waste disposal
---------------
This problem of waste disposal has been
examined in books by West and Loveless
and in articles by Jones et al., Coffee
and Street, and Abernathy.
```

To summarize the material, select the key information (a complete book or part of an article), condense it, and get on with other matters. Although a summary card needs documentation about the author, a page number is seldom cited because, as shown in Figure 78, the note summarizes the entire selection, not a specific passage.

Figure 78
Computer note summarizing a book

```
TV & reality              Epstein's book
------------------
Now dated but cited by various sources,
the 1973 book by Epstein seems to lay
the groundwork for this kind of work
because he shows in case after case how
the networks distorted news broadcasts
and failed to present reality.
```

Eventually, this summary note was incorporated into the final draft of Stefan Hall's research paper, an excerpt of which is shown in Figure 79. (See pages 247–63 for the complete paper.)

Figure 79
A portion of a finished manuscript that incorporates a summary note

```
Television viewers, engulfed in the
world of communication, participate in
the construction of symbolic reality by
their perception of and belief in the
presentation. Edward Jay Epstein laid the
groundwork for such investigation in 1973
by showing in case after case how the
networks distorted the news and did not,
perhaps could not, represent reality.
```

5d   WRITING PRÉCIS NOTES

A précis note differs from the summary note by its more polished style. It requires you to capture in just a few words the ideas of an entire paragraph, section, or chapter. Usually, a précis serves a specific purpose, so it deserves a polished style for eventual transfer into the paper.

You will need to use précis notes for several reasons:

1. To review an article or book
2. To annotate a bibliographic entry
3. To provide a plot summary
4. To create an abstract

You serve as a bridge between the source material and the reader, so you must condense (abridge) fairly and without bias. Success with the précis requires that you:

1. Condense the original with precision and directness. For example, reduce a long paragraph into a sentence, tighten an article into a brief paragraph, or summarize a book into a page.
2. Preserve the tone of the original. If the original is serious, suggest that tone in the précis. In the same way, retain moods of doubt, skepticism, optimism, and so forth.
3. Write the précis in your own language. However, retain exceptional phrases from the original, enclosing them in quotation marks. Guard against taking material out of context.
4. Provide documentation to the source and page in order to locate the source of your material at a later time, if necessary.

A sample précis note is shown in Figure 80.

Figure 80
*Keyboarded
précis note*

On the "fairness doctrine"   CQR 370

The CQ Researcher indicates that
Congress has begun efforts to implement
again the "fairness doctrine," which
the Federal Communications Commission
repealed in 1987. The law would require
stations to air equal sides of an
argument. Talk show hosts, as might be
expected, are fighting the legislation.

With three sentences, the writer has summarized the entire article. Eventually, this précis note was incorporated into a final draft for the student's research paper; as shown in Figure 81.

The précis note shown in Figure 82 summarizes two entire articles in only a few words.

> **Note: As shown in Figure 82, a précis note usually needs no citation to a page number because it reviews the entire work, not a specific passage.**

Eventually, as shown in Figure 83, this note was incorporated into Stefan Hall's research paper as an endnote. (See pages 247–63 for the complete paper.)

Political correctness--honesty to both
sides--seems foreign to many programs. In
fact, The CQ Researcher indicates that
Congress has begun efforts to implement
again the "fairness doctrine," which the
Federal Communications Commission repealed
in 1987. The law would require stations to
air equal sides of an argument. However,
the talk show hosts, as might be expected,
are fighting the legislation ("Will the
'Fairness Doctrine' Be Reborn?" 370).

Figure 81
*A portion of a
finished manuscript
incorporating a
précis note*

McClellan

On proliferation of talk shows

Steven McClellan has two closely
related articles on this subject, but
both are about the proliferation of
talk shows. He opens both with "Talk,
Talk, Talk." See bib cards.

Figure 82
*Sample précis note
for two journal
articles*

[1]McClellan has two closely related
articles: "Can We Talk . . . and Talk . . .
and Talk?" Broadcasting & Cable 124.4
(1994): 88-89, and "Talk, Talk, Talk: Cable
Can't Get Enough." Broadcasting & Cable
124.8 (1994): 42-43.

Figure 83
*An endnote for a
finished manuscript
that incorporates a
précis note*

Using the Précis to Write an Annotated Bibliography

An annotation is a précis that accompanies a bibliographic entry. As shown in Figure 84, it explains the contents of a source and briefly clarifies the nature of the work.

Figure 84
*Sample of an
annotated
bibliography as
keyboarded into the
computer*

Figure 84
*Sample of an
annotated
bibliography as
keyboarded into the
computer*

```
Steele, Janet. "TV's Talking Headaches."
     Columbia Journalism Review 31.2
     (1992): 49-52. This writer examines
     the networks' use of experts to
     comment on national and international
     events. She finds, however, that
     persons with real expertise in the
     history of a country, its language,
     and its customs are bypassed for
     experts who have contacts, can
     telephone the right people, and
     explain what's happening, whether it
     is true or not.
```

An annotation may extend beyond two or three sentences in order to establish the authority of the author, to explain the work's primary purpose, to discuss any bias by the author, and to compare this work with others. Figure 85 illustrates how the writer used the annotation as part of his research paper.

Figure 85
*A portion of a
finished manuscript
that incorporates an
annotation from a
note card*

```
The television hosts blatantly tell us that
what the guest says is true, for they back
it up with photography and commentary from
bona fide experts. Yet Janet Steele argues
that persons with real expertise in the
history of a country, its language, and its
customs are bypassed for experts who have
contacts, can telephone the right people,
and explain what's happening, whether it is
true or not (51-52).
```

(See also Section 4e, "Preparing an Annotated Bibliography," pages 112–14.)

Using the Précis in a Plot Summary Note

Another specialized type of précis is the plot summary. In just a few sentences it summarizes a novel, a short story, a drama, or a similar literary work, as shown by the computer note in Figure 86.

Great Expectations by Dickens describes young Pip, who inherits money and can live the life of a gentleman. But he discovers that his "great expectations" have come from a criminal. Because of that knowledge, his attitude changes from one of vanity to one of compassion.

Figure 86
Keyboarded plot summary note

Furnish a plot summary in your paper as a courtesy to your readers to cue them about the contents of a work. *Caution:* Make the plot summary a précis to avoid a full-blown retelling of the whole plot.

Using the Précis to Write an Abstract

An abstract is a brief description that appears at the beginning of an article. Usually written by the article's author, it helps readers decide whether to read or to skip the article. You will find entire volumes devoted to abstracts, such as *Psychological Abstracts* and *Abstracts of English Studies*. An abstract, such as the one shown in Figure 87, is required for most papers in the social and natural sciences.

This study examines the problems of child abuse, especially the fact that families receive attention after abuse occurs, not before. With statistics on the rise, efforts devoted to prevention rather than coping should focus on parents in order to discover those adults most likely to commit abuse because of heredity, their own childhood experiences, the economy, and mental depression. Viewing the parent as a victim, not just a criminal, will enable social agencies to institute preventive programs that may control abuse and hold together family units.

Figure 87
Sample abstract

(See also "Abstract," pages 203–04, for instructions about placing the abstract in your paper.)

5e   WRITING PARAPHRASED NOTES

A paraphrase is the most difficult note to write. It requires you to re-state in your own words the thought, meaning, and attitude of someone else. Throughout the paraphrased note, you need to maintain the sound of your voice, to sustain your style, and to avoid an endless string of direct quotations. A paraphrase is:

1. An *interpretation* of important reference material. As you do with the précis, you act as a bridge between the source material and the reader, but, unlike the précis, you must capture the wisdom of the source in approximately the same number of words. That is one of your duties as a researcher—to share prevailing scholarly opinions with your readers.
2. A careful *rewriting* as developed by careful reading and evaluation of the sources. It requires you to name the source (*who*), indicate the source's attitude with your verb (*how*), and rewrite the material (*what*).

Keep in mind these four rules for writing paraphrased notes:

1. Rewrite the original in about the same number of words.
2. Provide an in-text citation to author and page number. You may and often should credit the source at the beginning of the paraphrase and put the page number in parentheses at the end. In that way, your reader will know when the paraphrase begins and when it ends.
3. Retain *key* words and phrases from the original by enclosing them within quotation marks.
4. Preserve the tone of the original by suggesting moods of satire, anger, humor, doubt, and so on. Show the author's attitude with appropriate verbs: "Edward Zigler condemns . . . defends . . . argues . . . explains . . . observes . . . defines."

Caution: Double-check a finished paraphrase with the original source to be certain that the paraphrase truly rewrites the original and that it uses quotation marks with any words retained from the original.

Figure 88
Keyboarded notes to show, first, a quotation and, second, a paraphrase

```
Quotation:
    Heredity                                    Hein 294
    ------------
    Fred Hein explains, "Except for
    identical twins, each person's
    heredity is unique" (294).

Paraphrased note:
    Heredity                                    Hein 294
    ------------
    Fred Hein explains that heredity is
    special and distinct for each of us,
    unless a person is one of identical
    twins (294).
```

Figures 88 and 89 show the differences between a quotation note and a paraphrased note.

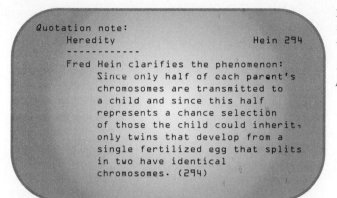

Figure 89
Keyboarded notes show, first, a long, indented quotation and, second, a long paraphrase

The use of active verbs, such as *specifies* and *affirms,* will convey your impression of the source's contribution. The verbs indicate the attitudes and the stance of the scholars.

The process of writing a rough draft goes quickly when you use paraphrased notes because they can so easily be transferred into your text. Writing does not go quickly when you have to shuffle through page after page of photocopied materials. For example, the following is an original interview article about television's influence on children:

> *Perspectives:* What about writing? Could television be used to aid its development?
>
> *Dr. Fransecky:* Yes, it could help a lot. Simple things. We always get concerned about kids doing book reports. Why don't we parallel that with video reports, using that critical framework which we have hopefully put in place? Have kids write critical reports of what they've seen, be it television newscasts, sexy jeans commercials, or whatever else. I think we'll be amazed at how perceptive and critical kids are. That's not very new or exciting information, but why shouldn't it be done?

The researcher's paraphrased note, based on this source, is shown in Figure 90.

```
Video reports                    Fransecky 718
------------------
In his interview Fransecky responds to
these questions: "What about writing?
Could television be used to aid its
development?" His affirmative answer
included the suggestion that children
write "video reports" as well as
traditional book reports, which could
criticize television across the board--
from news programs to "sexy jeans
commercials" (718).
```

Eventually, this paraphrased passage appeared in the student's research paper, slightly altered, as shown in Figure 91. Note that it follows MLA style.

```
     Writing is enhanced by television

viewing. In a recent interview, Roger

Fransecky responds to this question:

"Could television be used to aid [writing]

development?" He answers in the affirmative

to suggest that children might write "video

reports" in addition to book reports. The

reports could review a broad spectrum of

programming, from the news programs to

"sexy jeans commercials" (718).
```

When paraphrasing, remember to keep the length of the note about the same as the original but convert the original into your own language and style. Any key wording of the source is placed within quotation marks.

5f   WRITING PERSONAL NOTES

During your research, record *your* thoughts on the issues by writing plenty of personal notes. A research journal serves the same purpose. It is important for you to build your own discourse on the subject you have chosen for your paper. Write notes that advance a theory, defend an idea, make a comparison, and discover another point of view.

Remember, the content of a research paper is not a collection of ideas transmitted by experts in books and articles; it is an expression of your own ideas as supported by the scholarly evidence. Readers are primarily interested in *your* thesis sentence, *your* topic sentences, and *your* fresh view of the issues.

Developing personal notes or writing in a research journal is essential to the process. Personal notes allow you to personalize your discoveries, to reflect on the findings, to make connections, and to identify prevailing views and patterns of thought.

Personal note cards should conform to these standards:

1. The idea on the note card is yours.
2. The note is labeled "PER" "my idea," "mine," or "personal thought" so that later you can be certain it has not been borrowed.
3. The note contains a complete sentence or two so that you can transfer it into your text.
4. The note lists other authorities who address the same issue.
5. If you use a research journal instead of personal notes, the jottings in it are original and not copied from the sources.

Without personal notes, your writing will develop slowly. Let's consider two hypothetical instances. Student A sits down with his outline and notes drawn entirely from the sources. He faces a major hurdle: how to write his own paper while avoiding the temptation to string together an endless cycle of quotations and paraphrases. Student B uses her personal notes in combination with notes from the sources in order to write out her argument as supported by the sources. The difference is monumental.

Figure 92 illustrates two samples of personal notes.

PER
Objectivity on television, if it exists at all, gets skewed out of shape by forces within the television world as well as forces acting on the world of communication in general.

PER
It seems to me that Geraldo, Morton Downey, Jr., Oprah and all the others will sometimes uncover a bit of truth out of the weird people interviewed, but any sense of objectivity goes out the window.

Figure 92
Sample personal note cards

Eventually, these notes became part of Stefan Hall's research paper, as shown in Figure 93. (See pages 247–63 for complete paper.)

Figure 93
A portion of a finished manuscript that incorporates personal notes

> Geraldo, Morton Downey, Jr., and others sometimes uncover some truth about our society, but any objectivity is often skewed, whether intentionally or not, by forces within the television world as well as within the world of communication in general.

5g   AVOIDING PLAGIARISM

Plagiarism (purposely using another person's writing as your own) is a serious breach of ethics. Knowledgeable, ethical behavior is necessary whenever you handle sources and cite the words of other people. A plea of ignorance about plagiarism does not play well with most readers, especially writing instructors, so give credit whenever it is due. Above all, avoid any deliberate effort to deceive instructors and other readers of your research paper.

Documenting Your Sources for a Purpose

Research is a basic ingredient of business and professional life, whether by a lawyer, a retail merchandiser, or a hospital nurse. Any management position demands research expertise as well as the ability to examine critically and to write effectively about an issue, whether it be about a client's liability, a marketing decision, or the design of a nurse's workstation.

The inventor Thomas Edison depended upon documented research of others. He once said that he began his inventions where other inventors left off; he built upon their beginnings. How fortunate he was that his predecessors recorded their experiments. Scholarship involves the sharing of information. The primary reason for any research paper is to announce and publicize new findings. For example, a botanist explains her discovery of a new strain of ferns in Kentucky's Land Between the Lakes. A medical scientist reports the results of his cancer research. A sociologist announces the results of a two-year pilot study of Native Americans in the Appalachian region.

Similarly, you must explain your findings from a geology field trip, disclose research on illegal dumping of medical waste, or discuss the results of an investigation into overcrowding of school classrooms. Like Thomas

Edison's, your research—no matter what the subject—begins where others leave off. Because you cite experts in the field to support your thesis sentence, accuracy in your quotations and paraphrases is essential. When instructors see an in-text citation without quotation marks, they will assume that you are paraphrasing, not quoting. Be sure that their assumption is true.

Blending your chosen sources into your text is a major part of the research assignment. You will get credit if you:

Cite the source of the ideas you borrow.

Give appropriate credit to the speaker of a well-worded quoted phrase.

Name the authors of the best ideas on a topic that you have summarized.

Any research assignment involves critical thinking in that it tests your ability to assimilate ideas and then to disseminate them in clear, logical progression.

One of your roles as researcher is to share with the reader the fundamental scholarship on a narrow topic. You are serving the reader by explaining not merely subject matter but also the *literature* of the topic. Therefore, you will strengthen your paper by summarizing an important book, by paraphrasing passages of important articles, and by directly quoting key authorities. Rather than secretly stuffing your paper with plagiarized materials, announce boldly the name of your sources to let readers know the scope of your reading on the subject, as in the student's computer note shown in Figure 94.

Figure 94
A keyboarded note that clearly identifies the source

```
                            Roberts 43
Christianity and political activists
----------------
Commenting on the political activities of
the Christian coalition within the
Republican party, Steven V. Roberts makes
this observation in U.S. News and World
Report: "These incidents have triggered a
backlash among establishment Republicans
who fear that religious conservatives are
pulling their party too far to the right
and undermining their ability to win
national elections" (43).
```

This sentence serves the reader because it clearly identifies the political spokesperson of a national news magazine, it gives undeniable evidence of the writer's investigation into the subject, and it is intellectually honest.

One way to avoid plagiarism is to develop personal notes full of your own ideas on a topic. Discover how you feel about the issue. Then, rather than copy sources onto your pages of text, try to synthesize the ideas of the authorities with your own thoughts by using the précis and the paraphrase. Rethink and reconsider ideas gathered by your reading, make meaningful connections, and when you refer to a specific source—as you inevitably will—give it credit.

If you plagiarize, you will abandon critical thinking of your own and become intellectually inept. You will never have original ideas because you lean upon others—their ideas and their words.

Understanding Plagiarism So You Can Avoid It

Fundamentally, the plagiarist offers the words or ideas of another person as his or her own. There are two types of plagiarism that are grounds for failure in a course and even dismissal from high school, college, or graduate school. The first type is the use of another student's work; this is the worse violation. The second is the flagrant, dishonest use of sources without documentation and with no remorse (see Student Version A on page 142). Students who purposely cheat have no place in the classroom.

A gray area in plagiarism involves a student's carelessness that results in an error. For example, the writer may fail to enclose quoted material within quotation marks, even though an in-text citation is provided (perhaps because the note card was mislabeled or carelessly written). Perhaps the writer's paraphrase never quite becomes a paraphrase because too much of the original is left intact (see Student Version B on page 143). Although these cases are not flagrant instances of plagiarism, these students face the wrath of instructors who demand precision in citations. If for no other reason, the serious consequences of plagiarism require you to exercise caution any time you borrow from sources.

Admittedly, a double standard exists. Magazine writers and newspaper reporters quote people constantly without documentation. Nevertheless, academic writers must document original ideas borrowed from source materials. The reason goes back to the discussion about Thomas Edison toward the beginning of this section. Each scholar builds upon previous scholarship. As with Thomas Edison's, your research in any area perpetuates a chain reaction. You begin where others leave off by borrowing from others and by advancing your findings and theory. Then somebody else, perhaps, will continue your research and carry it to another level. Without proper documentation on your part, the flow of research grinds to a halt.

Consequently, you must conform to a few rules of conduct:

1. Acknowledge borrowed material by introducing the quotation or paraphrase with the name of the authority. This practice serves to indicate where the borrowed materials begin.

2. Enclose within quotation marks all quoted materials.
3. Make certain that paraphrased material has been *rewritten into your own style and language.* A simple rearrangement of sentence patterns is unacceptable.
4. Provide specific in-text documentation for each borrowed item. For example, MLA style requires name and page for all in-text references. Requirements differ for other fields, so see Chapter 10 on APA style and Chapter 11 for other styles.
5. Provide a bibliographic entry on the Works Cited page for every source cited in the paper.
6. Omit sources consulted but not cited in the text. This point is important. You do not want your instructor leafing back through the paper trying to find your use of a source that, in truth, was not cited.

These are the rules, but exceptions are made for information that may be considered common knowledge. For example, most sources on Franklin Pierce report many facts that are common knowledge as well as specific perspectives on the facts—his birth and death dates, 1804–1869; his support of the Compromise of 1850; his role at the age of 48 as fourteenth president of the United States from 1853–1857; and even his political support of the Kansas-Nebraska Act. Information of this sort requires *no* in-text citation, as shown in the following example:

```
Franklin Pierce supported the Compromise of 1850 in
an effort to resolve the slavery issue. Later, as
president, he gave his support to the Kansas-Nebraska
Act, which allowed slavery to spread west.
```

However, if you use one historian's idea that Pierce's handling of the slavery issue ruined his effectiveness as president, you must provide an in-text citation to the source, as shown in the following example:

```
An astute statesman would have seen the political
peril of the Kansas-Nebraska Act, but President Pierce
supported it and seriously damaged his political stature
(Reiff 409).
```

Let's look at another example. Because information that is common knowledge needs no documentation, no in-text citation is needed here:

```
George Bush launched the Desert Storm attack against
Iraq with the support of allies and their troops from
several nations.
```

However, theory, interpretation, or opinion about the facts requires documentation, as in this example:

```
Beyond his victory of the war against Iraq, President
Bush demonstrated great mastery in his diplomatic
unification of a politically diverse group of allies
(Wolford 46).
```

The next group of examples demonstrates the differences between genuine research writing and plagiarism. Shown first is the original reference material. It is followed by four student versions, two of which are plagiarized and two of which are not. Note that both acceptable versions are documented in proper MLA style.

Original Material

Despite the growth of these new technologies and the importance of the mass media in our lives, our schools have failed to do anything in the way of developing a systematic curriculum aimed at helping students to understand the form, content, ownership, and organization of the mass media.—David M. Considine, "Visual Literacy and the Curriculum: More to It Than Meets the Eye," *Language Arts* 64 (1987): 635.

While schools continue to operate as though print were the main means of communication in our culture, an increasingly high-tech society requires a new definition of literacy that encompasses visual, computer, and media literacy.—Considine 639.

Student Version A (Unacceptable)

```
Despite new technology that makes the mass media
important in our lives, the schools have failed to
develop a systematic curriculum aimed at helping
students to un-derstand television. In fact, schools
operate as though print were the main means of
communication in our culture. But young people have
a high-tech, visual sense of communication.
```

This piece of writing is a clear example of plagiarism. Material stolen without documentation is obvious. The writer has simply borrowed abundantly from the original source, even to the point of retaining the essential wording. The writer has provided no documentation whatsoever, nor has the writer named the authority. In truth, the writer implies to the reader that these sentences are an original creation when, actually, nothing belongs to the writer.

The next version is better, but it still demonstrates blatant disregard for scholarly conventions.

Student Version B (Unacceptable)

```
Modern communication technology is here to stay and
cannot be ignored. We live in the information age,
bombarded by television and radio in our homes and
automobiles, annoyed by ringing telephones, and
infatuated by computers and their modems for networking
across the nation. Despite this new technology that
makes the mass media important in our lives, the schools
have failed to develop a systematic curriculum aimed at
helping students to understand television. In fact,
schools operate as though print were the main means of
communication in our culture. But young people have a
high-tech, visual sense of communication (Considine
635-39).
```

Although this version provides original opening sentences by the student and a citation to the authority David Considine, it contains two serious errors. First, readers cannot know that the citation "(Considine 635–39)" refers to most of the paragraph; in fact, they can only assume that the citation refers to the final sentence. Second, the borrowing from Considine is not paraphrased properly; it contains far too much of Considine's language—words that should be enclosed within quotation marks.

The next version is correct and proper.

Student Version C (Acceptable)

```
Modern communication technology is here to stay and
cannot be ignored. We live in the information age,
bombarded by television and radio in our homes and
automobiles, annoyed by ringing telephones, and
infatuated by computers and their modems for networking
across the nation. David Considine sees the conflict
as chalkboards and talking by teachers versus an
environment of electronic marvels (635). He argues,
"While schools continue to operate as though print were
the main means of communication in our culture, an
increasingly high-tech society requires a new definition
of literacy that encompasses visual, computer, and media
literacy" (639).
```

This version represents a satisfactory handling of the source material. The authority is acknowledged at the outset of the borrowing, a key section has been paraphrased in the student's own words with a correct page citation to Considine's article, and another part has been quoted directly with a page citation at the end.

Let's suppose, however, that the writer does not wish to quote directly at all. The fourth example shows a paraphrased version with proper acknowledgment given to the source.

Student Version D (Acceptable)

```
Modern communication technology is here to stay and
cannot be ignored. We live in the information age,
bom-barded by television and radio in our homes and
automobiles, annoyed by ringing telephones, and
infatuated by computers and their modems for networking
across the nation. David Considine sees the conflict
as chalkboards and talking by teachers versus an
environment of electronic marvels (635). He argues
that our public schools function with print media
almost exclusively, while the children possess a complex
feel and understanding of modern electronics in their
use of computers, television, and other media forms
(639).
```

Although the entire paragraph is paraphrased in the student's own language and no direct quotation is employed, the authority is acknowledged and credited.

For additional examples, study the complete research paper by Stefan Hall, pages 247–63, and note especially how the writer weaves back and forth from personal commentary to a proper use of the sources.

6

Writing the Paper

Drafting a long paper involves many starts and stops, and your attention will be diverted by meals, class sessions, social functions, and daydreams. Therefore, do not expect a polished product at first. Treat the initial draft as exploratory, one that examines both your knowledge and the strength of your evidence. At this point, supporting evidence may be weak, and you may need to abandon the manuscript at times to retrace previous steps—reading, researching, and note taking.

If you get writer's block and find yourself staring at the wall, relax and learn to enjoy the break rather than get frustrated. Lean back in your chair, and change depression into prime time for reflecting. Nature has a way of reminding us that we need to pause now and then, catch our breath, and rethink our problems. Even if the manuscript is only a page or two, read back over your writing. Rereading might restart your thought processes.

These three rules for drafting may serve your needs:

1. *Be practical.* Write what you know and feel, not what you think somebody wants to hear. Write portions of the paper when you are ready, not when the outline sequence dictates. If necessary, leave blank spots on the page to remind you that more evidence will be required.
2. *Be uninhibited.* Write the first draft with a controlled frenzy to get words on the page rather than to create a polished document. The computer makes it easy to revise and polish the paper at a later date.
3. *Be cautious when borrowing from the sources.* Treat the sources with respect—citing names, using quotation marks where appropriate, and providing page numbers to the sources.

Write without procrastination or fear, reminding yourself that a first draft is a time for discovery. Later, during the revision period, you can strengthen skimpy paragraphs, refine your prose, and rearrange material to maintain the momentum of your argument.

Begin with these four tasks:

1. Refine your thesis sentence.
2. Write a preliminary title that identifies your key terms.
3. Understand your purpose and role as a writer.
4. Use a computer to keep your ideas in order, or use scissors to cut and tape.

6a   WRITING A FINAL THESIS SENTENCE

The thesis sentence, a proposition that you want to maintain, analyze, and prove, functions as the principal component of any theoretical presentation. A final thesis sentence will:

1. Control and focus the entire paper.
2. Give order to details of the essay by providing unity and a sense of direction.
3. Specify to the reader the point of the research.

For example, Stefan Hall (see his complete paper on pages 247–63) started with the topic "television talk shows." He narrowed his work to "truth and reality on television talk shows." Ultimately, he crafted this thesis sentence, which focused the direction of his writing:

```
Television objectivity is nothing more than an ideal
which can never be perfectly presented by any broadcast
nor perceived by any viewer.
```

Without such focus, Hall might have drifted into other areas, confusing himself and his readers.

Abandon your preliminary thesis if research leads you to new, different issues. For example, one writer began research on child abuse with this preliminary thesis: "A need for a cure to child abuse faces society each day." Investigation, however, narrowed her focus: "Parents who abuse their children should be treated as victims, not criminals." The writer moved, in effect, to a specific position from which to argue that social organizations should serve abusing parents in addition to their abused children.

Use the important words from your notes and rough outline to refine your thesis sentence. For example, during a reading of several novels or short stories by Ernest Hemingway, you might have jotted down certain repetitive images, themes or characters. The key words might be *death, loss of masculinity, the code of the hero,* or other issues that Hemingway explored time and again. These concrete ideas might point you toward a general thesis:

POSSIBLE THESIS SENTENCE The tragic endings of Hemingway's
stories force his various heroes into
stoic resignation to their fate.

POSSIBLE THESIS SENTENCE Hemingway's code of the hero includes
a serious degree of pessimism that
clouds the overstated bravado.

The final thesis should conform to several conventions, named in this checklist:

Final Thesis Checklist

1. **It expresses your position in a full, declarative sentence, which is not a question, not a statement of purpose, and not merely a topic.**
2. **It limits the subject to a narrow focus that grows out of research.**
3. **It establishes an investigative, inventive edge to the discovery, interpretation, or theoretical presentation.**
4. **It points forward to the conclusion.**
5. **It conforms to evidence on note cards and the title.**

If you have trouble focusing on a thesis sentence, ask yourself a few questions. One of the answers might serve as the thesis.

What does the research show?

THESIS Recent research demonstrates that self-guilt often
prompts a teenager to commit suicide.

What do I want this paper to do?

THESIS The public needs to understand that advertisers
who use blatant sexual images have little regard
for moral scruples and ordinary decency.

Can I tell the reader anything new or different?

THESIS The evidence indicates clearly that most well
water in the county is unsafe for drinking.

Do I have a solution to the problem?

Thesis Public support for safe houses will provide a
haven for children who are abused by their
parents.

Do I have a new slant and new approach to the issue?

Thesis Personal economics is a force to be reckoned with,
so poverty, not greed, forces many youngsters into
a life of crime.

Should I take the minority view of this matter?

Thesis Give credit where it is due: Custer may have lost
the battle at Little Bighorn, but Crazy Horse and
his men, with inspiration from Sitting Bull, <u>won</u>
the battle.

What exactly is my theory about this subject?

Thesis Trustworthy employees, not mechanical safeguards
on computers and software, will prevent theft of
software, sabotage of mainframes, and destruction
of crucial files.

These sample thesis sentences all use a declarative sentence that focuses the argument toward an investigative issue that will be resolved in the paper's general discussion and conclusion. *Note:* Express your thesis, usually, at the end of your introduction or at the very beginning (see Section 6f, pages 158–163).

6b   WRITING A TITLE

The title of a research paper should provide specific words of identification. A clearly expressed title, like a good thesis sentence, helps control your writing and keeps you on course. For example, one writer began with this title: "Television Reality Check." To make it more specific, the writer added another phrase: "Television Reality Check: The Fine Line Between Fact and Fiction on Talk Shows." Readers now have a clear concept about the contents of the research paper. Remember that titles of 10 or 12 words are fairly standard in scholarly writing.

Consider the following strategies for writing your title:

1.   Name a general subject, followed by a colon and phrase that renames the subject.

Poor title: Saving the Software
Better title: Computer Control: Software Safeguards and
Computer Theft

Key words: *software safeguards* and *computer theft*

2.   Name a general subject, and narrow it with a prepositional phrase.

Poor title: Gothic Madness
Better title: Gothic Madness in Three Southern Writers

Key words: *Gothic* and *southern writers*

3.   Name a general subject, and cite a specific work that will illuminate the topic.

Poor title: Religious Imagery
Better title: Religious Imagery in Faulkner's *The Sound and the Fury*

Key words: *religious imagery, Faulkner,* and The Sound and the Fury

4.   Name a general subject, followed by a colon, and followed by a phrase that describes the type of study.

Poor title: Black Dialect in Poetry
Better title: Black Dialect in Maya Angelou's Poetry: A Language Study

Key words: *black dialect, Maya Angelou's poetry,* and *language study*

5.   Name a general subject, followed by a colon and a question.

Poor title: AIDS
Better title: AIDS: Where Did It Come From?

Key words: AIDS* and *where

6.   Establish a specific comparison.

Poor title: A Comparison of Momaday and Storm
Better title: Religious Imagery in Momaday's *The Names* and Storm's *Seven Arrows*

Key words: *religious imagery, Momaday,* The Names, *Storm,* and Seven Arrows

Fancy literary titles may fail to label issues under discussion. The title "Let There Be Hope" offers no clue for a reader; use such a title with a personal essay or a short story, not with a research paper. A better title would be "Let There Be Hope: A View of Child Abuse." An even more precise title would be: "Child Abuse: A View of the Victims." For placement of the title, see "Opening Page or Title Page," pages 201–03.

6c   UNDERSTANDING YOUR PURPOSE AND ROLE AS A WRITER

Your writing style in a research paper needs to be factual, but it should also be human. Build on the intellectual framework (the facts of the study) and the emotional framework (your feelings about the topic). You can explain a problem with the weight of the evidence, but you cannot afford to be wholly objective, distant, and even cold. (See also "Drafting a Research Proposal," Section 1d, 18–24.)

As an objective writer, you need to offer evidence and analysis and keep a distance from the subject. You must examine a problem, make your claim (your thesis sentence), and produce your supporting evidence. As a subjective writer, you should argue with flashes of human passion about the subject. Complete objectivity, then, is unlikely for any research paper, which displays in fact and form an intellectual argument. Of course, you must avoid the extremes of subjective writing—demands, insistence, quibbling. Moderation of your voice, even during argument, suggests control of the situation, both emotionally and intellectually.

You can win the audience to your point of view in two ways:

1. Display a clearly discernible reasoning process, and project the image that you know and care about what you are doing and saying. This will give you an ethical appeal because the reader will recognize your deep interest in the subject and your carefully crafted argument.
2. Provide sufficient evidence. Make sure that you adequately use statistics, paraphrases, and direct quotations from authorities on the subject and that you quote extensively from primary sources. This will give you a logical appeal because the reader can see your proof. However, readers will differ according to the discipline, so you must approach them with a professional demeanor. (On this point, see "Identifying Your Audience for the Research Proposal," pages 20–21.)

For example, in an examination of autism, Pat Bracy is objective in rendering the logical evidence about two theories on the treatment of autism (see pages 318–32). At the same time, the ethical problem remains close to the surface: children need help with the affliction, but proper treatment is in question. So we hear Bracy making such statements as, "Since autism is sometimes outgrown, childhood treatment offers the best hope for the autistic person, who must try to survive in an alien environment." Bracy comes across as a concerned person confronting the facts and evidence on the subject.

6d   WRITING WITH A COMPUTER

Word processing has several advantages. First, it saves time because you only type the text once and you can make subsequent revisions quite easily. Second, the high speed printer will produce the various drafts for you. Third, the computer can store notes and retrieve them instantly, transferring them into your draft with the touch of a few keys or the mouse button. Fourth, it enables you to move blocks of typed material from one place to another. Fifth, in many instances it will review your writing style, check your spelling, and offer a thesaurus of available words.

Storing and Retrieving Notes, Documents, and Bibliographic Sources

Methods for writing your notes into a computer are explained in Chapter 5, pages 121–22, which explains two methods for writing and storing your notes, one that keeps all notes in a single file and one that creates each note as a separate, temporary file. Chapter 5 also discusses the importance of establishing a BIBLIO file for storing full information on your sources. It is from the BIBLIO file that you can produce the Works Cited page.

Pulling the Text Together On-Screen

Once you learn a few new commands, the word processing system on any computer functions much like a typewriter. If you did not use the word processor to store your notes, you should now gather all materials and begin keyboarding, much as you would at a regular typewriter. You can transfer your outline to the screen to guide your writing. Do this in one of two ways.

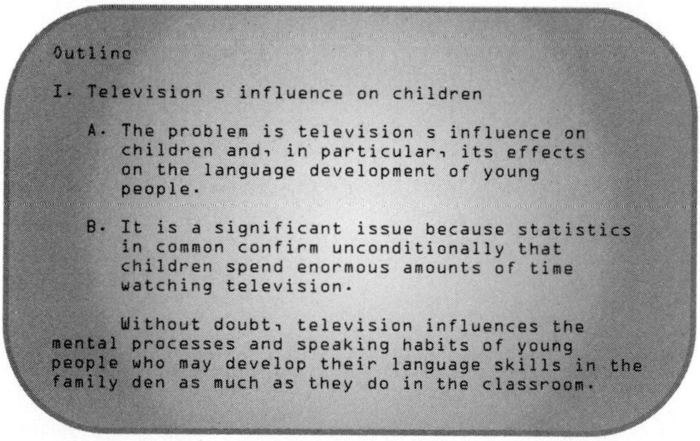

Figure 95
Working with word processing software on a computer

Method one requires the complete outline on file so that you can enter information onto the screen under any of the heads as you develop ideas. One student used this technique in preparing her research on television's influence on children, a portion of which is shown in Figure 95. You can transfer your notes to a specific location on the outline. This techniques allows you to work anywhere within the paper to match your interest of the moment with a section of your outline.

Method two requires word processing software that has a split-screen feature. With this method the software splits the screen so that in one section you can write text while in another, a section of your outline or even a section of your notes is held in place. (See Chapter 5, pages 121–22, for tips on developing your notes with a computer.) As shown in Figure 96, the split-screen reminds you of content necessary for the text.

Figure 96
Using the split-screen feature while writing with word processing software

```
I. Television s influence on children

   A. The problem is television's
      influence on children and, in
      particular, its effects on the
      language development of young
      people.
```

```
   Without doubt, television
influences the mental processes and
speaking habits of young people who
may develop their language skills in
the family den as much as they do in
the classroom.
```

You can transfer your notes to the text without rekeyboarding only if you used the word processing software to write them. If you wrote your notes into a single file, such as NOTES, begin writing your draft at the beginning of the file (Your notes will be pushed downward as you keyboard). When you need a certain note, scroll down to find it, MARK it or CUT it as a block, scroll up to your text, and MOVE it into place. Then blend it into your text discussion with necessary rewording. An important alternative, especially for a long set of notes (12 or more), is to develop each note as a separate file, using a different code word for each. You can then pause during your writing to ask the computer to READ, COPY, or PASTE a file into your text. For example, let's suppose you have labeled and filed your notes by number, name of author, or key words of your outline, such as TVTIME, TVABUSE, THESIS, TV&LANGU(age). (*Note:* Names of PC files are generally limited to eight characters.) You can retrieve those files and blend them into your rough draft. This system of having separate note files is more efficient than having only one file full of many notes because you do not have to scroll through note after note looking for the right one. However, you must keep a written record of file names and the contents of each file.

Transferring Graphics into the Text

You may create graphic designs and transfer them into your text. Many software programs allow you to create bar, line, or pie graphs as well as spreadsheets and other original designs. Some computer software includes ready-made graphics. Such materials can enhance the quality of your presentation. After you create a table or locate a graphic design, transfer it to the body of your text and resize it to fit your space. Use four-color art if your printer prints in four colors. (See the back cover of this textbook for an example of one student's use of color.)

Place a full-page graphic design on a separate sheet after making a reference to it, such as "see Table 7," on the previous page of text. Alternatively, place graphic designs in an appendix when you have several complex items that might distract the reader from your text message. (See page 261 for Stefan Hall's use of an appendix for two tables.) In all cases, conform to standard rules for numbering, labeling, and presenting tables and illustrations. (See pages 225–29 for rules and examples.) Finally, use graphic designs and tables *only* where appropriate. Do not substitute clip art for good, solid prose or use figures and text art to dazzle the reader when your information is shaky.

Safeguarding Your Work on a Computer

During your entry of text, be sure that you use the SAVE command to preserve the material every page or so. This command inscribes your writing onto the diskette or hard drive so that it will not be lost if the computer suddenly shuts down for any reason, such as a power failure or an accidental unplugging of the machine.

When you finish your initial keyboarding, there are two more things to do. First, copy the file onto two diskettes. Second, have the computer print a copy of your paper with double or triple spacing. (See also "Using the Computer to Edit Your Text," pages 175–77.)

6e   DRAFTING YOUR PAPER

At some point you must write a draft of the whole paper. You may work systematically through the outline, adhering to its order and using the note cards for evidence and support. Alternatively, you may start any-where in the outline and write what you know at the time, keeping the pieces of manuscript controlled by your thesis and overall plan.

Leave plenty of space as your write—wide margins, double spacing, and blank spaces between some paragraphs. The open areas will invite your revisions and additions at a later time. If available, use word process-ing so that once the draft is keyboarded, you will not need to keyboard *everything* for revisions (see pages 174 and 175–77).

Use your notes or research journal to:

Transfer personal notes, with modification, into the draft.
Transcribe précis notes and paraphrased materials directly into the
   text.
Quote primary sources.
Quote secondary sources from notes.

Write with caution when working from photocopied, downloaded, or scanned pages of articles or books. You will be tempted to borrow too much. Quote or paraphrase key phrases and sentences; do not quote an entire paragraph unless it is crucial to your discussion and you cannot eas-ily reduce it to a précis.

You may cite more than one source in a paragraph. For example, the following passage effectively cites two different sources:

```
Tabloid television is not so much news as entertainment.
One source notes that "the networks live by the dictum
'keep it short and to the point,'" so they make the news
"lively" (Kuklinsky and Sigelman 821). Many programs, Hard
Copy and A Current Affair come to mind, go for "show over
substance with an ongoing commentary to let listeners
know how they should be reacting and to keep emotional
involvement high" (Keller 201). The recreations of some
newscasts are designed for the same scintillating purpose,
"show over substance," an enhancement or abbreviation of
the facts, a breach of objectivity.
```

This sample paragraph illustrates four points. The writer:

1. Weaves the sources effectively into a whole
2. Cites each source separately, one at a time
3. Provides two different in-text citations
4. The writer, Stefan Hall, makes the use of the sources seem a nat-ural extension of his thinking

Readers want to discover your thoughts and ideas and then examine your sources for contrast with, evidence for, and support of them. You should explain, analyze, and support a thesis, not merely string together research information. For this reason, a paragraph should seldom contain only source material; it needs at least a topic sentence to establish a point for the research evidence.

Writing in the Proper Tense

Verb tense often distinguishes a paper in the humanities from one in the natural and social sciences. MLA style (for a paper in the humanities) uses the present tense to cite an author's work (e.g., "Johnson *explains*" or "the work of Elmford and Mills *shows*"). In contrast, APA style (for a paper in the natural and social sciences) uses the past or present perfect tense to cite an author's work (e.g., "Johnson *discovered*" or "the work of Elmford and Mills *has demonstrated*").

A paper in the humanities (MLA style) uses the historical present tense because it makes universal assertions.

Note the use of the present tense in these two examples:

```
"It was the best of times, it was the worst of times,"
writes Charles Dickens about the eighteenth century.

Johnson argues that sociologist Norman Wayman has a
"narrow-minded view of clerics and their role in the
community" (64).
```

MLA style requires the present tense for comments by you and by the sources because the ideas and the words of the writers remain in print and continue to be true in the universal present (e.g., "Richard Ellmann *argues*" or "Eudora Welty *writes*").

When using MLA style, employ the past tense *only* for reporting historical events. In the next example, the past tense is appropriate for all sentences except the last:

```
The year 1963 was dramatic for America in several ways.
John F. Kennedy died in Dallas. About 200,000 persons
marched on Washington where Martin Luther King, Jr.,
proclaimed, "I Have a Dream." The Atomic Test-Ban Treaty
was signed by the United States, Russia, and other
countries. Black student Harvey Gantt enrolled at
Clemson University to begin integration of South
Carolina schools. Gantt's story is a lesson in courage,
one worthy of study.
```

In contrast, a paper in the natural or social sciences (APA style) uses the past or present perfect tense because it shows what has been accomplished. For example:

```
Matthews (1989) designed the experiment and, since that
time, several investigators have used the method
(Thurman, 1990; Jones 1991).
```

However, APA style require's the present tense when you discuss the results (e.g., "the results confirm" or "diuretic therapy helps control hypertension"). See Chapter 10, "Using APA Style," for additional discussion.

Using the Language of the Discipline

Many words and phrases are peculiar to a certain topic. Therefore, while reading and taking notes, jot down words and phrases relevant to the study. Get comfortable with them so you can use them effectively. For example, a paper on child abuse requires the language of sociology and psychology, thereby demanding an acquaintance with:

```
aggressive behavior        incestuous relations
battered child             maltreatment
behavioral patterns        poverty levels
formative years            recurrence
guardians                  social worker
hostility                  stress
```

Similarly, a poetry paper might require the words *symbolism, imagery, rhythm, persona,* or *rhyme.* Every discipline and every topic has its own vocabulary. In fact, many writers compose a terminology list to strengthen noun and verb usage. However, nothing betrays a writer's ignorance of the subject matter more quickly than awkward and distorted use of technical terminology. For example, the following sentence uses big words, but it distorts and scrambles the language:

```
The enhancement of learning opportunities is often
impeded by a pathological disruption in a child's mental
processes.
```

The words may be large, but what does the sentence mean? Probably this:

```
Education is often interrupted by a child's abnormal
behavior.
```

Writing in the Third Person

Write your paper in the third person to avoid statements such as "I believe" and "It is my opinion." Rather than say, "I think objectivity on television is nothing more than an ideal," just drop the opening two words and say, "Objectivity on television is nothing more than an ideal." Readers will understand that the statement is your thought. (See the sample paper on pages 241–46 for an example of the correct use of voice.) However, as shown in the following example, always attribute human functions to yourself or other persons, not to nonhuman sources.

WRONG   `The total study considered several findings.`

CORRECT   `This writer considered the findings of several`
                  `sources.`

Writing with Unity and Coherence

Unity gives writing a single vision; coherence connects the parts. Your paper has *unity* if it explores one topic in depth, with each paragraph carefully expanding upon a single aspect of the narrowed subject. A good organizational plan will help you achieve unity (see Chapter 3, pages 81–96). The next passage moves with unity through a series of citations on a central idea.

> What is a talk show but a structured setting for people
> to talk about their problems or their lives? Structure
> means that producers conduct prior planning and
> rehearsals so that the seeds of subjectivity start to
> sprout even before the viewers are introduced into the
> equation. After the fact, editing is necessary to meet
> time restraints for the broadcast. Once editing enters
> the picture, the producers compromise objectivity,
> omitting something of the whole while emphasizing
> something else. The broadcasts of Oprah or Maury Povich
> may seem spontaneous, but a set structure shapes the
> presentations always.

Your paper has *coherence* if the parts are connected logically by the repetition of key words, the judicious use of pronouns and synonyms, and the effective placement of transitional words and phrases (e.g., *also, furthermore, therefore, in addition,* and *thus*). Pay special attention to the progression of ideas and the incorporation of quoted materials in the following example:

> Many talk shows utilize audience participation in
> the studio to create the illusion or the feeling of
> interaction between "real" people (the audience) and the
> guests. Wayne Edward Munson argues that by "positioning
> itself as more 'real' and effective in its interactive
> inscription of the spectator, the participatory talk
> show aspires to go beyond spectacle . . . " (dissertation

abstract). This interaction allows for a parallel to be made between the studio audience and home viewers since both are trying to make sense of the performance or questioning the validity or realness of the topics and the guests' stories. Yet talk shows are still just talk shows, spectacles, entertainment; therefore, members of the studio audience are acting out parts in the drama, like a Greek chorus, just as the host, the guest, and the television viewers are actors as well. Furthermore, some sort of interaction with the "characters" in this made-for-television "drama" happens all the time. If we read a book or attend a play, we question the text, we question the presentation, and we determine for ourselves what it means to us.

6f WRITING THE INTRODUCTION OF THE PAPER

Use the first few paragraphs of your paper to establish the nature of your study, but keep the introduction short and directed toward the issues. Some writers wait to write the introduction until they have developed the body and the conclusion.

Subject Identify your specific topic. Then define, limit, and narrow it to one issue.

Background Provide relevant historical data. Discuss a few key sources that touch on your specific issue. If writing about a major figure, give relevant biographical facts, not an encyclopedia-type survey. (See "Providing Background Information," pages 159–60.)

Problem The point of a research paper is to explore or resolve a problem, so identify and explain the complications that you see.

Thesis sentence Within the first few paragraphs, use your thesis sentence to establish the direction of the study and to point your readers toward your eventual conclusions. (See "Opening with Your Thesis Statement," which follows.)

How you work these essential elements into the framework of your introduction will depend upon your style of writing. They need not appear in this order, and you should not cram all of them into a short, opening paragraph. Feel free to write two or three paragraphs of the introduction, letting it run over onto page two, if necessary. When crafting your introduction, use more than one of the techniques described in the following paragraphs.

Opening with Your Thesis Statement

Generally, the thesis statement appears in the final paragraph of the general introduction, although one technique is to use it to begin the research paper. For example, one writer considered using this introduction that features the thesis sentence first:

> Television objectivity is nothing more than an ideal which can never be perfectly presented by any broadcast nor perceived by any viewer. Geraldo, Morton Downey, Jr., and others sometimes uncover some truth about our society, but objectivity is often skewed, whether intentionally or not, by forces within the television world as well as within the world of communication in general. Most television shows are nothing more than a presentation, an easily accessible and understandable entertainment for the masses. What we must accept is that television is like a novel, a history text, a play, or a newspaper.

—Thesis

Now look on page 251 to see how Stefan Hall actually positioned his thesis sentence at the end of the first paragraph.

Relating to the Well Known

This next introduction suggests the significance of the subject as it appeals to the popular interest and knowledge of the reader:

> Television flashes images into our living rooms, radios invade the confines of our automobiles, and local newspapers flash their headlines to us daily. However, one medium that has gained great popularity and influence within the past decade is the specialized magazine.

Popular appeal

Providing Background Information

A third opening technique offers essential background matter, which should not be confused with information that is irrelevant to the thesis. For example, explaining that Eudora Welty was born in Jackson, Mississippi, in 1909 would contribute little to the following introduction:

> In 1941 Eudora Welty published her first book of short stories, <u>A Curtain of Green</u>. That group of stories was followed by <u>The Wide Net</u> (1943) and <u>The Bride of the Innisfallen</u> (1955). Each collection brought her critical acclaim, but taken together the

Background

three volumes established her as one of America's
premier short story writers.

Reviewing the Literature

This opening technique cites only books and articles relevant to the
specific issue. As shown in the following example, it distinguishes your
point of view by identifying previous works and by explaining the logical
connections between them and your present work:

Review of literature —

<u>Billy Budd</u> possesses many characteristics of
the Bible. Melville's story depicts the "loss of
Paradise" (Arvin 294); it serves as a gospel story
(Weaver 37-38); and it hints at a moral and solemn
purpose (Watson 319). Throughout his tale, Melville
intentionally uses biblical references as a means of
portraying and distinguishing various characters,
ideas, and symbols, and of presenting different
moral principles by which people may govern their
lives. The story explores the biblical passions of
one man's confrontation with good and evil (Howard
327-28; Mumford 248).

Reviewing the History and Background of the Subject

This fifth method reviews the scholarly history of the chosen topic,
usually with quotations from the sources, as shown in the following:

Background information —

Autism, a neurological dysfunction of the
brain, which commences before the age of 30 months,
was identified by Leo Kanner (1943). Kanner studied
eleven cases, all of which showed a specific type of
childhood psychosis that was different from other
childhood disorders, although each was similar to
childhood schizophrenia. Kanner described the
characteristics of the infantile syndrome as:
1. Extreme autistic aloneness
2. Language abnormalities
3. Obsessive desire for the maintenance of sameness
4. Good cognitive potential
5. Normal physical development
6. Highly intelligent, obsessive, and cold parents
Rutter (1978) has reduced these symptoms to four
criteria: onset within 30 months of birth, poor

social development, late language development, and a
preference for regular, stereotyped activity. In the
United States, autism affects one out of 2,500
children, and it is not usually diagnosed until the
child is between two and five years of age (Koegel
and Schreibman 1981).

Taking Exception to Critical Views

A sixth technique for writing an introduction identifies the subject, establishes a basic view taken by the literature, and then differs with or takes exception to the critical position of other writers, as shown in the following example:

Lorraine Hansberry's popular and successful
<u>A Raisin in the Sun</u>, which first appeared on Broadway
in 1959, is a problem play of a black family's
determination to escape a Chicago ghetto to a better
life in the suburbs. There is agreement that this
escape theme explains the drama's conflict and its
role in the black movement (e.g., Oliver, Archer, and
especially Knight, who describes the Youngers as "an
entire family that has become aware of, and is
determined to combat, racial discrimination in a
supposedly democratic land" [34]). Yet another issue
lies at the heart of the drama. Hansberry develops a
modern view of black matriarchy in order to examine
both the co-hesive and the conflict-producing effects
it has on the individual members of the Younger family.

Exception
to prevailing
rules

Challenging an Assumption

Another opening technique, shown in the following example, establishes a well-known idea or general theory in order to question and analyze it, challenge it, or refute it.

Christianity dominates the religious life of
most Americans to the point that many assume that it
dominates the world population as well. However,
despite the denominational missionaries who have
reached out to every corner of the globe, only one
out of every four people on the globe is a Christian, and far fewer than that practice their faith.

Challenge
to an
assumption

Providing a Brief Summary

When the subject is a novel, a long poem, a book, or other work that can be summarized, a very brief summary refreshes the memory of the reader, as shown here:

Summary —
> Ernest Hemingway's novel <u>The Old Man and the</u>
> <u>Sea</u> narrates the ordeal of an old Cuban fisherman,
> Santiago, who manages to endure a test of strength
> when locked in a tug of war with a giant marlin that
> he hooks and later when he fights sharks that attack
> his prize catch. The heroic and stoic nature of this
> old hero reflects the traditional Hemingway code.

Defining Key Terms

Another opening method, the ninth technique, explains difficult terminology, as shown with the following example:

Definition —
> Black matriarchy, a sociological concept with
> origins in slavery, is a family situation, according
> to E. Earl Baughman, in which no husband is present
> or, if he is present, in which the wife and/or
> mother exercises the main influence over family
> affairs (80-81). Hansberry develops a modern view of
> black matriarchy in order to examine the conflict-
> producing effects it has on the individual members
> of the Younger family.

Supplying Data, Statistics, and Special Evidence

This final routine for an introduction uses special evidence to attract the reader and establish the subject. For example, the opening about autism by Pat Bracy (see pages 321–22) cites 11 cases studied by Kenner, lists 6 characteristics of autism, and mentions that one out of every 2500 children are affected.

Avoiding Certain Mistakes in the Opening

Avoid a purpose statement, such as "The purpose of this study is . . ." unless your writing reports empirical research, in which case you *should* explain the purpose of your study. (See Chapter 10, "Using APA Style.")

Avoid repetition of the title, which appears on the first page of the text anyway.

Avoid complex or difficult questions that may puzzle the reader. However, general rhetorical questions are acceptable.

Avoid simple dictionary definitions, such as "Webster defines *monogamy* as 'marriage with only one person at a time.'" See above (162) for an acceptable opening that features definition and page 165 for ways to define key terminology.

Avoid humor, unless the subject deals with humor or satire.

Avoid hand-drawn artwork and cute lettering unless the paper's nature requires it. (For example, it might be appropriate if your title is "The Circle as Advertising Symbol.") Do use computer graphics, tables, and other designs that are appropriate to your subject.

6g WRITING THE BODY OF THE RESEARCH PAPER

The body of the paper should feature a logical analysis of the major issues in defense of the thesis sentence. The presentation of ideas in well-reasoned statements with proper documentation may seem at first an ideal but distant dream. Just remember, however, that writing is the act of discovery that demands a mode of expression. The thought and expression will differ with every writer. Your unique view and expression have validity. As you write, your ideas and your notes will experience a metamorphosis; that is, you will transform scribbled notations into a series of neat, typewritten paragraphs. The transformation continues until the rough manuscript stops crawling or limping along and marches boldly to carry the banner of the argument. When finished, you will have traced, classified, compared, and analyzed the various issues.

The techniques described in the following paragraphs demonstrate how to build substantive paragraphs for your paper. The sample research papers (presented on pages 241–63 and 319–32) may also prove helpful in demonstrating how other writers built papers with well-developed paragraphs to explore their complex topics.

Using Chronology or Plot Summary to Relate a Time Sequence

Use a chronology and plot summary to trace historical events and to survey a story or novel. You should, almost always, discuss the significance of the events, as illustrated in this sample:

> John Updike's "A & P" is a short story about a young grocery clerk named Sammy, who feels trapped by the artificial values of the small town where he lives. — **Quick Summary**
>
> The store manager, Lengel, is the voice of the conservative values in the community. For him, the girls in swimsuits pose a disturbance to his store, so he expresses his displeasure by reminding the

girls that the A & P is not the beach (1088). Sammy,
a liberal, believes the girls may be out of place in
the A & P only because of its "fluorescent lights,"
"stacked packages," and "checkerboard green-and-
cream-rubber-tile floor," all artificial things
(1086).

> **Note: Keep the plot summary short, and relate it to your thesis, as shown by the first sentence in the preceding passage. Do not allow the plot summary to extend beyond one paragraph; otherwise, you may retell the entire story. Your task is to make a point, not retell the story.**

Comparing or Contrasting Critics, Literary Characters, and Issues

Employ comparison and contrast to compare two characters, to compare the past with the present, to compare positive and negative issues, or to show the two sides of a subject, as shown here:

Comparison and contrast —

To burn or not to burn the natural forests in
the national parks is the question. The pyrophobic
public voices its protests while environmentalists
praise the rejuvenating effects of a good forest
fire. It is difficult to convince people that not
all fire is bad. The public has visions of Smokey
the Bear campaigns and mental images of Bambi and
Thumper fleeting the roaring flames. Perhaps the
public could learn to see beauty in fresh green
shoots, like Bambi and Faline as they returned
to raise their young. Chris Bolgiano explains
that federal policy evolved slowly "from the basic
impulse to douse all fires immediately to a
sophisticated decision matrix based on the functions
of any given unit of land." Bolgiano declares that
"timber production, grazing, recreation, and
wilderness preservation elicit different fire-
management approaches" (23).

Developing Cause and Effect

Use cause and effect to develop the reasons for a circumstance or to examine the consequences. Stefan Hall, for example (see pages 247–63), explores the effects of talk shows on the social and moral fiber of the populace. Another example is shown here:

To see how the Hubble Law implies uniform,
centerless expansion of a universe, image that you
want to make a loaf of raisin bread. As the dough
rises, the expansion pushes the raisins away from
each other. Two raisins that were originally about
one centimeter apart separate more slowly than
raisins that were about four centimeters apart. The
uniform expansion of the dough causes the raisins to
move apart at speeds proportional to their distances.
Helen Write, in explaining the theory of Edwin Powell
Hubble, says the farther the space between them, the
faster two galaxies will move away from each other.
This is the basis for Hubble's theory of the expanding
universe (369).

— **Cause and effect**

Defining Your Key Terminology

Use definition to expand on a complex subject, as illustrated by the
following:

Football players and weightlifters often use
anabolic steroids to "bulk out." According to Oakley
Ray, "Steroids are synthetic modifications of
testosterone that are designed to enhance the anabolic
actions and decrease the 'androgenic effects.'" He
says the anabolic substance, which improves the growth
of muscles, is an action caused by testosterone, a
male sex hormone. Anabolism, then, increases the
growth of muscle tissue (Ray 81).

—**Definition**

Showing a Process

Draft a process paragraph, as shown here, which explains stage by
stage the steps necessary to achieve a desired end:

Blood doping is a process for increasing an
ath-lete's performance on the day of competition. To
per-form this procedure, technicians drain about one
liter of blood from the competitor about 10 months
prior to the event. This time allows the "hemoglobin
levels to return to normal" (Ray 79). Immediately
prior to the athletic event, the blood is reintroduced
by injection to give a rush of blood into the
athlete's system. Ray reports that the technique
produces an "average decrease of 45 seconds in the
time it takes to run five miles on a treadmill" (80).

—**Process**

Asking Questions and Providing Answers

Framing a question as a topic sentence gives you the opportunity to develop a thorough answer with specific details and evidence. Look at how a question and answer are used in this example:

Questions and answers —

> Does America have enough park lands? The lands now designated as national and state parks, forests, and wildland total in excess of 33 million acres. Yet environmentalists call for additional protected land. They warn of imbalances in the environment.

Dean Fraser, in his book, The People Problem, addresses the question of whether we have enough park land:

> Yosemite, in the summer, is not unlike Macy's the week before Christmas. In 1965 it had over 1.6 million visitors; Yellowstone over 2 million. The total area of federal plus state-owned parks is now something like 33 million acres, which sounds impressive until it is divided by the total number of annual visitors of something over 400 million. . . . (33)

We are running short of parks and playgrounds, which must give way to highways, housing projects, and industrial development.

Citing Evidence from the Source Materials

Citing evidence from the various authorities in the form of quotations, paraphrases, and summaries to support your topic sentences is another excellent way to frame a paragraph, as shown in the following example:

> Several critics reject the impression of Thomas Hardy as a pessimist. He is instead a realist who tends toward optimism.

Quotation of a secondary source —

> Thomas Parrott and Willard Thorp make this comment about Hardy in Poetry of the Transition:
>
>> There has been a tendency in the criticism of Hardy's work to consider him as a philosopher rather than as a poet and to stigmatize him as a gloomy pessimist. This is quite wrong. (413)

The author himself felt incorrectly labeled, for he
writes:

> As to pessimism. My motto is, first
> correctly diagnose the complaint--in this
> case human ills--and ascertain the cause:
> then set about finding a remedy if one
> exists. The motto of optimists is: Blind
> the eyes to the real malady, and use
> empirical panaceas to suppress the
> symptoms. (Life 383)

Quotation of a primary source

Hardy is dismayed by these "optimists" and has little
desire to be lumped within such a narrow perspective.

Using a Variety of Other Methods

Use *classification* to identify several key issues of the topic, and then use *analysis* to examine each in detail. For example, you might classify several types of fungus infections and do an analysis of each, such as athlete's foot, dermatophytosis, and ringworm.

Use specific *criteria of judgment* to examine performances and works of art. For example, you could analyze the films of George Lucas by a critical response to story, theme, editing, photography, sound track, special effects, and so forth.

Use *structure* for papers on architecture, poetry, fiction, and biological forms. For example, a short story might have six distinct parts that you can examine in sequence.

Use *location* and *setting* for papers in which geography and locale are key ingredients. For example, you might examine the settings of several novels by William Faulkner or build an environmental study around land features (e.g., lakes, springs, or sinkholes).

Use *critical responses to an issue* to evaluate a course of action. For example, an examination of President Harry Truman's decision to use the atomic bomb at the end of World War II would invite you to consider several minor reasons and then to study Truman's major reason(s) for his decision.

Dividing the body by important *issues* is standard fare in many research papers. Stefan Hall (see pages 247–63) uses the body of his paper to develop major issues about radio and television talk shows.

Many other methods exist for developing paragraphs; among them are *description, statistics, symbolism, point of view, scientific evidence, history, and character.* You must make the choices, basing your decision on your subject and your notes.

> *Note:* Drafting a paragraph or two on each method of development is one way to build the body of your paper, but only if each part fits the purpose and design of your work. Write a comparison paragraph, classify and analyze one or two issues, show cause and effect, and ask a question and answer it. Sooner than you think, you will draft the body of the paper.

Writing Paragraphs of Substance for the Body of the Paper

Give the reader sufficient evidence to support each of your topic sentences. The paragraphs in the body of a research paper ought to be about one-half page in length or longer. You can accomplish this task only by writing good topic sentences and by developing them fully. The writer of the paragraph below uses a question-and-answer sequence to build the paragraph, asking the question, "Who pays?" She answers it, "consumers pay," and she defends that answer with a quotation from an authority on the subject.

```
     If shoplifters with sticky fingers are looting
retail stores in ever larger numbers, a simple question
is this one: Who pays? Well, the bill comes to you and
the other honest shoppers who must make up the difference.
Consumers pay not only for shoplifting but also for the
cost of security measures. Jack Fraser, a retail executive,
states: "Stores are losing 1.94 percent of sales per year--
and that doesn't even include the expense of maintaining
the security staff and equipment. That's a lot of cash.
It cuts into profits" (qtd. in Schneider 38).--Rachel
Strosshofer
```

Almost every paragraph you write in the body of the research paper is, in one way or another, *explanatory*. You must state your position in a good topic sentence and then list and evaluate your evidence. Notice how the following writer defends his topic sentence with specific details. The accumulation of evidence builds a paragraph of substance.

```
     Let the real world into the public schools. Channel
One furnishes a satellite dish for every school and a
television set for every classroom. We should use this
technology. It can bring PBS programs and other news and
features to the students. We should use videotapes,
camcorders, audio cassettes with Walkman, electronic
piano keyboards, fax machines, and computers with
CD-ROM, E-Mail, modems, and other recent technology.
Some students have better electronic equipment at home
```

in their bedrooms than in their schools. A teacher, a desk, and a book are not adequate anymore. The Apple corporation has made gifts of computers to schools for many years now. It had a profit motive, but so what? Look at the trade-off. Worse, look at the alternative-- no computers at all in the schools.--Lawrence Thompson

6h WRITING THE CONCLUSION OF THE RESEARCH PAPER

Build a conclusion that goes beyond mere summary and repetition of the thesis sentence. A conclusion should reach a judgment to endorse one side of an issue, to discuss findings, or to offer directives. To put it succinctly, it should say something worthwhile. After all, the reader who stays with a long research paper has a right to a concluding statement. The following techniques suggest ways to build a comprehensive conclusion.

Restating the Thesis and Reaching Beyond It

As a general rule, restate your thesis sentence; however, do not assume that your reader will generate final conclusions about the issues. Instead, establish the essential mission of your study. For example:

A literary study of a novel should turn from analysis of the work to a discussion of the author's accomplishments (see page 170).
A business paper can establish guidelines and directives.
A geology study might discuss in depth the significance of the findings.

Notice in the next example how Stefan Hall begins his conclusion by restating his thesis and by then making his judgments. (See pages 247–63 for the complete paper.)

> Real or unreal, objectivity is something seldom, if ever, found on television. | **—Thesis**
> Ultimately, we must wonder why in the world 24 percent of the people surveyed watch talk shows on a regular basis, while 30 percent watch them sometimes (see Appendix, Table 2). We live the re-creations vicariously, briefly in 30 and 60 minute bites. According to one critic, the "programs provide instant, vivid, and easy to consume information about a wide and growing range of public affairs" (Kuklinski and Sigelman 810), but most of the guests appearing on these shows are not like us in any way. | **Explanantion of the thesis**
> Right? But we enjoy watching the freaks of our society or begrudging the super rich and their

struggles with fame. We enjoy this "infotainment,"
as Wayne Edward Munson calls it (dissertation
abstract). The New Yorker says that "Mostly, we just
[become] more and more aware of our own voyeurism"
(21). Nevertheless, tabloid television gives people
a way to feel good about themselves. They become
players in the virtual reality of the drama. They
are helping to define their own subjective reality
within the boundaries of the objective world and the
symbolic reality of television.

Closing with an Effective Quotation

Sometimes a source may provide a striking commentary that deserves special placement, as shown by the example:

Billy Budd, forced to leave the Rights of Man,
goes aboard the Bellipotent where law, not
morality, is supreme. His death is an image of the
crucifixion, but the image is not one of hope. William
Braswell best summarizes the mystery of the novel by

Quotation — suggesting that the crucifixion, for Melville, "had
long been an image of human life, more suggestive of
man's suffering than of man's hope" (146).

Returning the Focus of a Literary Study to the Author

While the body of a literary paper should analyze the characters, images, and plot, the conclusion should explain the author's accomplishments. The following is how one writer accomplished this:

Focus on By her characterization of Walter, Lorraine Hansberry
author has raised the black male above the typical
Hansberry stereotype. Walter is not a social problem, nor a
mere victim of matriarchy. Rather, Hansberry creates
a character who breaks out of the traditional
sociological image that dehumanizes the black male.
By creating a character who struggles with his fate
and rises above it, Hansberry has elevated the black
male. As James Baldwin puts it, "Time has made some
changes in the Negro face" (24).

Comparing Past to Present

You can use the conclusion rather than the introduction to compare past research with the present study or to compare the historical past with the contemporary scene. For example, after explaining the history of two schools of treatment for autism, Pat Bracy switches to the present, as shown in this excerpt. (See pages 319–32 for the complete paper.)

```
There is hope in the future that both the cause and
the cure for autism will be found. For the present,     Comparison
                                                        of present
new drug therapies and behavior modification offer      and the
some hope for the abnormal, SIB actions of autistics.   future
Since autism is sometimes outgrown, childhood
treatment offers the best hope for the autistic person
who must try to survive in an alien environment.
```

Offering a Directive or Solution

After analyzing a problem and synthesizing issues, offer your theory or solution, as demonstrated in the previous example from Pat Bracy's paper in which she suggests that "childhood treatment offers the best hope for the autistic person who must try to survive in an alien environment."

Discussing the Test Results

Discuss your findings, and identify any limitations of a scientific study, as shown:

```
     The results of this experiment were similar     Findings
to expectations, but perhaps the statistical          and
significance, because of the small subject size, was  limitations
biased toward the delayed conditions of the curve.    of the
                                                      study
The subjects were, perhaps, not representative of the
total population because of their prior exposure to
test procedures. Another factor that may have
affected the curves was the presentation of the data.
The images on the screen were available for five
seconds, and that amount of time may have enabled the
subjects to store each image effectively. If the time
period for each image were reduced to one or two
seconds, there could be lower recall scores, thereby
reducing the differences between the control group
and the experimental group.
```

(See also Chapter 10, "Using APA Style.")

Avoiding Certain Mistakes in the Conclusion

Avoid afterthoughts or additional ideas; now is the time to end the paper, not begin a new thought. However, it is acceptable to introduce empirical studies that discuss options and possible alterations that might affect test results (see "Discussing the Test Results," page 171).

Avoid the use of *thus, in conclusion,* or *finally* at the beginning of the last paragraph. Readers can see plainly the end of the paper.

Avoid ending the paper without a sense of closure.

Avoid questions that raise new issues; however, rhetorical questions that restate the issues are acceptable.

Avoid fancy artwork.

6i REVISING THE ROUGH DRAFT

After completing the rough draft, you face three important tasks:

1. *Revising*. This means altering, amending, and improving the entire work in a series of drafts.
2. *Editing* (see Section 6j). This means preparing the draft for a final printout or finished version by checking your style, word choice, and grammar.
3. *Proofreading* (see Section 6k). This means examining the final typed manuscript to spot any last-minute errors.

Although all three are vital to your success, revision and proofreading, in particular, are often overlooked.

Revising Your Various Drafts

Revision can turn a passable paper into an excellent one and change an excellent one into a radiant one.

Global Revision

First, revise the whole manuscript by performing these tasks:

1. Skim through the paper to check its unity. Does the paper maintain a central proposition from paragraph to paragraph? For example, the paper by Jay Wickham, found on pages 241–46, consistently examines character development in several stories by Flannery O'Connor. Wickham does not drift into other areas of literary criticism.
2. Transplant paragraphs, moving them to more relevant and effective positions.
3. Delete paragraphs and critical citations that do not further your cause.
4. Revise your outline to match these changes, especially if you must submit the outline with the paper.

Paragraph Revision

Second, revise each individual paragraph by performing these tasks:

1. Cut out wordiness and irrelevant thoughts, as painful as that might be, even to the point of deleting sentences that contribute nothing to the dynamics of the paper.
2. Combine any short paragraphs with others, or build the short paragraph into one of substance (see "Writing Paragraphs of Substance for the Body of the Paper," pages 168–169).
3. Revise long, difficult paragraphs by dividing them or by using transitions effectively (see "Writing with Unity and Coherence," pages 157–158).
4. For paragraphs that seem shallow and weak, add evidence, especially quotations from the primary source or critical citations from secondary sources.
5. Add your own input to paragraphs that rely too heavily on the source materials.

After these general activities, revise conscientiously the three main sections of the paper: the introduction, the body, and the conclusion.

Revision of the Introduction

Examine your opening for the presence of several items: the thesis sentence, a clear direction or plan of development, and a sense of your involvement. (See also Section 6f, pages 158–163.) Invite the reader into your investigation of a problem. For example, Jay Wickham in his paper on Flannery O'Connor (pages 241–46) establishes a recurring structural pattern in several stories and invites the reader to consider its implications for the main characters of four stories.

Revision of the Interior Paragraphs

Check the body of your paper for a clear sequence of major statements. Examine the body for appropriate and effective evidence in support of your key ideas. Examine it for transitions that move the reader effectively from one block of material to another. (See also Sections 6e, pages 154–158, and 6g, pages 163–169.)

Revision of the Conclusion

Examine the ending for a conclusion (1) drawn from the evidence, (2) developed logically from the introduction and the body, and (3) determined by your position on the issues. (See also Section 6h, pages 169–172.)

Using the Computer for Revision of the Whole Work

Once you have keyboarded the entire paper, you can redesign and realign sentences, paragraphs, and entire pages without bothering to cut the actual sheets and paste them back together. The computer cuts and pastes for you. You can add, delete, or rewrite material anywhere within the body.

Depending on your software, the commands used for moving material are MOVE, MOVE BLOCK, CUT, PASTE, COPY, and so forth. You will quickly learn them even if you haven't used them before. After each move, remember to rewrite and blend the words into your text. Then reformat your paragraph. To eliminate constant scrolling up and down the screen, use the FIND command to locate a section by using some key words and phrases. Use the FIND and REPLACE commands to change wording or spelling throughout the document.

When you are satisfied that the paper flows effectively point by point and fulfills the needs of your intended audience, begin editing with an exacting and demanding attitude toward correctness.

6j   EDITING BEFORE YOU TYPE THE FINAL MANUSCRIPT

The cut and paste revision period is complemented by careful editing of paragraphs, sentences, and individual words. Travel through the paper to study your sentences and word choice. Look for ways to tighten and condense. Read the paper aloud to discover awkward phrasing. Cut phrases and sentences that do not advance your main ideas or that merely repeat what your sources have already stated. Determine that coordinated, balanced ideas are appropriately expressed and that minor ideas are properly subordinated. Look for ways to change various forms of the verb *to be* (*is, are, was*) to stronger active verbs. Maintain the present tense in most verbs. Convert passive structures to active ones if possible. In particular, confirm that you have introduced paraphrases and quotations so that they flow smoothly into your text. Look to your individual wording for effectiveness within the context of your subject. Pause at pronouns to be sure referents are clear. Language should be elevated slightly in its formality, so be on guard against clusters of little monosyllabic words that fail to advance ideas.

Note the editing by one student in the example shown in Figure 97. The paragraph has been edited conscientiously. Remember to delete unnecessary material, add supporting statements and evidence, relate facts to one another, rearrange data, add new ideas, and rewrite for clarity. Review earlier sections of this text, if necessary, on matters of unity and coherence (pages 157–58) and writing the body (pages 163–69).

Figure 97
Example of editing on a manuscript page

```
                                       In some cases                              is
                                         ^One critic calls television^ "junk food"
                                       see
                                       (^Fransecky 717), and I think excessive
                                                          (see esp. Paul Witty as qtd. in Postman 41)
                                       viewing does distracts from other activities^.

                                       yet television can and does bring cultural
                                                    and        of our best     according to the evidence,
                                       programs^some good^novels. It does,^improve
                                                                                    /
                                       children's vocabularies, encourages their
                                                                          /
                                       reading, and inspires their writing.
                                                    and school                              s  the
                                       Television^should not be an antagonist^; it
                                       traditional classroom curriculum should seek and find harmony with the
                                       should complement school work. preschool television
                                                                                    curriculum.
```

Using the Computer to Edit Your Text

In some situations you may have a software program that examines the *style* of your draft. Such a program provides information on the total number of words, the number of sentences, the average number of words per paragraph, and so forth. It provides a list of your most active words and counts the number of monosyllabic and polysyllabic words. It may locate passive constructions, jargon words, and usage errors. Its analysis then suggests, for example, "Your short paragraphs suggest a journalistic style that may not be appropriate for scholarly writing" or "The number of words in your sentences exceeds the norm."

The software program may provide a readability score. For example, the Flesch Reading Ease Score is based on the number of words in each sentence and also the average number of syllables per word. The highest score, 100, represents a fourth-grade level. A Flesch score within the range of 40–50 is acceptable for a research paper. Another program, the Gunning Fog Index, examines sentence length, but it looks especially for words of three or more syllables. A score of 6 means an easy reading level, but research papers, because they use a specialized language, usually reflect a higher level, one of 9–12.

After a software program examines the style of your manuscript, you should revise and edit the text to improve certain stylistic weaknesses. However, you must edit and adjust your paper by *your* standards, regardless of the computer analysis. Remember, it is your paper, not the computer's. You may need to use some long words and write some long sentences, or you may prefer the passive voice in one particular sentence.

Some software programs can examine your grammar and mechanics, looking for a parentheses that you have opened but not closed, unpaired quotation marks, passive verbs, and other specific items that a computer can quickly mark and flag for your correction. Pay attention to the caution flags raised by this type of program.

A spelling checker moves quickly through the text to flag misspelled words and words not in the computer dictionary, such as proper names. You must then move through the text to correct misspellings. Regardless of the availability of such sophisticated software, you should move through the text and make all necessary editorial changes.

In particular, use the FIND or the SEARCH function of your computer system to move the cursor quickly to troublesome words and common grammatical errors. For example, if your experience with the use of *there, their,* and *they're* has been less than successful, search quickly for all instances of these words. By concentrating on one problem and tracing it through the entire paper, you can edit effectively. If your writing history suggests it, use the FIND command to examine especially one or more of the following:

1. *Words commonly misused.* Do you sometimes use *alot* rather than *a lot* and *to* rather than *too?* If so, use the SEARCH or FIND function to locate *alot* and *to* so you can correct any errors. Here is a list of words that are often problematic for people. You know your weaknesses, so search out usage problems that plague you.

a. accept/except
b. adapt/adopt
c. advice/advise
d. all ready/already
e. among/between
f. cite/site
g. criteria/criterion
h. data/datum
i. farther/further
j. its/it's
k. lay/lie
l. on to/onto
m. passed/past
n. suppose to/supposed to
o. use to/used to

Keep in mind that the spelling checker does not alert you to a properly spelled word that is misused, so your use of the SEARCH command may be necessary.

2. *Contractions.* Research papers are formal, so avoid contractions. You can easily correct them by using the FIND command to locate all apostrophes (').

3. *Pronouns.* Troublesome words include the pronouns *he, she, it, they, their* because referents can be unclear. For example, use FIND to locate each use of *he* to be sure it has a clear masculine referent, without ambiguity or bias, as shown in the next example:

```
Stonewall Jackson served General Lee valiantly in the
battles against Union forces. He was a man of raw
courage.
```

The cursor, blinking as it pauses at *He,* encourages a change to:

```
Stonewall Jackson served General Lee valiantly in the
battles against Union forces. Jackson, like Lee, was a
man of raw courage.
```

The FIND command for the word *this* might uncover:

```
Dr. Himmelwit stresses this point: "Book reading comes
into its own, not despite television but because of it"
(qtd. in Postman 33). This is not universally supported.
```

The first use of *this* is correct, but the second needs clarification, as with:

```
This view by Himmelwit is not universally supported.
```

4. *Unnecessary negatives.* Use the SEARCH function to locate *no, not,* and *never* in order to correct obtuse wording, as shown here:

```
A not unacceptable reading of Hawthorne is Fogle's
interpretation of The Scarlet Letter.
```

This correction turns the sentence into a positive assertion that is easily understood:

```
An acceptable reading of Hawthorne is Fogle's
interpretation of The Scarlet Letter.
```

5. *Punctuation.* Use the SEARCH command to locate all commas (,) and semicolons (;) to check your accuracy. Consult also Section 7h, pages 191–193, on punctuation of quotations. If you employ parentheses regularly, use the SEARCH function to locate opening parentheses so you can check visually for a closing one.

6. *Abbreviations.* Use the FIND and REPLACE functions to put into final form any abbreviated words or phrases employed in the early draft(s). For example, you might have saved time in drafting the paper by typing SL for *The Scarlet Letter.* Now is the time to use the FIND or SEARCH command to locate each instance of SL; use the REPLACE command to substitute the full title for the abbreviation automatically.

7. *Italics.* Have you underlined titles to show italics, or have you actually italicized them with the italics font? Were you consistent? Use the FIND function with your italics command (Ctrl-I, perhaps) and with your underlining command (Ctrl-U, perhaps). In this way, you can ensure styling consistency.

Editing to Avoid Sexist Language

You must exercise caution against using words that may stereotype any person, regardless of gender, race, nationality, creed, age, or disability. Reevaluate words for accuracy; there is no need to avoid gender, for example, when writing about the difficulty of working during the sixth month of pregnancy ("she began early labor") or a running back in the National Football League ("he rushed for 1000 yards").

If your writing is not precise, readers might make assumptions about race, age, and disabilities. To many people, a reference to a doctor or governor may bring to mind a white male, while a similar reference to a teacher or homemaker may bring to mind a woman. In truth, no characteristic should be assumed for all members of a group. The following are some guidelines to avoid discriminatory language:

1. Review the accuracy of your statement.

> DISCRIMINATORY   Old people walk with difficulty.
>
> > a. How old is *old?*
> > b. Do *all* old people walk with difficulty?
> > c. Are the elderly the only persons who walk with difficulty?
>
> NONDISCRIMINATORY   Some older people walk with difficulty. Or be specific: Persons afflicted with severe scoliosis walk with difficulty.

2. Use plural subjects so that nonspecific, plural pronouns are grammatically correct. For example, do you intend to specify that Judy Jones maintains *her* lab equipment in sterile condition or to indicate that technicians in general maintain *their* equipment in sterile condition? Be careful; the plural is easily overused and often inappropriate. For example, some people now use a plural pronoun with the singular *everybody, everyone, anybody, anyone, each one* in order to avoid the masculine reference (even though it is not correct grammar):

> SEXIST   Each author of the pre-Raphaelite period produced *his* best work prior to 1865.
>
> COLLOQUIAL   Each author of the pre-Raphaelite period produced *their* best work prior to 1865.
>
> GRAMMATICALLY CORRECT   *Authors* of the pre-Raphaelite period produced *their* best *works* prior to 1865.

3. Reword the sentence so that a pronoun is unnecessary:

> CORRECT   The doctor prepared the necessary surgical equipment without interference.
>
> CORRECT   Each technician must maintain the laboratory equipment in sterile condition.

4. Use pronouns denoting gender only when necessary to specify gender or when gender has been previously established. A new pronoun, *s/he,* has gained popularity for use in some letters and memos. However, it has not yet become an acceptable choice in academic applications.

The use of a specifier (*the, this, that*) is often helpful. In directions and informal settings, the pronoun *you* is appropriate, but *it is not appropriate in research papers.* Note these sentences:

> SPECIFY GENDER WITH A PRONOUN   Mary, as a new laboratory technician, must learn to maintain *her* equipment in sterile condition.

USE A DEMONSTRATIVE ADJECTIVE TO SPECIFY	The lab technician maintains *that* [not *his* or *hers*] equipment in sterile condition.
USE SECOND PERSON IN INFORMAL WRITING BUT NOT IN RESEARCH PAPERS	Each of you should maintain *your* equipment in sterile condition.

5.   The first mention of a person requires the full name (e.g., Ernest Hemingway or Joan Didion) but thereafter requires only the use of the surname (e.g., Hemingway or Didion). At first mention, use Emily Brontë, but thereafter use Brontë, *not* Miss Brontë. In general, avoid formal titles (e.,g., Dr., Gen., Mrs., Ms., Ms., Lt. or Professor). Avoid their equivalents in other languages (e.g., Mme, Dame, Monsieur).

Editing with an eye for inadvertent bias should serve to tighten up the expression of your ideas. However, beware of the pitfall. If your attempt to be unbiased draws more attention than your arguments, it will ultimately detract from the paper.

6k   PROOFREADING BEFORE THE FINAL COMPUTER PRINTOUT

After you have edited the text to your satisfaction, print a hard copy of the manuscript to check for double spacing, one-inch margins, running head with page numbers, and so forth. (See pages 201–05 for the details of page format.) Even if you used available software programs to check your spelling, grammar, and style, you must nevertheless proofread the final version for correctness of spelling, punctuation, alphabetization of entries on the Works Cited page, and so forth.

Note: **Before and during final printing of the manuscript, consult Section 8b, "Glossary: Techniques for Preparing the Manuscript in MLA Style," pages 205–40, which provides tips on handling technicalities of the title page, margins, content notes, and many other matters.**

If at all possible, print your final version on a laser printer or a letter-quality printer. Such printers with sheet-fed paper or razor-cut continuous forms paper produce a manuscript of the best typewriter quality. Regular perforated paper in continuous forms will leave ragged edges along the top, sides, and bottom of sheets. A dot matrix printer will not give the black sharpness of detail that many instructors require unless you use the double-strike feature that is available on most. This feature commands the printer to strike each letter twice, with the second strike slightly off center, giving letters a darker quality.

You are ultimately responsible for the manuscript, whether you type it, produce it on a computer, or have somebody else type it. At this stage, be doubly careful; typographical errors often count against a paper just as heavily as other shortcomings. If necessary, make necessary corrections neatly in ink; marring a page with a few handwritten corrections is better than leaving damaging errors in your text.

Specifically, use a few proofreading strategies, especially those geared to your particular style. Go through the paper several times to check for errors that plague your writing. You know which ones apply to you.

1. Check for errors in sentence structure, spelling, and punctuation.
2. Check for hyphenation and word division. Remember that **no** words should be hyphenated at the end of lines. If you are using a computer, turn off the automatic hyphenation.
3. Read each quotation to verify accuracy of your own wording and that of quoted materials. Look, too, for the correct use of quotation marks.
4. Double-check in-text citations to be certain that each one is correct and that each source is listed on the Works Cited page at the end of the paper.
5. Double-check the format—the title page, margins, spacing, content notes, and many other elements—as explained in Chapter 8, pages 201–64.

7

Blending Reference Material into Your Writing

One of your primary tasks is to blend your source material into your writing with unity and coherence. First, the sources contribute to the unity of your paper if they are useful to the argument. That is, all quotations, paraphrases, and summaries must explain and otherwise develop a topic sentence and your thesis. A collection of random quotations, even though they deal with the same topic, is unacceptable. Second, the sources contribute to coherence only if you relate them directly to the matter at hand. Introductions, transitions, repetition of key words—these tie the paraphrase or the quotation to your exposition. (See also "Writing with Unity and Coherence," pages 157–58.)

Your in-text citations should conform to standards announced by your instructor. This chapter explains the MLA style, as established by the Modern Language Association. Unless otherwise specified, use it for papers in composition, literature, English usage, and foreign languages. Instructors in courses other than these may require a different form of documentation, such as APA style, CBE (Council of Biological Editors) style, the number style, or the footnote style. (See Chapters 10 and 11 for styling according to these other formats.) A program that features writing across the curriculum may require you to use MLA style for all your papers, or it may expect you to switch styles according to your subject matter, such as APA style for a social issue, the number system for a paper on computer technology, or the footnote system for a history paper.

MLA style requires you to list an author and a page number in your text, usually within parentheses, and then at the end of your paper to provide a full bibliographic entry on a Works Cited page (see Section 9a, pages 266–67). Notice how this next passage uses names and page numbers in two different ways. In the first sentence, the writer uses the name of the authority to introduce the quotation and places the page number after the quotation. In the second, the writer places both the name and the page number at the end.

```
According to John Hartley, 19th century scientists
"discovered single cells that divided into two identical
offspring cells" (56). This finding eventually produced
the cell theory, which asserts, "All organisms are
composed of cells and all cells derive from other living
cells" (Justice 431).
```

> *Note:* **Do not place a comma between the name and the page number.**

7a   BLENDING A REFERENCE INTO YOUR TEXT

An important reason for writing a research paper is to gather and present source material on a topic. Therefore, you should display those sources prominently in your writing, not hide them or fail to cite them.

As a general policy, provide just enough information within the text to identify a source. Remember, your readers will have full documentation to each source on the Works Cited page. Sometimes you will need no parenthetical reference, as with: "Baird has devoted his entire text to the subject of Melville's mythology." No parenthetical reference is needed in this case if Baird has only one book in the Works Cited page. However, if you cite a specific part of a book, add page numbers, as shown here:

```
James Baird argues convincingly that Melville shaped a
new "symbolistic literature" (19).
```

Always try to use this standard citation because it informs the reader of the beginning and the end of borrowed materials, as explained next.

Beginning with the Author and Ending with a Page Number

Introduce a quotation or a paraphrase with the author's name, and close it with a page number, placed inside parentheses:

```
Herbert Norfleet states that the use of video games by
children improves their hand and eye coordination (45).
```

This paraphrase makes absolutely clear to the reader when the borrowed idea begins and when it ends.

In this next example, notice how unclear the use of the source is because the writer does not introduce borrowed material:

```
The use of video games by children improves their hand
and eye coordination. They also exercise their minds by
working their way through various puzzles and barriers.
"The mental gymnastics of video games and the competition
with fellow players are important to young children and
their development physically, socially, and mentally"
(Norfleet 45).
```

What was borrowed? Did only the final quotation come from Norfleet? In truth the entire paragraph, both the early paraphrasing and the quotation, came from Norfleet. Norfleet is the expert for this paragraph, so the paper should mention his name prominently, as shown in the revision below:

```
    Video games for children have opponents and
advocates. Herbert Norfleet defends the use of video
games by children. He says it improves their hand and
eye coordination and that it exercises their minds
as they work their way through various puzzles and
barriers. Norfleet states, "The mental gymnastics of
video games and the competition with fellow players are
important to young children and their physical, social,
and mental development" (45).
```

This paragraph demonstrates proper usage in these ways:

1. It credits the source properly and honestly.
2. It correctly uses both paraphrase and quotation.
3. It demonstrates the writer's research into the subject.

(See also Student Version B, page 143, which explains plagiarism.)

Putting the Name and Page Number at the End of Borrowed Material

You can, if you like, put cited names with the page number at the end of a quotation or paraphrase, but give your reader a signal to show when the borrowing begins, as this writer does:

```
One source explains that the DNA in the chromosomes
must be copied perfectly during cell reproduction. "Each
DNA strand provides the pattern of bases for a new
strand to form, resulting in two complete molecules"
(Justice, Moody, and Graves 462).
```

By opening with "One source explains," the writer signals when the borrowing begins.

In contrast, the reader cannot possibly tell in the following example which ideas are the authority's and which aren't.

```
Herman Melville used symbols of reincarnation,
innocence, primitive waters, the shadow that haunts all
people, and many others. He shaped a new "symbolistic
literature" for America (Baird 19).
```

See how the addition of several words to delineate the borrowing clarifies the source for the reader:

```
The book Ishmael by James Baird explains that Herman
Melville used symbols of reincarnation, innocence,
primitive waters, the shadow that haunts all people, and
many others. The writer argues that Melville shaped a
new "symbolistic literature" for America (Baird 19).
```

7b   CITING A SOURCE WHEN NO AUTHOR IS LISTED

When no author is shown on a title page, cite the title of an article, the name of the magazine, the name of a bulletin or book, or the name of the publisher, as shown in the following examples.

> *Note:* **Search for the author's name at the bottom of the opening page and at the end of the article.**

Citing the Title of a Magazine Article

```
Articles about the unusual names of towns, such as
Peculiar, Missouri; Kinmundy, Illinois; and Frostproof,
Florida, are a regular feature of one national magazine
("Name-Dropping" 63).
```

The Works Cited entry would read as follows: "Name-Dropping." *Country* June/July 1994: 63.

> *Note:* **You should shorten magazine titles to a key word for the citation, such as "Selling" for "Selling Products to Young Children," but give the full title in the Works Cited entry.**

Citing the Title of a Report

One bank showed a significant decline in assets despite an increase in its number of depositors (Annual Report 23).

Citing the Name of a Publisher or a Corporate Body

The report by the school board endorsed the use of Channel One in the school system and said that "students will benefit by the news reports more than they will be adversely affected by advertising" (Clarion County School Board 3-4).

7c IDENTIFYING NONPRINT SOURCES THAT HAVE NO PAGE NUMBER

On occasion you may need to identify nonprint sources, such as a speech, the song lyrics from a compact disc, an interview, or a television program. Since there is no page number, omit the parenthetical citation. Instead, as shown in the following examples, introduce the type of source (i.e., lecture, letter, interview, computer screen or paragraph number of a computer screen) so that readers do not expect a page number.

Thompson's lecture defined *impulse* as "an action triggered by the nerves without thought for the consequences."

Mrs. Peggy Meacham said in her phone interview that prejudice against young black women is not as severe as that against young black males.

John F. Kennedy held firm in his face to face confrontation with premier Khrushchev (screen 11).

7d USING A DOUBLE REFERENCE TO CITE SOMEBODY WHO HAS BEEN QUOTED IN A BOOK OR ARTICLE

Sometimes the writer of a book or article will quote another person from an interview or personal correspondence, and you will want to use that same quotation. For example, in a newspaper article in *USA Today,* page 9A, Karen S. Peterson writes this passage in which she quotes two other people:

> Sexuality, popularity, and athletic competition will create anxiety for junior high kids and high schoolers, Eileen Shiff says. "Bring up the topics. Don't wait for them to do it; they are nervous and they want to appear cool." Monitor the amount of time high schoolers spend working for money, she suggests. "Work is important, but school must be the priority."
>
> Parental intervention in a child's school career that worked in junior high may not work in high school, psychiatrist Martin Greenburg adds. "The interventions can be construed by the adolescent as negative, overburdening and interfering with the child's ability to care for himself."
>
> He adds, "Be encouraging, not critical. Criticism can be devastating for the teen-ager."

Suppose that you want to use the quotation above by Martin Greenburg. You will need to quote the words of Greenburg and also put Peterson's name in the parenthetical citation as the person who wrote the article, as shown in the following:

```
After students get beyond middle school, they begin to
resent interference by their parents, especially in
school activities. They need some space from Mom and
Dad. Martin Greenburg says, "The interventions can be
construed by the adolescent as negative, overburdening
and interfering with the child's ability to care for
himself [or herself]" (qtd. in Peterson 9A).
```

> *Note:* **Peterson's name will appear on a bibliography entry in your list of works cited, but Greenburg's will not because Greenburg is not the author of the article.**

In other words, you need a double reference that introduces the speaker and includes a clear reference to the book or article where you found the quotation or the paraphrased material. Without the reference to Peterson in the previous example, nobody could find the article. Without the reference to Greenburg, readers would assume that Peterson spoke the words. Peterson's name should appear in a bibliographic entry on your Works Cited page; Greenburg's name should not appear because Greenburg is not the author of the article.

Cite the original source if at all possible. If an author quotes from another writer's published essay or book, it is preferable to search for the original essay or book rather than use the double reference.

7e   CITING FREQUENT PAGE REFERENCES TO THE SAME WORK

When you make frequent references to the same novel, drama, or long poem, you need not repeat the author's name in every instance; a specific page reference is adequate, or you can provide act, scene, and line if appropriate. Note the following example:

> When the character Beneatha denies the existence of God in Hansberry's *A Raisin in the Sun,* Mama slaps her in the face and forces her to repeat after her, "In my mother's house there is still God" (37). Then Mama adds, "There are some ideas we ain't going to have in this house. Not long as I am at the head of the family" (37). Thus Mama meets Beneatha's challenge head on. The other mother in the Younger household is Ruth, who does not lose her temper, but through kindness wins over her husband (79-80).

> *Note:* **If you are citing from two or more novels in your paper, let's say John Steinbeck's *East of Eden* and *Of Mice and Men,* provide both title (in abbreviated form) and page unless the reference is clear: (*Eden* 56) and (*Mice* 12–13).**

7f   CITING MATERIAL FROM TEXTBOOKS AND LARGE ANTHOLOGIES

Reproduced below is a small portion of a textbook:

METAPHOR

The Skaters

Black swallows swooping or gliding
In a flurry of entangled loops and curves;
The skaters skim over the frozen river.
And the grinding click of their skates as they
impinge upon the surface,
Is like the brushing together of thin wing-tips
of silver.

John Gould Fletcher

—From *Patterns in Literature,* ed. Edmund J. Farrell, Ouida H. Clapp, and Karen Kuehner. Glenview: Scott, 1991. 814.

If you quote from Fletcher's poem and if that is all you quote from the anthology, cite the author and page in the text and put a comprehensive entry in the Works Cited list. Here is how the respective references would look:

In-Text Entry

In "The Skaters" John Gould Fletcher compares "the
grinding click" of ice skates to "the brushing together
of thin wing-tips of silver" (814).

Bibliographic Entry

Fletcher, John Gould. "The Skaters." Patterns in
    Literature. Ed. Edmund J. Farrell, Ouida H. Clapp,
    and Karen Kuehner. Glenview: Scott, 1991. 814.

Suppose, however, that you want to quote not only from Fletcher but also from the authors of the textbook and from a second poem in the book. In that case, you can make in-text citations to name and page, but your Works Cited entries can be shortened by cross-references, as shown here:

In-Text Entry

    In "The Skaters" John Gould Fletcher compares "the
grinding click" of ice skates to "the brushing together
of thin wing-tips of silver" (814). The use of metaphor
is central to his poetic efforts. One source emphasizes
Fletcher's use of metaphor, especially his comparison of
"the silhouettes of a group of graceful skaters to a
flock of black swallows" (Farrell, Clapp, and Kuehner
814). Metaphor gives us a fresh look, as when Lew Sarett
in his "Requiem for a Modern Croesus" uses coins to make
his ironic statement about the wealthy king of sixth
century Lydia:

            To him the moon was a silver dollar, spun
        Into the sky by some mysterious hand; the sun
            Was a gleaming golden coin--
                His to purloin;
        The freshly minted stars were dimes of delight
            Flung out upon the counter of the night.
            In yonder room he lies,
            With pennies in his eyes. (814)

> *Note:* **Center the lines of poetry if necessary rather than indent them 10 spaces or one inch. (See also Section 7i, pages 193–195.)**

In addition, let's suppose that you also decide to cite a portion of Dickens's novel, *Great Expectations*, from this same anthology. Your Works Cited page will require four entries, mixed in with other entries in alphabetic order. Because of alphabetic order, Dickens, in the example below, comes before Farrell even though the anthology is the primary source. (See also Section 9b, "Cross References" 277.)

Bibliographic Entries

```
Dickens, Charles. Great Expectations. Farrell, Clapp,
     and Kuehner. 675-785.
Farrell, Edmund J., Ouida H. Clapp, and Karen Kuehner,
     eds. Patterns in Literature. Glenview: Scott, 1991.
Fletcher, John Gould. "The Skaters." Farrell, Clapp, and
     Kuehner. 814.
Sarett, Lew. "Requiem for a Modern Croesus." Farrell,
     Clapp, and Kuehner. 814.
```

> *Note:* **The bibliographic entry to the Farrell, Clapp, and Kuehner book is primary; the others make cross-references to it.**

7g ADDING EXTRA INFORMATION TO IN-TEXT CITATIONS

As a courtesy to your reader, add extra information within the citation. Show parts of books, different titles by the same writer, or several works by different writers. For example, your reader may have a different anthology than yours, so a clear reference, such as "(*Great Expectations* 681; ch. 4)," will enable the reader to locate the passage. The same is true with a reference to "(*Romeo and Juliet* 2.3.65–68)." With it the reader can find the passage in any edition of Shakespeare's play.

Here is what extra textual information within citations would look like in a variety of situations:

One of Several Volumes

These two citations provide three vital facts: (1) an abbreviation for the title, (2) the volume used, and (3) the page number(s).

```
In a letter to his Tennessee Volunteers in 1812 General
Jackson chastised the "mutinous and disorderly conduct"
of some of his troops (Papers 2: 348-49).

Joseph Campbell suggests that man is a slave yet also
the master of all the gods (Masks 1: 472).
```

Two or More Works by the Same Writer

In this example the writer makes reference to two different novels, both abbreviated. Full titles are *Tess of the D'Urbervilles* and *The Mayor of Casterbridge.*

```
Thomas Hardy reminds readers in his prefaces that "a
novel is an impression, not an argument" and that a
novel should be read as "a study of man's deeds and
character" (Tess xxii; Mayor 1)
```

The complete titles of the two works by Campbell that are referenced in the following example are *The Hero with a Thousand Faces* and *The Masks of God,* a four-volume work.

```
Because he stresses the nobility of man, Joseph Campbell
suggests that the mythic hero is symbolic of the "divine
creative and redemptive image which is hidden within us
all . . . " (Hero 39). The hero elevates the human mind
to an "ultimate mythogenetic zone--the creator and
destroyer, the slave and yet the master, of all the
gods" (Masks 1: 472).
```

Several Authors in One Citation

Sometimes a citation refers to several different writers who treat the same topic. In such a case, put them in alphabetical order (as shown in the following example) to match that of the Works Cited page, or place them in the order of importance to the issue at hand. That is, list first the source that you most recommend to the reader.

```
Several sources have addressed this aspect of gang
warfare as a fight for survival, not just for control of
the local turf (Robertson 98-134; Rollins 34; Templass
561-65).
```

Additional Information with the Page Number

As a courtesy to your reader, identify notes, sections, or special editions, as shown here:

```
Horton (22; n. 3) suggests that Melville forced the
symbolism, but Welston (199-248; esp. 234) reaches an
opposite conclusion.
```

Classical prose works such as *Moby Dick* or *Paradise Lost* may appear in two or more editions. Courtesy dictates that you provide extra information to chapter, section, or part so that readers can locate a quotation in any edition of the work. See how this writer handles a reference to *Moby Dick:*

```
Melville uncovers the superstitious nature of Ishmael by
stressing Ishmael's fascination with Yojo, the little
totem god of Queequeg (71; ch. 16).
```

(See also Section 7f, 187–189.)

7h PUNCTUATING CITATIONS PROPERLY AND WITH CONSISTENCY

Position page citations outside quotation marks but inside the final period. The exception is long indented quotations, which do not use quotation marks at all. In MLA style, use no comma between the name and the page within the citation (for example, Jones 16–17 *not* Jones, 16–17). Do not use *p.* or *pp.* with the page number(s) in MLA style.

Commas and Periods

Place commas and periods inside quotation marks unless the page citation intervenes. The following example shows (1) how to put commas and periods inside the quotation marks, (2) how to interrupt a quotation to insert the speaker's name, (3) how to use single quotation marks within the regular quotation marks, and (4) how to place the period after a page citation.

```
"Modern advertising," says Rachel Murphy, "not only
creates a marketplace, it determines values." She adds,
"I resist the advertiser's argument that they 'awaken,
not create desires'" (192).
```

Suppose this is the original material:

> The Russians had obviously anticipated neither the quick discovery of the bases nor the quick imposition of the quarantine. Their diplomats across the world were displaying all the symptoms of improvisation, as if they had been told nothing of the placement of the missiles and had received no instructions what to say about them.—From: Arthur M. Schlesinger, Jr., *A Thousand Days,* (New York: Houghton, 1965) 820.

Citations from this source could be punctuated in one of the following methods in accordance with MLA style:

"The Russians ," writes Schlesinger, "had obviously anticipated neither the quick discovery of the [missile] bases nor the quick imposition of the quarantine " (820).

Schlesinger notes, "Their diplomats across the world were displaying all the symptoms of improvisation . . . " (820).

Schlesinger observes that the Russian failure to anticipate an American discovery of Cuban missiles caused "their diplomats across the world" to improvise answers as "if they had been told nothing of the placement of the missiles . . . " (820).

Note that the last example correctly makes the capital *T* of *their* lowercase to match the grammar of the restructured sentence, and it does not use ellipsis points before *if* because the phrase flows smoothly into the text.

Semicolons and Colons

Both semicolons and colons go outside the quotation marks, as illustrated by these three examples:

Zigler admits that "the extended family is now rare in contemporary society "; however, he stresses the greatest loss as the "wisdom and daily support of older, more experienced family members" (42).

Zigler laments the demise of the "extended family ": that is, the loss of the "wisdom and daily support of older, more experienced family members" (42).

Brian Sutton-Smith says, "Adults don't worry whether their toys are educational " (64); nevertheless, parents want to keep their children in a learning mode.

This third example shows how to place the page citation after a quotation and before a semicolon.

Question Marks and Exclamation Marks

When a question mark or an exclamation mark comes at the end of a quotation, keep it inside the quotation marks. Put the citation to a page number in the text, immediately after the name of the source, as shown here:

```
The philosopher Thompson (16) asks, "How should we order
our lives?"

"How should we order our lives," asks Thompson (16),
when we face "hostility from every quarter"?

Thompson (16) passionately shouted to union members, "We
can bring order into our lives even though we face
hostility from every quarter!"
```

Single Quotation Marks

When a quotation appears within another quotation, use single quotation marks for the shorter one, as shown in the next example. Should another quotation appear also within the shorter one, use double quotation marks for it.

```
George Loffler (32) confirms that "the unconscious
carries the best of human thought and gives man great
dignity, but it also has the dark side so that we cry,          Place the
                                                                period
in the words of Shakespeare's Macbeth, 'Hence, horrible         inside the
                                                                quotation
shadow! Unreal mockery, hence.'"                                marks.
```

Remember that the period always goes inside quotation marks unless the page citation intervenes, as shown in the following:

```
George Loffler confirms that "the unconscious carries
the best of human thought and gives man great dignity,
but it also has the dark side so that we cry, in the            Place the
                                                                period after
words of Shakespeare's Macbeth, 'Hence, horrible shadow!        the page
Unreal mockery, hence'" (32).                                   citation.
```

7i   INDENTING LONG QUOTATIONS OF PROSE AND POETRY

Citing Long Passages of Prose

Set off long prose quotations of more than four lines by indenting 10 additional spaces from the left margin or indenting one inch. Do not use quotation marks with the indented material. Double-space between the text and the quote material. Place the parenthetical citation *after* the final mark of punctuation, as shown below:

Television gives us symbolic reality but dresses it in
the robes of "real" or "objective" reality. Two political
commentators make this observation:

> Every day the network news organizations face
> the task of reducing complex, multifaceted
> issues to simple, unambiguous stories that
> consume no more than a minute or two of
> precious air time. To avoid the accusation of
> being unfair, they also face the pressure to
> present "both sides" of the controversies they
> cover. (Kuklinski and Sigelman 814)

Even Oprah and Donahue, numbers one and two respectively
in most watched talk shows (see Appendix, Table 1),
have established styles for conducting their shows and
commercially viable structures that the facts must
squeeze into. Sometimes a little reality falls out when
this squeezing occurs.

Note: **If you quote more than one paragraph, indent all paragraphs 3 extra spaces or a quarter inch unless the first sentence quoted does not begin a paragraph in the original source (see Section 7k, pages 196–198).**

Citing Long Passages of Poetry

Set off more than three lines of poetry by indenting 10 additional spaces or one inch from the left margin, as shown below:

The king cautions Prince Henry:

> Thy place in council thou has rudely lost,
> Which by thy younger brother is supplied,
> And art almost an alien to the hearts
> > Of all the court and princes of my blood.
>
> > > (3.2.32-35)

Refer to act, scene, and lines only after you have established Shakespeare's *Henry IV, Part 1* as the central topic of your study; otherwise, write "(*1H4* 1.1.15–18)." (See also "Arabic Numerals," pages 214–17.)

Quoting Short Passages of Poetry

Incorporate short quotations of poetry (two or three lines) into your text, as one writer does with a quotation of T. S. Eliot:

```
Eliot's "The Waste Land" (1922) remains a springtime
search for nourishing water: "Sweet Thames, run softly,
for I speak not loud or long" (3.12) says the speaker in
"The Fire Sermon," while in Part 5 the speaker of "What
the Thunder Said" yearns for "a damp gust / Bringing
rain" (5.73-74).
```

As the example demonstrates:

1. Set off the quoted material with quotation marks.
2. Indicate separate lines by using a slash mark (/) with a space before and after it.
3. Place line documentation within parentheses immediately following the final quotation mark and inside the period.
4. Use Arabic numerals for books, parts, volumes, and chapters of works; acts, scenes, and lines of plays; cantos, stanzas, and lines of poetry (see "Arabic Numerals," pages 214–217).

Signaling Turnovers for Long Lines of Poetry

When quoting a line of poetry that is too long for your right margin, indent the continuation line 3 spaces or a quarter inch more than the greatest indentation. See how one writer uses this format when quoting from another poem by T. S. Eliot:

```
            In the first section of Ash-Wednesday Eliot
lets despair spill out:
            Because I cannot drink
            There, where trees flower, and springs flow,
                 for there is nothing again
            Because I know that time is always time
          And place is always and only place. . . .
Thus the theme of the exile reaches its low ebb, and
Eliot turns to the religious theme.
```

7j ALTERING INITIAL CAPITALS IN SOME QUOTED MATTER

In general, you should reproduce quoted materials exactly, yet one exception is permitted for logical reasons. If the quotation forms a grammatical part of the sentence in which it occurs, you need not capitalize the first word of the quotation, even though it is capitalized in the original. In the following example, *The,* which is capitalized as the first word in the original sentence, is made lowercase because it continues the grammatical flow of the student's sentence.

```
Another writer argues that "the single greatest
impediment to our improving the lives of America's
children is the myth that we are a child-oriented
society" (Zigler 39).
```

Restrictive connectors, such as *that* or *because,* create restrictive clauses, thereby eliminating a need for the comma. Without a comma, the capital letter is unnecessary.

However, when your quotation follows a formal introduction that is set off by a comma or colon (as shown in this next example), you must capitalize the first word as in the original.

```
Another writer argues, "The single greatest. . . ."
```

or

```
Zigler states: "The single greatest. . . ."
```

but

```
Zigler says that "the single greatest. . . ."
```

7k USING ELLIPSIS POINTS TO OMIT PORTIONS OF QUOTED MATTER

Omit quoted material with spaced ellipsis points (. . .). Use a fourth dot to end a sentence. Ellipsis points must *not* be used to change the spirit or essential meaning of the original, that is, to take a quotation out of context. Quote your sources in correct grammatical structure. The following examples are illustrations for using ellipses in a variety of contexts:

1. Ellipsis points for material omitted from the middle of a sentence:

Three spaced ellipsis points
```
Phil Withim objects to the idea that "such episodes are
intended to demonstrate that Vere . . . has the intelligence
and insight to perceive the deeper issue" (118).
```

2. Ellipsis points for material omitted from the end of a source:

Ellipsis points with period after the page citation
```
R. W. B. Lewis declares that "if Hester has sinned, she
has done so as an affirmation of life, and her sin is
the source of life . . . "(62).
```

or

Four spaced ellipsis points
```
R. W. B. Lewis (62) declares that "if Hester has sinned,
she has done so as an affirmation of life, and her sin
is the source of life. . . ."
```

> *Note:* **As shown in the preceding example, if quoted material ends a sentence, use a period with no space and then three spaced ellipsis points.**

3. Ellipsis points for material omitted from the beginning of a source:

> He states: ". . . the new parent has lost the wisdom
> and daily support of older, more experienced family
> members" (Zigler 34).

Actually, the passage would read better without the ellipsis points or with your bracketed insertion of "[The]":

> He states that "the new parent has lost the wisdom and
> daily support of older, more experienced family members"
> (Zigler 34).

or

> He states: "[The] new parent has lost the wisdom and
> daily support of older, more experienced family members"
> (Zigler 34).

4. Ellipsis points for a complete sentence(s) omitted from the middle of a source:

> Zigler reminds us that "child abuse is found more
> frequently in a single (female) parent home in which the
> mother is working. . . . The unavailability of quality day
> care can only make this situation more stressful" (42).

5. Ellipsis points for a line(s) of poetry omitted:

> Do ye hear the children weeping, O my brothers,
>   Ere the sorrow comes with years?
> They are leaning their young heads against their
> mothers,
>   And <u>that</u> cannot stop their tears.
> . . . .
> They are weeping in the playtime of the others,
>   In the country of the free. (Browning 382)

6. Ellipsis points for paragraphs omitted:

```
Zigler makes this observation:
```

Indent three extra spaces or a quarter inch ⟶

```
          With many others, I am nevertheless optimistic
      that our nation will eventually display its
      inherent greatness and successfully correct the
      many ills that I have touched upon here. . . .
          Of course, much remains that could and
      should be done, including increased efforts in
      the area of family planning, the widespread
      implementation of the availability of homemaker
      and child care services, and a reexamination of
      our commitment to doing what is in the best
      interest of every child in America. (42)
```

> *Note:* **If you are quoting two or more paragraphs, indent the first line of each paragraph an extra 3 spaces (quarter inch) in addition to the standard indentation of 10 spaces (one inch).**

Many times you can be more effective if you incorporate parts of the quotation rather than quote the whole passage sprinkled with many ellipsis points. For example:

```
    The long-distance marriage, according to William
Nichols, "works best when there are no minor-aged
children to be considered," the two people are "equipped
by temperament and personality to spend a considerable
amount of time alone," and both are able to "function in
a mature, highly independent fashion" (54).
```

71   USING BRACKETS TO INSERT YOUR WORDS INSIDE QUOTED MATTER

Use brackets for interpolation, which means the insertion of new matter into a text or quotation. The use of brackets signals several different kinds of insertions. Note the following:

1. Use brackets to clarify:

This same critic indicates that "we must avoid the temptation to read it [The Scarlet Letter] heretically" (118).

2. Use brackets to establish correct grammar within an abridged quotation:

"John F. Kennedy [was] an immortal figure of courage and dignity in the hearts of most Americans," notes one historian (Jones 82).

He states: "[The] new parent has lost the wisdom and daily support of older, more experienced family members" (Zigler 34).

3. Use brackets to note the addition of underlining or italics:

He says, for instance, that the "extended family is now rare in contemporary society, and with its demise the new parent has lost the wisdom [my emphasis] and daily support of older, more experienced family members" (Zigler 42).

4. Use brackets with *sic* to indicate errors in the original:

Lovell says, "John F. Kennedy, assassinated in November of 1964 [sic], became overnight an immortal figure of courage and dignity in the hearts of most Americans" (62).

Note: **The assassination occurred in 1963. However, do not burden your text with the use of** *sic* **for historical matter in which misspellings are obvious, as with:**
> **"Faire seemely pleasauance each to other makes."**

5. Use brackets to enclose parenthetical material within parentheses:

The escape theme explains the drama's racial conflict
(see esp. Knight, who describes the Younger family as
one that opposes "racial discrimination in a supposedly
democratic land" [34]).

or

Consult the tables at the end of the report (i.e., the
results for the experimental group [n = 5] are also
listed in Figure 3, page 16).

6. Use brackets to present fractions:

$$\underline{a} = [(1 + \underline{b})/\underline{x}]^{1/2}$$

To present fractions in a line of text, use a slash mark (/) and parentheses first ( ), then brackets [( )], and finally braces {[( )]}. Some keyboards do not have brackets or braces; if that is the case, leave extra space for the brackets and braces when keyboarding and write them in with ink.

8 *Handling Format*

This chapter addresses questions about formatting a research paper—margins, spacing, page numbers, and so forth. Section 8a shows you how to design the final manuscript, and Section 8b explains matters of usage in an alphabetized glossary. Section 8c provides a short literary paper, and Section 8d gives an example of a longer, more formal research paper.

8a PREPARING THE FINAL MANUSCRIPT IN MLA STYLE

The format of a research paper consists of the following parts:

1. Title page
2. Outline
3. Abstract
4. Text of the paper
5. Content endnotes
6. Appendix
7. Works Cited

Items 4 and 7 are required for a paper in the MLA style; use the other items to meet the needs of your research. *Note:* Items 1, 3, 4, and 7 are required for a paper in APA style (see Chapter 10), but the order differs for Items 5–7.

Title Page or Opening Page

A research paper in MLA style does not need a separate title page unless you include an outline, abstract, or other prefatory matter. If you choose not to use a title page, place your identification in the upper left corner of your opening page, as shown in Figure 98:

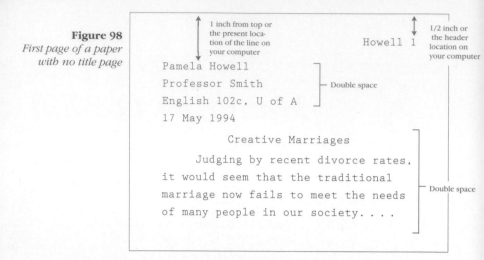

Figure 98
First page of a paper with no title page

Pamela Howell
Professor Smith
English 102c, U of A
17 May 1994

Creative Marriages
    Judging by recent divorce rates,
it would seem that the traditional
marriage now fails to meet the needs
of many people in our society. . . .

However, if you include prefatory matter, such as an outline, you need the title page with centered divisions for the title, the author, and the course identification, as illustrated in Figure 99. Adjust it to fit the demands of your instructor.

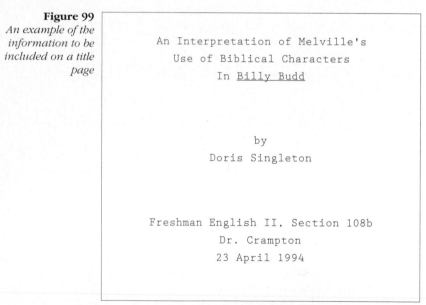

Figure 99
An example of the information to be included on a title page

An Interpretation of Melville's
Use of Biblical Characters
In Billy Budd

by
Doris Singleton

Freshman English II, Section 108b
Dr. Crampton
23 April 1994

Follow these guidelines for writing a title page:

1. Use an inverted pyramid to balance two or more lines of the title.
2. Use capitals and lowercase letters without underscoring or italicizing and without quotation marks. Published works that appear

as part of your title require underscoring or italics (for books, for example) or quotation marks (for short stories, for example). Do not use a period after a centered heading.
3. Place your full name below the title, usually in the center of the page.
4. Employ separate lines, centered, to provide the course information, institution, instructor, date, or program (e.g., Honors Program).
5. Provide balanced, even margins for all sides of the title page.
6. Use your computer to print a border on this page, if you so desire, but not on any other pages.

> *Note:* **APA style requires a different setup for the title page; see page 319 for guidelines and an example.**

Outline

Print your outline into the finished manuscript only if your instructor requires it. Place it after the title page on separate pages, and number these pages with lowercase Roman numerals beginning with ii (e.g., ii, iii, iv, v) at the top right-hand corner of the page just after your last name (e.g., Spence iii). For information on writing an outline, see Section 3c, pages 90–93, and the sample outlines on pages 248–50.

Abstract

Include an abstract for a paper in MLA style only if your instructor requires it. (APA style requires the abstract; see Section 10e, page 318.) An abstract provides a brief digest of the paper's essential ideas in about 100 words. To write one, borrow from your introduction, use some of the topic sentences from your paragraphs, and use one or two sentences from your conclusion.

Place the abstract on the first page of text (page 1) one double space below the title and before the first lines of the text. Indent the abstract 5 spaces or a half inch from the left as a block, and indent the first line an additional 5 spaces or a half inch. Use quadruple spacing at the end of the abstract to set it off from the text, which follows immediately. You may also place the abstract on a separate page between the title page and the first page of text.

Remember that the abstract is usually read first and may be the *only* part read; therefore, make it accurate, specific, objective, and self-contained (i.e., so that it makes sense alone without references to the main text). Note the example given in Figure 100:

Figure 100
*Sample abstract
on the first page of
the paper*

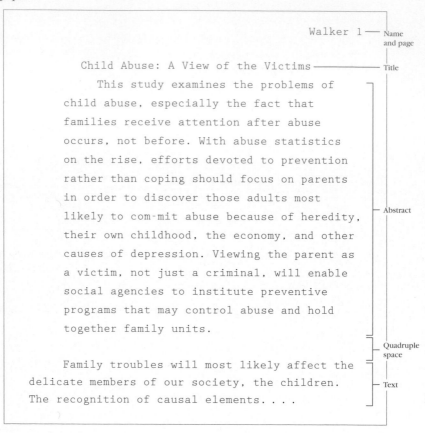

Walker 1 —— Name
and page

Child Abuse: A View of the Victims ———— Title

   This study examines the problems of
child abuse, especially the fact that
families receive attention after abuse
occurs, not before. With abuse statistics
on the rise, efforts devoted to prevention
rather than coping should focus on parents
in order to discover those adults most
likely to com-mit abuse because of heredity,
their own childhood, the economy, and other
causes of depression. Viewing the parent as
a victim, not just a criminal, will enable
social agencies to institute preventive
programs that may control abuse and hold
together family units.

—— Abstract

—— Quadruple
space

   Family troubles will most likely affect the
delicate members of our society, the children.
The recognition of causal elements. . . .

—— Text

Text of the Paper

Double-space throughout the entire paper except for the title page (see page 202) and the separation of the abstract from the first line of text (see above). In general, you should *not* use subheads or numbered divisions for short papers, 10 pages or less. Instead, use continuous paragraphing without subdivisions or headings. However, long papers and most scientific and business reports require subheads (see "Headings," page 224).

If the closing page of your text runs short, leave the remainder of the page blank. Do not write "The End" or provide artwork as a closing signal. Do not start Notes or Works Cited on this final page of text.

See also these sections:

Chapter 6 for a discussion of the three dominant parts of the text—
   the introduction (Section 6f, pages 158–163), the body (Section

6g, pages 163–169), and the conclusion (Section 6h, pages 169–172).

"Drafting Your Paper" (Section 6e, pages 154–158) to learn more about such matters as tense, voice, and language.

Section 8a, pages 201–03, for details about name, page number, and course identification for your first page of text.

Content Endnotes

Label this page "Notes," centered toward the top edge of the sheet, at least one double space below the page numbering sequence in the upper right corner. Double-space between the "Notes" heading and the first note. Number the notes in sequence with raised superscript numerals (see 254–57) to match those within your text. Double-space all entries, and double-space between them. See "Content Endnotes," pages 219–20, and see also the sample Notes page, found on page 260.

Appendix

Place additional material, if necessary, in an appendix preceding the Works Cited page. It is the logical location for numerous tables and illustrations, computer data, questionnaire results, complicated statistics, mathematical proofs, and detailed descriptions of special equipment. Double-space the material for the appendix(es) and begin each appendix on a new sheet. Continue the page numbering sequence in the upper right corner of the sheet. Label the page "Appendix," centered at the top of the sheet. If you have more than one appendix, use "Appendix A," "Appendix B," and so forth. See page 261 for an example.

Works Cited

Center the heading "Works Cited" 1 inch from the top edge of the sheet. Continue the page numbering sequence in the upper right corner. Double-space throughout. Set the first line of each entry flush left, and indent turnover lines 5 spaces or a half inch. If your software supports it, use the command for a hanging indent. For samples and additional information, see Chapter 9, "Works Cited: MLA Style," pages 265–306, and also the sample Works Cited found on pages 246 and 262–63.

8b   GLOSSARY: TECHNIQUES FOR PREPARING THE MANUSCRIPT IN MLA STYLE

The alphabetic glossary that follows in this section will answer most of your miscellaneous questions about matters of form, such as margins, pagination, dates, and numbers. For matters not addressed in the glossary, consult the index, which will direct you to appropriate pages elsewhere in this text.

Abbreviations   Employ abbreviations often and consistently in notes and citations, but avoid them in the text. *Tip:* When drafting your text, abbreviate long titles, difficult names, or hard-to-spell terms (e.g., *Tess* for *Tess of the D'Urbervilles* or *T* for *tourniquet*), and then expand the abbreviation with your software's FIND and REPLACE commands before printing the final copy.

In the entries for the Works Cited page, always abbreviate technical terms (e.g., anon., e.g., diss.), institutions (e.g., acad., assn., Cong.), dates (e.g., Jan., Feb.), states (e.g., OH, CA), and names of publishers (e.g., McGraw, UP of Florida). (See also "Names of Persons," page 231, for comments on the correct abbreviations of honorary titles.)

Abbreviations for Technical Terms and Institutions

abr.	abridged
AD	*anno Domini* ("in the year of the Lord"); precedes numerals with no space between letters (e.g., AD 350)
anon.	anonymous
art., arts.	article(s)
assn.	association
assoc.	associate, associated
BC	before Christ; follows numerals with no space between letters (e.g., 500 BC)
bk., bks.	book(s)
ca., c.	*circa* ("about"); used to indicate an approximate date (e.g., ca. 1812)
cf.	*confer* ("compare" one source with another); not, however, to be used in place of *see* or *see also*
ch., chs., chap, chaps.	chapter(s)
col., cols.	column(s)
comp.	compiled by or compiler
diss.	dissertation
doc.	document
ed., eds.	editor(s), edition, or edited by
e.g.	*exempli gratia* ("for example"); preceded and followed by a comma
enl.	cnlarged (e.g., enl. ed.)
esp.	especially, as in "12–15, esp. 13"
et al.	*et alii* ("and others"); *John Smith et al.* means "John Smith and other authors"
etc.	*et cetera* ("and so forth")
et pas.	*et passim* ("and here and there"); see *passim*
et seq.	*et sequens* ("and the following"); *9 et seq.* means "page nine and the following page"; compare *f.* and *ff.*
f., ff.	and the following; *8f.* means "page eight and the following page"; but exact references are sometimes preferable, for example, "45–51, 55, 58" instead of "45ff." Acceptable also is "45+."

fig.	figure
fl.	*floruit* ("flourished"); used to indicate the dates on which a person reached greatness (e.g., fl. 1420–50); used when birth and death dates are unknown
ibid.	*ibidem* ("in the same place"); used to indicate the immediately preceding title, normally capitalized and underscored or set in italics (e.g., *Ibid.,* p. 34)
i.e.	*id est* ("that is"); preceded and followed by a comma
illus.	illustrated by, illustrations, or illustrator
infra	"below"; used to refer to a succeeding portion of the text; compare *supra*. Generally, it is best to write "see below."
intro., introd.	introduction (by)
loc. cit.	*loco citato* ("in the place [passage] cited")
ms., mss. (Ms., Mss.)	Manuscript(s) (e.g., [Cf. the mss. of Glass and Ford])
n, nn	note(s) (e.g., 23n2, 51n. 52nn 2–4.)
narr.	narrated by, narrator
n.d.	no date (in a book's title or copyright page)
no., nos.	number(s)
n.p.	no place (of publication); no publisher
n. pag.	no pagination listed
ns	new series
op. cit.	*opere citato* ("in the work cited")
p., pp.	page(s); do not use *ps.* for "pages"
passim	"here and there throughout the work," for example, "67, 72, et passim," but also acceptable is "67+"
proc.	proceedings
pseud.	pseudonym
pt., pts.	part(s)
rev.	revised, revised by, revision, review, or reviewed by
rpt.	reprint, reprinted
sec(s).	section(s)
ser.	series
sess.	session
sic	"thus"; placed in brackets to indicate an error in the quoted passage and the writer is quoting accurately; see example on page 199.
st., sts.	stanza(s)
St., Sts.	Saint(s)
sup.	*supra* ("above"); used to refer to a preceding portion of the text; it is just as easy to write "above" or "see above"
supp.	supplement(s)
s.v., s. vv.	*sub voce (verbo)* ("under the word or heading")
trans., tr.	translator, translated, translated by, or translation
ts., tss.	typescript(s)

viz.	*videlicet* ("namely")
vol., vols.	volume(s) (e.g., vol. 3)
vs., v.	versus ("against"); used in citing legal cases

Abbreviations for Days of the Week and Months

Sun.	Jan.	July
Mon.	Feb.	Aug.
Tues.	Mar.	Sept.
Wed.	Apr.	Oct.
Thurs.	May	Nov.
Fri.	June	Dec.
Sat.		

Abbreviations for States and Geographic Names

AL	Alabama	MT	Montana
AK	Alaska	NE	Nebraska
AZ	Arizona	NV	Nevada
AR	Arkansas	NH	New Hampshire
CA	California	NJ	New Jersey
CO	Colorado	NM	New Mexico
CT	Connecticut	NY	New York
DE	Delaware	NC	North Carolina
DC	District of Columbia	ND	North Dakota
FL	Florida	OH	Ohio
GA	Georgia	OK	Oklahoma
GU	Guam	OR	Oregon
HI	Hawaii	PA	Pennsylvania
ID	Idaho	PR	Puerto Rico
IL	Illinois	RI	Rhode Island
IN	Indiana	SC	South Carolina
IA	Iowa	SD	South Dakota
KS	Kansas	TN	Tennessee
KY	Kentucky	TX	Texas
LA	Louisiana	UT	Utah
ME	Maine	VT	Vermont
MD	Maryland	VI	Virgin Islands
MA	Massachusetts	VA	Virginia
MI	Michigan	WA	Washington
MN	Minnesota	WV	West Virginia
MS	Mississippi	WI	Wisconsin
MO	Missouri	WY	Wyoming

Abbreviations for Publishers' Names

Use the shortened forms below as guidelines. Some of these publishers no longer exist, but their imprints remain on copyright pages of books.

Abrams	Harry N. Abrams, Inc.

ALA	American Library Association
Allen	George Allen and Unwin Publishers, Inc.
Allyn	Allyn and Bacon, Inc.
Barnes	Barnes and Noble Books
Basic	Basic Books
Beacon	Beacon Press, Inc.
Bobbs	The Bobbs-Merrill Co., Inc.
Bowker	R. R. Bowker Co.
Cambridge UP	Cambridge University Press
Clarendon	Clarendon Press
Columbia UP	Columbia University Press
Dell	Dell Publishing Co., Inc.
Dodd	Dodd, Mead, and Co.
Doubleday	Doubleday and Co., Inc.
Farrar	Farrar, Straus, and Giroux, Inc.
Free	The Free Press
Gale	Gale Research Co.
GPO	Government Printing Company
Harcourt	Harcourt Brace and Company.
Harper	Harper and Row Publishers, Inc.
HarperCollins	HarperCollins Publishers, Inc.
Harvard UP	Harvard University Press
Heath	D. C. Heath and Co.
Holt	Holt, Rinehart, and Winston, Inc.
Houghton	Houghton Mifflin Co.
Indiana UP	Indiana University Press
Knopf	Alfred A. Knopf, Inc.
Lippincott	J. B. Lippincott Co.
Little	Little, Brown, and Co.
Macmillan	Macmillan Publishing Co., Inc.
McGraw	McGraw-Hill, Inc.
MIT P	The MIT Press
MLA	The Modern Language Association of America
Norton	W. W. Norton and Co., Inc.
Oxford UP	Oxford University Press
Prentice	Prentice-Hall, Inc.
Putnam's	G. P. Putnam's Sons
Random	Random House, Inc.
St. Martin's	St. Martin's Press, Inc.
Scott	Scott, Foresman and Co.
Scribner's	Charles Scribner's Sons
Simon	Simon and Schuster, Inc.
State U of New York P	State University of New York Press
U of Chicago P	University of Chicago Press
UP of Florida	University Press of Florida
Washington Square P	Washington Square Press

Abbreviations for Books of the Bible   Use parenthetical documentation for biblical references in the text. That is, place the entry within parentheses immediately after the quotation, for example:

> After the great flood God spoke to Noah, "And I will
> establish my covenant with you; neither shall all flesh
> be cut off any more by the waters of a flood; neither
> shall there any more be a flood to destroy the earth"
> (Gen. 9.11).

Do not italicize or underscore titles of books of the Bible. Abbreviate books of the Bible except some very short titles, such as Ezra and Mark.

Acts	**Acts of the Apostles**
1 and 2 Chron.	1 and 2 Chronicles
Col.	Colossians
1 and 2 Cor.	1 and 2 Corinthians
Dan.	Daniel
Deut.	Deuteronomy
Eccles.	Ecclesiastes
Eph.	Ephesians
Esth.	Esther
Exod.	Exodus
Ezek.	Ezekiel
Gal.	Galatians
Gen.	Genesis
Hab.	Habakkuk
Hag.	Haggai
Heb.	Hebrews
Hos.	Hosea
Isa.	Isaiah
Jer.	Jeremiah
Jon.	Jonah
Josh.	Joshua
Judg.	Judges
Lam.	Lamentations
Lev.	Leviticus
Mal.	Malachi
Matt.	Matthew
Mic.	Micah
Nah.	Nahum
Neh.	Nehemiah
Num.	Numbers
Obad.	Obadiah
1 and 2 Pet.	1 and 2 Peter
Phil.	Philippians

Philem.	Philemon
Prov.	Proverbs
Ps. (Pss.)	Psalm(s)
Rev.	Revelation
Rom.	Romans
1 and 2 Sam.	1 and 2 Samuel
Song Sol.	Song of Solomon
1 and 2 Thess.	1 and 2 Thessalonians
1 and 2 Tim.	1 and 2 Timothy
Zech.	Zechariah
Zeph.	Zephaniah

Abbreviations for Literary Works

Shakespeare   In parenthetical documentation, use italicized or underscored abbreviations for titles of Shakespearean plays, as shown in this example:

```
Too late, Capulet urges Montague to end their feud, "O
brother Montague, give me thy hand" (Rom. 5.3.296).
```

Here is a complete list of abbreviations for Shakespeare's plays:

Ado	*Much Ado About Nothing*
Ant.	*Antony and Cleopatra*
AWW	*All's Well That Ends Well*
AYL	*As You Like It*
Cor.	*Coriolanus*
Cym.	*Cymbeline*
Err.	*The Comedy of Errors*
Ham.	*Hamlet*
1H4	*Henry IV, Part 1*
2H4	*Henry IV, Part 2*
H5	*Henry V*
1H6	*Henry VI, Part 1*
2H6	*Henry VI, Part 2*
3H6	*Henry VI, Part 3*
H8	*Henry VIII*
JC	*Julius Caesar*
Jn.	*King John*
LLL	*Love's Labour's Lost*
Lr.	*King Lear*
Mac.	*Macbeth*
MM	*Measure for Measure*
MND	*A Midsummer Night's Dream*
MV	*The Merchant of Venice*
Oth.	*Othello*

Per.	*Pericles*
R2	*Richard II*
R3	*Richard III*
Rom.	*Romeo and Juliet*
Shr.	*The Taming of the Shrew*
TGV	*Two Gentlemen of Verona*
Tim.	*Timon of Athens*
Tit.	*Titus Andronicus*
Tmp.	*Tempest*
TN	*Twelfth Night*
TNK	*The Two Noble Kinsmen*
Tro.	*Troilus and Cressida*
Wiv.	*The Merry Wives of Windsor*
WT	*The Winter's Tale*

Use italics or underscoring for these abbreviations of Shakespeare's poems:

Luc.	*The Rape of Lucrece*
PhT	*The Phoenix and the Turtle*
PP	*The Passionate Pilgrim*
Son.	*Sonnets* ("Sonnet 14" in the text but "Son. 14" in a parenthetical notation)
Ven.	*Venus and Adonis*

Chaucer   Use the following abbreviations in parenthetical documentation. Italicize or underscore the book but not the individual tales:

CkT	The Cook's Tale
ClT	The Clerk's Tale
CT	*The Canterbury Tales*
CYT	The Canon's Yeoman's Tale
FranT	The Franklin's Tale
FrT	The Friar's Tale
GP	The General Prologue
KnT	The Knight's Tale
ManT	The Manciple's Tale
Mel	The Tale of Melibee
MerT	The Merchant's Tale
MilT	The Miller's Tale
MkT	The Monk's Tale
MLT	The Man of Law's Tale
NPT	The Nun's Priest's Tale
PardT	The Pardoner's Tale
ParsT	The Parson's Tale
PhyT	The Physician's Tale
PrT	The Prioress's Tale
Ret	Chaucer's Retraction

RvT	The Reeve's Tale
ShT	The Shipman's Tale
SNT	The Second Nun's Tale
SqT	The Squire's Tale
SumT	The Summoner's Tale
Th	The Tale of Sir Thopas
WBT	The Wife of Bath's Tale

Other Literary Works   Wherever possible in your in-text citations, use the initial letters of the title. For example, a reference to page 18 of Melville's *Moby-Dick* could appear as follows: (*MD* 18). Use the following italicized abbreviations as guidelines:

Aen.	*Aeneid* by Vergil
Ag.	*Agamemnon* by Aeschylus
Ant.	*Antigone* by Sophocles
Bac.	*Bacchae* by Euripides
Beo.	*Beowulf*
Can.	*Candide* by Voltaire
Dec.	*Decameron* by Boccaccio
DJ	*Don Juan* by Byron
DQ	*Don Quixote* by Cervantes
Eum.	*Eumenides* by Aeschylus
FQ	*The Faerie Queene* by Spenser
Gil.	*Epic of Gilgamesh*
GT	*Gulliver's Travels* by Swift
Il.	*Iliad* by Homer
Inf.	*Inferno* by Dante
MD	*Moby-Dick* by Melville
Med.	*Medea* by Euripides
Nib.	*Nibelungenlied*
Od.	*Odyssey* by Homer
OR	*Oedipus Rex* by Sophocles
PL	*Paradise Lost* by Milton
SA	*Samson Agonistes* by Milton
SGGK	*Sir Gawain and the Green Knight*
SL	*Scarlet Letter* by Hawthorne

Accent Marks   When you quote, reproduce accents exactly as they appear in the original. You may need to use the character sets embedded within the computer software (see "Character Sets," page 219). Use ink if your typewriter or word processor does not support the marks.

```
"La tradición clásica en españa," according to Romana,
remains strong and vibrant in public school instruction
(16).
```

Acknowledgments   Generally, acknowledgments are unnecessary, and a preface is not required. Use a superscript reference numeral to your first sentence, and then place any obligatory acknowledgments or explanations in a content endnote (see also pages 219–22):

> [1] I wish here to express my thanks to Mrs. Horace A. Humphrey for permission to examine the manuscripts of her late husband.

> *Note:* **Acknowledge neither your instructor nor typist for research papers, though such acknowledgments are standard with graduate theses and dissertations.**

Ampersand   Avoid using the ampersand symbol (&) unless custom demands it (e.g., A & P). Use *and* for in-text citations in MLA style (e.g., Smith and Jones 213–14), *but do use* an ampersand in APA style references (e.g., Spenser & Wilson, 1994, p. 73).

Annotated Bibliography   An annotation describes the essential details of a book or article. Place it just after the facts of publication. Follow these suggestions:

1. Explain the main purpose of the work.
2. Briefly describe the contents.
3. Indicate the possible audience for the work.
4. Note any special features.
5. Warn of any defect, weakness, or suspected bias.

Provide enough information in three to six sentences for a reader to have a fairly clear image of the work's purpose, contents, and special value. Turn to Section 4e, pages 112–14, to see an annotated bibliography.

Apostrophe   To form the possessive of singular nouns, add an apostrophe and *s* (e.g., the typist's ledger). Add only the apostrophe with plural nouns ending in *s* (e.g., several typists' ledgers). Add the apostrophe and *s* to singular proper nouns of people and places even if the noun ends in an *s* (e.g., Rice's story, Rawlings's novel, Arkansas's mountains, *but* the Rawlingses' good fortune). Exceptions are the names of *Jesus* and *Moses* (e.g., Jesus' scriptures, Moses' words) and hellenized names of more than one syllable ending in *es* (e.g., *Euripides'* dramas). Use apostrophes to form the plurals of letters (e.g., a's and b's) but not to form the plural of numbers or abbreviations (e.g., ACTs in the 18s and 19s, the 1980s, sevens, three MDs).

Arabic Numerals   Both MLA and APA styles require Arabic numerals whenever possible for volumes, books, parts, and chapters of works; acts, scenes, and lines of plays; cantos, stanzas, and lines of poetry.

Use Arabic figures to express all numbers 10 and above (e.g., 154, 1,269, the 15th test, the remaining 12%). Write as Arabic numerals any numbers below 10 that cannot be spelled out in one or two words (e.g., 3½, 6.234).

For inclusive numbers that indicate a range, give the second number in full for numbers through 99 (e.g., 3–5, 15–21, 70–96). In MLA style with three digits or more, give only the last two in the second number unless more digits are needed for clarity (e.g., 98–101, 110–12, 989–1001, 1030–33, 2766–854). In APA style with three digits or more, give all numbers (e.g., 110–112, 1030–1033, 2766–2854).

Place commas between the third and fourth digits from the right, the sixth and seventh, and so on (e.g., 1,200 or 1,200,000). Exceptions are page and line numbers, addresses, the year, and ZIP codes (e.g., page 1620; at 12116 Nova Road; in 1985; or New York, NY 10012).

Use the number *1* in every case for numbers, not the lowercase *l* or uppercase *L,* especially if you are keyboarding on a word processor or computer.

Numbers Expressed as Figures in Your Text Use figures in your text according to the following examples:

1. All numbers 10 and above:
   the subjects who were 25 years old
       but a twenty-five-year-old female
   the collection of 48 illustrations

2. Numbers that represent ages, dates, time, size, score, amounts of money, and numerals used as numerals:
   ages 6 through 14
   AD 200 *but* 200 BC
   in 1991–92 *or* from 1991 to 1992, *but not* from 1991–92
   March 5, 1991 *or* 5 March 1991, *but not* both styles
   1990s *or* the nineties
   six o'clock *or* 6:00 p.m.
   7 pounds
   4 feet
   $9.00 or $9
   32–34 *or* pages 32–34, *but not* pp. 32–34
   lines 32–34, *but not* ll. 32–34
   page 45, *but not* the forty-fifth page
   6% *but* use "six percent" in discussions with few numbers
   scores in the 92–96 percentile
   from 1965 through 1970

3. Statistical and mathematical numbers:
   6.213
   0.5, *but not* .5
   consumed exactly 0.45 of the fuel

4. Numbers that precede units of measurement:
    a 5-milligram tablet
    use 7 centimeter of this fluid
5. Numbers below 10 grouped with higher numbers:
    3 out of 42 subjects
    tests 6 and 13
    but 15 tests in three categories (Tests and categories are differ-
    ent groups; they are not being compared.)

Numbers Expressed as Words in Your Text   Spell out numbers
in the following instances:

1. Numbers less than 10 that are not used as measurements:
    three students
    one who should know
    a group of six professors
    six proposals
    three-dimensional renderings
2. Numbers less than 10 that are grouped with other numbers be-
    low 10:
    five sessions with six examinations in each session
    the fifth of eight participants
3. Common fractions:
    one fifth of the student population
    eighty-eight errors
    thirty-four times
    a one-third majority
4. Any number that begins a sentence:
    Thirty participants elected to withdraw.
5. The numbers *zero* and *one* when used alone:
    zero-base budget planning
    a one-line paragraph
    one response *but* 1 of 15 responses
6. References to centuries:
    twentieth century
    twentieth-century literature

Numbers as Both Figures and Words   Combine words and figures in these situations:

1. Back to back modifiers:
    twelve 6-year-olds *or* 12 six-year-olds, *but not* 12 6-year-olds
2. Large numbers:
    an operating budget of $4 million

Numbers in Documentation   Use numbers with in-text citations
and Works Cited entries according to the following examples:

(*Ham.* 5.3.16–18)
(*Faust* 2.140)
(2 Sam. 2.1–8)
(Fredericks 23–24) (MLA style)
(Fredericks, 1995, pp. 23–24) (APA and CBE style)
Rpt. as vols. 13 and 14
Glass ms. 210
102nd Cong., 1st sess. S 2411
16 mm., 29 min.
Monograph 1962-M2
College English 15 (Winter 1995): 3–6 (MLA style)
Memory and Cognition, 3, 562–590 (APA style)
J. Mol. Biol. 149:15–39; 1995 (CBE style)
Journal of Philosophy 29 (1995): 172–89 (footnote style)

Asterisks   Do not use asterisks (*) for tables, illustrations, or content endnotes (see pages 225–29). Use numbers for tables and illustrations (e.g., Table 2, Fig. 3) and letters for notes (see Figure 106, page 229).

Bible   Use parenthetical documentation for biblical references in the text (2 Chron. 18.13). Do not underscore or italicize the books of the Bible. For abbreviations, see pages 210–211.

Borders   Computers offer you the opportunity to build borders around pages, paragraphs, and graphic designs. Use this feature with restraint. Place the title page within a full-page border if you like, but *not* pages of your text. Use a border with a fill pattern, if desired, for graphs, charts, highlighted text, and other material that deserves special emphasis.

Bullets and Numbers   Computers can supply several bullet or number styles, which are indented lines that begin with a circle, square, diamond, triangle, number, or letter. Use this feature for a list, as shown in the paper by Patti Bracy (see page 353).

Capitalization

Capitalize Some Titles   For books, journals, magazines, and newspapers, capitalize the first word, the last word, and all principal words, including words that that follow hyphens in compound terms (e.g., French-Speaking Islands). Do not capitalize articles, prepositions that introduce phrases, coordinating conjunctions, and the *to* in infinitives when these words occur in the middle of the title (e.g., *The Last of the Mohicans*). For titles of articles and parts of books, capitalize as for books (e.g., "Writing the Final Draft" or Appendix 2). If the first line of the poem serves as the title, reproduce it exactly as it appears in print (e.g., anyone lived in a pretty how town).

Note: APA style capitalizes only the first word and proper names in reference titles (including the first word of subtitles), as shown here:

APA style

Baron, J. N., & Bielby, W. (1980). Bring the firms back in: Stratification, segmentation and the organization of work. American Sociological Review, 45, 737-765.

Study the appropriate style for your field as found in Chapters 9, 10, and 11.

Capitalize After a Colon   When a *complete* sentence follows a colon, MLA style skips one space and does *not* capitalize the first word unless the colon introduces a rule or principle; APA style also skips one space but *does* capitalize the first word after the colon.

MLA style:

The consequences of this decision will be disastrous: each division of the corporation will be required to cut twenty percent of its budget within this fiscal year.

Franklin warns: A penny saved is a penny earned

APA style:

They have agreed on the outcome: Informed subjects perform better than do uniformed subjects.

Capitalize Some Compound Words   Capitalize the second part of a hyphenated compound word only when it is used in a heading with other capitalized words:

Low-Frequency Sound Equipment

but

Low-frequency sound distortion is caused by several factors.

Capitalize Trade Names   Use capitals for trade names, such as:

Pepsi   Plexiglas   du Pont   Dingo   Corvette   Xerox

Capitalize Proper Names   Capitalize proper names used as adjectives *but not* the words used with them:

Einstein's theory   Salk's vaccine

Capitalize Specific Departments or Courses   Capitalize the specific names of departments or courses, but use lowercase when they are used in a general sense.

Department of Psychology *but* the psychology department

Psychology 314 *but* an advanced course in psychology

Capitalize Nouns Used Before Numerals or Letters   Capitalize the noun when it denotes a specific place in a numbered series:

```
During Test 6, we observed Group C, as shown in Table 5
and also Figure 2.
```

However, do *not* capitalize nouns that name common parts of books or tables followed by numerals:

```
chapter 12        page ix        column 14
```

Character Sets   Most computers provide characters that are unavailable on your keyboard. These are special letters, signs, and symbols, such as Φ, Σ, â, ▶. The software instructions will help you find and utilize these marks and icons.

Clip Art   Pictures, figures, and drawings are available on many computers, but avoid the temptation to embed them in your document. Clip art, in general, conveys an informal, sometimes comic effect, one that is inappropriate to the serious nature of most research papers.

Content Endnotes   As a general rule, put important matters in your text. Use a content endnote to display research problems, conflicts in the testimony of experts, matters of importance that are not germane to your discussion, interesting tidbits, credit to people and sources not mentioned in the text, and other tangential matters that you think will interest the readers. After you have embedded most of your computer files into your draft, check the remaining files to find appropriate material for content endnotes.
   Content endnotes should conform to these rules:

1. Content endnotes are *not* documentation notes. Use in-text citations to document your sources, not content endnotes. *Note:* Instructors in some fields, especially history, philosophy, and the fine arts, may ask for documentation footnotes; if so, see "Footnotes for Documentation," pages 223 and 358–60.
2. The content endnotes should be placed on a separate page(s) following the last page of text. Do not write them as footnotes at the bottom of pages. See pages 358–60 for specifications on typing endnotes.
3. At a computer, a word processing code can be used to produce superscript numbers (e.g., [1]) or numbers within slash marks after the end punctuation mark (e.g., /1/). *Note:* The computer superscript numerals often appear in a smaller size and different font. At a typewriter, place superscript numerals within the text by turning the roller of the typewriter so that the Arabic numeral strikes about half a space above the line, like this:[3] Each superscript numeral should immediately follow the material to which it

refers, usually at the end of a sentence, with no space between the superscript numeral and a word or mark of punctuation, as shown in this example:

Third, a program to advise college students about
politically correct language and campus attitudes[1]
may incite demonstrations by both faculty and students
against the censorship of free speech by both faculty
and students.

Note: **The preceding superscript numeral refers to Note 1 under "Related Matters Not Germane to the Text," which follows. See also the sample paper on pages 247–63 for its use of superscript numerals and content endnotes.**

---

4. Sources mentioned in endnotes must appear in your Works Cited page even if they are not mentioned in the main body of text.

The samples below demonstrate various types of content endnotes.

Related Matters Not Germane to the Text

[1] The problems of politically correct language are
explored in Adams, Tucker (4-5), Zalers, and also Young
and Smith (583). These authorities cite the need for
caution by administrators who would impose new measures
on speech and behavior. Verbal abuse cannot be erased by
a new set of unjust laws. Patrick German offers several
guidelines for implementing an effective but reasonable
program (170-72).

Blanket Citation

[2] On this point see Giarrett (3-4), de Young (579),
Kinard (405-07), and Young (119).

[3] Cf. Campbell (<u>Masks</u> 1: 170-225; <u>Hero</u> 342-45),
Frazer (312), and Baird (300-44).

Literature on a Related Topic

[4] For additional study of the effects of alcoholics
on children, see especially the <u>Journal of Studies on
Alcohol</u> for the article by Wolin et al. and the
bibliography on the topic by Orme and Rimmer (285-87).
In addition, group therapy for children of alcoholics
is examined in Hawley and Brown.

Major Source Requiring Frequent In-Text Citations

[5] All citations to Shakespeare are to the Parrott edition.

[6] Dryden's poems are cited from the California edition of his <u>Works</u> and documented in the text with first references to each poem listing volume, page, and lines and with subsequent references citing only lines.

Reference to Source Materials

[7] Cf. James Baird who argues that the whiteness of Melville's whale is "the sign of the all-encompassing God" (257). Baird states: "It stands for what Melville calls at the conclusion of the thirty-fifth chapter of <u>Moby Dick</u> 'the inscrutable tides of God'; and it is of these tides as well that the great White Whale himself is the quintessential emblem, the iconographic representation" (257).

[8] On this point see also the essay by Patricia Chaffee in which she examines the "house" as a primary image in the fiction of Eudora Welty.

Explanation of Tools, Methods, or Testing Procedures

[9] Water samples were drawn from the identical spot each day at 8:00 a.m., noon, 4:00 p.m., and 8:00 p.m., with testing done immediately on site.

[10] The control group continued normal dietary routines, but the experimental group consumed nuts, sharp cheeses, and chocolates to test acne development of its members against that of the control group.

[11] The initial sample was complete data on all twins born in Nebraska between 1920 and 1940. These dates were selected to provide test subjects 60 years of age or older.

Note: **A report of an empirical study in APA style would require an explanation of tools and testing procedures in the text under "Method." See Section 3b, page 87, and Chapter 10, pages 318–22**

Statistics   (See also "Illustrations and Tables," pages 225–229.)

[12] Database results show 27,000 pupil-athletes in 174 high schools with grades 0.075 above another group of 27,000 nonathletes at the same high schools. Details on the nature of various <u>reward structures</u> are unavailable.

Acknowledgments for Assistance or Support

[13] Funds to finance this research were graciously provided by the Thompson-Monroe Foundation.

[14] This writer wishes to acknowledge the research assistance of Pat Luther, graduate assistant, Department of Physics.

Variables or Conflicts in the Evidence

[15] Potlatch et al. included the following variables: the positive acquaintance, the equal status norm, the various social norms, the negative stereotypes, and sexual discrimination (415-20). However, racial barriers cannot be overlooked as one important variable.

[16] The pilot study at Dunlap School, where sexual imbalance was noticed (62 percent males), differed sharply from test results compared with those of other schools. The male bias at Dunlap thereby caused the writer to eliminate those scores from the totals.

Copyright Law   "Fair use" of the materials of others is permitted without the need for specific permission as long as your purpose is noncommercial for purposes of criticism, scholarship, or research. Under those circumstances, you can quote from sources and reproduce artistic works within reasonable limits. The law is vague on specific amounts that can be borrowed, suggesting only the "substantiality of the portion used in relation to the copyrighted work as a whole." In other words, you should be safe in reproducing the work of another as long as the portion is not substantial. To protect your own work, keyboard in the upper right-hand corner of your manuscript, "Copyright © 19__ by ____." Fill in the blanks with the proper year and your name. To register a work, order a form from the U.S. Copyright Office, Library of Congress, Washington, D.C. 20559.

Corrections   Because the computer can produce a printed copy quickly, you should make all proofreading corrections before printing a finished manuscript. With a typed paper, however, you may make corrections neatly using correction fluid, correction paper, or tape to cover and type over any errors. Add words or short phrases directly above a line, not in the margins. Keep such corrections to a minimum; retype pages that require four or more corrections. Do not strike over a letter, paste inserts onto the page, write vertically in the margins, or make handwritten notes on the manuscript pages.

Covers and Binders   Most instructors prefer that you submit manuscript pages with one staple in the upper left corner. Unless required or permitted to do so, do not use a cover or binder.

Dates   See "Arabic Numerals," pages 214–217.

Definitions   For definitions and translations within your text, use single quotation marks without intervening punctuation, for example:

```
The use of et alii 'and others' has diminished in
scholarly writing.
```

Endnotes for Documentation of Sources   An instructor or supervisor may prefer traditional superscript numerals within the text and documentation endnotes at the end of paper. If so, see Chapter 11, pages 360–61.

Etc.   (et cetera) Avoid using this term, which means "and so forth," by adding extra items to the list or by writing "and so forth."

Footnotes for Documentation   If your instructor requires you to use footnotes, see Chapter 11, pages 358–60, for a discussion and examples.

Fonts   Most computers offer a variety of typefaces. Courier (`Courier`), the typewriter font, is always a safe choice, but you may use others, such as a nonserif typeface like Helvetica (**Helvetica**) or a serif typeface like Times Roman (**Times Roman**). Use the same font consistently throughout for your text, but shift to different fonts if desired for tables, illustrations, and other matter. See the sample paper by Jay Wickham, pages 241–46, for an example.

Foreign Cities   In general, spell the names of foreign cities as they are written in original sources. However, for purposes of clarity, you may substitute the English equivalent or provide both spellings with one in parentheses:

```
Köln (Cologne)           Braunschweig (Brunswick)
München (Munich)         Praha (Prague)
```

Foreign Languages   Underscore or italicize foreign words used in an English text:

```
Like his friend Olaf, he is aut Caesar, aut nihil,
either overpowering perfection or ruin and destruction.
```

Do not underscore or italicize quotations in a foreign language:

> Obviously, he uses it to exploit, in the words of Jean
> Laumon, "une admirable mine de themes poetiques."

Do not underscore or italicize foreign titles of magazine or journal articles, but do underscore or italicize the foreign names of the magazines or journals:

> Arrigoitia, Luis de. "Machismo, folklore y creación en
>   Mario Vargas Llosa." <u>Sin nombre</u> 13.4 (1983): 19-25.

Do not underscore or italicize foreign names of places, names of institutions, proper names, or titles that precede proper names:

> Racine became extremely fond of Mlle Champmeslé, who
> interpreted his works at the Hotel de Bourgogne.

For titles of French, Italian, and Spanish works, capitalize the first word, the proper nouns, but not the adjectives derived from proper nouns:

> La noche de Tlatelolco: Testimoniosde historia oral
>
> Realismo y realidad en la narrativa argentina

For titles of German works, capitalize the first word, all nouns, and all adjectives derived from names of persons:

> Über die Religion: Reden an die Gebildeten unter ihren
> Verächtern

Graphics   If they will contribute in a demonstrable way to your research study, you may create graphic designs and import them into your document. Computer software offers various methods for performing this task. See "Illustrations and Tables," pages 225–229, for basic rules; see also the paper by Pat Bracy, found on pages 319–32, for examples.

Headers and Footers   The software of your computer will automatically insert your name and the page number at the top, right margin of each page for MLA style (e.g., Morris 3). Use a numbering or a header command to set an automatic numbering sequence. For APA style you will need a shortened title and page number with 5 spaces between the shortened title and the page number (see page 319 for an example). Footers are seldom used.

Headings   Begin every major heading (for example, the ones on the title page and opening page, Notes, Appendix, Works Cited) on a new page of your paper. Center the heading in capital and lowercase letters 1 inch from the top of the sheet. Use a double space between the heading and the first line of text. (APA style also requires double spaces between headings and text, but see Chapter 10 for use of extra space above and below an equation and above a side heading.) Number *all* text pages, including those with major headings. (See also "Spacing," pages 236–237.) Short papers, 10 pages or less, need only major headings (A-level), but the advent of desktop publishing makes it possible for long research papers and scientific papers to gain the look of professional typesetting. Use the following guide-line for writing subheads in your paper:

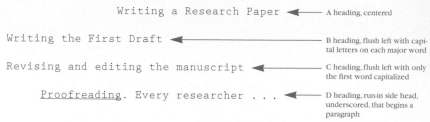

Writing a Research Paper ◀——— A heading, centered

Writing the First Draft ◀——————————— B heading, flush left with capital letters on each major word

Revising and editing the manuscript ◀——— C heading, flush left with only the first word capitalized

Proofreading. Every researcher . . . ◀——— D heading, run-in side head, underscored, that begins a paragraph

Hypertext Link   A hypertext link is simply a signal within your text that links a key word or phrase to another document. It assumes that your audience will read your document on the computer. Using your software appropriately, you can insert a "button" or a highlighted hypertext term. If the reader clicks the mouse on the word or touches certain keys (e.g., F2 or Ctrl-G), the reader will be automatically transported to another part of the text, perhaps an appendix, an endnote, or a spreadsheet. You may wish to use this technique for instructors who will read your work at their computers.

Hyphenation   Do not hyphenate words at the end of lines. If necessary, turn off your computer's automatic hyphenation command. See also "Punctuation," pages 232–35.

Illustrations and Tables   Illustrations include a variety of nontext items, such as blueprints, charts, diagrams, drawings, graphs, photos, photostats, maps, and so on. Make sure you use the different kinds of graphs appropriately. A line graph serves a different purpose than a circle (pie) chart, and a bar graph plots different information than a scatter graph. Note the sample shown in Figure 101.

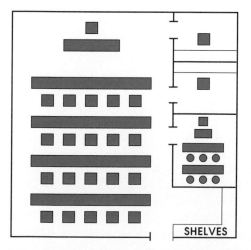

Figure 101
Sample illustration in a paper

Figure 4: Audio Laboratory with Private Listening Rooms and a Small Group Room

Tables are a systematic presentation of materials, usually in columns, as shown in Figure 102.

Figure 102
Sample table in a
paper

Table 8.1

Response by Class on Nuclear Energy Policy

	Freshmen	Sophomores	Juniors	Seniors
1. More nuclear power	150	301	75	120
2. Less nuclear power	195	137	111	203
3. Present policy is acceptable	87	104	229	37

Your illustrations or tables should conform to the following guidelines:

1. Present only one kind of information in each illustration, and make it as simple and brief as possible. Frills and fancy artwork may distract rather than attract the reader.
2. Place small illustrations and tables within your text; place large illustrations, sets of illustrations, or complex tables on separate pages in an appendix (see "Appendix," page 205).
3. Place the illustration or table as immediately *after* your text discussion as possible. The illustration or table should not precede the first mention of it in text.
4. Make certain that the text adequately explains the significance of the illustration. Describe the illustration so that your reader may understand your observations without reference to it, but avoid giving too many numbers and figures in your text.
5. Label the illustration so that your reader can understand it without reference to your text discussion.
6. In the text refer to illustrations and tables by number (for example, "Figure 5") or by number and page reference (for example, "Table 4, 16"). Do not use vague references (such as, "the table above," "the following illustration," or "the chart below").
7. Number tables consecutively throughout the paper with Arabic numerals, preceded by the word *Table* (for example, "Table 2"). Place the numbered designation one double space above the caption, flush left *above* the table, as shown in Figure 103. Alternatively, you may place the numbered designation on the same line as the caption.

Figure 103
*Sample table with
in-text citation*

Table 8.2
Mean Scores of Six Values Held by College Students,
According to Sex

All Students		Men		Women	
Pol.	40.61	Pol.	43.22	Aesth.	43.86
Rel.	40.51	Theor.	43.09	Rel.	43.13
Aesth.	40.29	Econ.	42.05	Soc.	41.62
Econ.	39.45	Soc.	37.05	Econ.	36.85
Soc.	39.34	Aesth.	36.72	Theor.	36.50

Source: Carmen J. Finley et al. (165).

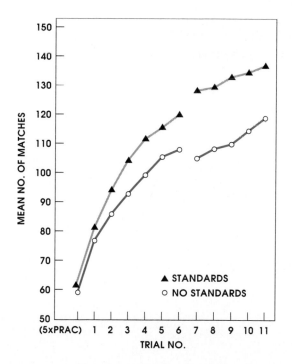

Figure 104
*Sample illustration
with clear labels
and caption*

Figure 6: Mean Number of Matches by Subject
        with and without Standard (by Trail).
        Source: Lock and Bryan (289).

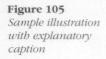

Figure 105
*Sample illustration
with explanatory
caption*

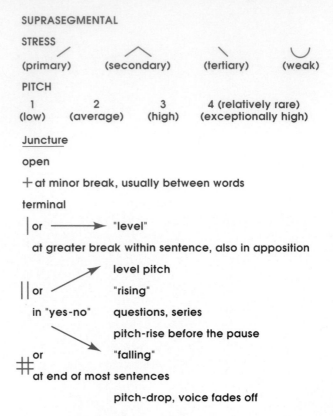

Figure 9: Phonemes of English. Generally, this figure follows the Trager-Smith system, used widely in American linguistics. Source: Anna H. Live (1066).

8. Use Arabic numbers to number illustrations consecutively throughout the paper, preceded by the word *Figure* (for example, "Figure 4") or the abbreviation *Fig.* (for example, "Fig. 6"). Place the numbered designation one double space above the caption, and position it flush left on the second line *below* the illustration. Alternatively, you may place the numbered designation on the same line as the caption, as shown in Figures 104 and 105.

9. Always insert a caption that explains the material, placed flush left *above* the table and *below* the illustration. Use either all-capital letters or capital letters only for the first letter of each important word, but do not mix the two styles in the same paper.

10. Insert a caption or number for each column of a table, centered above the column or, if space considerations make it necessary, inserted diagonally or vertically above it.

Figure 106
*Sample table with
in-text citations and
notes*

Table 8.3

Inhibitory Effects of Sugars on the Growth of Clostridium
Histoylticum (11 Strains) on Nutrient Agar

Sugar added 2%	Aerobic incubation (hr)		Anaerobic incubation (hr)	
	24	48	24	48
None	11[a]	11	11	11
Glucose	0	0	11	11
Maltose	0	0	11	11
Lactose	1	1	11	11
Sucrose	3	6	11	11
Arabinose	0	0	0	0
Inositol	0	0	11	11
Xylose	0	0	0	0
Sorbitol	2	7	11	11
Mamnitol	9	10	11	11
Rhamnose	0	0	11	11

Source: Nishida and Imaizumi (481).

[a]No. of strains that gave rise to colonies in the
presence of the sugar.

11. When inserting an explanatory or reference note, place it below
    both a table and an illustration. Use a lowercase letter as the iden-
    tifying superscript, not an Arabic numeral, as shown in Figure 106.
12. Abbreviate sources as in-text citations (see Figures 103–106), and
    present full documentation in the Works Cited page.

Indentation   Indent text paragraphs 5 spaces or a half inch. Indent long
quotations (4 lines or more) 10 spaces or one inch from the left margin.
The opening sentence to a quoted paragraph receives no extra indentation
even if it is indented in the original. However, if you quote two or more
paragraphs, indent the beginning of each paragraph an extra 3 spaces or a
quarter inch (see page 194). Turnover lines on the Works Cited page indent 5 spaces or a half inch. Indent the first line of content footnotes 5
spaces or a half inch. Other styles (APA or CBE) have different requirements (see Chapters 10 and 11, pages 307–64).

Italics   If your word processing system and your printer can reproduce italic lettering, use it. Otherwise, indicate italics by underscoring. (See also "Underscoring" pages 238–240.

Keyboarding   Submit the paper in printed or typed form, although some instructors will accept handwritten manuscripts if they are neat, legible, and written in blue or black ink on ruled paper. Print on only one side of the page. In addition to the Courier font (traditional with typewriters), you may use the clear, legible typefaces supported by computer software (Helvetica, Times Roman, Bodini, and others), but keep in mind that whichever one you choose must be clear and legible (see "Fonts," page 223). Right justification, which spaces out a line of type to fill a predetermined line length, is not acceptable because it creates incorrect spacing. Use no hyphens at the ends of lines. Avoid widows and orphans, which are short, single lines at the top or the bottom of the page, respectively. Some computers can be used to correct this problem. Use special features—boldface, italics, graphs, color—with discretion. The writing, not the graphics, will earn the credits and the better grades. You are ultimately responsible for correct pagination and accuracy of the manuscript. See also Section 6i, "Revising the Rough Draft," pages 172–174.

Length of the Research Paper   A reasonable length for a research paper is ten pages, but setting an arbitrary length is difficult. The ideal length for your work depends on the nature of the topic, the reference material available, the time allotted to the project, and your initiative as the researcher and writer. Your instructor or supervisor may set definite guidelines concerning the length of your paper. If not, try to generate a paper of 2000 to 3000 words, which comes to about ten keyboarded pages, excluding the title page, outline, endnotes, and Works Cited page. *Tip:* When you run the spelling checker, the final screen will usually give the total number of words.

Margins   A basic 1-inch margin on all sides is recommended. Place your page number ½ inch down from the top edge of the paper and 1 inch from the right edge. Your software will provide a ruler, menu, or style palette that allows you to set the margins. *Tip:* If you develop a header, the running head may appear 1 inch from the top, in which case your first line of text will begin 1½ inches from the top.

Monetary Units   Spell out monetary amounts only if you can do so in no more than two words. Conform to the style shown in the following examples:

> $10 *or* ten dollars
> $14.25 *but not* fourteen dollars and twenty-five cents
> $4 billion *or* four billion dollars

$10.3 billion

$63 *or* sixty-three dollars

the fee is one hundred dollars ($100) *or* the fee is one hundred
(100) dollars

two thousand dollars *or* $2,000

thirty-four cents

In business and technical writing that frequently uses numbers, use
numerals with appropriate symbols:

$99.45   6 @ $15.00   £92

Names of Persons   As a general rule, first mention of a person requires
the full name (e.g., Ernest Hemingway, Margaret Mead) and thereafter requires only usage of the surname (e.g., Hemingway, Mead). (APA style
uses the last name only.) Omit formal titles (e.g., Mr., Mrs., Dr., Hon.) in
text and note references to distinguished persons, living or dead. Convention suggests that certain prominent figures require a title (e.g., Lord By-
ron, Dr. Johnson, Dame Edith Sitwell) while others, for no apparent
reason, do not (e.g., Tennyson, Browne, or Hillary rather than Lord Tennyson, Sir Thomas Browne, or Sir Edmund Hillary). Where custom dictates, you may employ simplified names of famous persons (e.g., Dante
rather than the surname Alighieri or Michelangelo rather than Michelangelo Buonarroti). You may also use pseudonyms where custom dictates (e.g.,
George Eliot, Maxim Gorky, Mark Twain). Refer to fictional characters by
names used in the fictional work (e.g., Huck, Lord Jim, Santiago, Capt.
Ahab).

Numbering

Pagination   Use a header to number your pages in the upper right-
hand corner of the page. Depending on the software, you can create the
head with the numbering command or the header command. It may appear ½–1 inch down from the top edge of the paper and 1 inch from the
right edge. Precede the number with your last name unless anonymity is
required, in which case you may use a shortened version of your title
rather than your name, as in APA style (see page 319). Otherwise, type the
heading, and then double-space to your text.

**Note: If your computer program numbers pages automatically at
the bottom of the sheet and you don't know how to change the
configuration, leave the numbering at the bottom and put only
your name in the upper right corner.**

Use lowercase Roman numerals (ii, iii, iv) on any pages that precede the text. If you have a separate title page, count it as a page i, but do not actually keyboard the numeral on the page. You *should* put a page number on your opening page of text, even if you include course identification (see page 202).

Items in a Series   Within a sentence, incorporate a series of items into your text with parenthetical numbers or lowercase letters (a, b, c):

```
College instructors are usually divided into four ranks:
(1) instructors, (2) assistant professors, (3) associate
professors, (4) full professors.
```

Present longer items in an enumerated list:

```
College instructors are divided into four ranks:

    1. Full professors generally have 15 or more years
of experience, have a Ph.D. or other terminal degree,
and have achieved distinction in teaching and scholarly
publications.
    2. Associate professors . . .
```

Paper   Print on one side of white bond paper, 16- or 20-pound weight, 8½ by 11 inches. If you write the final draft in longhand, use ruled theme paper. If you write the paper by word processor or computer, use the best quality paper available and select letter quality if you have a dot matrix printer. Avoid erasable paper. Carefully strip continuous sheet computer paper of the side bars, separate the pages, and staple the manuscript. Do not enclose the manuscript within a cover or binder unless your instructor asks you to do so.

Percentages   Spell out percentages when they can be expressed in one or two words. For example:

percent *not* per cent
one hundred percent *but* 150 percent
forty-five percent *but* 45 1/2 percent *or* 45 ½%

In business, scientific, and technical writing that requires frequent use of percentages, write all percentages as numerals with appropriate symbols:

100%   45 ½%   12%   6 @ 15.00   £92 $99.45

Proofreaders' Marks   Be familiar with the most common proofreaders' marks so that you can correct your own copy or mark it for a keyboarder. (See the inside back cover of this book for a list of them.)

Punctuation   Consistency is an important component to proper punctuation. Careful proofreading of your paper for punctuation errors will generally improve the clarity and accuracy of your writing.

Commas   Use commas between items listed in a series of three or more, including before the *and* or *or* that precedes the last item. For example:

```
Reader (34), Scott (61), and Wellman (615-17) agree with
Steinbeck on this point.
```

The comma follows a parenthesis if your text requires the comma:

```
How should we order our lives, asks Thompson (22-23),
when we face "hostility from every quarter"?
```

The comma goes inside single quotation marks as well as double quotation marks:

```
Such irony is discovered in Smith's article, "The
Sources of Franklin's 'The Ephemera,'" but not in most
text discussions.
```

Colons   Use colons to introduce examples or further elaboration on what has been said in the first clause. Semicolons join independent clauses. (For proper use of colons and semicolons within quotations, see Sections 7h and 7i, pages 191–195, and for usage within documentation, see Section 9b, "The Title of the Book," 270). Skip only 1 space after the colon or semicolon. Do not capitalize the first word after a colon unless the colon introduces a rule or a principle (see also page 218). Do not use a colon where a semicolon is appropriate for joining independent clauses. Here a colon is used to introduce an elaboration or definition:

```
Weathers reminds us of crucial differences in rhetorical
profiles that no writer should forget: colloquial wording
differs radically from formal wording, and a plain texture
of writing differs greatly from a rich texture.
```

Semicolons   Use semicolons to join two distinct independent clauses:

```
Weathers reminds us of crucial differences in rhetorical
profiles that no writer should forget; the writer who
does forget may substitute colloquial wording where
formal is appropriate or may use a plain texture where
rich texture is needed.
```

Dashes   Use dashes to set off special parts of the text that require emphasis. On a computer use the character set, which will give you an unbroken line. Otherwise, keyboard two hyphens with no blank space before or after, as shown here:

```
Two issues--slow economic growth and public debt--may
prevent an early recovery for the banking industry.
```

Exclamation Marks   Exclamation marks make an emotional ending to a sentence. They should be avoided in research writing. A forceful declarative sentence is preferable.

Hyphens Use hyphens to divide the syllables of words. Both MLA and APA styles discourage division of words at the end of a line. It is preferable to leave the lines short. If you are using a word processing program with automatic hyphenation, you can usually disengage it.

If you must use hyphenation, always double-check word division by consulting a dictionary. Do not hyphenate proper names. Avoid separating two letters at the end or beginning of a line (for example, use "dependable," not "de-pendable").

When using hyphenated words, follow these general rules:

1. Do not hyphenate unless the hyphen serves a purpose:
    a water treatment program *but* a water-powered turbine

2. Compound adjectives that *precede* a noun usually need a hyphen, but those that follow do not:
    same-age children *but* children of the same age

3. When a common base serves two or more compound modifiers, omit the base on all except the last modifier, but retain the hyphens on every modifier:
    right- and left-hand margins
    5-, 10-, and 15-minute segments

4. Write most words with prefixes as one word:
    overaggressive   midterm   antisocial   postwar

    There are exceptions:
    self-occupied   post-Renaissance   self-protection   post-1980

    Consult a dictionary regularly to resolve doubts on such narrow problems as anti-Reagan *but* antisocial.

5. Use a hyphen between pairs of coequal nouns:
    scholar-athlete   trainer-coach

Periods Use periods to signal the end of complete sentences of the text, endnotes, footnotes, and all bibliographic entries. Use one space after a period. When periods are used between numbers to indicate related parts (e.g., 2.4 for act 2, scene 4), use no space. The period normally follows the parenthesis. (The period is placed within the parenthesis only when the parenthetical statement is a complete sentence, as in this instance.) See also Section 7k, pages 196–198, for an explanation of the period in conjunction with ellipsis points.

Brackets Use brackets to enclose words of the text. Use brackets to enclose phonetic transcription, mathematical formulas, and interpolations into a quotation. An interpolation is the insertion of your words into the text of another person. Insert them by hand if brackets are not on your keyboard. (See Section 7l, pages 198–200, for examples.)

Quotation Marks Also use quotation marks to enclose words of the text. Use them to enclose all quotations used as part of your text except for long indented quotations (the indentation signals the use of a quotation). Quotations require proper handling to maintain the style of the original; they also require precise documentation. (See examples and discussions in Chapter 7, pages 181–200.)

In addition, use quotation marks for titles of articles, essays, short stories, short poems, songs, chapters of books, unpublished works, and episodes of radio and television programs.

Use quotation marks for words and phrases that you purposely misuse, misspell, or use in a special sense:

```
The "patrons" turned out to be criminals searching for a
way to launder their money.
```

However, a language study requires underscoring for all linguistic forms (letters, words, and phrases) that are the subject of discussion (for example, "The word *patron*"). Use double quotation marks around parenthetical translations of words or phrases from another language:

```
José Donoso's El jardin de al lado, ("The Garden Next
Door") dramatizes an artistic crisis that has ethical
and political implications.
```

Use single quotation marks for definitions that appear without intervening punctuation (for example, *nosu* 'nose'). In other cases use double quotation marks for foreign phrases and sentences and single quotation marks for your translation.

```
It was important to Bacon that the 1625 collection
appear in France as "un oeuvre nouveau," 'a new work,'
(14:536).
```

Parentheses   Use parentheses to enclose words and numbers in your text in the following situations:

1. In-text citations:

```
Larson (23-25) and Mitchell (344-45) report . . .
```

2. Independent matter:

```
The more recent findings (see Figure 6) show . . .
```

3. Headings for a series:

```
The tests were (1) . . . , (2) . . . , and (3) . . .
```

4. First use of an abbreviation:

```
The test proved reaction time (RT) to be . . .
```

Roman Numerals   Use capital Roman numerals for titles of persons (e.g., Elizabeth II) and primary sections of an outline (see pages 90–96). Use lowercase Roman numerals (iii, iv, v) for preliminary pages of text, as for a preface or introduction. Otherwise, use Arabic numerals (e.g., Vol. 5,

Act 2, Plate 32, 2 Sam. 2.1–8, or *Iliad* 2. 121–30), *except* when writing for some instructors in history, philosophy, religion, music, art, and theater, in which case you may need to use Roman numerals (e.g., III, Act II, I Sam. ii.1–8, *Hamlet* I.ii. 5–6). Here is a list of Roman numerals:

	Units	*Tens*	*Hundreds*
1	I	X	C
2	II	XX	CC
3	III	XXX	CCC
4	IV	XL	CD
5	V	L	D
6	VI	LX	DC
7	VII	LXX	DCC
8	VIII	LXXX	DCCC
9	IX	XC	CM

Thus, XXI equals 21, CX equals 110, and CLV equals 155.

Running Heads   Repeat your last name in the upper right corner of every page just in front of the page number (see the sample paper, pages 247–63). APA style requires a short title at the top of each page just above the page number (see "Short Titles in the Text," immediately following).

Short Titles in the Text   Use abbreviated titles of books and articles mentioned often in the text after a first, full reference. For example, after initial usage *Backgrounds to English as Language* should be shortened to *Backgrounds* both in the text, notes, and in-text citations (see also page 190) but not in the bibliographic entry. Mention *The Epic of Gilgamesh* and thereafter use *Gilgamesh*. (*Note:* Be certain to italicize the shortened title.)

When keyboarding a manuscript according to APA style, shorten your own title to the first two or three words and place it at the top right corner of each page for identification purposes (for example, "Discovering Recall Differences of the Aged" should be shortened to "Discovering" or "Discovering Recall Differences"). See pages 319–32 for examples of the short title as a page heading.

Slang   Avoid the use of slang. When using it in a language study, enclose in double quotation marks any words to which you direct attention. Words used as words, however, require underscoring: the word *bruit* from Middle English means noise (see page 240).

Spacing   As a general rule, double-space everything—the body of the paper, all indented quotations, and all reference entries. Footnotes, if used, should be single-spaced, but endnotes should be double-spaced (see pages 360–61). APA style (see pages 307–32) double-spaces after all headings and separates text from indented quotations and from figures by double spacing. APA advocates quadruple spacing above and below statistical and mathematical expressions.

Space after punctuation according to these guidelines:

1. Use 1 space after commas, semicolons, and colons (see also "Capitalize After a Colon," page 218).
2. Use 1 space after punctuation marks at the end of sentences.
3. Use 1 space after periods that separate parts of a reference citation.
4. Do not use space before or after periods within abbreviations (for example, i.e., e.g., a.m.).
5. Use 1 space between initials of personal names (e.g., M. C. Bone).
6. Do not use a space before or after a hyphen (e.g., a three-part test), but use 1 space before and after a hyphen used as a minus sign (e.g., $a - b + c$) and 1 space before but none after a hyphen used for a negative value (e.g., -3.25).
7. Do not use a space before or after a dash (e.g., the evidence—interviews and statistics—which was published).

Spelling   Spell accurately. Always use the computer to check spelling if the software is available. When in doubt, consult a dictionary. If the dictionary says a word may be spelled in two separate ways, the first spelling is the preferred spelling. Be consistent in the form employed, as with *theater* and *theatre,* unless the variant form occurs in quoted materials. Use American (as opposed to English) spelling throughout.

Statistical and Mathematical Copy   Use the simplest form of equation that can be made by ordinary mathematical calculation. If an equation cannot be produced entirely by keyboard, enter what you can and fill in the rest with ink. As a general rule, keep equations on one line rather than two:

ACCEPTABLE $\dfrac{a + b}{x + y}$

BETTER $(a + b)/(x + y)$

APA style requires quadruple line spacing above and below an equation.

Superscript Numerals in the Text   On a computer, use the appropriate keys as explained in the product manual or in the Help index (e.g., Shift-F1, Ctrl-PY, and so forth), or place the number with slash marks (e.g., "the end of the sentence./3/"). At a typewriter, create a raised numeral by turning the roller of the typewriter so that the Arabic numeral strikes about half a space above the line, like this.[14] See also Section 11c, "Using the Footnote System."

Table of Contents A table of contents is unnecessary for undergraduate research papers, but *do* write a table of contents for a graduate thesis or dissertation (see "Theses and Dissertations," which follows). Many computers can be used to develop a table of contents.

Theses and Dissertations The author of a thesis or dissertation must satisfy the requirements of the university's graduate program. Therefore, even though you may use MLA style or APA style, you must abide by certain additional rules with regard to paper; typing; margins; and introductory matter such as title page, approval page, acknowledgment page, table of contents, abstract, and other matters. Use both the graduate school's guidelines and those of this book to maintain the appropriate style and format.

Titles Within Titles For a title to a book that includes another title indicated by quotation marks, retain the quotation marks, as shown here:

    O. Henry's Irony in "The Gift of the Magi"

For a title of an article within quotation marks that includes a title to a book, as indicated by underscoring, retain the underscoring or use italics:

    "Great Expectations as a Novel of Initiation"

    "*Great Expectations* as a Novel of Initiation"

For the title of an article within quotation marks that includes another title indicated by quotation marks, enclose the shorter title within single quotation marks:

    "A Reading of O. Henry's 'The Gift of the Magi'"

For an underscored title to a book that incorporates another title that normally receives underscoring or italics, do not underscore or italicize the shorter title or place it within quotation marks:

    Interpretations of Great Expectations

    Using Shakespeare's Romeo and Juliet *in the Classroom*

Underscoring

Titles Use italics, not underscoring, if your computer can produce it. Otherwise, underscoring takes the place of italics in a keyboarded manuscript. Use a continuous line for titles with more than one word. Italicize or underscore the titles of the following types of works:

Type of Work	Example
aircraft	*Enola Gay*
ballet	*The Nutcracker*
book	*Earthly Powers*
bulletin	*Production Memo 3*
drama	*Desire under the Elms*
film	*Treasure of the Sierra Madre*
journal	*Journal of Sociology*
magazine	*Newsweek*
newspaper	*The Nashville Banner*
novel	*The Scarlet Letter*
opera	*Rigoletto*
painting	*Mona Lisa*
pamphlet	*Ten Goals for Successful Sales*
periodical	*Scientific American*
poem	*Idylls of the King* (only if book length)
radio show	*Grand Ole Opry*
recording	*The Poems of Wallace Stevens*
sculpture	*David*
ship	*Titanic*
short novel	*Billy Budd*
symphony	Beethoven's *Eroica*
	but
	Beethoven's Symphony no. 3 in A (to identify form, number, and key)
television	*Tonight Show* (program title, not a single episode)
yearbook	*The Pegasus*

In contrast, place quotation marks around the titles of articles, essays, chapters, sections, short poems, stories, songs, lectures, sermons, reports, and individual episodes of television programs.

If separately published, underscore titles of essays, lectures, poems, proceedings, reports, sermons, and stories. However, these items are usually published as part of an anthology (for example, a compilation of sermons or a collection of stories), in which case you would underscore the title of the anthology.

Do not underscore the titles of sacred writings (e.g., Genesis, Old Testament); series (e.g., The New American Nation Series), editions (e.g., Variorum Edition of W. B. Yeats), societies (e.g., Victorian Society), courses (e.g., Greek Mythology), divisions of a work (e.g., preface, appendix, canto 3, scene 2), or descriptive phrases (e.g., Nixon's farewell address or Reagan's White House years).

Individual Words for Emphasis   The use of underscoring to emphasize certain words or phrases is discouraged. A better alternative is to position the key word in such a way as to accomplish the same purpose. For example:

UNDERSCORING FOR EMPHASIS   Perhaps an answer lies in preventing abuse, not in makeshift remedies after the fact.

BETTER   Prevention of abuse is a better answer than makeshift remedies after the fact.

Some special words and symbols require underscoring.

1. Species, genera, and varieties:

Penstemon caespitosus subsp. thompsoniae

2. Letters, words, or phrases cited as a linguistic sample:

the letter e in the word let

3. Letters used as statistical symbols and algebraic variables:

trial n of the t test or $C(3, 14) = 9.432$

Word Division   Avoid dividing any word at the end of a line. Leave the line short rather than divide a word (see "Hyphens," page 234).

8c   SAMPLE PAPER: A SHORT ESSAY WITH DOCUMENTATION

The following paper demonstrates correct form for short papers that use only a few secondary sources. Keep in mind that a short paper, like the long, formal research paper, requires correct in-text citations and a list of references. This paper is shown in Helvetica typeface, one of the fonts available on many computers. Most instructors will accept papers printed in Helvetica and other typefaces. You may also use italics rather than underscoring and various other features of the computer.

Wickham 1

Jay Wickham

Professor Thompson

Heritage 1020

5 May 1995

Same Construction, Different Walls: Structural Similarities
in the Short Stories of Flannery O'Connor

Flannery O'Connor uses a recurring structural pattern
in the development of the main characters in four short
stories: "Greenleaf," "Good Country People," "Revelation,"
and "Everything That Rises Must Converge." The pattern
consists of three stages: (1) the author makes use of the
omniscient point of view, allowing the reader to be privy
to all the characters' thoughts and motives; (2) then a
disconcerting and jolting climax occurs, usually very harsh
for the character; and (3) readers finally discover how this
climax affects the characters.

The five main characters of these stories (Mrs. May,
Hulga, Mrs. Turpin, Julian, and his mother) are all based on
a common denominator in their character makeup—that of
emotional contempt for the world they inhabit and, even
more, contempt for themselves. O'Connor sets up these
characters with inflated egos, then she pulls the rug out
from under the characters in a climactic moment.
Ironically, each character is smashed by something he or
she held in contempt.

Critic Richard Poirer, writing on O'Connor's structure
of climax, argues that "she propels her characters towards
the cataclysms where alone they can have a tortured
glimpse of the need and chance for redemption" (qtd. in
CA 721). The aftermath of those destructive moments is
rather grim. The character dies or withdraws in shame and
despair. David Havird goes so far as to say that O'Connor

Use an inverted pyramid style for the title (see Section 8a, page 202).

Identify the literary work early in the paper (see Section 6f, pages 158–163).

Use parenthetical numbers to list three or more ideas (see "Items in a Series," page 232).

Provide a thesis sentence to control the analysis of the literary works (see Sections 1d, pages 21–24, and 6a, pages 146–148).

The citation means that Poirer was quoted in Contemporary Authors, a book that the writer properly abbreviates in the text citations (see page 213).

Wickham 2

wants "to knock these proud female characters down a
notch. . . by forcing upon them, in a sexually and often
violent way, the humbling knowledge that they are after
all women" (915).

In "Greenleaf" Mrs. May is (1) a woman with two lazy and
ungrateful sons; (2) a woman who encourages her sons to
go to church, even though she herself "did not, of course,
believe any of [religion] was true" (O'Connor 316); and (3) a
woman who envies her despised neighbors, the Greenleafs,
who become successful. Most frustrating to her is the fact
that the Greenleafs succeed because she made it possible.
The Greenleafs have made good in the wake of her failures.

Mrs. May is gored by the bull belonging to the
Greenleafs, just as they have served as the thorn in her
side. Mrs. May dies almost instantly, but not before
O'Connor describes her as "leaning over . . . as if to
whisper some final discovery into the bull's ear" (O'Connor
334). This final sentence suggests that Mrs. May had
learned something, but the story gives no hint as to what
that might be, and just as well. Robert Drake calls it a "dark
vision of modern damnation and redemption" (*CA* 721).
Havird calls it a rape that brings a moment of grace to the
masculine woman (15-26).

In "Good Country People," Hulga is a misanthropic Ph.D.
with a wooden leg. Hulga is not satisfied with the quality of
her life and perhaps justifiably so; a real leg would be nice,
just as helpful sons would be nice for Mrs. May. Hulga takes
her emotional pain out on others around her, scoffing at
them for the miserable people they are, not realizing her
own inadequacies.

Being a conceited intellectual, she has lived with the
idea that the people around her, including her mother, are
simpletons. Hulga regards her mother as a woman who
refuses to use her mind, and would likely try to solve

Introduce quotations with the speaker's name, and end them with the parenthetical citation (see Section 7a, pages 182–184).

The writer uses brackets to interpolate his own word, reli-gion, into the quoted material (see Section 7l, pages 198–200).

Use three ellipsis points to indicate the omission of words from a quotation (see Section 7k, pages 196–198).

Wickham 3

heartache with a peanut-butter and jelly sandwich; but when Manley Pointer pulls out his flask and his condoms, she is left with the realization that she, the self-acknowledged brilliant one, has been undone by a simple country boy who steals her wooden leg. He departs and says (O'Connor 291), "Hulga, you ain't so smart. I been believing in nothin' ever since I was born!" Her contempt does her no good now.

> Put a page citation in front of a quotation to avoid interfering with an exclamation point or a question mark (see pages 192–93).

In "Revelation," Mrs. Turpin is a pious and prejudiced woman, yet she is another character who looks down on others around her. She takes comfort in the knowledge that people less important than herself exist so that she can look down on them, including the ugly girl in the waiting room.

At this point in the story, Mrs. Turpin has been prattling on for quite some time, to anyone in the waiting room who will converse with her, lauding all the while the many gifts a gracious God has given her. As she goes on and on, the ugly girl gets angry and finally explodes in a furious attack on Mrs. Turpin. The girl, finally restrained by orderlies, shouts to Mrs. Turpin, "Go back to hell where you came from, you old wart hog" (O'Connor 500).

About this scene, Robert Brinkmeyer says, "Human pretensions are not merely undercut but utterly destroyed; they are shown to be worthless and insignificant if not terribly evil" (57). In "Revelation" the reader follows the main character home to see the long-term effects. Mrs. Turpin's self-image has been destroyed. It causes her to scream and shake her fist at God, to question for the first time why she is what she is. Her answer is life-shattering, for she turns her high-powered and pious contempt on herself. She begins to feel her own worthlessness. Only by this grotesque initiation does she arrive at her revelation. (On this point see Rowley, who gives a Jungian reading on "individuation" to the story.)

> Leave a line short rather than use the hyphen to divide a word at the end of a line (see page 234).

> Reference to an entire article needs no in-text citation to a page number (see pages 345–52).

Wickham 4

Of her themes concerning piety, O'Connor writes:

> If other ages felt less, they saw more, even
> though they saw with the blind, prophetical,
> unsentimental eye of acceptance, which is to
> say, of faith. In the absence of this faith, now, we
> govern by tenderness. It is a tenderness which,
> long cut off from the person of Christ, is wrapped
> in theory. When tenderness is detached from the
> source of tenderness, its logical outcome is terror.
> (qtd. in Morrow 145)

In "Everything That Rises Must Converge" Julian is a college graduate and, like Hulga, is overly proud of his intellect. He is misanthropic, especially toward his mother. Alienated from others, he has an insensitive personality, one that hates easier than it loves. His mother, on the other hand, is a friendly lady unaccustomed to questioning the feelings or impulses in her heart. She judges the right and wrong of situations by what Julian believes to be a worn-out set of values.

Both Julian and his mother are also characterized by their racial prejudices. Julian is respectful of blacks, but he has no notion of how to interact. His mother, having grown up on a plantation, presumes to know how to treat blacks. However, a black woman strikes Julian's mother with a heavy purse when Julian's mother offers a penny to a black child. The blow causes Julian's mother to have a stroke, and she soon collapses. She has been destroyed by her own prejudices, in the sense that she could not anticipate that a black woman would be offended by her condescending offer. She never saw the blow coming.

In a domino effect, her stroke becomes Julian's moment of destruction. After taunting his mother, then realizing her serious condition, he runs from the scene into the night. The guilt of the moment follows close behind. The person he most condemned—his mother—has been eradicated.

Wickham 5

Perhaps that is why he ran; he cannot face the fact that he truly held his mother in contempt. He discovers "his own ignorance and cruelty" (Brinkmeyer 71). Thus "the tide of darkness seemed to sweep him back to her, postponing from moment to moment his entry into the world of guilt and sorrow" (O'Connor 420).

Every author has a different method of creating characters. O'Connor seems to have decided for these four stories that if something works well once, it will work well again. In terms of character development, these stories are structurally the same because all four correspond to the same theme in terms of characterization: live by the sword, die by the sword. The jolting climax of each story "produces a shock for the reader," says O'Connor, who adds, "and I think one reason for this is that it produced a shock for the writer" (qtd. in Brinkmeyer 39).

Blend quotations into your sentences smoothly, as shown in these two examples (see Section 7a, pages 182–184).

Wickham 6

Works Cited

Brinkmeyer, Robert. *The Art and Vision of Flannery O'Con-nor.* Baton Rouge: Louisiana State UP, 1989.

Contemporary Authors. Detroit: Gale, 1967.

Havird, David. "The Saving Rape: Flannery O'Connor and Patriarchal Religion." *The Mississippi Quarterly* 47 (1993): 15-26.

Morrow, Suzanne P. *Flannery O'Connor: A Study of the Short Fiction.* Boston: Twayne, 1988.

O'Connor, Flannery. *The Complete Stories.* New York: Farrar, 1962.

Rowley, Rebecca K. "Individuation and Religious Experi-ence: A Jungian Approach to O'Connor's 'Revelation.'" *Southern Literary Journal* 25 (1993): 92-103. InfoTrac: Expanded Academic Index. CD-ROM. Information Access. 20 Apr. 1995.

Note abbrevia-
tion for a uni-
versity press
(see pages
208–09).

Remember to
include the
primary source,
the collection of
stories, as well
as the secondary
sources
(see Section 9a,
pages 266–67).

8d   SAMPLE PAPER: A FORMAL RESEARCH PAPER

The following paper illustrates the style and form of the fully devel-oped research paper. It includes a title page, outline pages, a variety of in-text citations, superscript numerals to content endnotes, and a fully developed Works Cited page. Notations in the margins signal special cir-cumstances in matters of form and style.

Television Reality Check: The Fine Line between Fact
and Fiction on Talk Shows

The title page is
a three-part
balance of title,
author, and
course informa-
tion (see pages
201–03)

by

Stefan Hall

Composition 1020

Professor James D. Lester

17 August 1994

See also the
preliminary pa-
pers discussed
in Section 4e,
pages 112–14,
and Section 4f,
pages 114–18.

Use lowercase Roman numerals for preliminary pages (see pages 232).

This writer uses the topic outline (see pages 90–96).

Repeat your thesis at the beginning of the outline, although it may take a different form in the paper itself (sexe pages 146–47).

Use standard outline symbols (see pages 90–96).

The headings for both the introduction (I) and conclusion (III) are content-oriented like other outline entries (see pages 90–96).

Outline

Thesis: Television objectivity is nothing more than an ideal which can never be perfectly presented by any broadcast nor perceived by any viewer.

I. Distorting the truth with television news and talk shows

A. Skewing and distorting objectivity

1. Recognizing television as a presentation, like a drama

2. Contriving an illusion (Schiller quote)

3. Falsifying the line between fact and fiction (Keller quote)

B. Perceiving objectivity in television broadcasts

II. Finding the scholarly issues in the way we construct reality

A. Identifying three categories (Cohen, Adoni, and Bantz quote)

1. Recognizing the objective social reality

2. Accepting a symbolic social reality

3. Building our own subjective social reality

B. The producers: dressing television as "real" or "objective"

1. Presenting both sides of a controversy (Kuklinski quote)

2. Squeezing out reality to conform to a format

3. Rehearsing and editing to compromise objectivity

C. The audience: viewing and accepting television

1. Accepting or rejecting television as fact or fiction

2. Constructing social reality despite biased reporting

Hall iii

      3. Acting as both the creator and the product of our social world (Cohen et al. quote)

      4. Creating truth by juggling objective reality (sensory data) and symbolic reality (television)

      5. Realizing the difference between news objectivity and entertainment drama (McClellan quote)

   D. Compromising the truth

      1. Selling witnesses to the highest bidder

      2. Exploiting the "gullible" factor of viewers

      3. Exercising power over our interpretation (Schiller quote)

      4. Using biased and tainted testimony from experts

   E. Using a studio audience

      1. Building interaction between "real" people (the audience) and the guests (Munson quote)

      2. Acting out parts in the drama, like a Greek chorus

   F. Manipulating the images

      1. Using re-creations instead of the actual scenes

      2. Editing to skew the truth and obliterate objectivity

      3. Emphasizing "show over substance" (Keller quote)

III. Recognizing ourselves (the viewers) as one of the players

   A. Acting within one's own subjective drama

      1. Shaping our lives with our own perceptions of reality

      2. Discerning the difference between truth
         and "trumped up reality" (Keller quote)
  B. Living on the edge, vicariously
      1. Enjoying the weird life styles
      2. Participating in the "infotainment"
         (Munson)
      3. Becoming players in the virtual reality of
         the overall drama

Hall 1

Television Reality Check: The Fine Line between
Fact and Fiction on Talk Shows

Television news and talk shows profess the
truth of our society. They present the facts for
the viewers in an objective manner for the
edification of our minds that thrive on reality. Or
do they? Oprah Winfrey, Morton Downey, Jr., and
others sometimes uncover some truth about our
society, but objectivity is often skewed, whether
intentionally or not, by forces within the
television world as well as within the world of
communication in general. Most television shows
are nothing more than a presentation, an easily
accessible and understandable entertainment for
the masses. What we must accept is that television
is like a novel, a history text, a play, or a
newspaper. Dan Schiller in his book <u>Objectivity and
the News</u> says that we accept television news as
reality because "news--akin to any literary or
cultural form--must rely upon conventions. . . . to
contrive the illusion of objectivity" (2), while
Teresa Keller proclaims that "the problem is that
the line between news/entertainment, fact/fiction,
accuracy/effect is more than blurred--it's
intentionally trampled" (202). We need to avoid the
word <u>objectivity</u> when talking about television news
and talk shows because objectivity is nothing more
than an ideal which can never be perfectly presented
by any broadcast nor perceived by any viewer.

The scholarly issue at work here is the
construction of reality. Writing for the Sage
Library of Social Research, Cohen, Adoni, and Bantz
label the construction a social process "in which
human beings act both as the creators and products

Both running head and page number are given (but see page 236).

Repeat the title on the first page of text.

For tips on building opening paragraphs, see Section 6f, pages 158–163.

Use parenthetical citations to your sources (see Section 7a pages 182–184).

The thesis comes late in the opening; it could also appear early (see pages 158–59).

The writer shifts to a new issue in accordance with his outline (see Section 3c, pages 90–93).

Hall 2

of the social world" (34). These writers identify three categories (34-35):

1. Objective social reality, which is "the objective world existing outside the individual and confronting him or her as facts."

2. Symbolic social reality, which "consists of any form of symbolic expression of objective reality such as art, literature, media contents, or communicative behavior."

3. Subjective social reality, "where both the objective and symbolic realities serve as an input for the construction of the individual's own reality."

Television gives us symbolic reality but dresses it in the robes of "real" or "objective" reality. Two political commentators make this observation:

> Every day the network news organizations face the task of reducing complex, multifaceted issues to simple, unambiguous stories that consume no more than a minute or two of precious air time. To avoid the accusation of being unfair, they also face the pressure to present "both sides" of the controversies they cover. (Kuklinski and Sigelman 814)

Even Oprah and Donahue, numbers one and two respectively in most watched talk shows (see Appendix, Table 1), have established styles for conducting their shows and commercially viable structures that the facts must squeeze into. Sometimes a little reality falls out when this squeezing occurs.

What is a talk show but a structured setting for people to talk about their problems or their lives? Structure means that producers conduct prior planning and rehearsals so that the seeds of

Hall 3

subjectivity start to sprout even before the viewers
are introduced into the equation. After the fact,
editing is necessary to meet time restraints for the
broadcast. Once editing enters the picture, the
producers compromise objectivity, omitting something
of the whole while emphasizing something else.
The broadcasts of Oprah or Maury Povich may seem
spontaneous, but a set structure shapes the
presentation always.

> The writer effectively summarizes the basic problem and then moves to the next issue.

    Television viewers, engulfed in the world of
communication, participate in the construction of
symbolic reality by their perception of and belief
in the presentation. Edward Jay Epstein laid the
groundwork for such investigation in 1973 by
showing in case after case how the networks
distorted the news and did not, perhaps could not,
represent reality. Today, the scholars say that
"symbolic reality as it appears in television news
. . . tends to present conflicts as less complex,
more intense and more solvable than they really
are" (Cohen, Adoni, and Bantz 35). The distinct
purpose of communicative language is for one person
to try to relate a meaning to another, an implied
togetherness intrinsic to the word <u>communication</u>.
Therefore, the viewer of these various television
shows must bring part of the sense to the overall
meaning. This requires two activities. The viewers
must be willing to accept or reject television
programs as fact or fiction, and viewers must be
able to construct for themselves a social reality
from the bits and pieces of edited and extrapolated
material that Rush Limbaugh or Dan Rather spit out
nightly. Cohen, Adoni, and Bantz make this
observation:

> Even paraphrased materials should be introduced and documented in the text (see Section 5e, pages 134–36).

> This paragraph blends personal observations with paraphrase; short quotations; and a long, indented quotation (see Chapter 7, pages 181–200).

        The process of reality construction is
        defined as social because it can be
        carried out only through social interaction,

either real or symbolic. The social
construction of reality is a dialectical
process in which human beings act both as
the creators and as the products of their
social world. (34)

Use parentheses to add clarifying words to your own text, but use brackets to insert your words into a quotation (see Section 7l, pages 198–200).

Thus, viewers must not only deal discriminately with
supposed truths thrust upon them by society,
especially television, but also create their own set
of truths and beliefs by juggling objective reality
(sensory data) and symbolic reality (television news).

How many times do we ask, "Hey, is this true?"
What do we believe, or what are we willing to
believe? The nature of a constructed reality relies
upon both the television shows' presentations and
the perceptions of the viewers, both of which are
highly subjective. Steve McClellan's article, "What
Is Reality? The Thin and Blurring Line,"[1] suggests

Superscript numerals signal content endnotes (see pages 358–64). Do not use superscript numerals and endnotes for documentation of sources unless you need to cluster several sources.

that people seem not to realize the difference
between news programs (such as NBC Evening News)
and entertainment drama (Hard Copy) as sources of
information (38).

Tabloid television sensationalizes to attract
viewers, utilizing any means necessary to stimulate
the people into watching just long enough for the
next commercial to accost them. Jim Paratore, a
movie executive, says that "there is a feeding
chain" on the reality stories because "many of the
guests that the talk shows are booking are also the
story subjects for the magazine shows" (qtd. in
McClellan 38). So the next time Phil Donahue or

Note the form used for a quote within another writer's work (see Section 7d, pages 185–186).

Morton Downey, Jr., tells a guest to stick to the
subject or the next time Oprah looks into the camera
and professes her grief, objectivity disappears, and
a biased judgment is being made for the audience to
either follow or dismiss. Political correctness--
honesty to both sides--seems foreign to many
programs. In fact, The CQ Researcher indicates that

Hall 5

Congress has begun efforts to implement again
the "fairness doctrine," which the Federal
Communications Commission repealed in 1987. The
law would require stations to air equal sides of
an argument. Talk show hosts, as might be expected,
are fighting the legislation ("Will the 'Fairness
Doctrine' Be Reborn?" 370).

The facts are compromised in several ways.
Erica Goode and Katia Hetter in their article, "The
Selling of Reality," report that an agent for a
16-year-old orphan peddled the boy's story to a
book agent, a television show, and two movie
producers (49+). We also know that some of the
principal witnesses in the O. J. Simpson case
compromised their testimony by talking to publicity
agents before talking with police investigators.
When Hard Copy features a quotation from an
eyewitness, must we assume that it is reality? Some
persons have a high "gullible" factor.[2] The
interpretation or perception of any given
presentation becomes the reality constructed by
the individual that is unique to that individual;
after all, what is interpretation if it is not a
construction of sense. Symbolic reality, namely
talk shows and tabloid news shows like Oprah or
Hard Copy or America's Most Wanted, tends to impose
upon and warp this sense of perception so that
"social conflicts have been disguised, contained,
and displaced through the imposition of news
objectivity, a framework legitimating the exercise
of social power over the interpretation of reality"
(Schiller 196). In other words, our perception of
reality is a combination of (1) the tidbits Peter
Jennings and Sally Jessy Raphael throw our way and
(2) what we perceive as believable. Patricia Joyner
Priest's dissertation suggests that there is a
"perceived status conferred by appearing on

Use a title
when
no author is
listed (see
pages 184–85).

Use superscript
numbers to
signal a
content note
(see pages
358–64).

Note the blend of paraphrase and quotation so that the text follows smoothly with proper introductions and in-text citations (see Section 7a, pages 182–184).

television" (abstract). Priest further adds that the "deviant labels [attached to the 'freaks' or guests] which formerly engulfed informants are replaced with a new and favorable status-determining trait: 'as seen on TV.'" Seemingly, the viewers learn the labels for guests (homosexual, hermaphrodite, pedophile) and file these labels into their sense of reality. The television hosts blatantly tell us that what the guest says is true, for they back it up with photography and commentary from bona fide experts. Yet the expert opinions can be taken out of context, or, even worse, could be biased from the start (Steele 49-52). Sometimes we are still left wondering what to believe.

Many talk shows utilize audience participation in the studio to create the illusion or the feeling of interaction between real people (the audience) and the guests. Wayne Edward Munson argues that by "positioning itself as more real and effective in its interactive inscription of the spectator,

See on the use of *sic* page 199.

the participatory talkshow [sic] aspires to go beyond spectacle. . . ." This interaction allows for a parallel to be made between studio audience and home viewers since both are trying to make sense of the performance or questioning the validity or realness of the topics and the guests' stories.

This section develops negative and positive viewpoints. For tips on building the body of your paper, see Section 6g, pages 163–169, and the section on paradigms, Section 3b, pages 87–90.

Yet talk shows are still just talk shows, spectacles, entertainment; therefore, members of the studio audience are acting out parts in the drama, like a Greek chorus, just as the host, the guest, and the television viewers are actors as well. Furthermore, some sort of interaction with the "characters" in this made-for-television "drama" happens all the time. If we read a book or attend a play, we question the text, we question the presentation, and we determine for ourselves what it

Hall 7

means to us. Just as the interactive audience purports to bring more overall realness and meaning to a program by questioning the guests or expressing opinions, so does the discriminating viewer sitting at home help in constructing the overall meaning by questioning and emoting. The key is perception in both cases. Although the studio audience is a part of what we perceive, they are also a model for our own attempts to make sense of the presentation. Members of the studio audience, like the guests, become characters for the viewers to relate to.

Another form of subjectivity arises in that all television programs involve, to some extent, a reliance upon photographic realism. Many talk shows and news telecasts even initiate re-creations or employ experts to stress their subjective realities. Schiller says the use of photography underlines and extends the "belief in a direct and completely accurate symmetry between art and reality" (94). Yet the discriminating viewer may think otherwise. We all know that a photograph can be taken out of context, can be manipulated, can be made from any angle that the photographer desires. The producers decide beforehand what section of the video they will show in order to affect the viewers' reactions. If actual film is unavailable, they recreate it, often without telling us, which is yet another form of editing that can skew the objectivity.

Recently, a young man (not Rodney King) claimed he was beaten by a police officer for no reason that he could think of other than racism.[3] The incident was captured on film, perfectly preserving the exact reality of the incident. Yet some witnesses claim that the young man instigated the struggle and even threw several punches at the officer before any action was taken by the officer.

The video recording had not been on the scene for
the entire altercation. So are we to believe the
video if it is not complete? Viewers constantly see
the edited video clips of newscasts and talk shows
along with the edited story, and they often take
for granted that it is objective; however, we have
established the fact that television is a symbolic
social reality.

Tabloid television is not so much news as
entertainment. One source notes that "the networks
live by the dictum 'keep it short and to the
point,'" so they make the news "lively" (Kuklinsky
and Sigelman 821). Many programs, <u>Hard Copy</u> and
<u>A Current Affair</u> come to mind, go for "show over
substance with an ongoing commentary to let
listeners know how they should be reacting and to
keep emotional involvement high" (Keller 201). The
re-creations of some newscasts are designed for the
same scintillating purpose, "show over substance,"
an enhancement or abbreviation of the facts, a
breach of objectivity.

The viewers, unaware of what to believe or not
to believe, are just one piece in the whole (along
with producers and newscasters and the presentation
itself) that makes up a sketch of symbolic reality.
The viewer is a player in his or her own subjective
drama. As we sit and watch Oprah and Sally Jessy
Raphael and Donahue and Geraldo and <u>A Current Affair</u>
and <u>Hard Copy</u>, we are constantly editing the shows
ourselves in our own minds, shaping the presentation
with our personalized hammers of perception and
cudgels of reality. That is how the human brain
works to make sense of the world. As Teresa Keller
puts it, "Stories are woven around a small part of
the truth," (204), but exactly "how important is it
to discern the difference" (202) between what is
real and what is just trumped up reality?

Blend
quotations into
your text
smoothly (see
Chapter 7 pages
181–200).

Some lines may
appear ex-
tremely short
but do not hy-
phenate words
at the end of
lines (see page
234).

Hall 9

Real or unreal, objectivity is something seldom, if ever, found on television. Ultimately, we must wonder why in the world 24% of the people surveyed watch talk shows on a regular basis, while 30% watch them sometimes (see Appendix, Table 2). We live the re-creations vicariously and briefly in 30- and 60-minute bites. According to one critic, the "programs provide instant, vivid, and easy to consume information about a wide and growing range of public affairs" (Kuklinski and Sigelman 810), but most of the guests appearing on these shows are not like us in any way. Right? But we enjoy watching the freaks of our society or begrudging the super rich and their struggles with fame. We enjoy this "infotainment," as Wayne Edward Munson calls it. The New Yorker says, "Mostly, we just [become] more and more aware of our own voyeurism" (21). Nevertheless, tabloid television gives people a way to feel good about themselves. They become players in the virtual reality of the drama. They are helping to define their own subjective reality within the boundaries of the objective world and the symbolic reality of television.

The writer reasserts his thesis. The conclusion now officially begins. Note how the writer develops a full judgment on the issue and does not merely summarize the paper.

For tips on writing paragraphs of the conclusion, see Section 6h, pages 169–172.

Hall 10

Notes

This note offers
additional
literature on a
point (see page
220).

    1. McClellan has two closely related articles,
both about the proliferation of talk shows: "Can We
Talk . . . and Talk . . . and Talk?" <u>Broadcasting &
Cable</u> 124.4 (1994): 88-89, and "Talk, Talk, Talk:
Cable Can't Get Enough," <u>Broadcasting & Cable</u> 124.8
(1994): 42-43.

Content
endnotes
appear on a
separate page.
For tips on
writing content
endnotes, see
pages 219–22.

    2. I don't mean to sound completely negative
about what we witness on television, but we should
use reasonable discretion. Every person makes
his or her adjustment based on what I call the
"gullible" factor. They are too trustful and
therefore susceptible.

    3. This source is hearsay because I cannot
cite the precise source. I heard this story on the
radio, perhaps NPR, but I cannot be certain.

Hall 11

Appendix

Table 1: Harris Poll

See pages 225–229 for guidelines on the use of tables and illustrations.

QUESTION: Which one of the (television) talk show hosts do you most like to watch?

Oprah Winfrey	31%
Phil Donahue	11
Regis Philbin and Kathie Lee Gifford	10
Geraldo Rivera	8
David Letterman	8
Arsenio Hall	6
Sally Jessy Raphael	6
Jay Leno	6
Montel Williams	6
Charlie Rose	2
Joan Rivers	1
None	4
Not sure	2

Source: Dialog File 468: Public Opinion.

Table 2: Princeton Survey Research Associates

QUESTION: I'd like to know how often, if ever, you read certain types of publications, listen to the radio, or watch certain types of T.V. (television) shows. For each that you read tell me if you do it regularly, sometimes, hardly ever or never. How often do you . . . watch television talk shows such as Oprah, Donahue or Geraldo?

Regularly	24%
Sometimes	30
Hardly ever	19
Never	27

Source: Dialog File 468: Public Opinion.

Start
Works Cited
on a new page.

For tips on
writing the
bibliographic
entries, see
Chapter 9,
pages 265–306.

Entry for a
magazine (see
page 286).

An electronic
source (see
pages 291–98).

A typical entry
for a journal
article (see
pages 283–85).

An entry for
two authors
(see page 274).

A journal entry
may include the
issue number
(see pages
283–84).

A reference to a
dissertation (see
pages 300 and
296).

An entry with
no author (see
page 274).

Works Cited

Cohen, Akiba A., Hanna Adoni, and Charles R. Bantz.
    Social Conflict and Television News. Newbury Park:
    Sage, 1990.

Epstein, Edward J. News from Nowhere. New York: Random,
    1973.

Goode, Erica, and Katia Hetter. "The Selling of
    Reality." U.S. News and World Report 25 July 1995:
    49+.

Harris Poll. Interview with 1,262 adults. File 468:
    Public Opinion. 28 June 1993. Online. DIALOG. 5
    Aug. 1994.

Keller, Teresa. "Trash TV." Journal of Popular Culture
    26 (1993): 195-206.

Kuklinski, James H., and Lee Sigelman. "When
    Objectivity Is Not Objective: Network Television
    News Coverage of U.S. Senators and the 'Paradox of
    Objectivity.'" The Journal of Politics 54 (1992):
    810-33.

McClellan, Steve. "What Is Reality? The Thin and
    Blurring Line." Broadcasting and Cable 123.15
    (Apr. 12, 1993): 37-38.

Munson, Wayne Edward. "Talking about Talk: The
    Talkshow, Audience Participation, and the
    Postmodern (Interactive Media)." DAI 52 (1992):
    724A. New York U, 1990. Dissertation Abstracts
    Online. Online. DIALOG. 5 Aug. 1994.

"Notes and Comments." The New Yorker 10 Aug. 1992:
    21-22.

Priest, Patricia Joyner. "Self-Disclosure on
    Television: The Counter-Hegemonic Struggle of
    Marginalized Groups on 'Donahue.'" DAI 53 (1994):
    2147A. Dissertation Abstracts Online. Online.
    DIALOG. 5 Aug. 1994.

Hall 13

Princeton Survey Research Associates. Interview with
    1,516 adults. File 468: Public Opinion. 16 July
    1993. Online. DIALOG. 5 Aug. 1994.

Schiller, Dan. <u>Objectivity and the News: The</u>
    <u>Public and the Rise of Commercial Journalism</u>.
    Philadelphia: Philadelphia UP, 1981.

Steele, Janet. "TV's Talking Headaches." <u>Columbia</u>
    <u>Journalism Review</u> 31.2 (1992): 49-52.

"Will the 'Fairness Doctrine' Be Reborn?" <u>The CQ</u>
    <u>Researcher</u> 4 (29 Apr. 1994): 370.

A book entry (pages 268–73). Include any subtitles separated from the main title by a colon.

9 *Works Cited: MLA Style*

After writing your paper, prepare a Works Cited page to list your reference materials. List only the ones actually used in your manuscript, including works mentioned within content endnotes and in captions of tables and illustrations. If you carefully developed your working bibliography as a computer file (see pages 31–34), preparing the Works Cited page will be relatively simple. Your list of sources, arranged alphabetically, can provide the necessary information.

Although Works Cited is the most commonly used heading for the reference page, it is not the only choice. Select a heading that indicates the nature of your list.

1. Label the page with the heading *Works Cited* if your list includes only the printed works quoted and paraphrased in the paper.
2. Use the label *Sources Cited* if your list includes nonprint items (e.g., an interview or speech) as well as printed works.
3. Reserve the heading *Bibliography* for a complete listing of *all* works related to the subject, an unlikely prospect for an undergraduate paper.

(See also Annotated Bibliography, pages 112–13.)
Works pertinent to the paper but not quoted or paraphrased, such as an article on related matters, can be mentioned in a content endnote (see pages 219–20) and then listed on the Works Cited page. On this point, see especially material on the Notes page of the sample paper, page 260.

Keyboard your Works Cited page according to the MLA standards that follow. (For a variety of formats used in other disciplines, see Chapters 10 and 11.)

9a FORMAT FOR THE WORKS CITED PAGE

Arrange items in alphabetic order by the surname of the author using the letter-by-letter system. Ignore spaces in the author's surname. Consider the first names only when two or more surnames are identical. Note how the following examples are alphabetized letter by letter:

De Morgan, Augustus
Dempsey, William H.

MacDonald, Lawrence
McCullers, Carson
McPherson, James Alan
McPherson, Vivian M.

Saint-Exupéry, Antoine de
St. James, Christopher

When two or more entries cite coauthors that begin with the same name, alphabetize by the last names of the second authors:

Harris, Muriel, and David Bleich
Harris, Muriel, and Stephen M. Fishman

When no author is listed, alphabetize by the first important word of the title. Imagine lettered spelling for unusual items. For example, "#2 Red Dye" should be alphabetized as though it were "Number Two Red Dye."

The list of sources may also be divided into separate alphabetized sections, for example, for primary and secondary sources, for different media (film, books, CD-ROM), for differences in subject matter (biography, autobiography, letters), for different periods (Neoclassic period, Romantic period), and for different areas (German viewpoints, French viewpoints, American viewpoints).

Place the first line of each entry flush with the left margin, and indent succeeding lines 5 spaces or one half inch. Double-space each entry, and also double-space between entries. Use 1 space after periods and other marks of punctuation.

Set the title *Works Cited* 1 inch down from the top of the sheet, and double-space between it and the first entry. A sample page is illustrated as Figure 167. (See also the sample Works Cited pages on pages 241–63 and 319–32.)

Note: **If you are writing the paper on a computer, you may use italicize book titles rather than underscore them.**

---

*Sample Works Cited
page*

                                        Robertson 12

                        Works Cited

Berg, Orley. <u>Treasures in the Sand: What Archaeology</u>
      <u>Tells Us about the Bible</u>. New York: Pacific, 1993.

The Bible. Revised Standard Version.

Bulfinch, Thomas. <u>Bulfinch's Mythology</u>. 2 vols. New
      York: Mentor, 1962.

Campbell, Joseph. <u>The Hero with a Thousand Faces</u>.
      Cleveland: Meridian, 1956.

---. <u>The Masks of God</u>. 4 vols. New York: Viking, 1970.

Chickering, H. "Hearing Ariel's Songs." <u>Journal of</u>
      <u>Medieval Renaissance Studies</u> 24 (1994): 131-72.

Henderson, Joseph L., and Maud Oakes. <u>The Wisdom</u>
      <u>of the Serpent: The Myths of Death, Rebirth,</u>
      <u>Resurrection</u>. New York: Collier, 1971.

Homer. <u>The Iliad</u>. Trans. Richmond Lattimore. Chicago: U
      of Chicago P, 1951.

Laird, Charlton. "A Nonhuman Being Can Learn Language."
      <u>College Composition and Communication</u> 23 (1972):
      142-54.

Lévi-Strauss, Claude. "The Structural Study of Myth."
      <u>Myth: A Symposium</u>. Ed. Thomas A. Sebeok.
      Bloomington: Indiana UP, 1958. 45-63.

Riccio, B. D. "Popular Culture and High Culture: Dwight
      MacDonald, His Critics and the Ideal of Cultural
      Hierarchy in Modern America." <u>Journal of American</u>
      <u>Culture</u> 16 (1993): 7-18.

Robinson, Lillian S. "Criticism--and Self-Criticism."
      <u>College English</u> 36 (1974): 436-45.

9b   BIBLIOGRAPHIC FORM: BOOKS

Enter information about books in the following order. Items 1, 3, and 8 are required; add other items according to the circumstances explained in the text that follows.

1. Author(s)
2. Chapter or part of the book
3. Title of the book
4. Editor, translator, or compiler
5. Edition
6. Volume number of the book
7. Name of the series
8. Place, publisher, and date
9. Page numbers
10. Total number of volumes

Name of the Author(s)   List the author's name, surname first, followed by given name or initials and then a period.

> Alexander, Shoshana. In Praise of Single Parents:
>   Mothers and Fathers Embracing the Challenge. New
>   York: Houghton, 1994.

Always give authors' names in the fullest possible form, for example, "Cosbey, Robert C." rather than "Cosbey, R. C." unless, as indicated on the title page of the book, the author prefers initials. However, APA style (see Chapter 10, 307–332) requires last name and initials only (e.g., Cosbey, R. C.).

When an author has two or more works, do not repeat his or her name with each entry. Rather, insert a continuous three-hyphen line flush with the left margin, followed by a period. Also, list the works alphabetically by the title (ignoring *a, an,* and *the*). In the following example, the *C* of *Composing* precedes the *F* of Fault.

> Miller, Richard E. "Composing English Studies: Towards a
>   Social History of the Discipline." CCC 45 (1994):
>   164-79.
> ---. "Fault Lines in the Contact Zone." College English
>   56 (1994): 389-408.

The three hyphens stand for exactly the same name(s) as in the preceding entry. However, do not substitute three hyphens for an author who has two or more works in the bibliography when one is written in collaboration with someone else.

> Bizzell, Patricia. "Opportunities for Feminist Research
>   in the History of Rhetoric." Rhetoric Review 11
>   (1992): 50-58.

```
---. "The Praise of Folly, The Woman Rhetorician, and
    Post-Modern Skepticism." Rhetoric Society Quarterly
    22 (1992): 7-17.
Bizzell, Patricia, and Bruce Herzberg. The Rhetorical
    Tradition: Readings from Classical Times to the
    Present. Boston: Bedford-St. Martin's, 1990.
```

If the person edited, compiled, or translated the work that follows on the list, place a comma after the three hyphens and write "ed.," "comp.", or "trans.," respectively, before you give the title. This label does not affect the alphabetic order by title.

```
Finneran, Richard J. Editing Yeat's Poems. New York: St.
    Martin's, 1983.
---, ed. W. B. Yeats: The Poems. New ed. New York:
    Macmillan, 1983.
```

Chapter or Part of the Book   List the chapter or part of the book on the Works Cited page only when it is separately edited, translated, or written or when it demands special attention. For example, if you quote from a specific chapter of a book, let's say Chapter 13 of James A. Hall's novel, *Hard Aground,* the entry should read:

```
Hall, James A. Hard Aground. New York: Dell, 1993.
```

Your in-text citation should list specific page numbers, so there is no reason to mention a specific chapter, even though it is the only portion of Hall's book that you read.

However, if you cite from one work in a collection of works by the same author or from an anthology of works by many different authors, provide the specific name of the work and the corresponding page numbers. This next writer cites one story from a collection of stories by the same author:

```
Kenan, Randall. "Run, Mourner, Run." Let the Dead Bury
    Their Dead. San Diego: Harcourt, 1992. 163-91.
```

Edited anthologies supply the names of authors as well as editors. Almost always cite the author first. Conform to the rules given in these examples.

1. If you paraphrase or quote portions of an essay by Lonne Elder, write this entry:

```
Elder, Lonne. "Ceremonies in Dark Old Men." New Black
    Playwrights: An Anthology. Ed. William Couch, Jr.
    Baton Rouge: Louisiana State UP, 1968. 55-72.
```

2. If you cite lines from Aristophanes' drama *The Birds* in your paper, write this entry:

Aristophanes. <u>The Birds</u>. <u>Five Comedies of Aristophanes</u>.
Trans. Benjamin B. Rogers. Garden City: Doubleday,
1955. 110-54.

3. If you cite material from a chapter of one volume in a multivolume set, write an entry like this:

Child, Harold. "Jane Austen." <u>The Cambridge History of</u>
<u>English Literature</u>. Ed. A. W. Ward and A. R. Waller.
Vol. 12. London: Cambridge UP, 1927. 159-68.

Although not required, you may also provide the total number of volumes.

Saintsbury, George. "Dickens." <u>The Cambridge History of</u>
<u>English Literature</u>. Ed. A. W. Ward and A. R. Waller.
Vol. 13. New York: Putnam's, 1917. 257-71. 14 vols.

In cases where you cite several different authors from the same anthology, you should make cross-references (see page 277).

Title of the Book   Show the title of the work, underscored or italicized, followed by a period. Separate any subtitle from the primary title by a colon and 1 space, even though the title page has no mark of punctuation or the card catalog entry has a semicolon.

Styron, William. <u>A Tidewater Morning: Three Tales from</u>
<u>Youth</u>. New York: Random, 1993.

If a title includes the title of another article or book, special rules apply (see "Titles within Titles," page 287). You may need to omit an underscore or italics on one of the titles, as in this next example:

Schilling, Bernard N. <u>Dryden and the Conservative Myth:</u>
A Reading of Absalom and Achitophel. New Haven:
Yale UP, 1961.

Name of the Editor, Translator, or Compiler   Mention an editor, translator, or compiler of a collection after the title with the abbreviations *Ed., Trans.,* or *Comp.,* respectively, as shown here:

Yeats, W. B. <u>The Poems of W. B. Yeats</u>. Ed. Richard J.
Finneran. New ed. New York: Macmillan, 1983.

However, if your in-text citation refers to the work of the editor, translator, or compiler (e.g., "The Ciardi edition caused debate among Dante scholars"), use this form:

Ciardi, John, trans. <u>The Purgatorio</u>. By Dante. New York:
NAL, 1961.

Edition of the Book Indicate the edition used, whenever it is not the first, in Arabic numerals (e.g., "3rd ed.") or as "Rev. ed.," "Abr. ed.," and so forth, without further punctuation.

> Schulman, Michael, and Eva Meckler. <u>Bringing Up a Moral</u>
>
> <u>Child</u>. Rev. ed. New York: Doubleday, 1994.

Name of the Series If the book is one in a published series, show the name of the series, without quotation marks or underscoring, the series number of this work in Arabic numerals (for example, "no. 3" or simply "3"), and a period.

> Brown, J. R., and Bernard Harris. <u>Restoration Theatre</u>.
>
> Stratford-upon-Avon Studies 6. London: Arnold,
>
> 1965.

Volume Number If you are citing from two or more volumes of a multi-volume work, show the number of volumes in Arabic numerals (e.g., "4 vols."), as shown here:

> Seale, William. <u>The President's House: A History</u>. 2
>
> vols. Washington: White House Historical Assn.,
>
> 1986.

If you are citing from volumes that were published over a period of years, provide the inclusive dates at the end of the citation. Should the volumes still be in production, write "to date" after the number of volumes and leave a space after the hyphen that follows the initial date.

> Cassidy, Frederic, ed. <u>Dictionary of American Regional</u>
>
> <u>English</u>. 2 vols. to date. Cambridge: Belknap-
>
> Harvard UP, 1985- .
>
> Parrington, Vernon L. <u>Main Currents in American Thought</u>.
>
> 3 vols. New York: Harcourt, 1927-32.

If you are citing from only one volume of a multivolume work, provide the number of that volume with information for that volume only. For your in-text citation, you need to specify only page numbers, for example, (Seale 45–46). See page 282 for additional examples.

> Seale, William. <u>The President's House: A History</u>. Vol.
>
> 1. Washington: White House Historical Assn., 1986.

Although additional information is not required, you may provide the inclusive page numbers, the total number of volumes, and the inclusive dates of publication.

> Daiches, David. "The Restoration." <u>A Critical History of</u>
>
> <u>English Literature</u>. 2nd ed. Vol. 2. New York:
>
> Ronald, 1970. 537-89. 2 vols.

> Wellek, René. <u>A History of Modern Criticism, 1750-1950</u>.
>   Vol. 5. New Haven: Yale UP, 1986. 8 vols. 1955-92.

If you are using only one volume of a multivolume work and the volume has an individual title, you can cite the one work without mentioning the other volumes in the set.

> Crane, Stephen. <u>Wounds in the Rain</u>. <u>Stephen Crane: Tales</u>
>   <u>of War</u>. Charlottesville: UP of Virginia, 1970.
>   95-284.

As a courtesy to the reader, you may include supplementary information about an entire edition.

> Crane, Stephen. <u>Wounds in the Rain</u>. <u>Stephen Crane: Tales</u>
>   <u>of War</u>. Charlottesville: UP of Virginia, 1970. Vol.
>   6 of <u>The University of Virginia Edition of the</u>
>   <u>Works of Stephen Crane</u>. Ed. Fredson Bowers. 95-284.
>   10 vols. 1969-76.

Place, Publisher, and Date   Indicate the place, publisher, and date of publication.

> Sperry, Stuart M. <u>Keats the Poet</u>. Princeton: Princeton
>   UP, 1994.

For foreign cities, include the abbreviation for the country (or of the province if the city is in Canada) only if necessary for clarity.

> Morgan, John A. <u>Drama at Stratford</u>. Manchester, Eng.:
>   Wallace, 1995.

If more than one place of publication appears on the title page, the first city mentioned is sufficient. If successive copyright dates are given, use the most recent (unless your study is specifically concerned with an earlier, perhaps definitive, edition). A new printing does not constitute a new edition. For example, if the text has a 1940 copyright date and a 1975 printing, use 1940 unless other information is given, such as "facsimile printing" or "1975 third printing rev."

> Bell, Charles Bailey, and Harriett P. Miller. <u>The Bell</u>
>   <u>Witch: A Mysterious Spirit</u>. 1934. Facsim. ed.
>   Nashville: Elder, 1972.
> <u>The Oxford Dictionary of Quotations</u>. 3rd ed. Oxford,
>   Eng.: Oxford UP, 1979.

If the place, publisher, date of publication, or pages are not provided, use one of these abbreviations:

n.p.   No place of publication listed
n.p.   No publisher listed
n.d.   No date of publication listed
n. pag.   No pagination listed

Lewes, George Henry. <u>The Life and Works of Goethe</u>. 1855.

    2 vols. Rpt. as vols. 13 and 14 of <u>The Works J. W.</u>

    <u>von Goethe</u>. Ed. Nathan Haskell Dole. London:

    Nicolls, n.d. 14 vols.

Perrine, Laurence. "A Monk's Allegory." <u>A Limerick's</u>

    <u>Always a Verse: 200 Original Limericks</u>. San Diego:

    Harcourt, 1990. N. pag.

Provide the publisher's name in a shortened form, such as "Bobbs" rather than "Bobbs-Merrill Co., Inc." (See page 208–09 for a list of publishers' abbreviations.) A publisher's special imprint name should be joined with the official name, for example, Anchor-Doubleday, Jove-Berkley, Ace-Grossett, Del Rey-Ballantine, and Mentor-NAL.

Faulkner, William. "Spotted Horses." <u>Three Famous Short</u>

    <u>Stories</u>. New York: Vintage-Random, 1963.

If you cite materials from CD-ROM or database printouts, special rules apply. See pages 291–98 for an explanation of this type of entry:

Williams, T. Harry. <u>The Military Leadership of the</u>

    <u>North and the South</u>. 1960. <u>US History on CD-ROM</u>.

    Parsippany: Bureau Development, 1990.

Page Number(s) to a Section of a Book   Cite pages to help a reader find a particular section of a book.

Knoepflmacher, U. C. "Fusing Fact and Myth: The New

    Reality of <u>Middlemarch</u>." <u>This Particular Web:</u>

    <u>Essays on</u> Middlemarch. Ed. Ian Adam. Toronto: U of

    Toronto P, 1975. 55-65.

See also "Chapter or Part of the Book," pages 269–270.

Sample Bibliographic Entries: Books

Author

Ladd, Jerrold. <u>Out of the Madness: From the Projects to</u>

    <u>a Life of Hope</u>. New York: Warner, 1994.

Author, Anonymous

The Song of Roland. Trans. Frederick B. Luquines. New
    York: Macmillan, 1960.

Author, Anonymous but Name Supplied

[Madison, James]. All Impressments Unlawful and
    Inadmissible. Boston: Pelham, 1804.

Author, Pseudonymous but Name Supplied

Slender, Robert [Philip Freneau]. Letters on Various and
    Important Subjects. Philadelphia: Hogan, 1799.

Author, Listed by Initials with Name Supplied

A[lden], E[dmund] K. "Alden, John." Dictionary of American
    Biography. New York: Scribner's, 1928. 146-47.

Author, More Than One Work by the Same Author

Hansberry, Lorraine. A Raisin in the Sun. New York:
    Random, 1959.
---. To Be Young, Gifted and Black. Ed. Robert Nemiroff.
    Englewood Cliffs: Prentice, 1969.

For additional examples, see pages 268–69.

Authors, Two

Schulman, Michael, and Eva Meckler. Bringing Up a Moral
    Child. Rev. ed. New York: Doubleday, 1994.

Authors, Three

Chenity, W. Carole, Joyce Takano Stone, and Sally A.
    Salisbury. Clinical Gerontological Nursing: A Guide
    to Advanced Practice. Philadelphia: Saunders, 1991.

Authors, More Than Three   Use *et al.*, which means "and others," or
list all the authors. See the two examples that follow:

Balzer, LeVon, Linda Alt Berene, Phyllis L. Goodson,
    Lois Lauer, and Irwin L. Slesnick. Life Science.
    Glenview: Scott, 1990.
Lewis, Laurel J., et al. Linear Systems Analysis. New
    York: McGraw, 1969.

Author, Corporation or Institution   A corporate author can be an
association, a committee, or any group or institution when the title page
does not identify the names of the members.

```
Committee on Telecommunications. Reports on Selected
     Topics in Telecommunications. New York: Natl. Acad.
     of Sciences, 1970.
```

List a committee or council as the author even when the organization is also the publisher, as in this example:

```
American Council on Education. Annual Report, 1991.
     Washington: ACE, 1991.
```

Alphabetized Works, Encyclopedias, and Biographical Dictionaries

Treat works arranged alphabetically as you would an item in a collection, but omit the name of the editor(s), the volume number, and the page number(s). If the author is listed, begin the entry with the author's name; otherwise, begin with the title of the article. If the article is signed with initials, look elsewhere in the work for a complete name. Well-known works, such as the first two examples that follow, need only the edition and the year of publication; you may omit the place of publication and the publisher.

```
Garrow, David J. "Martin Luther King." The World Book
     Encyclopedia. 1990 ed.
"Kiosk: Word History." The American Heritage Dictionary
     of the English Language. 3rd ed. 1992.
```

However, less-familiar reference works need a full citation, as shown in this next example:

```
Perrin, Porter G. "Puns." Writer's Guide and Index to
     English. 4th ed. Glenview: Scott, 1968.
```

Place within quotation marks the titles to a synopsis or description of a novel or drama, even though the novel or the drama would normally be underscored or italicized.

```
"Antigone." Masterpieces of World Literature. Ed. Frank
     N. Magill. New York: Harper, 1989. 44-46.
```

The Bible

Do not underscore or italicize the word *Bible* or the books of the Bible. Common editions need no publication information. Do underscore or italicize special editions of the Bible.

```
The Bible. [Denotes King James version.]
The Old Testament. The Bible. CD-ROM. Parsippany: Bureau
     Development, 1990.
The Bible. Revised Standard Version.
The Geneva Bible. 1560. Facsim. rpt. Madison: U of
     Wisconsin P, 1961.
```

The New Open Bible. Large print ed. Nashville: Nelson,
    1990.

A Book Published before 1900 For older books that are now out of
print, you may omit the publisher. Use a comma, not a colon, to separate
the place of publication from the year.

Dewey, John. The School and Society. Chicago, 1899.

Classical Works

Homer. The Iliad. Trans. Richmond Lattimore. Chicago: U
    of Chicago P, 1951.

Committee Report, Published as a Book

National Committee on Careers for Older Americans. Older
    Americans: An Untapped Resource. Washington: AED,
    1979.

See also "Author, Corporation or Institution," pages 274–75.

Component Part of an Anthology or Collection In general, works
in an anthology have been published previously, but the prior publication
data may not be readily available; if it is not, use this form:

Updike, John. "A & P." Fiction 100. Ed. James H. Pickering.
    4th ed. New York: Macmillan, 1982. 1086-89.

Provide the inclusive page numbers for the piece, not just the page or
pages that you have cited in the text.

Hawthorne, Nathaniel. The Scarlet Letter. The Scarlet
    Letter and Other Writings by Nathaniel Hawthorne.
    Ed. H. Bruce Franklin. Philadelphia: Lippincott,
    1967. 22-233.

Hoy, Cyrus. "Fathers and Daughters in Shakespeare's
    Romances." Shakespeare's Romances Reconsidered. Ed.
    Carol McGinnis Kay and Henry E. Jacobs. Lincoln: U
    of Nebraska P, 1978. 77-90.

Use the following form if you can quickly identify the original publication information:

Scott, Nathan, Jr. "Society and the Self in Recent
    American Literature." The Broken Center. New Haven:
    Yale UP, 1966. Rpt. in Dark Symphony: Negro
    Literature in America. Ed. James A. Emanuel and
    Theodore L. Gross. New York: Free, 1968. 539-54.

```
Updike, John. "A & P." Pigeon Feathers and Other
     Stories. New York: Knopf, 1962. Rpt. in Fiction
     100. Ed. James H. Pickering. 4th ed. New York:
     Macmillan, 1982. 1086-89.
```

If you use several works from the same anthology, you can shorten the citation by citing the short work and by making cross-references to the larger one. (See "Cross-References," immediately following, for specific details.)

Cross-References   If you are citing several selections from one anthology or collection, provide a reference to the anthology followed by individual references to the selections used from the anthology along with cross-references to the editor(s) of the anthology.

```
Emanuel, James A., and Theodore L. Gross, eds. Dark
     Symphony: Negro Literature in America. New York:
     Free, 1968.
Hughes, Langston. "Mulatto." Emanuel and Gross 204-06.
Scott, Nathan, Jr. "Society and the Self in Recent
     American Literature." Emanuel and Gross 539-54.
```

Note also the following examples in which the first entry refers to the one that follows:

```
Eliot, George. "Art and Belles Lettres." Westminster
     Review. USA ed. April 1856. Partly rpt. Eliot, A
     Writer's Notebook.
---. A Writer's Notebook, 1854-1879, and Uncollected
     Writings. Ed. Joseph Wiesenfarth. Charlottesville:
     UP of Virginia, 1981.
```

However, add an abbreviated title to the cross-reference if you list two or more works under the editor's name.

```
Anson, David. "Searing, Nervy and Very Honest." Axelrod
     and Cooper, Guide 303-04.
Axelrod, Rise B., and Charles R. Cooper. Reading Critically,
     Writing Well. New York: St. Martin's, 1987.
---. The St. Martin's Guide to Writing. New York: St.
     Martin's, 1994.
Forster, E. M. "My Wood." Axelrod and Cooper, Reading
     111-14.
Murayama, Veronica. "Schizophrenia: What It Looks Like,
     How It Feels." Axelrod and Cooper, Guide 181-84.
```

Edition Note any edition beyond the first, as shown below:

> Keith, Harold. <u>Sports and Games</u>. 6th ed. Scranton:
> Crowell, 1976.
>
> Stone, Lawrence. <u>The Crisis of the Aristocracy:</u>
> <u>1558-1660</u>. Abr. ed. London: Oxford UP, 1971.

Indicate that a work has been prepared by an editor, not the original author.

> Melville, Herman. <u>Moby-Dick</u>. Ed. with Introd. by Alfred
> Kazin. Riverside ed. Boston: Houghton, 1956.

If you wish to show the original date of the publication, place the year immediately after the title, followed by a period.

> Hardy Thomas. <u>Far from the Madding Crowd</u>. 1874. Ed.
> Robert C. Schweik. A Norton critical ed. New York:
> Norton, 1986.

Editor List the editor first only if your in-text citation refers to the work of the editor (for example, the editor's introduction or notes). Your in-text citation will give a specific page; for example, a content footnote by David Bevington would be cited in the text as "(Bevington 316n)." The Works Cited entry should then be written as follows:

> Bevington, David, ed. <u>The Complete Works of Shakespeare</u>.
> 4th ed. New York: Harper, 1992.

In other cases, you may wish to show the inclusive page numbers to a foreward, preface, afterward, and some other commentary by an editor.

> Bryant, Jennings, and Daniel R. Anderson, eds. Preface.
> <u>Children's Understanding of Television: Research on</u>
> <u>Attention and Comprehension</u>. New York: Academic,
> 1983. iv-xii.

Encyclopedia

> Garrow, David J. "Martin Luther King, Jr." <u>The World</u>
> <u>Book Encyclopedia</u>. 1990 ed.

See also "Alphabetized Works, Encyclopedias, and Biographical Dictionaries" on page 275.

Introduction, Preface, Foreword, or Afterword If you are citing an introduction, a preface, a foreword, or an afterword, use the following forms. An introduction to an anthology uses this next form:

> Lester, Julius. Introduction. <u>The Negro Caravan</u>. Ed.
> Sterling A. Brown, Arthur P. Davis, and Ulysses
> Lee. Rpt. ed. Salem: Ayer, 1991. vi-xii.

If the writer of the piece is different from the author of the complete work, use the writer's full name after the word *By*.

> Lowell, Robert. Foreword. <u>Ariel</u>. By Sylvia Plath. New
>   York: Harper, 1966. vii-ix.

If the writer of the prefatory matter is also the author of the primary work, use only the last name after the word *By*.

> Vonnegut, Kurt. Prologue. <u>Jailbird</u>. By Vonnegut. New
>   York: Delacorte, 1979. 1-3.

Note: Use the form above when you cite from the prologue only and not from the main text.

Manuscript Collections in Book Form

> <u>Cotton Vitellius</u>. Ms. A. XV. British Museum, London.
>
> Chaucer, Geoffrey. <u>The Canterbury Tales</u>. Harley ms.
>   7334. British Library, London.

See also "Manuscripts (ms) and Typescripts (ts)," page 302.

Play, Classical

> Racine, Jean. <u>Phaedra</u>. Trans. Robert Lowell. <u>World
>   Masterpieces</u>. Ed. Maynard Mack et al. Continental
>   ed. Vol. 2. New York: Norton, 1956. 102-46. 2 vols.
>
> Shakespeare, William. <u>Macbeth</u>. <u>Shakespeare: Twenty-Three
>   Plays and the Sonnets</u>. Ed. T. M. Parrott. New York:
>   Scribner's, 1953.

Play, Modern

> Eliot, T. S. <u>The Cocktail Party</u>. <u>The Complete Poems and
>   Plays: 1909-1950</u>. New York: Harcourt, 1952.
>   295-387.
>
> Greene, Graham. <u>The Complaisant Lover</u>. New York: Viking,
>   1959.

Poem, Classical

> Ciardi, John, trans. <u>The Purgatorio</u>. By Dante. New York:
>   NAL, 1961. 26n.

Note: Use the form above only if the citation is to Ciardi's prefatory matter or notes to the text. Otherwise, cite Dante:

> Dante. <u>The Divine Comedy</u>. Trans. Lawrence G. White. New
>   York: Pantheon, 1948.

Poem, Modern Collection   Use this form if you cite one short poem from a collection:

> Eliot, T. S. "The Love Song of J. Alfred Prufrock." The
>   Complete Poems and Plays 1909-1950. New York:
>   Harcourt, 1952. 3-7.

Use this next form if you cite one book-length poem:

> Eliot, T. S. Four Quartets. The Complete Poems and Plays
>   1909-1950. New York: Harcourt, 1952. 115-45.

Do not cite specific poems and pages if you cite several different poems of the collection. Your in-text citations should cite the specific poems and page numbers (see pages 193–95).

> Eliot, T. S. The Complete Poems and Plays 1909-1950. New
>   York: Harcourt, 1952.

Republished Book   If you are citing from a republished book, such as a paperback version of a book published originally in hardback, provide the original publication date after the title followed by the publication information for the book from which you are citing.

> Lowes, John Livingston. The Road to Xanadu: A Study
>   in the Ways of the Imagination. 1930. New York:
>   Vintage-Knopf, 1959.

Although it is not required, you may wish to provide supplementary information about the republished version. Give the type of reproduction to explain that the republished work is, for example, a facsimile reprinting of the text.

> Hooker, Richard. Of the Lawes of Ecclesiasticall
>   Politie. 1594. Facsim. rpt. Amsterdam: Teatrum
>   Orbis Terrarum, 1971.

Give facts about the original publication. In this next example, the republished book was originally published under a different title.

> Arnold, Matthew. "The Study of Poetry." Essays: English
>   and American. Ed. Charles W. Eliot. 1886. New York:
>   Collier, 1910. Rpt. of the General Introduction to
>   The English Poets. Ed. T. H. Ward. 1880.

Series, Numbered and Unnumbered

> Commager, Henry Steele. The Nature and the Study of
>   History. Soc. Sci. Seminar Ser. Columbus: Merrill,
>   1965.

```
Jefferson, D. W. "'All, all of a piece throughout':
    Thoughts on Dryden's Dramatic Poetry." Restoration
    Theatre. Ed. J. R. Brown and Bernard Harris.
    Stratford-upon-Avon Studies 6. London: Arnold,
    1965. 159-76.
Wallerstein, Ruth C. Richard Crashaw: A Study in Style
    and Poetic Development. U of Wisconsin Studies in
    Lang. and Lit. 37. Madison: U of Wisconsin P, 1935.
```

Sourcebooks and Casebooks

```
Ellmann, Richard. "Reality." Yeats: A Collection of
    Critical Essays. Ed. John Unterecker. Twentieth
    Century Views. Englewood Cliffs: Prentice, 1963.
    163-74.
```

If you can identify the original facts of publication, include that information also.

```
Ellmann, Richard. "Reality." Yeats: The Man and the
    Masks. New York: Macmillan, 1948. Rpt. in Yeats: A
    Collection of Critical Essays. Ed. John Unterecker.
    Twentieth Century Views. Englewood Cliffs: Pren-
    tice, 1963. 163-74.
```

If you cite more than one article from a casebook, use cross-references (see page 277).

Title of a Book in Another Language
For French titles, use lowercase letters except for the first word and all proper nouns. For titles in German, Italian, Spanish, and Latin, use lowercase letters except for the first word and all words normally capitalized. Provide a translation in brackets if you think it necessary (e.g., *Étranger* [*The Stranger*] or Praha [Prague]).

```
Brombert, Victor. Stendhal et la voie oblique. New
    Haven: Yale UP, 1954.
Castex, P. G. Le rouge et le noir de Stendhal. Paris:
    Sedes, 1967.
```

See also "Titles within Titles," page 238.

```
Levowitz-treu, Micheline. L'amour et la mort chez
    Standhal. Aran: Editions due Grand Chéne, 1978.
```

Compare this form with that for a journal entry (see page 287).

Translator

```
Condé, Maryse. Segu. Trans. Barbara Bray. New York:
    Ballantine, 1982.
```

List the translator's name first only if the translator's work is the focus of your study.

> Shorey, Paul, trans. <u>The Republic</u>. By Plato. Cambridge:
>   Harvard UP, 1937. 162n.

Volumes, a Work of Several Volumes   See pages 271–72 for an explanation and additional examples to this bibliographic form.

> Parrington, Vernon L. <u>Main Currents in American Thought</u>.
>   3 vols. New York: Harcourt, 1927-32.
>
> Ruskin, John. <u>The Works of Ruskin</u>. Ed. E. T. Cook and
>   Alexander Wedderburn. 39 vols. London: Allen; New
>   York: Longmans, 1903-23.

Volumes, One of Several Volumes

> Dryden, John. "The Romantic Poets. <u>Poems 1649-1680. The
>   Works of John Dryden</u>. Ed. Edward Niles Hooker et
>   al. Vol. 1. Berkeley: U of California P, 1956.

Volumes, Component Part of One of Several Volumes   See pages 271–72 for an explanation and additional examples to this bibliographic form.

> Daiches, David. "The Romantic Poets." <u>A Critical History
>   of English Literature</u>. 2nd ed. Vol. 2. New York:
>   Ronald, 1970. 117-86.
>
> Hawthorne, Nathaniel. "My Kinsman, Major Molineaux." <u>The
>   American Tradition in Literature</u>. Ed. Sculley
>   Bradley, R. C. Beatty, and E. Hudson Long. 3rd ed.
>   Vol. 1. New York: Norton, 1967. 507-22. 2 vols.

9c   BIBLIOGRAPHIC FORM: PERIODICALS

For journal or magazine articles, use the following order:

1. Author(s)
2. Title of the article
3. Name of the periodical
4. Series number (if it is relevant)
5. Volume number (for journals)
6. Issue number (if needed)
7. Date of publication
8. Page numbers

Name of the Author(s) Show the author's name flush with the left margin, without a numeral and with succeeding lines indented 5 spaces. Enter the surname first, followed by a comma, a given name or initials, and then a period.

```
O'Keefe, Maura. "Linking Marital Violence: Mother-
     Child/Father-Child Aggression and Child Behavior
     Problems." Journal of Family Violence 9 (1994):
     63-79.
```

Title of the Article Show the title within quotation marks followed by a period (unless the title has its own end mark) inside the closing quotation marks.

```
Baum, Rosalie Murphy. "Early-American Literature:
     Reassessing the Black Contribution." Eighteenth
     Century Studies 27 (1994): 533-49.
```

Name of the Periodical Give the name of the journal or magazine, underscored or italicized, with no following punctuation. Omit any introductory article to the title of the periodical or newspaper.

```
Boose, Lynda E. "Othello's Handkerchief: 'The
     Recognizance and Pledge of Love.'" English
     Literary Renaissance 5 (1975): 360-74.
```

Volume, Issue, and Page Numbers for Journals Most journals are paged continuously through all issues of an entire year, so listing the month of publication is unnecessary. For example, page numbers and a volume number are sufficient for you to find an article in *Eighteenth Century Studies* or *English Literary Renaissance*. However, some journals have separate pagination for each issue. If that is the case, you need to add an issue number following the volume number, separated by a period.

```
Cann, Johnson, and Deborah Smith. "Volcanoes of the Mid-
     Ocean Ridges and the Building of New Oceanic
     Crust." Endeavor 18.2 (1994): 61-66.
```

Add the month if more information would ease the search for the article: "20.5 (Nov. 1954): 4–6."

Specific Date, Year, and Page Numbers for Magazines With magazines, neither the volume nor the issue number helps in finding an article. For example, one volume of *Time* (52 issues a year) has page 16 repeated 52 times. For this reason, you need to insert an exact date (month and day) for weekly and fortnightly publications.

```
Norland, Rod. "Deadly Lessons." Newsweek 9 Mar. 1992:
     22-24.
```

The month suffices for monthly and bimonthly publications.

> Andrews, Peter. "The Media and the Military." <u>American
>   Heritage</u> July-Aug. 1991: 78-85.

Supply inclusive numbers (202–09, 85–115, or 1112–24), but if an article is paged here and there throughout the issue (for example, on pages 74, 78, and 81–88), write only the first page number and a plus sign (+) with no intervening space.

> Gaylin, Jody. "Secrets of Marriages That Last." <u>Parents
>   Magazine</u> Aug. 1991: 74+.

Sample Bibliographic Entries: Periodicals

Address, Published

> Humphries, Alfred. "Computers and Banking." Address to
>   Downtown Kiwanis Club, Nashville. 30 Aug. 1994.
>   Rpt. in part <u>Tennessee Monthly</u> 31 Aug. 1994: 33-34.
> Nixon, Richard. "Address to Veterans of Foreign Wars."
>   19 Aug. 1974. Rpt. in <u>Weekly Compilation of
>   Presidental Documents</u> 10 (26 Aug. 1974): 1045-
>   50.

Author, Anonymous

> "Fiddling While Peace Burns." <u>Economist</u> 2 Apr. 1994: 14.

Interview, Published

> Satire, William. Interview. <u>Playboy</u> Nov. 1992: 63+.

Journal, with All Issues for a Year Paged Continuously

> Garrett, Norman. "Technology in the Service of Language
>   Learning." <u>Modern Language Journal</u> 75 (1991):
>   74-101.

Journal, with Each Issue Paged Anew   Add the issue number after the volume number because page numbers alone are not sufficient to locate the article within a volume of 6 or 12 issues when each issue has separate pagination.

> Naffziger, Douglas W., Jeffrey S. Hornsby, and Donald F.
>   Kuralko. "A Proposed Research Model of
>   Entrepreneurial Motivation." <u>Entrepreneurship:
>   Theory and Practice</u> 18.3 (Spring 1994): 29-42.

If a journal uses only an issue number, treat it as a volume number.

```
Wilson, Katharina M. "Tertullian's De cultu foeminarum
     and Utopia." Moreana 73 (1982): 69-74.
```

Journal, Volume Numbers Embracing Two Years Some journals that publish only 4 or 6 issues a year bind 8 issues or 12 issues, respectively, thereby putting two years together. Use the form shown in the following example:

```
Callenbach, Ernest. "The Unbearable Lightness of
     Leaving." Film Quarterly 44-45 (Fall 1991): 2-6.
```

Magazine, Monthly

```
Stap, Don. "Along a Ridge in Florida, an Ecological
     House Built on Sand." Smithsonian Sept. 1994:
     36-44.
```

Magazine, Weekly

```
Norland, Rod. "Deadly Lessons." Newsweek 9 Mar. 1992:
     22-24.
```

Monograph

```
Martin, Judith N., Michael L. Hecht, and Linda K.
     Larkey. "Conversational Improvement Strategies for
     Interethnic Communication: African American and
     European American Perspectives." Communication
     Monographs 61.3 (Sept. 1994): 236-55.
```

Notes, Queries, Reports, Comments, Letters Magazine and journals publish many pieces that are not full-fledged articles. Identify this type of material (e.g., "Letter" or "Comment") if the title of the article or the name of the journal does not make clear the nature of the material.

```
Brown, Amanda. "Comment and Response." College English
     56 (1994): 93-95.
"Challenges to Intellectural Freedom Rise by Seven
     Percent." Bulletin. Library Journal 1 Mar. 1994:
     13.
Holden, Michael. "Scholarship at Whose Service?" Letter.
     PMLA 109 (1994): 442-43.
"Prioritizing the Powerless." Letter. Library Journal 1
     Mar. 1994: 3.
```

Reprint of a Journal Article

```
Simonds, Robert L. "The Religious Right Explains the
     Religious Right." School Administrator 9 (Oct.
     1993): 19-22. Rpt. in Education Digest Mar. 1994:
     19-22.
```

If the article is reprinted in an information service that gathers together several articles on a common topic, such as Social Issues Resources Series (SIRS), use the form shown in the following example (see also page 302):

```
Edmondson, Brad. "AIDS and Aging." American Demographics
     Mar. 1990: 28+. The AIDS Crisis. Ed. Eleanor
     Goldstein. Vol. 2. Boca Raton: SIRS, 1991. Art. 24.
```

Review, in a Magazine or Journal   Name the reviewer and the title of the review. Then write "Rev. of" and the title of the work being reviewed, followed by a comma and the name of the author or producer. If necessary, identify the nature of the work within brackets immediately after the title.

```
Steck, Richard. "The Next Best Thing to Being There."
     Rev. of Remote Access [Computer software], by
     Custom Software. PC World 1.5 n.d.: 97-99.
```

If the name of the reviewer is not provided, begin the entry with the title of the review.

```
"Recent Books." Rev. of Writing as a Road to Self-
     Discovery, by Barry Lane. CCC 45 (May 1994): 279.
```

If the review has no title, omit it from the entry.

```
Rogers, Michael. Rev. of Keats the Poet, by Stuart
     Sperry. Library Journal 15 Mar. 1994: 105.
```

If the review is neither signed or titled, begin the entry with "Rev. of" and alphabetize the entry under the title of the work reviewed.

```
Rev. of Anthology of Danish Literature, ed. F. J.
     Billeskov Jansen and P. M. Mitchell. Times Literary
     Supplement 7 July 1972: 785.
```

As shown in the example above, use an appropriate abbreviation (e.g., *ed, comp., trans.*) for the work of someone other than an author.

Series   Between the name of the publication and the volume number, identify a numbered series with an ordinal suffix (*2nd, 3rd*) followed by the abbreviation *ser.* For publications divided between the original series and a new series, show the series with *os* or *ns,* respectively.

```
Hill, Christopher. "Sex, Marriage and the Family in
     England." Economic History Review 2nd ser. 31
     (1978): 450-63.
```

```
Terry, Richard. "Swift's Use of 'Personate' to Indicate
     Parody." Notes and Queries ns 41.2 (June 1994):
     196-98.
```

Title, Omitted

```
Berkowitz, David. Renaissance Quarterly 32 (1979):
     396-493.
```

Title, Quotation within the Article's Title

```
Ranald, Margaret Loftus. "'As Marriage Binds, and
     Blood Breaks': English Marriage and Shakespeare."
     Shakespeare Quarterly 30 (1979): 68-81.
```

Title, within the Article's Title

```
Dundes, Alan. "'To Love My Father All': A Psychoanalytic
     Study of the Folktale Source of King Lear."
     Southern Folklore Quarterly 40 (1976): 353-66.
```

Title, Foreign

```
Rebois, Charles. "Les effets du 12 Juin." Le Figaro
     Magazine 2 juillet 1994: 42-43.
Stivale, Charles J. "Le vraisemblable temporel dans Le
     rouge et le noir." Stendhal Club 84 (1979):
     299-313.
```

See also "Title of a Book in Another Language," page 281.

9d BIBLIOGRAPHIC FORM: NEWSPAPERS

Provide the name of the author; the title of the article; the name of the newspaper as it appears on the masthead, omitting any introductory article (e.g., *Wall Street Journal,* not *The Wall Street Journal*); and the complete date—day, month (abbreviated), and year. Omit any volume and issue numbers.

Provide a page number as listed (e.g., 21, B-6, 14C, D3). For example, *USA Today* uses "6A," but *The New York Times* uses "A6." There is no uniformity among newspapers on this matter, so list the page accurately as an aid to your reader. If the article is not printed on consecutive pages (for example, if it begins on page 1 and skips to page 8), write the first page number followed by a plus sign (+).

Newspaper in One Section

```
Hanuszczak, Sharon. "Environmental Program Stalled."
     Chicago Defender 18 July 1994: 6.
```

Newspaper with Lettered Sections

Olivas, Michael A. "Mr. Justice Marshall, Dissenting."
    Chronicle of Higher Education 17 July 1991: B1-B3.

Newspaper with Numbered Sections

Storch, Charles. "Soul Searchings of 2 Black Writers Win
    Heartlands." Chicago Tribune 24 Aug. 1994, sec. 2:
    1.

Newspaper Editorial with No Author Listed

"Sales Tax Increase Is a Question of Priorities."
    Editorial. Tennessean [Nashville] 4 Sept. 1994: 4D.

Newspaper Article with City Added

In the case of locally published newspapers, add the city in square brackets (see also the sample entry immediately above).

Powers, Mary. "Finding Advances in the Search for Strep
    Vaccine." Commercial Appeal [Memphis] 7 July 1991:
    C3.

Newspaper Edition or Section for **The New York Times**

The Saturday edition of *The New York Times* is usually published as one complete section, so a lettered section is unnecessary. If you show the edition, place it after the year and before the page number, as shown in this next example:

Andrews, Edmund L. "Telephone Price War Heats Up." New
    York Times 7 Jan. 1995, natl. ed.: 39+.

On Monday through Friday, *The New York Times* usually has four sections, *A, B, C, D.* When citing an article from the weekly paper, you need to show the section used.

Zuint, Michael. "Market Place." New York Times 9 Jan.
    1995: D4.

The Sunday edition of *The New York Times* has numbered sections, individually paged, to cover art, business, travel, and so forth. If you cite from one of these sections, provide the section number. Otherwise, cite the lettered section.

Frant, Maureen. "A Cosmopolitan Food Scene in
    Jerusalem." New York Times 8 Jan. 1995, sec. 5: 6+.

Newspaper in a Foreign Language

Richard, Michel Bole, and Frédéric Fritscher. "Frederick
    DeKlerk, l'homme qui a aboli l'apartheid." Le Monde
    3 juillet 1991: 1.

Serialized Article in a Newspaper or Periodical   A series of articles, published in several issues under the same general heading, requires identification of the different issues. If each article that you cite has the same author and title, include the bibliographic information in one entry.

```
Meserole, Harrison T., and James M. Rambeau.
     "Articles on American Literature Appearing in
     Current Periodicals." American Literature 52
     (1981): 688-705; 53 (1981): 164-80, 348-59.
```

If each article that you cite has different authors and/or different titles, list each one separately. Indicate the number of this article in the series, and give the name of the series. If the series features the same author(s), alphabetize by the first letters of the titles.

```
Thomas, Susan, and Brad Schmitt. "Kids Find Their Fun in
     Danger." Tennessean [Nashville] 1 Sept. 1994: 1A+.
     Pt. 5 of a 30-day journal, Taking Back Our Kids: An
     Inner City Diary, begun 28 Aug. 1994.
---. "Little Love, Less Hope, Lost Lives." Tennessean
     [Nashville] 28 Aug. 1994: 1A+. Pt. 1 of a 30-day
     journal, Taking Back Our Kids: An Inner City Diary.
---. "This Is a Horrible Street." Tennessean [Nashville]
     29 Aug. 1994: 1A+. Pt. 2 of a 30-day journal,
     Taking Back Our Kids: An Inner City Diary, begun 28
     Aug. 1994.
```

9e   BIBLIOGRAPHIC FORM: GOVERNMENT DOCUMENTS

Since the nature of public documents is so varied, the form of the entry cannot be standardized. Therefore, you should provide sufficient information so that the reader can easily locate the reference. As a general rule, place information in the bibliographic entry in this order (but see "Executive Branch Documents" if you know the author of the work).

1. Government
2. Body or agency
3. Subsidiary body
4. Title of document
5. Identifying numbers
6. Publication facts

When you cite two or more works by the same government, substitute three hyphens for the name of each government or body that you repeat.

```
United States. Cong. House.
---. ---. Senate.
---. Dept. of Justice.
```

Congressional Papers   Senate and House sections are identified by an *S* or an *H,* respectively, with document numbers (e.g., S. Res. 16) and page numbers (e.g., H2345-47).

```
United States. Cong. Senate. Subcommittee on Juvenile
     Justice of the Committee on the Judiciary. Juvenile
     Justice: A New Focus on Prevention. 102nd Cong., 2nd
     sess. S. Hearing 102-1045. Washington: GPO, 1992.
---. ---. ---. Violent Crime Control Act 1991. 102d
     Cong., 1st sess. S 1241. Washington: GPO, 1991.
```

If you provide a citation to the *Congressional Record,* you should abbreviate it and provide only the date and page numbers.

```
Cong. Rec. 25 Aug. 1994: 12566-75.
```

See "Material Accessed through a Computer Service," page 296, if you wish to cite the name.

Executive Branch Documents

```
United States. Dept. of State. Foreign Relations of the
     United States: Diplomatic Papers, 1943. 5 vols.
     Washington: GPO, 1943-44.
Clinton, Bill. Health Security: The President's Report
     to the American People. Pr Ex 1.2:H34/4. Washington:
     GPO, 1993.
```

Documents of State Governments   Publication information on state papers varies widely, so provide sufficient data for your reader to find the document.

```
Tennessee. Board of Regents. 1992-1993 Statistical Report.
     Nashville: State of Tennessee, 1994. TBR A-001-92.
Tennessee. Department of Education. "Giles County."
     1993-1994 Directory of Public Schools. Nashville:
     State of Tennesee, n.d.
Tennesee. Tennessee State Library and Archives. Tennessee
     Election Returns, 1796-1825. Microfilm. Nashville:
     State of Tennessee, n.d. JK5292 T46.
```

Legal Citations and Public Statutes

```
California. Const. Art. 2, sec. 4.
```

Environmental Protection Agency et al. v. Mink et al. US
    Reports, CDX. 1972.

15 US Code. Sec. 78h. 1964.

Illinois. Revised Statutes Annotated. Sec. 16-7-81.
    1980.

Noise Control Act of 1972. Pub. L. 92-574. 1972. Stat.
    86.

People v. McIntosh. California 321 P. 3d 876, 2001-6.
    1970.

State v. Lane. Minnesota 263 N. W. 608. 1935.

US Const. Art. 2, sec. 1.

9f ELECTRONIC SOURCES (CD-ROM, THE INTERNET, E-MAIL, DATABASES)

New technology makes it possible for you to have access to information at your computer that was only a dream five years ago. A single CD-ROM can hold enormous amounts of information, such as the text of every Shakespeare play, which makes it possible for you to copy sections of these works onto your floppy disk or hard disk and then to incorporate the material into your paper without having to rekey it.

In another fashion, Internet opens a cornucopia of information from millions of sources. In addition, E-Mail enables you to send and access messages from around the globe.

However, you must cite every electronic source that you use in your paper. In general, provide the author(s); the title of the work; publication information for printed works, including the date; the medium (e.g., online, CD-ROM, E-Mail); the name of the computer service or the network; and the date that you accessed the work. It may help you to know the meaning of a few terms:

Analogue Numerical data represented by measurable variables, such as electrical signals

BITNET (Because It's Time Network) A bulletin board available via E-Mail

CD-ROM (compact disc with read-only memory) Storage for about 250,000 pages of text, which serves as an alternative to online sources

Diskette A floppy plastic disk that can serve as a medium of publication

E-Mail (electronic mail) A system for sending messages by computer

FTP (File Transfer Protocol) Guidelines for the transfer of files by computer via a network

Internet A high-speed network for sharing a variety of communications by computer

Online Information that is retrievable by computer from a network

Magnetic Tape A plastic tape coated with iron oxide for use in magnetic recording of sounds, words, and other signals

Telnet A protocol within the Internet system that allows messages to be sent and accessed electronically

Citing Sources Found on CD-ROM   CD-ROM technology provides information in four different ways, and each method of transmission requires an adjustment in the form of the entry for your Works Cited page.

1. *CD-ROM, full-text articles with publication information for the printed source.* Full-text articles from a selected set of periodicals are provided on CD-ROM by national distributors, such as Information Access Company (InfoTrac), UMI-ProQuest (ProQuest), SilverPlatter, or SIRS CD-ROM Information Systems. If your library has such a service, you can sit at the computer, use the indexing system, find an article of interest, and print it. This electronic system enables you to conduct a search that might require hours under the old method of searching printed indexes and then going in search of the printed magazines and journals.

   This bibliographic form requires that you first provide full information about the printed source or the analogue: the author(s); the title of the article; the title of the periodical in which it appears in print; the volume number, if relevant; the year of publication; and the page number(s). Next, you must give full information about the electronic source: the database, underscored or italicized; the medium, CD-ROM; the name of the national distributor, such as SilverPlatter; and the month and year that you accessed the information. Conform to the examples that follow:

DePalma, Antony. "Mexicans Renew Their Pact on the

    Economy Retaining the Emphasis on Stability." <u>New

    York Times</u> 25 Sept. 1994: 4. <u>New York Times Ondisc</u>.

    CD-ROM. UMI-ProQuest. Jan. 1995.

Mann, Thomas E., and Norman J. Ornstein. "Shipshape? A

    Progress Report on Congressional Reform." <u>Brookings

    Review</u> Spring 1994: 40-45. <u>SIRS Researcher</u>. CD-ROM.

    Boca Raton: SIRS, 1994. Art. 57.

See also page 302 for citing SIRS in its loose-leaf form.

Silver, Daniel J. "The Battle of the Books." Rev. of <u>The

    Western Canon: The Books and Schools of the Ages</u>,

    by Harold Bloom. <u>Commentary</u> 98.6 (1994): 60-63.

    <u>Resource/One</u>. CD-ROM. UMI-ProQuest. Feb. 1995.

```
Wessel, David. "Fed Lifts Rates Half Point, Setting
     Four-Year High." Wall Street Journal. 2 Feb.
     1995: A2+. Wall Street Times Ondisc. CD-ROM.
     UMI-ProQuest. Feb. 1995.
```

Note: When you cite from electronic sources, complete information may not be readily available—for example, the original publication data may be missing. In such cases, provide what is available.

```
Silver, Daniel J. "The Battle of the Books." Rev. of The
     Western Canon: The Books and School of the Ages, by
     Harold Bloom. Resource/One. CD-ROM. UMI-ProQuest.
     Feb. 1995.
```

2. *CD-ROM, full-text articles with no publication information for a printed source.* Sometimes the original printed source of an article or report is not provided by the distributor of the CD-ROM database. In such a case, provide information in this order: the author(s) if provided; the title of the article, in quotation marks; date, if provided; the title of the database, underscored or italicized; the medium, CD-ROM; the name of the distributor; and the month and year that you accessed the information. Conform to the examples that follow:

```
"Faulkner Biography." Discovering Authors. CD-ROM.
     Detroit: Gale, 1993. May 1994.
"U.S. Population by Age: Urban and Urbanized Areas."
     1990 U.S. Census of Population and Housing. CD-ROM.
     US Bureau of the Census. 1990. Jan. 1995.
```

3. *Texts of complete books and other publications on CD-ROM.* Many CD-ROM now contain the text to complete books. For example, you can now have access to the Bible or the plays of Shakespeare on CD-ROM. Therefore, cite this type of source as you would a book, and then provide information to the electronic source that you accessed. You may also cite, in your text, the screen numbers or page numbers to these electronic sources, such as (para. 25), (lines 43–54), or (screen 15). Conform to the examples that follow:

```
The Bible. The Old Testament. CD-ROM. Parsippany: Bureau
     Development, 1990.
English Poetry Full-Text Database. Rel. 2. CD-ROM.
     Cambridge, Eng.: Chadwyck, 1993.
"John F. Kennedy." InfoPedia. CD-ROM. N.p.: Future
     Vision, n.d.
```

Poe, Edgar Allan. "Fall of the House of Usher."
    Electronic Classical Library. CD-ROM. Garden
    Grove: World Library, 1993.

Williams, T. Harry. The Military Leadership of the
    North and the South. 1960. US History on CD-ROM.
    Parsippany: Bureau Development, 1990.

Wilson, Gohan. The Ultimate Haunted House. CD-ROM.
    Redman: Microsoft, 1992.

4. *CD-ROM abstracts to books and articles provided by the national distributors.* As a service to readers, the national distributors have members of their staff write abstracts of articles and books if the original authors have not provided such abstracts. As a result, an abstract that you find on Infotrac and ProQuest is not the writing of the original author, so you should not quote such abstracts. See page 134 for information on paraphrasing from the abstracts. However, these SilverPlatter databases *do* have abstracts written by the original authors:

PsychLIT (a database to psychology articles)
CINAHL (a database to nursing articles)

In either case, you need to show in the works cited entry that you have cited from the abstract, not the complete article or book. Provide publication facts for the printed source. Follow that with the word *Abstract,* followed by a period. Then give the name of the database, the medium, the national distributor, and the date you accessed the material. Conform to the examples that follow:

Figueredo, Aurelio J., and Laura Ann McCloskey. "Sex,
    Money, and Paternity: The Evolutionary Psychology
    of Domestic Violence." Ethnology and Sociobiology
    14 (1993): 353-79. Abstract. PsychLIT. CD-ROM.
    SilverPlatter. Jan. 1995.

O'Keefe, Maura. "Linking Marital Violence, Mother-
    Child/Father-Child Aggression, and Child Behavior
    Problems." Journal of Family Violence 9.1 (1994):
    63-79. Abstract. InfoTrac: Expanded Academic Index.
    CD-ROM. Information Access. Dec. 1994.

Silver, Daniel J. "The Battle of the Books." Rev. of The
    Western Canon: The Books and School of the Ages, by
    Harold Bloom. Abstract. UMI-ProQuest. Feb. 1995.

```
Steele, Janet. "TV's Talking Headaches." Columbia
    Journalism Review 31.2 (1992): 49-52. Abstract.
    InfoTrac: Expanded Academic Index. CD-ROM.
    Information Access. July 1994.
```

Citing a Source That You Access in More Than One Medium   Some
distributors issue packages that include different media, such as CD-ROM
and accompanying microfiche or a diskette and an accompanying videotape. Cite such publications as you would a nonperiodical CD-ROM (see
item 3 above) with the addition of the media available with this product.

```
Franking, Holly. Negative Space: A Computerized Video
    Novel. Vers. 1.0. Diskette, videocassette. Prairie
    Village: Diskotech, 1990.
Jolly, Peggy. "A Question of Style." Exercise Exchange
    26.2 (1982): 39-40. ERIC. CD-ROM, microfiche.
    SilverPlatter. 17 Feb. 1995. ED236601, fiche 1.
Silver, Daniel J. "The Battle of the Books." Rev. of The
    Western Canon: The Books and School of the Ages, by
    Harold Bloom. Resource/One. CD-ROM, microfiche S-
    637. UMI-ProQuest. Feb. 1995.
```

Citing a Source Found on a Diskette   Cite a diskette as you would a
book with the addition of the word *Diskette.* Conform to the examples that
follow:

```
Lester, James D. Grammar: Computer Slide Show. Diskette.
    Clarksville: Austin Peay State U, 1995.
"Nuclear Medicine Technologist." Guidance Information
    System. 17th ed. Diskette. Cambridge: Riverside-
    Houghton, 1992.
```

Citing a Source Found on a Magnetic Tape   Write this entry as you
would for a book with the addition of the words *Magnetic tape.* If relevant,
show the edition (3rd ed.), release (Rel. 2), or version (Ver. 3). Conform to
the example that follows:

```
Statistics on Child Abuse--Montgomery County, Tennessee.
    Rel. 2. Magnetic tape. Clarksville: Harriett Cohn
    Mental Health Center, 1993.
```

Citing a Source Found on an Online Database   To access an online
database by a computer service, you will need to get on a telephone line
by modem and receive electronically the material from the national vender,

such as DIALOG, Dow Jones News Retrieval, CompuServe, Nexis, and Prodigy. See pages 39–42 for an explanation of the procedure. To access an online database by a computer network, such as the Internet or BIT-NET, you will use special codes that connect you electronically to numerous special-interest networks.

Therefore, your works cited entries will need to show that your source is online, that it can be accessed through a specific computer service or computer network, and that it had an original publication date as well as the date you accessed it.

Material Accessed through a Computer Service   When you access material through a computer service, some files will refer to material that is available in printed form, others will not. Use the following form to list a database source that also appears in print. *Note:* Enclose the date within parentheses only when it follows a volume number.

> Bronner, E. "Souter Voices Concern over Abortion Curb."
>
> <u>Boston Globe</u> 31 Oct. 1990: 1. Online. DIALOG. 22
>
> Nov. 1991.

> Priest, Patricia Joyner. "Self-Disclosure on Television:
>
> The Counter-Hegemonic Struggle of Marginalized
>
> Groups on 'Donahue.'" Diss. New York U, 1990. <u>DAI</u>
>
> 53.7 (1993): 2147A. <u>Dissertation Abstracts Online</u>.
>
> Online. DIALOG. 10 Feb. 1994.

Note: The abstracts of *DAI* are written by the authors; you may feel free to quote directly from them.

> United States. Cong. House. <u>A Bill to Restructure the</u>
>
> <u>Federal Budget Process</u>. 102nd Cong., 2nd sess. H
>
> 6089. 1 Oct. 1992. <u>GENFED</u>. Online. Lexis. 3 May
>
> 1993.

> Waxman, Henry A. "Conference Report on S. 323, Family
>
> Planning Amendments Act of 1992." <u>Cong. Rec.</u> 6 Aug.
>
> 1992: 7686. <u>Lexis Library</u>. Online. Lexis. 14 Jan.
>
> 1993.

If complete information is not available (for example, no printed source is listed), cite what is available.

> "Alexander Hamilton." <u>Academic American Encyclopedia</u>.
>
> Online. CompuServe. 5 Jan. 1995.

> Glicken, Morley D. "A Five-Step Plan to Renew Your
>
> Creativity." <u>National Business Employment Weekly</u>.
>
> Online. Dow Jones News Retrieval. 4 May 1994.

Electronic Text Accessed through a Computer Network   Computer networks, such as Internet, can display millions of documents, but they have no efficient indexing systems. This presents several problems. First, when you cite from such sources, you often have no page numbers. (See page 185 for details on handling this problem in your in-text citations.) Second, some information has no author and, sometimes, no author and no title. In such an instance, you need to be creative by writing, for example, "Document on Nuclear Disarmament" or "Comments on the Federal Deficit." Third, your instructor may require you to provide the electronic address that will enable other persons to access the document. Some of these addresses are difficult to find, so you may need your instructor to educate you on methods for finding electronic addresses. (For example, in Gopher the equal sign (=) produces a window that shows technical data, including the address.) In addition, the addresses are often very long, so take care in typing them. (See the entry for "2020 Views" below.) If you give the address, precede it with the word *Available.*

Use this form if your instructor does not require the electronic address:

> "Facts & Figures." <u>Chronicle of Higher Education</u>. 10
>   Feb. 1995. Online. Gopher. 15 Feb. 1995.

> "Silicone Gel Breast Implant Recall Urged by Health
>   Research Group." <u>The Gray Sheet</u>. 20 Jan. 1992: 7.
>   Online. Internet. 1 Aug. 1994.

If your instructor requires the electronic address, use a form similar to these:

> Bailey, Charles W., Jr. "Overview." 5 Mar. 1991. Online.
>   BITNET. 6 July 1991. Available Bailey: prvlnl.
>   BITNET. Pacs L@uhupvmi

> Buckley, Nat. "Green Teachers." <u>National Consortium for
>   Environmental Education and Training</u>. 1994. Online.
>   Gopher. 16 Feb. 1995. Available Gopher:
>   //nceet.snre.umich.edu:70/00/.g-i/grnTchers.read

> Carroll, L. "The Rabbit Sends in a Little Bill" (Ch. 4).
>   In <u>Alice's Adventures in Wonderland</u> (The
>   Millennium Fulcrum edition 2.7a). 1991. Online.
>   Internet. 3 Jan. 1995. Available FTP:
>   quake.think.com Directory: pub/etext/1991 File:
>   alice-in-wonderland.txt

> "2020 Views: Balancing Today against Tomorrow: Feeding
>   and Protecting the Earth." <u>2020 News & Views
>   Newsletter</u>. 7 June 1994. Online. Gopher. 16 Feb.
>   1995. Available Gopher: cgnet. com:70/00/CGIAR

```
%20news%20and%20information/2020%20News%20%26%20
Views%20Newsletter/1994-07%20-%20June5Newsletter
/2020%20Views%3a%20Balancing%20Today%20Against%20
Tomorrow%3a%20Feeding%20%26%20Protecting%20the%20
Earth
```

In some situations, you may prefer to give the E-Mail address so that other scholars can contact the sender for the electronic address and/or more information.

```
Rickert, N. W. "Consciousness and Simulation." Psycoloquy:
     Refereed Electronic Journal of Peer Discussion 3.47
     (Sept. 1992). Online. Available E-Mail: psyc@pucc
     Message: Get psyc 92-00077 (Sept. 1992).
```

Material Accessed through E-Mail   Electronic mail may be treated as a letter or memo (see page 000). Provide the name of the sender, a title or subject if one is listed, a description of the mail (e.g., "E-Mail to Greg Norman"), and the date of transmission.

```
Morgan, Melvin S. E-Mail to the author. 16 Feb. 1995.
Taylor, Stephanie. "Mail How-To #1." E-Mail to Harned
     users. 26 Sept. 1994.
```

Public posting on electronic bulletin boards, news groups, and other E-Mail networks require additional information: the description *Online posting,* the name(s) of the news group, the name of the network, and the date of access.

```
Singer, Roslyn A. "Newspeak and Newtspeak." 7 Feb.
     1995. Online posting. H-Net History of Rhetoric
     Discussion List. BITNET. 16 Feb. 1995.
```

Your instructor may require the electronic address, which necessitates this form:

```
Singer, Roslyn A. "Newspeak and Newtspeak." 7 Feb.
     1995. Online posting. H-Net History of Rhetoric
     Discussion List. BITNET. 16 Feb. 1995. Available H-
     Rhetor%uicvm. bitnet@uga.cc.uga.edu
```

9g   BIBLIOGRAPHIC FORM: OTHER SOURCES

Advertisement   Provide the name of the advertisement or the name of the product, the label *Advertisement,* and publication information.

```
Delta Faucets. Advertisement. ESPN. 16 Feb. 1995.
```

Jenkins & Wynne Ford/Mercury. Billboard advertisement.
    Clarksville. Aug. 1994.
"You've Got Some Royal Caribbean Coming." Advertisement.
    <u>New Yorker</u> 20 Feb. 1995: 163.

Art Work   If you actually experience the work itself, use the form shown
by the next two entries:

Remington, Frederic. <u>Mountain Man</u>. Metropolitan Museum
    of Art, New York.
Wyeth, Andrew. <u>Hay Ledge</u>. Private Collection of Mr. and
    Mrs. Joseph E. Levine.

If the art work is a special showing at a museum, use the form of this next
example:

"Gertrude Vanderbilt Whitney: Printmakers' Patron."
    Whitney Museum of American Art, New York. 22 Feb.
    1995.
Mortenson, Ray. "Photographs of Lakes and Ponds in the
    Hudson Highlands." Borden Gallery, New York. 26
    Feb. 1995.

Use this next form to cite reproductions in books and journals:

Lee-Smith, Hughie. <u>Temptation</u>. 1991. <u>A History of
    African-American Artists: From 1792 to the Present</u>.
    Ed. Romare Bearden and Harry Henderson. New York:
    Pantheon, 1993.
Raphael. <u>School of Athens</u>. The Vatican, Rome. <u>The World
    Book-Encyclopedia</u>. 1976 ed.

If you indicate the date of the original, place the date immediately after the
title.

Raphael. <u>School of Athens</u>. 1510-1511. The Vatican, Rome.
    <u>The World Book-Encyclopedia</u>. 1976 ed.

Broadcast Interview

Dole, Robert. Interview with David Brinkley. <u>This Week
    with David Brinkley</u>. ABC. WKRN, Nashville. 19 Feb.
    1995.
Wolfe, Tom. Interview. <u>The Wrong Stuff: American
    Architecture</u>. Dir. Tom Bettag. Videocassette.
    Carousel, 1983.

Bulletin

Economic Research Service. <u>Demand and Price Situation</u>.
Bull. DPS-141, 14 pp. Washington: Dept. of
Agriculture, Aug. 1994.

French, Earl. <u>Personal Problems in Industrial Research</u>
<u>and Development</u>. Bull. No. 51. Ithaca: New York
State School of Industrial and Labor Relations,
1993.

Cartoon

Danzig. Cartoon. <u>Christian Science Monitor</u> 1 Sept. 1994:
6.

If you cannot decipher the name of the cartoonist, use this form:

Cartoon. <u>New Yorker</u> 12 Sept. 1994: 92.

Computer Software

<u>Aldus Pagemaker 5.0</u>. Computer software. Seattle: Aldus,
1994.

Matthews, Martin S., and Carole B. Matthews. <u>Corel!5</u>
<u>Made Easy: The Basics and Beyond</u>. Berkeley:
Osborne-McGraw-Hill, 1994.

Conference Proceedings, Published

Miller, Wilma J., ed. <u>Writing across the Curriculum</u>.
Proc. of Fifth Annual Conference on Writing
across the Curriculum, Feb. 1995, U of Kentucky.
Lexington: U of Kentucky P, 1995.

Dissertation, Published

Nykrog, Per. <u>Les fabliaux: Etude d'histoire littéraire</u>
<u>et de stylistique</u> médiévale. Diss. Aarhus U, 1957.
Copenhagen: Munksgaard, 1957.

Dissertation, Unpublished

Burks, Linda Carol. "The Use of Writing as a Means of
Teaching Eighth-Grade Students to Use Executive
Processes and Heuristic Strategies to Solve
Mathematics Problems." Diss. U of Michigan, 1992.

Dissertation, Abstract Only   Use this form when you cite from *Dissertation Abstracts International* (*DAI*). The page number features *A, B,* or *C* to designate the series used: A, Humanities; B, Sciences; C, European dissertations.

> Burks, Linda Carol. "The Use of Writing as a Means of
>   Teaching Eighth-Grade Students to Use Executive
>   Processes and Heuristic Strategies to Solve
>   Mathematics Problems." Diss. U of Michigan. 1992.
>   <u>DAI</u> 54 (1993): 4019A.

See also material on CD-ROM abstracts, pages 294–295, and "Material Accessed through a Computer Service," page 296.

Film or Video Recording   Cite the title, the director, the distributor, and the year.

> <u>Scent of a Woman</u>. Dir. Martin Brest. Universal Pictures,
>   1992.

If relevant to your study, add the names of performers, writers, or producers after the name of the director.

> <u>Mask</u>. Dir. Charles Russell. Perf. Jim Carey. New Line
>   Prod., 1994.

If the film is a videocassette, filmstrip, slide program, or videodisc, add the type of medium before the name of the distributor. Add the date of the original film, if relevant, before the name of the medium.

> <u>Mask</u>. Dir. Charles Russell. Perf. Jim Carey. 1994.
>   Videocassette. New Line Home Video, 1995.

If you are citing the accomplishments of the director or a performer, begin the citation with that person's name.

> Pacino, Al, perf. <u>Scent of a Woman</u>. Dir. Martin Brest.
>   1992. Videocassette. MCA Universal, 1993.

If you cannot find certain information, such as the original date of the film, cite what is available.

> Altman, Robert, dir. <u>The Room</u>. Perf. Julian Sands, Linda
>   Hunt, and Annie Lennox. Videocassette. Prism, 1987.

Interview, Unpublished   For an interview that you conduct, name the person interviewed, the type of interview (e.g., telephone interview, personal interview, E-Mail interview), and the date.

> Safire, William. Telephone interview. 5 Mar. 1995.

See also "Interview, Published," page 284, and "Broadcast Interview," page 299.

Letter, Personal

> Weathers, Walter. Letter to the author. 5 Mar. 1995.

Letter, Published

Eisenhower, Dwight. Letter to Richard Nixon. 20 April
    1968. <u>Memoirs of Richard Nixon</u>. By Richard Nixon.
    New York: Grosset, 1978.

Loose-Leaf Collections If you cite an article from SIRS, *Opposing Viewpoints,* or other loose-leaf collections, provide both the original publication data and then add information for the loose-leaf volume, as shown in this next example:

Hodge, Paul. "The Andromeda Galaxy." <u>Mercury</u> July-Aug.
    1993: 98+. <u>Physical Science</u>. Ed. Eleanor Goldstein.
    Vol. 2. Boca Raton: SIRS, 1994. Art. 24.

Manuscripts (ms) and Typescripts (ts)

Glass, Malcolm. Jour. 3, ms. M. Glass Private Papers,
    Clarksville.
Tanner. Ms. 346. Bodleian Lib., Oxford, Eng.
Williams, Ralph. Notebook 15, ts. Williams Papers.
    Vanderbilt U, Nashville.

Map

<u>County Boundaries and Names</u>. United States Base Map GE-
    50, No. 86. Washington: GPO, 1987.
<u>Virginia</u>. Map. Chicago: Rand, 1987.

Microfilm or Microfiche

Chapman, Dan. "Panel Could Help Protect Children."
    <u>Winston-Salem Journal</u> 14 Jan. 1990: 14. <u>Newsbank:
    Welfare and Social Problems</u> 12 (1990): fiche 1,
    grids A8-11.
Jolly, Peggy. "A Question of Style." <u>Exercise Exchange</u>
    26.2 (1982): 39-40. <u>ERIC</u> ED2336601, fiche 1.
Tuckerman, H. T. "James Fenimore Cooper." Microfilm.
    <u>North American Review</u> 89 (1859): 298-316.

Mimeographed Material

Smith, Jane L. "Terms for the Study of Fiction." Mimeo-
    graphed. Athens. 1995.

Miscellaneous Materials (Program, Leaflet, Poster, Announcement)

"Earth Day." Poster. Louisville. 23 Mar. 1995.

"Gospel Arts Day." Program. Nashville: Fisk U. 18 June
    1994.

Monograph

Tennessee Teachers Group. <u>Kindergarten Practices, 1995</u>.
    Monograph 1995-M2. Knoxville: Author, 1995.

See also "Monograph," page 285, for a monograph published in a journal.

Musical Composition

Mozart, Wolfgang A. <u>Jupiter</u>. Symphony no. 41.

Wagner, Richard. <u>Lohengrin</u>.

Treat a published score as you would a book.

Legrenzi, Giovanni. "La Buscha." Sonata for Instruments.
    <u>Historical Anthology of Music</u>. Ed. Archibald T.
    Davison and Willi Apel. Cambridge: Harvard UP,
    1950. 70-76.

Pamphlet   Treat pamphlets as you would a book.

Federal Reserve Board. <u>Consumer Handbook to Credit
    Protection Laws</u>. Washington: GPO, 1993.

Westinghouse Advanced Power Systems. <u>Nuclear Waste
    Management: A Manageable Task</u>. Madison: Author,
    n.d.

Performance   Treat a performance (e.g., play, opera, ballet, or concert)
as you would a film, but include the site (normally the theater and city)
and the date of the performance.

<u>Lakota Sioux Indian Dance Theatre</u>. Symphony Space, New
    York. 18 Feb. 1995.

<u>Oedipus at Colonus</u>. By Sophocles. Trans. Theodore H.
    Banks. Pearl Theatre, New York. 8 Feb. 1995.

<u>Sunset Boulevard</u>. By Andrew Lloyd Webber. Dir. Trevor
    Nunn. Perf. Glenn Close, George Hearn, Alan
    Campbell, and Alice Ripley. Minskoff Theatre,
    New York. 7 Feb. 1995.

If your text emphasizes the work of a particular individual, begin with the
appropriate name.

Cytron, Sara. "Take My Domestic Partner--Please." Conf.
    on Coll. Composition and Communication Convention.
    Grand Hyatt Hotel, Washington. 24 Mar. 1995.

```
Gregory, Dick, comedian. Village Vanguard, New York. 22
     Feb. 1995.
Marcovicci, Andrea, cond. "I'll Be Seeing You: Love Songs
     of World War II." American Symphony Orchestra. Avery
     Fisher Hall, New York. 15 Feb. 1995.
```

Public Address or Lecture   Identify the nature of the address (e.g., Lecture, Reading), include the site (normally the lecture hall and city), and the date of the performance.

```
Evans, Nekhena. Lecture. Brooklyn Historical Soc., New
     York. 26 Feb. 1995.
Freedman, Diane P. "Personal Experience: Autobiographical
     Literary Criticism." Address. MLA Convention.
     Marriott Hotel, San Diego. 28 Dec. 1994.
Kinnel, Galway. Reading of Smart, Rilke, Dickinson, and
     others. Manhattan Theatre Club, New York. 20 Feb.
     1995.
```

Recording on Record, Tape, or Disk   If you are not citing a compact disc, indicate the medium (e.g., audiocassette, audiotape [reel-to-reel tape], or LP [long-playing record]).

```
"Chaucer: The Nun's Priest's Tale." Canterbury
     Tales. Narr. in Middle English by Robert Ross.
     Audiocassette. Caedmon, 1971.
John, Elton. "This Song Has No Title." Goodbye Yellow
     Brick Road. LP. MCA, 1974.
Sanborn, David. "Soul Serenade." Upfront. Elektra, 1992.
Tchaikovsky. Romeo and Juliet. Fantasy-Overture after
     Shakespeare. New Philharmonia Orchestra London.
     Cond. Lawrence Siegel. Classical Masters, 1993.
```

Do not underscore, italicize, or enclose within quotation marks a private recording or tape. However, you should include the date recorded, if available, as well as the location and the identifying number.

```
Walpert, Wanda A. Folk Stories of the Smokey Mountains.
     Rec. 6 Feb. 1995. Audiotape. U of Knoxville.
     Knoxville. UTF.34.82.
```

Cite a libretto, liner notes, or booklet that accompanies a recording in the form shown in the following example:

```
Brooks, Garth. Booklet. No Fences. By Brooks. Capital
     Nashville, 1990.
```

Report   Unbound reports are placed within quotation marks; bound reports are treated as books.

> Coca-Cola Company. <u>1994 Annual Report</u>. Atlanta: Author,
>   1994.
>
> Linden, Fabian. "Women: A Demographic, Social and
>   Economic Presentation." Report. The Conference
>   Board. New York: CBS/Broadcast Group, 1973.

Reproductions and Photographs

> Blake, William. <u>Comus</u>. Plate 4. Photograph in Irene
>   Taylor. "Blake's <u>Comus</u> Designs." <u>Blake Studies</u> 4
>   (Spring 1972): 61.
>
> Michener, James A. "Structure of Earth at Centennial,
>   Colorado." Line drawing in <u>Centennial</u>. By Michener.
>   New York: Random, 1974. 26.
>
> Snowden, Mary. <u>Jersey Pears</u>. 1982. <u>American Realism:
>   Twentieth Century Drawings and Watercolors</u>. New
>   York: Abrams, 1986. 159.

Table, Illustration, Chart, or Graph   Tables or illustrations of any kind published within works need a detailed citation.

> Abken, Peter A. "Over-the-Counter Financial Derivatives:
>   Risky Business?" Chart No. 2. <u>Economic Review</u> 79.2
>   (Mar.-Apr. 1994): 7.
>
> Alphabet. Chart. Columbus: Scholastic, 1994.
>
> Corbett, Edward P. J. Syllogism graph. <u>Classical
>   Rhetoric for the Modern Student</u>. New York: Oxford
>   UP, 1965.

Television or Radio Program   If available or relevant, provide information in this order: the title of the episode (in quotation marks), the title of the program (underscored or italicized), the title of the series (not underscored or in quotation marks), the name of the network, the call letters and city of the local station, and the broadcast date. Add other information (such as narrator) after the episode or program narrated or directed or performed. Place the number of episodes, if relevant, before the title of the series.

> "<u>Frankenstein</u>: The Making of the Monster." <u>Great Books</u>.
>   Narr. Donald Sutherland. Writ. Eugenie Vink. Dir.
>   Jonathan Ward. Learning Channel. 8 Sept. 1993.
>
> "News Headlines." Narr. Sadie Sakleford. <u>Weekend
>   Edition</u>. Narr. Diane Hanson. <u>NPR News</u>. NPR. WPHN,
>   Nashville. 19 Feb. 1995.

Middlemarch. By George Eliot. Adapt. Andrew Davies. Dir.
Anthony Pope. Perf. Juliet Aubrey and Patrick
Malahide. 6 episodes. Masterpiece Theatre. Introd.
Russell Baker. PBS. WCDN, Nashville. 10 Apr.-15 May
1994.

Nutrition & Aids. Narr. Carolyn O'Neil. CNN. 19 Feb.
1995.

Prairie Home Companion. NPR. WPHN, Nashville. 18 Feb.
1995. "Some of Our Planes Are Missing." Narr.
Morley Safer. Prod. David Fitzpatrick. *60 Minutes*.
CBS. WTVF, Nashville. 19 Feb. 1994.

Thesis   See "Dissertation, Unpublished," page 300.

Transparency

Sharp, La Vaughn, and William E. Loeche. *The Patient
and Circulatory Disorders: A Guide for Instructors*.
54 transparencies, 99 overlays. Philadelphia:
Lippincott, 1969.

Unpublished Paper

Elkins, William R. "The Dream World and the Dream
Vision: Meaning and Structure in Poe's Art."
Unpublished paper. Little Rock, 1995.

Videotape

The Gate to the Mind's Eye. A Computer Animation
Odyssey. Dir. Michael Boydstein. Music by Thomas
Dolly. Videocassette. BMG Video, 1994.

A Portrait of the Artist as a Young Man. By James
Joyce. Dir. Joseph Strick. Perf. Bosco Hogan.
Videocassette. Mystic Fire Video, 1989.

Sevareid, Eric, narr. *CBS News*. 11 Mar. 1975. Media
Services Videocassette. Vanderbilt U, 1975.

Thompson, Paul. "W. B. Yeats." Lecture. Videocassette.
Memphis U, 1995.

Voice Mail

Warren, Vernon. "Memo to Lester." Voice mail to the
author. 6 Jan. 1995.

10 Using APA Style

Your instructor may require you to write the research paper in APA style, which is governed by the *Publication Manual of the American Psychological Association,* fourth edition, 1994. This style has gained wide acceptance in academic circles.

> *Note:* APA style is used in the social sciences, and versions similar to it are used in the biological sciences, business, and the earth sciences.

You need to understand two basic ideas that govern this style. First, a scientific paper attempts to show what has been proven true by research in a narrowly defined area, so it requires the past tense when you cite the work of scientists (e.g., Johnson stipulated *or* the work of Elmford and Mills showed). Second, the scientific community considers the year of publication to be vital information, so they feature it immediately after any named source in the text (e.g., Johnson & Marshall, 1991). These two primary distinctions, and others, are explained in this chapter.

10a WRITING IN THE PROPER TENSE FOR AN APA-STYLED PAPER

Verb tense is an indicator that distinguishes papers in the humanities from those in the natural and social sciences. MLA style, as shown in previous chapters, requires you to use the present tense when you refer to a cited work (e.g., Johnson stipulates *or* the work of Elmford and Mills shows). In contrast, APA style requires you to use the past tense (e.g., Marshall stipulated) or the present perfect tense (e.g., the work of Elmford and Mills has demonstrated). APA style does require the present tense when you discuss the results of an experiment or study (e.g., the results confirm *or* the study indicates) and when you mention established knowledge (e.g., the therapy offers some hope *or* salt contributes to hypertension).

A paper in the humanities (MLA style) makes universal assertions, so it uses the historical present tense, as shown in the following examples:

"It was the best of times, it was the worst of times," `writes` Charles Dickens about the eighteenth century.

Johnson `argues` that sociologist Norman Manway has a "narrow-minded view of clerics and their role in nineteenth-century fiction" (64).

A scientific study makes a specific claim and requires the past tense or the present perfect tense with citations to a scientist's work, as shown here:

Matthews (1989) `designed` the experiment, and since that time several investigators `have used` the method (Thurman, 1990; Jones, 1991).

Note the differences in the verbs of these next two passages whenever the verbs refer to a cited work:

MLA style	APA style
What we must accept is that television is like a novel, a history text, a play, or a newspaper. Dan Schiller `says` that we accept television news as reality because "news--akin to any literary or cultural form-- must rely upon conventions. . . . to contrive the illusion of objectivity" (2), while Teresa Keller `proclaims` that "the problem is that the line between news/entertainment, fact/ fiction, accuracy/effect is more than blurred--it's intentionally trampled" (202).	What we must accept is that television is like a novel, a history text, a play, or a newspaper. Schiller (1994) `has said` that we accept television news as reality because "news--akin to any literary or cultural form--must rely upon conventions. . . . to contrive the illusion of objectivity" (p. 2), while Keller (1993) `has proclaimed` that "the problem is that the line between news/entertainment, fact/fiction, accuracy/ effect is more than blurred--it's intentionally trampled" (p. 202).

MLA style	**APA style**
The scholarly issue at work here is the construction of reality. Cohen, Adoni, and Bantz `label` the construction a <u>social</u> process "in which human beings act both as the creators and products of the social world" (34). These writers `identify` three categories (34-35).	The scholarly issue at work here is the construction of reality. Cohen, Adoni, and Bantz (1994) `have labeled` the construction a <u>social</u> process "in which human beings act both as the creators and products of the social world" (p. 34). These writers `have identified` three categories.

As illustrated in the preceding example on the left, MLA style requires that you use the present tense both for personal comments and for introducing sources. In MLA style the ideas and words of the authorities, theoretically, remain in print and continue to be true in the universal present. APA style, shown on the right, requires that you use the present tense for generalizations and references to stable conditions, but it requires the past tense for sources cited (e.g., The sources have tested [present perfect] a hypothesis *or* the sources reported [past tense] the results of the test). This next sentence uses tense correctly for APA style:

The danger of steroid use `exists` for every age group, even youngsters. Lloyd and Mercer (1991) `reported` on six incidents of liver damage to 14-year-old swimmers who used steroids.

As shown above in the example, use the present tense (*exists*) for established knowledge and the present perfect or the past tense (*reported*) for a citation.

10b USING IN-TEXT CITATIONS IN APA STYLE

APA style, unlike MLA style, uses these conventions for in-text citations.

1. Cites last names only
2. Cites the year, within parentheses, immediately after the name of the author
3. Cites page numbers always with a direct quotation, seldom with a paraphrase
4. Uses "p." or "pp." before page numbers

An in-text citation in APA style requires the last name of the author and the year of publication:

> The study of Conniff (1994) showed that one federal
> agency, the Bureau of Land Management (BLM), failed to
> protect the natural treasures of public land holdings,
> and Struble (1995) offered evidence that BLM serves the
> needs of ranchers, not the public.

If you do not use the author's name in your text, place the name within the parenthetical citation:

> It has been shown that the Bureau of Land Management
> often sacrifices wildlife and the environment to benefit
> miners and ranchers (Conniff, 1994; Struble, 1995).

Provide a page number when you quote the exact words of a source, and do use "p." or "pp." with page numbers:

> Conniff (1994, p. 33) explained that the bureau must
> "figure out how to keep the land healthy while also
> accommodating cowpokes, strip miners, dirt bikers,
> birdwatchers and tree huggers, all vocal, all willing
> to sue for their conflicting rights."

Note: Use a page number with a paraphrase only to identify a passage that might be difficult to find.

Always put the year immediately after the name of the authority; the page number may alternatively appear at the end of the quotation:

> Jones (1994) found that "these data of psychological
> development suggest that retarded adolescents are
> atypical in maturational growth" (p. 215).

Write a quotation of 40 words or more as a separate block, indented 5 spaces from the left margin. (*Note:* MLA style uses 10 spaces.) Because it is set off from the text in a distinctive block, do not enclose it with quotation marks. Do not indent the first line an extra 5 spaces; however, do indent the first line of any additional paragraphs that appear in the block an extra 5 spaces, that is, 10 spaces from the left margin. Set parenthetical citations outside the last period.

> Albert (1994) reported the following:
>
>> Whenever these pathogenic organisms attack the human
>> body and begin to multiply, the infection is set in
>> motion. The host responds to this parasitic invasion
>> with efforts to cleanse itself of the invading agents.

> When rejection efforts of the host become
> visible (fever, sneezing, congestion), the disease
> status exists. (pp. 314-315)

When one work has two or more authors, use "&" in citations only, not in the text, as shown in the following examples:

> It has been reported (Werner & Throckmorton, 1995) that
> toxic levels exceeded the maximum allowed levels each
> year since 1983.

> Werner and Throckmorton (1995) offered statistics on
> their analysis of water samples from six rivers and
> announced without reservations that "the waters are
> unfit for human consumption, pose dangers to swimmers,
> and produce contaminated fish that may cause salmonella"
> (pp. 457-458).

For three, four, or five authors, name them all in the first entry (e.g., Torgerson, Andrews, Smith, Lawrence, & Dunlap, 1995), but thereafter use "et al." (e.g., Torgerson et al., 1995). For six or more authors, employ "et al." in the first and in all subsequent instances (e.g., Fredericks et al., 1995).

Use small letters (a, b, c, and so forth) to identify two or more works published in the same year by the same author (e.g., Thompson (1994a) and Thompson (1994b)). Then use "1994a" and "1994b" in your References page (see page 314 for an example). If necessary, specify additional information:

> Horton (1994; cf. Thomas, 1993, p. 89) suggested an
> intercorrelation of these testing devices. But after
> multiple-group analysis, Welston (1995, esp. p. 211)
> reached an opposite conclusion.

If you make an in-text citation to an article or chapter of a textbook, casebook, or anthology, use the in-text citation to refer only to the person(s) you cite:

> One writer stressed that two out of every three new jobs
> in the 1990s will go to women (Bailey, 1995).

The list of references will make clear that this reference to Bailey is cited from an anthology (see "Textbook, Casebook, Anthology," pages 314–15).

Use a double reference to cite somebody who has been quoted in a book or article. That is, use the original author(s) in the text and cite your source for the information in the parenthetical citation.

> In other research, Massie and Rosenthal (1975) studied
> home movies of children diagnosed with autism, but

```
determining criteria was difficult due to the differences
in quality and dating of the available videotapes (cited
in Osterling & Dawson, 1994, p. 248).
```

The Reference page will list Osterling and Dawson, the source used, but Massie and Rosenthal need not be included in the list of references. If you do so, use this form:

```
    Massie, L., & Rosenthal, M. (1975). Diagnosing
autism via film. In J. Osterling & G. Dawson, p. 248.
```

Corporate authors should be spelled out at the first reference, followed by the abbreviation:

```
One source has questioned the results of the use of
aspirin for arthritis treatment in children (American
Medical Association [AMA], 1991).
```

The abbreviation may be used thereafter: (AMA, 1991).

When a work has no author listed, cite the title as part of the in-text citation (or use the first few words of the material):

```
The cost per individual student has continued to rise
rapidly ("Money Concerns," 1994, p. 2).
```

10c PREPARING A WORKING DRAFT OR PUBLISHING THE MANUSCRIPT

The editors of the APA style manual make a distinction between a working draft that writers submit to editors and a published manuscript that appears in a professional journal. While they show examples of a working draft, they suggest that students who write a long, formal research paper, thesis, or dissertation will probably want to publish their papers by the use of desk-top publishing to give it a polished form. In most cases, however, your instructors will expect a working draft.

What does this mean in practical terms?

1. The working draft will be written, usually, with the courier typeface, the one found on most typewriters. The published manuscript may use other fonts, serif or nonserif, according to your choice of fonts at the computer.
2. The working draft will use underscoring; the published manuscript may use italics.
3. The working draft will have an unjustified right margin with uneven lines; the published manuscript may use right justification because your selected font will feature proportional spacing.
4. The working draft will use paragraph indention for the works cited; the published manuscript will use hanging indention.

These distinctions are shown and explained in this chapter. What is important for you, however, are the wishes of your instructor. Therefore, when you are assigned a research paper in APA style, ask the instructor, "Do you want a working draft or a published manuscript?" Then act accordingly, using one of the two styles.

10d PREPARING THE LIST OF REFERENCES

Use "References" as a title for your bibliographic page. Every reference used in your text should appear in your alphabetic list of references at the end of the paper. Alphabetize the entries, and double-space throughout. Use only 1 space after each period.

You have a choice about the form of the entries. The editors of the new 1994 APA style manual recommend two forms (see Section 10c above). One is for a working draft, and the other is for a published manuscript.

Working Draft with Paragraph Indention and Underscoring for Titles

        Lifton, B. J. (1994). <u>Journey of the</u> adopted <u>self:</u>
A quest for wholeness.</u> New York: HarperCollins.

        O'Keefe, M. (1994, March). Linking marital violence,
mother-child/father-child aggression, and child behavior
problems. <u>Journal of Family Violence, 9,</u> 63-79.

The underlining extends to include any punctuation mark after the titles, as shown in the example above.

Published Manuscript with Hanging Indention and Italics for Titles

Lifton, B. J. (1994). *Journey of the adopted self: A
        quest for wholeness.* New York: HarperCollins.

O'Keefe, M. (1994, March). Linking marital violence,
        mother-child/father-child aggression, and child
        behavior problems. *Journal of Family Violence, 9,*
        63-79.

Books

Book (Basic Format)   For the working draft, indent the first line 5 spaces. For the published manuscript, use the hanging indention, that is, indent the first line five, six, or seven spaces (note: the tab key with some computer fonts will indent more than five spaces). List the author (surname first with initials for given names), year of publication within parentheses, title of the book underscored and with only first word of the title and any subtitle capitalized (but do capitalize proper nouns), place of publication, and publisher. In the publisher's name omit the words *Publishing, Company,* or *Inc.,* but otherwise give a full name: Houghton Mifflin, Florida State University Press, HarperCollins.

```
     Alexander, S. (1994). In praise of single parents:
Mothers and fathers embracing the challenge. New York:
Houghton Mifflin.
```

List chronologically two or more works by the same author. For example, Fitzgerald's 1994 publication would precede his 1995 publication.

```
Fitzgerald, R. F. (1994). Controlling oil spills.
Fitzgerald, R. F. (1995). Alaska and its oil reserves.
```

References with the same author in the same year are alphabetized and marked with lowercase letters (a, b, c, and so forth) immediately after the date:

```
Fitzgerald, R. F. (1995a). Water purification systems.
Fitzgerald, R. F. (1995b). Water waste today.
```

Entries of a single author precede those of multiple-authors beginning with the same surname without regard for the dates:

```
Fitzgerald, R. F. (1995). Water purification systems.
Fitzgerald, R. F., & Smithson, C. A. (1994). Water maps.
```

References with the same first author and different second or third author should be alphabetized by the surname of the author that is different:

```
Fitzgerald, R. F., & Smithson, C. A. (1994). Water maps.
Fitzgerald, R. F., & Waters, W. R. (1995). Alaska
pipelines.
```

Part of a Book List the author(s), date of publication, chapter or section title, editor(s) (with name in normal order) preceded by "In" and followed by "(Ed.)" or "(Eds.)," the name of the book (underscored), page number(s) to the specific section of the book cited (placed within parentheses), place of publication, and publisher. For example:

```
     Hartley, J. T., Harker, J. O., & Walsh, D. A.
(1980). Contemporary issues and new directions in adult
development of learning and memory. In L. W. Poon (Ed.),
Aging in the 1980s: Psychological issues (pp. 239-252).
Washington, DC: American Psychological Association.
```

Textbook, Casebook, Anthology First, make a primary reference to the anthology:

```
     Vesterman, W. (Ed.). (1991). Readings for the 21st
century. Boston: Allyn & Bacon.
```

Thereafter, make cross-references to the primary source, in this case to Vesterman, as shown in the following examples. *Note:* These entries should be mingled with all others on the reference page in alphabetic order; as a result, cross-references may appear before or after the primary source. The year cited should be the date when the cited work was published, not when the Vesterman book was published; such information is usually found in a headnote, footnote, or list of credits at the front or back of the anthology.

>   Bailey, J. (1988). Jobs for women in the nineties.
> In Vesterman, pp. 55-63.
>   Fallows, D. (1982). Why mothers should stay home.
> In Vesterman, pp. 69-77.
>   Steinem, G. (1972). Sisterhood. In Vesterman, pp.
> 48-53.
>   Vesterman, W. (Ed.). (1991). <u>Readings for the 21st</u>
> <u>century.</u> Boston: Allyn & Bacon.

The alternative to the style shown in the previous examples is to provide a complete entry for every one of the authors cited from the casebook (in which case you do not need a separate entry to Vesterman). For example:

>   Bailey, J. (1988). Jobs for women in the nineties.
> In W. Vesterman (Ed.), <u>Readings for the 21st century</u>
> (pp. 55-63). Boston: Allyn & Bacon.
>   Fallows, D. (1982). Why mothers should stay home.
> In W. Vesterman (Ed.), <u>Readings for the 21st century</u>
> (pp. 69-77). Boston: Allyn & Bacon.
>   Steinem, G. (1972). Sisterhood. In W. Vesterman
> (Ed.), <u>Readings for the 21st century</u> (pp. 48-53).
> Boston: Allyn & Bacon.

Book with a Corporate Author, Third Edition

>   American Psychiatric Association. (1980).
> <u>Diagnostic and statistical manual of mental disorders</u>
> (3rd ed.). Washington, DC: Author.

Encylcopedia, Entry in   List the author(s), year of publication, title of the article, title of the encyclopedia (underscored), volume, page, place of publication, and publisher.

>   Woodley, D. J. (1990). Acne. In <u>World book</u>
> <u>encyclopedia</u> (Vol. 1, p. 25). Chicago: World Book.

If no author is listed, begin with the title of the article, as shown here:

>   Brazil. (1970). <u>Harper encyclopedia of the modern</u>
> <u>world</u> (Vol. 2, pp. 256-271). New York: Harper & Row.

Periodicals

Journal   List the author(s), year of publication, title of the article without quotation marks and with only the first word, proper nouns, and words after colons capitalized, name of the journal (underscored) and with all major words capitalized, volume number (underscored), inclusive page numbers not preceded by "p." or "pp."

> Mielke, K. W. (1988). Television in the social
> studies classroom. <u>Social Education, 52,</u> 362-365.

Magazine   List the author(s), the date of publication (year, month without abbreviation, and the specific day for weekly and fortnightly magazines), title of the article without quotation marks and with only the first word capitalized, name of the magazine (underscored) with all major words capitalized, volume number, and inclusive page numbers, not preceded by "p." or "pp."

> Sherman, J. (1994, September). Like the factories
> he designed, Albert Kahn lived to work. <u>Smithsonian, 25,</u>
> 49-59.

Newspaper   List the author(s), date of publication (year, month, and day), title of article with only first word and proper nouns capitalized, complete name of newspaper (underscored) in capitals, and the section with all discontinuous page numbers. Use "p." or "pp." with newspaper articles.

> Raymond, C. (1990, September 12). Global migration
> will have widespread impact on society, scholars say.
> <u>The Chronicle of Higher Education,</u> pp. A1, A6.

Abstract of a Published Article from a Secondary Source

> Misumi, J., & Fujita, M. (1982). Effects of PM
> organizational development in supermarket organization.
> <u>Japanese Journal of Experimental Social Psychology, 21,</u>
> 93-111. (From <u>Psychological Abstracts,</u> 1982, <u>68,</u> Abstract
> No. 11474).

Abstract of an unpublished work

> Havens, N. B. (1982). Verbalized symbolic play of
> pre-school children in two types of play environments
> (Doctoral dissertation, Temple University, 1982).
> <u>Dissertation Abstracts International, 42,</u> 5058A.

Abstract on CD-ROM

Wood, W., Wong, F. Y., & Chachere, J. G. (1991). Effects of media violence on viewers' aggression in unconstrained social interaction [CD-ROM]. Psychological Bulletin, 109, 371-384. Abstract from: InfoTrac File: Expanded Academic Index: AN 10852239.

Review

Dewar, Alison. (1994). Media Review [Review of the book The body, schooling and culture]. Journal of Teaching in Physical Education, 14, 121-123.

If the review has no title, use the form shown in this next example:

Nelson, C. R. (1994, March 15). [Review of the book In praise of single parents: Mothers and fathers embracing the challenge]. Library Journal, 63, 91.

Report

Lance, J. G. (1990). Housing regulations (KU No. 90-16). Lawrence, KS: Media Center.

Nonprint Material

Corborn, W. H. (1990, November 3). "On facing the fears caused by nightmares" [Interview on cassette tape]. Lexington, KY.

Purple, W. C. (Producer). (1990). Hitting the backhand [Videotape]. Nashville: Sports Network.

Note: Personal communications (e.g., letters and personal interviews) are not recoverable data for other researchers. Therefore, do not include them in the reference list. Cite them in the text only, using initials as well as surname, a description of the material, and an exact date:

On this point, W. W. Giltrap (telephone interview, January 12, 1995) has explained the obsessive-compulsive disorders as "exaggerations accompanied by repetition," such as the need to brush one's teeth 20 or 30 times a day.

Electronic Media

Landers, J., Woolfe, R. T., & Balcher, C. (1990). Geometry games: Level two [Computer software]. Emporia, KS: Mediaworks.

Watson, M. W. (1995, February). Solitude and the
homosexual person [7 paragraphs]. <u>Psycoloquy</u> [On-line
serial], <u>6</u>(12). Available E-mail: psyc@pucc Message: Get
psyc 95-35217.

10e WRITING THE ABSTRACT

You should provide an abstract with every paper written in APA style. An abstract is a brief but thorough summary of the contents of your paper. It is read first and may be the only part read, so it must be:

1. *Accurate* in order to reflect both the purpose and content of the paper.
2. *Self-contained* so that it (a) explains the precise problem and defines terminology, (b) describes briefly both the methods used and the findings, and (c) gives an overview of your conclusions (but see item 4 immediately below).
3. *Concise and specific* in order to remain within a range of 80 to 120 words.
4. *Nonevaluative* in order to report information, not to appraise or assess the value of the work.
5. *Coherent and readable* in a style that uses an active, vigorous syntax and that uses the present tense to describe results (e.g., the findings confirm) but the past tense to describe testing procedures (e.g., I attempted to identify).

For theoretical papers, the abstract should include:

- The topic in one sentence
- The purpose, thesis, and scope of the paper
- The sources used (e.g., published articles, books, personal observation)
- Your conclusions and the implications of the study

For a report of an empirical study (see also Section 3b, pages 87–90), the abstract should include:

- The problem and hypothesis in one sentence, if possible
- The subjects (e.g., species, number, age, type)
- The method, including procedures and apparatus
- The findings
- Your conclusions and the implications of the study

10f SAMPLE PAPER IN APA STYLE

The following paper demonstrates the format and style of a paper written to the standards of a working draft in APA style.

The **working draft** is the more traditional form as produced by a typewriter with the courier typeface, with underlining for italics, with a ragged right margin, and with references indented as paragraphs, the idea being that the typesetting system at a publishing house will convert the manuscript to a published form.

The **published form** gives you more freedom with regard to fonts, margins, borders, hanging indentions, and other desk-top publishing features. Check with your instructor if you want to present your paper in the published form. In either case, the paper requires a title page that establishes the running head, an abstract, in-text citations to name and year of each source used, and a list of references.

Marginal notations, below, explain specific requirements.

```
                                           Autism      1


              Running Head: AUTISM
```

This running head will appear at the top of each page.

```
                  Autism: Early Intervention
                in Diagnosing and Educating
                      the Autistic Child

                      Patti M. Bracy

              Austin Peay State University
```

Autism   2

Place the abstract separately on page 2.

Do not use a paragraph indentation for this abstract.

The abstract should not exceed 120 words in length.

                                  Abstract

Autism has been reported as a neurological
dysfunction of the brain that afflicts infants
before age 30 months. Theories about the causes
and the necessary treatment have differed ever since
Kanner (1943) reported his findings that autism
differed from other childhood disorders. Attempts
to treat and detect autism have resulted in new
classifications of the term autism and the discovery
that many children may benefit from early behavioral
training. By diagnosing autism in infants and
toddlers, some autistic children may be trained to
live more independent, normal lives. In recent
years, an attempt has been made to diagnose children
with autism earlier than the standard 4 years by
using home movies to determine early behavioral
characteristics of autism in infants and toddlers.

Autism: Early Intervention in Diagnosing and
Educating the Autistic Child

Autism, a neurological dysfunction of the
brain, which commences before the age of 30 months,
was discovered by Leo Kanner (1943), who studied
11 cases, all of which showed a specific type of
childhood psychosis that was different from other
childhood disorders, although each was similar to
childhood schizophrenia. He described the syndrome
as:

- Extreme autistic aloneness
- Language abnormalities
- Obsessive desire for the maintenance of
  sameness
- Good cognitive potential
- Normal physical development
- Highly intelligent, obsessive, and cold
  parents

Rutter (1978) reduced these symptoms to four
criteria: onset within 30 months of birth, poor
social development, late language development, and
a preference for regular, stereotyped activity.
The American Psychiatric Association (1987) has
limited the definition of autism to three primary
characteristics which must be present before the
age of 3 years:

1. Qualitative impairment in reciprocal social
   interaction
2. Impairment in communication and imaginative
   activity
3. Markedly restricted repertoire of
   activities and interests

Cite the year
immediately
after the name
of the source.

See page 87 for
a discussion of
the paradigm
for the scientific
paper.

Use the past
tense or present
perfect tense
when citing
sources.

In the United States, autism affects one out of
2,500 children and is not usually diagnosed until
the child is between 2 and 5 years of age (Koegel &
Schreibman, 1981). Typically, the child is diagnosed
around the age of 4 years (Siegel, Pliner, Eschler,
& Elliott, 1988). The remarkable story of one
father's ordeal with an autistic child has been
recorded (Martin, 1994).

In recent years, studies have focussed on
infantile and preschool characteristics of autism
in order to detect children with autism earlier.
Many children with autism, if detected early enough
and if enrolled in intensive early intervention
programs, may be admitted into the mainstream of
regular education without any special services
(Lovaas, 1987; Strain & Hoyson, 1988, cited in
Powers, 1992). Early intervention seems to be the
preferred action, especially since the "facilitated
communication" technique was condemned with
vitriolic criticism in 1994. Facilitated
communication requires a person to guide the
autistic's hand over a computer keyboard, but the
person doing the guiding may have more input than
the autistic person (see esp. Berger, 1994).

Accordingly, special qualifying characteristics
have been devised in order to successfully identify
infants with autism. A public policy directive
(PL99-457) has provided money to fund the design of
programs geared especially for the infant or toddler
with disabilities and for their families (Powers,
1992).

Cause

Rutter (1978) listed three possible causes:
behavioral syndrome, organic brain disorder, or a

Margin notes:

Use arabic numbers in the text.

Use "&" in citations, not in the text.

Use underscored headings to mark divisions within a paper in APA style.

range of biological and psychosocial factors. In 1994, Rutter acknowledged that the "organic basis of autism" was generally agreed upon (Rutter, Bailey, Bolton, & Le Couteur, 1994, p. 311).

Gallagher, Jones, and Byrne (1990) surveyed professionals in the mental health field for opinions about the causes of autism. Gallagher et al. explained the study in this manner:

> The results of the segment of the analysis exhibited in Table 1 [shown on the next page] can be summarized straightforwardly: Biogenic factors clearly dominate psychiatrists' current attitudes toward etiological theories of infantile autism. Among the biogenic factors, by far the prominent choice is "biochemical imbalance," with a perceived strength-of-relationship mean value about midway between "related" and "strongly-related." (p. 936)

For three to five authors, list all authors at first use; thereafter use "et al." with the lead author's name.

Explain tables in the text.

Indent long quotations of 40 words or more 5 additional spaces, and omit the quotation marks.

Page numbers go outside the final period after a long quotation.

Behavior

The behavior of the autistic child has been reported (Fay, 1986; Happé, 1994; Osterling & Dawson, 1994; Rimland, 1984; Vandershaf, 1987). A typical autistic child withdraws into self-imposed privacy, avoids social contact, and avoids the touching hands of others. The child often rocks rhythmically and silently. He or she cannot or will not answer questions, and many autistics cannot or will not speak. Some of them senselessly copy the voices of others, a syndrome called echolalia. Others only emit a few sounds.

They speak "at" people, not "to" them, and they usually avoid eye contact. Many autistic children are hyperactive. They fling their hands,

See pages 225–29 for information on using illustrations and tables.

Autism   6

Table 1

Psychiatrists' Attitudes Toward Etiological Theories of Infantile Autism

Etiological theory	Mean value	Rank
Biochemical imbalance	3.491	1
Genetic inheritance	3.078	2
Brain lesion	3.014	3
Metabolic dysfunction	2.832	4
Prenatal factors	2.821	5
Chromosomal mutation	2.623	6
Maternal deprivation	1.933	7
Cold "intellectualized" parenting	1.752	8
Immune system deficiency	1.718	9
Maternal age	1.714	10
Birth order	1.361	11

Use this form to cite the source of a table.

Note. From "A National Survey of Mental Health Professionals Concerning the Causes of Early Infantile Autism," by B. J. Gallagher, B. J. Jones and M. Byrne, 1990, Journal of Clinical Psychology, 46, p. 936.

flick their fingers, blink their eyes repeatedly, and commit self-injurious behavior (SIB), especially when placed in an unfamiliar area.

Establish abbreviations before you use them alone.

Rutter (1978) has reported four ritualistic behaviors commonly seen with autism:

1. Autistic children may select toys of a specific shape or structure and play.
2. An autistic child may become overattached to a certain toy. The child will want that toy with him or her at all times. Should it be taken away, the child will usually throw a tantrum.

Autism   7

3. The child may have unusual concern for
   numbers, geometric shapes, bus routes, and
   colors.
4. The child maintains a specific routine and
   order, and the child gets perturbed if it
   is changed. (pp. 139-140)

<u>Early Behavior Indications</u>

In an effort to identify autistic children
earlier, Osterling and Dawson (1994) studied
videotapes of autistic children's first birthdays.
In almost every instance, the studied videotape
correctly identified the autistic child under 13
months old. The conclusive behaviors observed by
Osterling and Dawson's study consisted of pointing,
showing objects, looking at others, and orienting
to name. How often a child looked at others was
determined to be the best predictor of autism (see
the Appendix for a bar graph that depicts differences in infants judged to be normal or autistic).

<u>Retrospective Research</u>

In an effort to determine autism as quickly as
possible in infants and toddlers, several studies
have been performed based on a parent's remembrances
before a child was diagnosed with autism (Dahlgren &
Gillberg, 1989; Ornitz, Guthrie, & Farley, 1977).
The problem with these studies was that a parent's
memories after a 4-year interlude were generally
unreliable (Osterling & Dawson, 1994). In an effort
to substantiate the claim that parents generally
suspected a problem long before their children
reached diagnosis, another means of assessment was

Use the past
tense to cite
the work of a
scientist.

Summarize
experiments
and testing
procedures in
your text.

deemed to be necessary to record objectively earlier behaviors of infants and toddlers.

In other research, Massie and Rosenthal (1975) studied home movies of children diagnosed with autism, but determining criteria was difficult due to the differences in quality and dating of the available videotapes (cited in Osterling & Dawson, 1994, p. 248). In some instances, dating was difficult to establish with any close degree of accuracy.

In another study (Adrien et al., 1991, 1992) infants with and without behavioral abnormalities in social, affective, motor, and attentional abilities were studied using home movies. Using an infant behavior checklist, differences were detected during the infants' first year that corresponded to the childrens' current diagnoses (cited in Osterling & Dawson, 1994, p. 248).

For six or more authors, use "et al." in the first and all subsequent instances.

Videotapes of first birthdays were used (Osterling & Dawson, 1994) to determine the differences in behavior of normal and autistic children. Eleven diagnosed autistic children, and 11 normal children were studied. Four questions were used:

1. Are differences between autistic and normal children's behavior apparent at 1 year of age?
2. Can specific behaviors be identified that distinguish autism?
3. Does the early development of children with autism differ between those with and without later documented cognitive delay?
4. Is there any evidence to support the existence of late-onset autism?

<u>Methods</u>

The videotapes of 11 children with autism and 11
children with normal development were used to
determine whether there were differences that could
be noted in the tapes. Although differences were
noted in the settings and quality of the birthday
tapes, factors such as number of people (adults and
children) in groupings, and number of minutes child
was alone on the tape were factored in to provide
consistency.

Established autistic-like and behaviorally
appropriate characteristics were assigned codes,
and the presence or absence of these
characteristics during a 1-minute period were
identified by raters who did not know which
children were autistic or not. The behaviors coded
included:

> Social behaviors consist of looking at
> another's face, looking at the face of another
> while smiling, seeking contact
> with an adult, and imitating the behavior
> of another. Affective behaviors consisted
> of distress and tantrums. Joint attention
> behaviors consisted of pointing, vague point-
> ing (reaching for something in a
> communicative way), showing an object to
> another. Communicative behaviors included
> babbling, saying a word, using a
> conventional gesture such as waving goodbye,
> and following the verbal directions of
> another. Specific autistic behaviors included
> self-stimulatory behavior, covering ears,
> failing to orient to name being called, star-
> ing blankly into space, and

blunt affect. (Osterling & Dawson, 1994, p.
251)

The results of frequencies in the behaviors
of the children are shown in Figure 1 of the
Appendix, page 14. Social and joint attention
behaviors show a marked difference between normal
and autistic children. Communicative behaviors
show a difference but are not as statistically
viable as the first two behaviors. Also the
autistic children showed more autistic symptoms
than the normal children. The study showed that
there are identifiable traits associated with
infant autism.

Discussion

> The discussion should evaluate and interpret the implications of your study.

Early intervention has proven to be beneficial
in educating and assisting children with autism,
especially if the home environment is not adequate
to provide social, physical, cognitive, or emotional
development (Berkson, 1993). Many times, children
that are not diagnosed until school age will not
respond as well to treatment; their defects may have
caused further delay in their normal progress.
Therefore, every effort should be made to identify
infants and preschoolers at risk for autism.

There is hope in the future that both the cause
and the cure for autism will be found. For the
present, early identification and intervention offer
some hope for the children at risk for autism and
their families. Since autism is sometimes outgrown,
childhood treatment offers the best hope for the
autistic person who must try to survive in an alien
environment.

References

Adrien, J., Faure, M., Perrot, A., Hameury, L., Garreau, B., Barthelemy, C., & Sauvage, D. (1991). Autism and family home movies: Preliminary findings. <u>Journal of Autism and Developmental Disorders, 21,</u> 43-49.

Adrien, J., Perrot, A., Sauvage, D., Leddet, I., Larmande, C., Hameury, L., & Barthelemy, C. (1992). Early symptoms in autism from family home movies. <u>Acta Paedopsychiatrica, 55,</u> 71-75.

American Psychiatric Association. (1987). <u>Diagnostic and statistical manual of mental disorders</u> (3rd ed., rev.). Washington, DC: Author.

Berger, J. (1994 February 12). Shattering the silence. <u>New York Times,</u> p.21.

Berkell, D. (1992). <u>Autism: Identification, education, and treatment.</u> Hillsdale, NJ: Lawrence Erlbaum Associates.

Berkson, G. (1993). <u>Children with handicaps: A review of behavioral research.</u> Hillsdale, NJ: Lawrence Erlbaum Associates.

Dahlgren, S., & Gillberg, C. (1989). Symptoms in the first two years of life: A preliminary population study of infantile autism. <u>European Archives of Psychiatry and Neurological Sciences, 238,</u> 169-174.

Fay, M. (1986, September). Child of silence. <u>Life, 9,</u> 84-89.

Gallagher, B., Jones, B., & Byrne, M. (1990). A national survey of mental health professionals concerning the causes of early infantile autism. <u>Journal of Clinical Psychology, 46,</u> 934-939.

Happé, G. (1994). Annotation: Current psychological theories of autism: The "theory of mind" account and rival theories. <u>Journal of Child Psychology and Psychiatry, 35</u>(2), 215-229.

Journal article.

Book.

Magazine article.

Kanner, L. (1943). Autistic disturbances of affective contact. <u>Nervous Child, 2,</u> 217-250.

Koegel, R., & Schreibman, L. (1981). <u>Teaching autistic and other severely handicapped children.</u> Austin: Pro-ed.

Lovaas, O. I. (1987). Behavioral treatment and normal educational and intellectual functioning in young autistic children. <u>Journal of Consulting and Clinical Psychology, 55,</u> 3-9.

Martin, R. (1994). <u>Out of silence: A journey into language.</u> New York: Holt.

Ornitz, E., Guthrie, D., & Farley, A. (1977). The early development of autistic children. <u>Journal of Autism and Childhood Schizophrenia, 7,</u> 207-229.

Osterling, J., & Dawson, G. (1994). Early recognition of children with autism: A study of first birthday home videotapes. <u>Journal of Autism and Developmental Disorders, 24,</u> 247-257.

Powers, M. (1992). Early intervention for children with autism. In D. Berkell, pp. 225-252.

Rimland, B. (1984). <u>Infantile autism.</u> New York: Appleton-Century-Crofts.

Rutter, M. (1978). Diagnosis and definition of childhood autism. <u>Journal of Autism and Childhood Schizophrenia, 8,</u> 139-161.

Rutter, M. (1983). Cognitive deficits in the pathogenesis of autism. <u>Journal of Child Psychology and Psychiatry, 26,</u> 513-531.

Rutter, M., Bailey, A. Bolton, P., & Le Couteur, A. (1994). Autism and known medical conditions: Myth and substance. <u>Journal of Child Psychology and Psychiatry, 35</u>(2), 311-322.

Siegel, B., Pliner, C., Eschler, J., & Elliott, G. R. (1988). How children with autism are diagnosed: Difficulties in identification of children with multiple developmental delays. <u>Developmental and Behavioral Pediatrics, 9</u>(4), 199-204.

Vandershaf, S. (1987, March). Autism: A chemical excess? <u>Psychology Today, 21,</u> 15-16.

Appendix

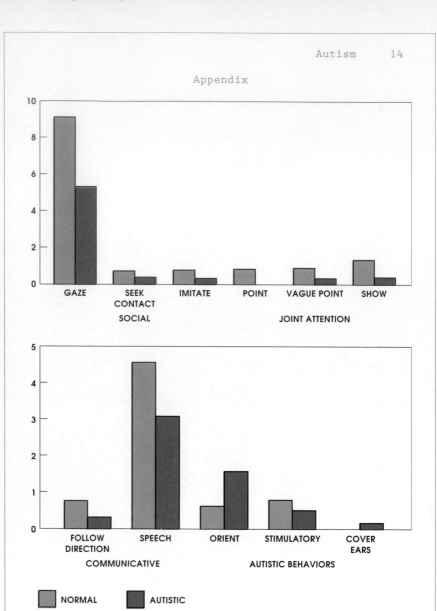

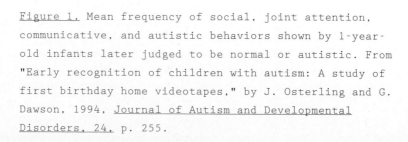

Figure 1. Mean frequency of social, joint attention, communicative, and autistic behaviors shown by 1-year-old infants later judged to be normal or autistic. From "Early recognition of children with autism: A study of first birthday home videotapes," by J. Osterling and G. Dawson, 1994, Journal of Autism and Developmental Disorders, 24, p. 255.

11

Form and Style for Other Disciplines

Every academic discipline has distinctive forms for displaying scholarship, as shown in Chapters 1–9 for literature and modern languages and in Chapter 10 for psychology. When writing papers in physics, biology, music, and other fields, you may need to cite works according to one of these additional formats:

1. The *name and year system* for use in the social sciences, biological and earth sciences, education, linguistics, and business.
2. The *number system* for use in the applied sciences, such as chemistry, computer science, mathematics, physics, and medicine.
3. The *footnote system* for use with papers in the fine arts (art, theater, and music) and humanities (history, philosophy, and religion, but excluding language and literature, which use the MLA style).

Guide, by Discipline

Agriculture, Name and Year, 339
Anthropology, Name and Year, 339
Archaeology, Name and Year, 339
Art, Footnote, 363
Astronomy, Name and Year, 341
Biology, Name and Year, 341
Bio-medical, Number, 351
Botany, Name and Year, 341
Business, Name and Year, 344
Chemistry, Number, 347
Computer Science, Number, 348
Dance, Footnote, 362
Economics, Name and Year, 344
Education, Name and Year, 335
Engineering, Number, 349
Geography, Name and Year, 336
Geology, Name and Year, 342
Health, Number, 351
History, Footnote, 362
Home Economics, Name and Year, 335
Linguistics, Name and Year, 336

Guide, by Discipline

Mathematics, Number, 349
Medicine, Number, 351
Music, Footnote, 363
Nursing, Number, 351
Philosophy, Footnote, 361
Physical Education, Name and
    Year, 337
Physics, Number, 350
Political Science, Name and Year,
    338

Psychology, Name and Year,
    338
Religion, Footnote, 361
Social Work, Name and Year,
    338
Sociology, Name and Year,
    338
Theater, Footnote, 363
Theology, Footnote, 361
Zoology, Name and Year, 341

11a   USING THE NAME AND YEAR SYSTEM

When writing research papers by the name and year system, conform to the following rules (see also Section 10b):

1.   Place the year within parentheses immediately after the authority's name:

```
Smith (1995) ascribes no species-specific behavior to
human beings. However, Adams (1994) presents data that
tend to be contradictory.
```

2.   If you do not mention the authority's name in your sentence, insert the name, year, and even page number(s) in parentheses:

```
Hopkins (1994) found some supporting evidence for a
portion of the questionable data (Marr & Brown, 1994, pp.
23-32) through point bi-serial correlation techniques.
```

3.   For two authors, employ both names (e.g., (Torgerson & Andrews, 1994)). For three to six authors, name them all in the first entry (e.g., (Torgerson, Andrews, & Dunlap, 1994)), but thereafter use "et al.," (e.g., (Torgerson et al., 1995)). For seven or more authors, employ "et al." in the first and all subsequent instances (e.g., (Fredericks et al., 1995).

4.   Use small letters (*a, b, c*) to identify two or more works published in the same year by the same author (e.g., Thompson (1994a) and Thompson (1994b)). Then use "1994a" and "1994b" in your References page (see page 314 for an example).

5.   If necessary, specify additional information. For example:

```
Horton (1995; cf. Thomas, 1993, p. 89) suggests an
intercorrelation of these testing devices. But after
multiple-group analysis, Welston (1995, esp. p. 211)
reached an opposite conclusion.
```

6.   In the case of a direct quotation or paraphrase to a specific page, you must include the author(s), year, *and* page number(s), as follows:

a.   A quotation or paraphrase in the middle of a sentence:

```
He stated, "These data of psychological development
suggest that retarded adolescents are atypical in
maturational growth" (Jones, 1994, p. 215), but he
failed to clarify which data were examined.
```

b.   A quotation or paraphrase at the end of a sentence:

```
Jones (1994) found that "these data of psychological
development suggest that retarded adolescents are
atypical in maturational growth" (p. 215).
```

c.   A long quotation set off from the text in a block (and therefore without quotation marks):

```
Albert (1994) found the following:
     Whenever these pathogenic organisms attack the
     human body and begin to multiply, the infection is
     set in motion. The host responds to this parasitic
     invasion with efforts to cleanse itself of the in-
     vading agents. When rejection efforts of the host
     become visible (fever, sneezing, congestion), the
     disease status exists. (pp. 314-315)
```

7.   Every reference used in your text should appear in your alphabetic list of references at the end of the paper. Because the format differs by discipline, consult the list on pages 333–34 to find the instructions appropriate for your discipline.

Using the Name and Year System for Papers in the Social Sciences

Education	Geography	Home Economics
Linguistics	Physical Education	Political Science
Psychology	Sociology and Social Work	

The disciplines of the social sciences employ the name and year system. In general, the stipulations of the *Publication Manual of the American Psychological Association* (see Chapter 10) have gained wide acceptance, but variations exist by discipline.

Education

In-Text Citation   Use the name and year system as explained on pages 334–35, or in Section 10b, pages 309–312.

List of References   Use the APA style with hanging indention as described in Chapter 10, p. 313, and as illustrated by this list:

```
                    References
Barron, Lloyd H., & Sawanakunanont, Yinda. (1994).
    Strategies utilized one year after participation in
    an in-service elementary science program. Journal
    of Elementary Science Education, 6(2), 52-62.
Casella, Vicki. (1988). Computers-in-the-curriculum
    workshop. Instructor, 97, 128-29.
Dahlberg, Lucy Ann. 1990. Teaching for the information
    age. Journal of Reading, 34, 199-210.
Edelwich, John, and Brodsky, Alex (1980). Burn-Out. New
    York: Human Services Press.
```

> *Note:* **The form of these entries conforms in general to the APA style and to the format of several education journals, such as the** *Journal of Educational Research,* **the** *Elementary School Journal,* **and** *Educational and Psychological Measurement.*

Geography

See the form and style for Sociology and Social Work, page 338.

Home Economics

Use the name and year system as explained on pages 334–35 or in Section 10b, pages 309–312.

Linguistics: LSA (Linguistic Society of America) Style

In-Text Citation   In-text citations for linguistic studies almost always include a specific page reference to the work along with the date, separated by a colon. For example:

```
(Jones 1993: 12-18)
Gifford's recent reference (1994: 162)
```

Therefore, follow basic standards for the name and year system (see pages 334–35) with a colon to separate the year and page number(s).

List of References   As shown in the following example, label the list "References" and alphabetize the entries. Place the year immediately after the name of the author(s). For journal entries, use a period rather than a colon or comma to separate the volume and page. There is *no* use of italics or underscoring. Linguistic journals are abbreviated; others are not. A sample list of references follows:

References

Aristar, Allen. 1994. Review of typology and
     universals, by William Croft. Lg. 70.172-175.

Beal, Carole R., and Susan L. Belgrad. 1990. The
     development of message evaluation skills in young
     children. Child Development 61.705-713.

Birner, Betty J. 1994. Information status and word
     order: An analysis of English inversion. Lg.
     70.233-259.

Burnam, Tom. 1988. A misinformation guide to grammar.
     Writer's Digest 68.36-39.

Chomsky, Noam. 1965. Aspects of the theory of syntax.
     Cambridge, MA: MIT Press

------. 1975. Reflections on language. New York:
     Pantheon.

De Boysson-Bardies, Bénédicte, and Marilyn M. Vihman.
     1991. Adaptation to language: Evidence from
     babbling and first words in four languages. Lg.
     67.287-319.

Jacobsson, Bengt. 1988. Should and would in factual
     that-clauses. English Studies 69.72-81.

Ross, John R. 1967. Constraints on variables in
     syntax. MIT dissertation.

Singer, Murry, Arthur C. Graesser, and Tom Trabasso.
     1994. Minimal or global interference during
     reading. Journal of Memory and Language 33.421-441.

> *Note:* **The form of these entries conforms in general to that ad-
> vocated by the Linguistic Society of America, *LSA Bulletin,* No. 71
> (December 1976), 43–45; the annual December issue; and the
> form and style practiced by the journal *Language.***

Physical Education

In-Text Citation   Use the name and year system as explained on pages 334–35 or in Section 10b, pages 309–312.

List of References Follow the form and style for Education, pages 335–36.

Political Science

In-Text Citation Use the name and year system as explained on pages, 334–35, or in Section 10b, pages 309–312.

List of References Follow the form and style for Sociology, see below, this page.

Psychology: APA Style

See Chapter 10.

Sociology and Social Work

In-Text Citation Use the name and year system as explained on pages 334–35 and in Section 10b, pages 309–312.

List of References Use APA style (see Chapter 10) or the format shown here, which duplicates the style of the *American Journal of Sociology*.

```
                         References
Berezin, Mabel.  1994.  "Cultural Form and Political
     Meaning: State-subsidized Theater, Ideology, and
     the Language of Style in Fascist Italy." American
     Journal of Sociology 99:1237-86.
Dowrick, Stephanie.  1994.  Intimacy and Solitude.  New
     York: Norton.
Epstein, Edwin M.  1980.  "Business and Labor under the
     Federal Election Campaign Act of 1971."  Pp.
     107-151 in Parties, Interest Groups, and Campaign
     Finance Laws, edited by Michael J. Malbin.
     Washington, DC: American Enterprise Institute for
     Public Policy Research.
Gest, Ted.  1994.  "Crime's Bias Problem."  U.S. News &
     World Report July 25:31-32.
```

Using the Name and Year System for Papers in the Biological and Earth Sciences

Agriculture	**Anthropology**	**Archaeology**	**Astronomy**
Biology	**Botany**	**Geology**	**Zoology**

The disciplines of this major grouping employ the name and year system. In general, the rules of APA style (see Chapter 10) match the documentation standards of these disciplines, especially for the in-text citations. However, stylistic variations do exist for the reference lists, as explained and demonstrated below.

Agriculture

In-Text Citation   Use the name and year system as explained on pages 334–35 or in Section 10b, pages 309–312.

List of References   In general, the form and style follows that for other disciplines using the name and year system. In this field, use hanging indentions of 5 spaces, abbreviations, journal titles,and no spaces between volume, issue, and page numbers.

References

Akayezu, J. M., et al. 1994. Evaluation of calf starters containing different amounts of crude protein for growth of Holstein calves. J. of Dairy Sci. 77.7:1882-89.

Benson, D. 1994. Dirt: The lowdown on growing a garden with style. New York: Dell.

Brotherton, I. 1990. On the voluntary approach to resolving rural conflict. Environ. & Plan Ag. 64:923.

Celis, W. 1988. Tax changes hit groups in land conservation. Wall Street J. Jan. 26:38.

Corring, T., A. Aumaitre, and G. Durand. 1978. Development of digestive enzymes in the piglet from birth to 8 weeks. Nutr. Metab. 22:231.

> *Note:* **The form of these entries conforms, in general, to that found in numerous agriculture journals, especially** *Animal Science,* *Journal of Animal Science,* **and** *Journal of the American Society for Horticultural Science.*

Anthropology and Archaeology

In-Text Citation   Use the name and year system as explained on pages 334–35 or in Section 10b, pages 309–312.

List of References Label the list "References Cited," and set the author's name and the date to the left, as shown here:

References Cited

Anderson, Jonathan W.

1994 Review of Spiritual Discourse: Learning with an Islamic Master, by Frances Trix. American Anthropologist 96:480-481.

Bastien, Joseph

1978 Mountain of the Condor: Metaphor and Ritual in an Andean Ayllu. American Ethnological Society Monograph 64. St. Paul, MN: West Publishing Co.

Binford, Louis R.

1962 Archaeology as Anthropology. American Antiquity 28:217-225.

Briody, Elizabeth K., and Marietta L. Baba

1991 Explaining Differences in Repatriation Experiences: The Discovery of Coupled and Decoupled Systems. American Anthropologist 93:322-344.

Dubinskas, Frederick A.

1988a [ed.] Making Time: Ethnographies of High-Technology Organizations. Philadelphia, PA: Temple University Press.

1988b Janus Organizations: Scientists and Managers in Genetic Engineering Firms. In Making Time: Ethnographies of High-Technology Organizations. Pp. 170-232. Philadelphia, PA: Temple University Press.

Dye, Daniel S.

1949 A Grammar of Chinese Lattice. 2nd ed. Harvard-Yenching Monograph Series VI. Cambridge: Harvard University Press.

Jennings, J. D.

1978 Origins. In J. D. Jennings, ed. Ancient Native Americans. Pp. 1-41. San Francisco: Freeman.

McLaren, Peter L.

1988 The Liminal Servant and the Ritual Roots of Critical Pedagogy. Language Arts 65:164-180.

Note: **The form of these entries is based upon the stylistic format of the journal** *American Anthropologist.*

Astronomy

See format and style for geology, pages 342–44.

Biology/Botany/Zoology: CBE (Council of Biology Editors) Style

The Council of Biology Editors has issued a new 1994 edition of its style manual, *Scientific Style and Format: The CBE Manual for Authors, Editors, and Publishers*. This guide advocates two citation and reference styles: (1) the name and year system for general biological studies (shown following) and (2) the number system for bio-medical papers (see "Using the Number System for Papers in the Medical Sciences," pages 351–52, especially the list of references on pages 356–57).

In-Text Citation Use a variation of the name and year system as explained on pages 334–35 or in Section 10b, pages 309–312, but do not use a comma between the name and year, as demonstrated with this example:

> This investigation (Logan 1994) has broken new ground in its findings on the herb as a medicinal agent. Walker and Tidwell (1995, pp. 45-56) suggest that "many other herbs may have these same effects, but research remains limited." Caution has been advised (Morgan 1994) because one herb has been identified as a potential poison if misapplied (Borders and Funderberg 1994).

Note: Do use a comma to distinguish between same-year (Smith 1994a, 1994b) or different-year citations (Johnson 1994, 1995).

List of References Alphabetize the list, and label it "Cited References." Keyboard the first line of each entry flush left; indent the second line and other succeeding lines 2 spaces. For books, list the author(s) with initials jammed together (JM.), year of publication, title, place, publisher, and total number of pages (optional). For articles, list the author(s), year of publication, article title, journal title, volume number, and inclusive pages. Add the issue number and/or a specific date for magazines and journals paged anew with each issue.

Cited References

Argyres, A., Schmitt, J. 1991. Microgeographic structure of morphological and life history traits in a natural population of <u>Impatiens capensis</u>. Evolution 45:178-89.

Atwell, J. 1994. Characterization of pilin genes from seven serologically defined prototype strains of <u>moraxella bovis</u>. Journal of Bacteriology 176:4875-82.

Bateson, P. 1978. Sexual imprinting and optimal out-crossing. Nature 273:659-660.

Bertin, RI. 1982. Paternity and fruit production in trumpet creeper (<u>Campsis radicans</u>). American Naturalist 119:694-709.

Ephron, B. 1982. The jackknife, the bootstrap, and other resampling plans. Philadelphia: Society for Industrial and Applied Mathematics.

Handel, S. 1983. Pollination ecology, plant population structure, and gene flow. In: Real, L., editor. Pollination biology. Orlando: Academic Press. p 163-211.

> *Note:* **The form of these entries conforms in general to the style of** *Scientific Style and Format: The CBE Manual for Authors, Editors, and Publishers.* **6th ed. (New York: Cambridge University Press, 1994).**

Geology

The United States Geological Survey sets the standards for geologic papers, as explained in the following.

In-Text Citation Use the name and year system as explained on pages 334–35 or in Section 10b, pages 309–12, and as demonstrated with this example:

In view of Niue's position as a former volcanic island rising from a submarine plateau (Schowater, 1994), it might be further speculated that it has a late-stage, silicic, peralkaline phase (Thomas, 1994, pp. 344-345). Such melts readily lose significant amounts of uranium and other elements on crystallization (Holt et al., 1991; Haffty and Nobel, 1992; Day and Webber, 1994), which are available to contemporary or later hydrothermal systems (Wallace, 1992).

List of References Label the bibliography "Literature Cited," and list only those works mentioned in the paper. If you list references not used in the paper, label the page "Selected Bibliography." Alphabetize the list. For books, list the author(s), followed by a comma; the year of publication, followed by a comma; the title of the work with only the first word, proper names, and first word after a colon capitalized, followed by a colon; the place of publication, followed by a comma; the publisher, followed by a comma; total pages, followed by a period. For journals, list the author, followed by a comma; the year of publication, followed by comma; the title of the article with only the first word, proper nouns, and first word after a colon capitalized, followed by a colon; the name of the journal, abbreviated but not italicized or underscored, followed by a comma; the volume number with lower case *v.* (e.g., v. 23), followed by a comma; the inclusive page numbers preceded by one *p.* Add other notations for issue number, maps, illustrations, plates, and so forth (see the Mattson entry in the following list of references).

Literature Cited

Banner, J. L., and Kaufman, J., 1994, The isotopic record of ocean chemistry and diagenesis preserved in non-luminescent brachiopods from Mississippian carbone rocks, Illinois and Missouri: Geo. Soc. of Amer. Bull., v. 106, p. 1074-1082.

Bowler, S., 1990a, Unprecedented damage as earthquake occurs close to surface: New Sci., v. 126, 30 June, p. 31.

----- 1990b, When will a big quake hit eastern US?: New Sci., v. 127, 29 Sept., p. 26.

----- 1991, Alaska quake spurs huge wave: New York Times, 22 Feb., p. A18.

Donath, F. A., 1963, Strength variation and deformational behavior in anisotropic rock, p. 281-197 <u>in</u> Judd, Wm. R., Editor, State of stress in the earth's crust: New York, American Elsevier Publishing Co., Inc., 732 p.

Friedlander, G., Kennedy, J. W., and Miller, J. M., 1964, Nuclear and radiochemistry: New York, John Wiley and Sons, 585 p.

Heard, H. C., Turner, F. J., and Weiss, L. E., 1965, Studies of heterogeneous strain in experimentally deformed calcite, marble, and phyllite: Univ. of Calif. Pub. in Geol. Sci., v. 46, p. 81-152.

Hill, M. L., and Troxel, B. W., 1966, Tectonics of Death Valley region, California: Geol. Soc. of Amer. Bull., v. 77, p. 435-438.

Mattson, Peter H., 1979, Subduction, buoyant braking,
   flipping, and strike-slip faulting in the northern
   Caribbean: J. of Geol., v. 87, no. 3, p. 293-304, 3
   figs., map.

Note: **The form of these geology entries conforms to the style of**
Geological Society of America Bulletin* and to *Suggestions to Au-
***thors of the Reports of the United States Geological Survey,* 6th**
ed. (Washington, D.C.: Dept. of the Interior, 1991), and to the
Journal of Geology* and *Journal of Geological Education.

Using the Name and Year System for Papers in Business and Economics

In-Text Citation   Use the name and year system as explained on pages 334–35 or in Section 10b, pages 309–312.

List of References   Consult with your instructor. Many business instructors endorse APA style (see Section 10d, pages 313–318) because it is used in many business journals, such as *Journal of Marketing Education, Applied Financial Economics,* and *Applied Economics.* For other instructors, you may need to modify APA style to conform with another set of business journals, such as *Journal of Marketing* or *Journal of Marketing Research.* If modification is required, do so in this manner:

1. Separate two authors with *and,* not *&.*
2. Use capitals for all major words in titles of books and articles.
3. Enclose the title of an article within quotation marks.
4. Use commas to separate items in a journal reference.
5. Do not italicize or underscore the volume number.

References

Addison, J. T., and Hirsch, B. T. (1989), "Union
   Effects on Productivity, Profits and Growth: Has
   the Long Run Arrived?" <u>Journal of Labor Economics</u>,
   7, 72-105.
Anderson, J. E. (1981), "Cross-Section Tests of
   the Heckscher-Ohlin Theorem: Comment," <u>American
   Economic Review</u>, 71, 1037-1039.
Antyoulatos, A. A. (1994), "Credit Rationing and Ratio-
   nal Behavior," <u>Journal of Money, Credit and
   Banking</u>, 26, 182-202.

Carter, A. (1970), <u>Structural Change in the American Economy</u>. Cambridge: Harvard University Press.

Celis, W. (March 1, 1991), "Study Urges a Preschool Role for Businesses," <u>New York Times</u>, A2.

Chirls, S. B. (Jan. 7, 1988), "Yule Workout Leaves Retailers in Good Shape," <u>Daily News Record</u>, 1-2.

Deardorff, A. V. (1979), "Weak Links in the Chain of Comparative Advantage," <u>Journal of International Economics</u>, 9, 197-209.

Deardorff, A. V. (1980), "The General Validity of the Law of Comparative Advantage," <u>Journal of Political Economy</u>, 88, 941-957.

Dooley, M., and Isard, P. (May 1979), "The Portfolio-Balance Model of Exchange Rates," International Finance Discussion Paper No. 141, Federal Reserve Board.

Doti, J. (Jan. 1978), "An Economic Theory of Shopping Behavior," Center for Economic Research Report No. 3, Chapman College.

Ellis, J. (June 1985), "Starting a Small Business Inside a Big One," <u>Money</u>, 85-86, 88, 90.

"An Updated Yardstick for GNP Growth," <u>Business Week</u>, (10 June 1985), 18.

> *Note:* The form of these economics entries is based in general upon the style and format of *Applied Economics* and the *Economics Journal.*

11b USING THE NUMBER SYSTEM

The number system is used in the applied sciences (chemistry, computer science, engineering, mathematics, and physics) and in the medical sciences (bio-medicine, health, medicine, and nursing). In simple terms, it requires an in-text *number,* rather than the year, and references at the end of the paper are numbered to correspond to the in-text citations. Writers in these fields conform to several general regulations that apply to all applied sciences.

After completing a list of references, assign a number to each entry. Use one of two methods for numbering the list: (1) arrange references in alphabetic order, and number them consecutively (in which case, of course, the numbers will not appear in consecutive order in the text); or (2) forego an alphabetic arrangement, and number the references consecutively as they appear in the text, interrupting that order when entering references cited earlier.

The bibliographic entries are always preceded by a numeral. When writing a rough draft, use the numbers as in-text citations. You can, of course, use the number with the name of the authority. In both cases the number serves as a key reference to the source, as listed at the end of the paper. If you quote a source, add specific page numbers to the bibliographic entry (see examples in the reference lists that follow) or add page numbers to your in-text citations. Conform to the following guidelines:

1.   Place the number within parentheses (1) or brackets [2] alone or with the name(s) of the source:

> In particular, the recent paper by Hershel, Hobbs,
> and Thomason (1) has raised many interesting questions
> related to photosynthesis, some of which were answered
> by Skelton (2).

An alternative, used by several disciplines and their journals, is to use a raised superscript number:

> In particular, the recent paper by Hershel, Hobbs,
> and Thomason[1] has raised many interesting questions
> re-lated to photosynthesis, some of which were answered
> by Skelton.[2]

2.   If your text does not mention the authority's name, employ one of the following two methods:

   a. Insert the number only, enclosing it within parentheses or brackets, or using a superscript number:

> It is known (1) that the DNA concentration of a nucleus
> doubles during interphase.

> It is known[1] that the DNA concentration of a nucleus
> doubles during interphase.

   b. Insert both name and number:

> Additional observations include alterations in
> carbonhydrate metabolism (Evans, 3), changes in ascorbic
> acid incorporation into the cell (Dodd and Williams, 11)
> and adjoining membranes (Holt and Zimmer, 7).

3.   If necessary, add specific data to the entry:

> "The use of photosynthesis in this application is
> crucial to the environment" (Skelton,[8] p. 732).

The results of the respiration experiment published by Jones (3, Table 6, p. 412) had been predicted earlier by Smith (5, Proposition 8).

Using the Number System for Papers in the Applied Sciences

Chemistry	**Computer Science**	**Engineering**
Mathematics	**Physics**	

The disciplines of the applied sciences employ the number system, but variations by field exist both in text citations and in entries of the list of references.

Chemistry: ACS (American Chemical Society) Style

In-Text Citation   You may use one of two styles. Check with your chemistry instructor for his or her preference.

1. Use raised superscript numerals as references occur:

The stereochemical features of arene molecules chemisorbed on metal surfaces cannot be assessed precisely.[3-5]

2. Place the reference numbers within parentheses:

However, composite statistics from theoretical calculations (6) and chemical studies (7-10) indicate that benzene is often chemisorbed.

Number your references in consecutive order as used, *not* in alphabetic order. If a reference is repeated, use the original number, not a new one.

List of References   Label the list "References." List entries as they occur in the text, not in alphabetic order. The basic forms for chemical entries are demonstrated in the following example. Titles of journal articles are not listed at all. Dates of journal articles are placed in boldface (**1994**) or marked for boldface (1994), but dates of books are not. A sample list follows:

References

(1) Mouscadet, J., et al. J. Biol. Chem. 1994, 269, 21635-21643.

(2) Duffey, J. L.; Kurth, M. L. J. Organ. Chem. 1994, 59, 3783-3785.

(3) "Selected Values of Chemical and Thermodynamic Properties." Natl. Bur. Stand. (U.S.) Circ. 1950, No. 500.

(4) Humphries, R. B. In <u>High School Chemistry</u>, 3rd ed.;
    Lamm, Nancy, Ed.; Lumar Press: New York, 1984; Vol.
    III, Ch. 6.

(5) Terrel, L. <u>J. Chem</u>. <u>1960</u>, <u>34</u>, 256; <u>Chem. Abstr</u>.
    <u>1961</u>, <u>54</u>, 110a.

(6) Cotton, F. A. <u>J. Am. Chem. Soc</u>. <u>1968</u>, <u>90</u>, 6230.

(7) (a) Sievert, A. C.; Muetterties, E. L. <u>Inorg. Chem</u>.
    <u>1981</u>, <u>20</u>, 489. (b) Albright, T. A., unpublished
    data, <u>1984</u>.

Note: The in-text citation may refer to 7, 7a, or 7b.

(8) Jones, R. C. <u>Modern Chemistry</u>; Zurtcher: New York,
    1991; pp 152-198.

Note: **The form of these chemistry entries conforms to the** *ACS Style Guide: A Manual for Authors and Editors.* **Ed. Janet S. Dodd. (Washington, D.C.: American Chemical Society, 1986).**

Computer Science

In-Text Citation   Use raised superscript numerals (as shown for Chemistry, page 347) and then number them in consecutive order by appearance in the paper, not in alphabetic order.

List of References   Label the list "Works Cited." Number the references according to their appearance in the text, not by alphabetic order. For books, titles are italicized or underscored; the publisher precedes the city of publication; and specific page(s) of books need not be listed, but in-text citation should specify pages for paraphrases and direct quotations. For journals, the title of the article is provided within quotation marks, with first word, title, proper nouns, and first word after a colon capitalized; the title of the journal and volume number are italicized or underscored; and the issue number is provided whenever available, preceding the date and page number(s). A sample follows:

Works Cited

1. Globus, A.; and Raible, E. "Fourteen ways to say
   nothing with scientific visualization." <u>Computer</u> <u>27</u>
   (July 1994), 73-83.

2. Stonebraker, M. "Future trends in database systems."
   <u>IEEE Trans. Knowledge and Data Eng</u>. <u>1</u> (1) (Mar.
   1989), 33-44.

3. Aho, A. V.; Hopcroft, J. E.; and Ullman, J. D. <u>The Design and Analysis of Computer Algorithms</u>. Addison-Wesley, Reading, Mass., 1974.

4. Gligor, V. D.; and Shattuck, S. H. "On deadlock detection in distributed systems." <u>IEEE Trans. Softw. Eng</u>. <u>SE-6</u> (5) (Sept. 1980), 435-40.

5. Sklansky, J.; and Wassel, G. N. <u>Pattern Classifiers and Trainable Machines</u>. Springer-Verlag, New York, 1981.

6. Holt, R. C. "Some deadlock properties of computer systems." <u>Computer Surv</u>. <u>4</u> (3) (Sept. 1972), 179-96.

7. Nelson, T. "On the Xanadu project." <u>Byte</u> <u>15</u> (Sept. 1990), 298-99.

Engineering

See the form and style for Physics, pages 350–51.

Mathematics: AMS (American Mathematical Society) Style

In-Text Citation   First alphabetize and then number the list of references. Label the list "References." All in-text citations are then made to the reference number, which you should place in your text within brackets as boldface or marked as boldface (wavy line). For example:

In addition to the obvious implications it is already known from [5] that every d-regular Lindelof space is D-normal. Further results on D-normal spaces will appear in [8], which is in preparation. The results obtained here and in [2], [3], and [5] encourage further research.

List of References   For books, the titles are italicized or underscored, the publisher precedes the city of publication, and the specific page(s) of books need not be listed. For journals, the title of the article is italicized or underscored, the journal title is *not* italicized or underscored, the volume is placed in boldface or marked for boldface (wavy line), the year of publication follows within parentheses, and the complete pagination of the article comes last. A sample list follows:

References

1. R. Artzy, <u>Linear geometry</u>, Addison-Wesley, Reading, Mass., 1965.

2. H. Colonius and D. Vorberg, <u>Distribution inequalities for parallel models with unlimited capacity</u>, J. Math. Psy. <u>38</u> (1994), 35-58.

3. I. M. Isaacs and D. S. Passman, <u>Groups with representations of bounded degree</u>, Canad. J. Math. <u>16</u> (1964), 299-309.

4. -------, <u>Characterization of groups in terms of the degrees of their characters</u>, Pacific J. Math. <u>15</u> (1965), 877-903.

5. L. J. Meconi, <u>Number bases revisited</u>, Sch. Science & Math. <u>90</u> (1990), 396-403.

6. O. Solbrig, <u>Evolution and systematics</u>, Macmillan, New York, 1966.

Note: **The form of these entries conforms to *A Manual for Authors of Mathematical Papers,* rev. ed. (Providence, R.I.: American Mathematical Society, 1990).**

Physics: AIP (American Institute of Physics) Style

In-Text Citation   Use raised superscript numerals, like this.[12] Number the list of references in consecutive order of in-text usage, not in alphabetic order.

List of References   For books, titles are italicized or underscored, the name of the publisher precedes the place of publication, and specific page reference *should* be provided. For journals, the title of the article is omitted entirely, the title of the journal is abbreviated and *not* italicized or underscored, the volume is placed in boldface or marked for boldface (wavy line), and the year within parentheses follows the pagination. A sample list follows:

References

[1] T. Fastie, W. G., Physics Today <u>44</u>, 37-44 (1991).

[2] C. D. Motchenbacher and F. C. Fitchen, <u>Low-Noise Electronic Design</u> (Wiley, New York, 1973), p. 16.

[3] L. Monchick, S., Chem. Phys. <u>71</u>, 576 (1979).

[4] F. Riesz and B. Nagy, <u>Functional-Analysis</u> (Ungar, New York, 1955), Secs. 121 and 123.

[5] G. E. Brown and M. Rho, Phys. Lett. <u>82</u>B, 177 (1979); G. E. Brown, M. Rho, and V. Vento, Phys. Letts. <u>84</u>B, 383

(1979); Phys Rev Ḏ2̱2̱, 2838 (1980); Phys Rev. Ḏ2̱4̱, 216
(1981).

[6]Marc D. Levenson, Phys. Today 3̱0̱(5), 44-49 (1977).

Note: **The form of these entries conforms to** *Style Manual for
Guidance in the Preparation of Papers for Journals Published
by the American Institute of Physics,* **3rd ed. (New York: American Institute of Physics, 1978).**

Using the Number System for Papers in the Medical Sciences

Health   Medicine   Nursing   Bio-Medicine

Like other applied sciences, the medical sciences, as a general rule,
employ the number system. Variations among medical journals do exist, so
consult your instructor about the proper format.

In-Text Citation   For citations that occur in the text, use numbers in
parentheses or superscript numerals. See the explanation and examples in
Section 11b, pages 345–46.

List of References   Label the list "References." Do not alphabetize
the list; rather, number it to correspond to sources as you cite them in the
text. For books, list the author(s); the title, italicized or underscored and
with all major words capitalized; the place; the publisher; and the year of
publication. For journals, list the author; the title of the article without quotation marks and with proper nouns, first words, and the first word after a
colon capitalized; the name of the journal, italicized or underscored and
with major words capitalized and abbreviated *without* periods (but followed by a period); the year followed by a semicolon; the volume followed by a colon; and the page number(s). A sample list follows:

References

1. Tardiff, K., et al. Homicide in New York City:
Cocaine use and firearms. JAMA 1994;272:43-52.
2. Miner, K. J., Baker, J. A. Media coverage of
suntanning and skin cancer: Mixed messages of health and
beauty. J Health Ed. 1994;25:234-238.
3. Antonovsky, A. Health, Stress, and Coping. San Francisco, Jossey-Bass, 1979.
4. Ayman, D. The personality type of patients with
arteriolar essential hypertension. Am J Med Sci.
1983;186:213-233.

5. Nash, P. <u>Authority and Freedom in Education</u>. New York, Wiley, 1966.

6. Green, M. I., Haggery, R. J. (eds). <u>Ambulatory Pediatrics</u>. Philadelphia, W. B. Saunders, 1968.

Note: **The form of these entries represents a general standard as established by (1) the American Medical Association,** *Style Book: Editorial Manual,* **6th ed. (Acton, Mass.: Publishing Sciences Group, Inc., 1976); (2)** *Scientific Style and Format: The CBE Manual for Authors, Editors, and Publishers;* **and by numerous medical journals, such as** *JAMA, Nutrition Reviews, Journal of American College Health,* **and others.**

Sample Paper Using the Number System

The following paper demonstrates the format for a paper in the applied sciences and the medical sciences. It is recommended that you use numbers within parentheses rather than raised superscript numbers in order to simplify the task of keyboarding the paper. However, your instructor may require the superscript numbering.

Autism 1

Patti M. Bracy

May 8, 1994

      Autism: Early Intervention in Diagnosing and

             Educating the Autistic Child

      Autism, a neurological dysfunction of the brain

which commences before the age of thirty months, was

discovered by Leo Kanner (1), who studied 11

cases, all of which showed a specific type of

childhood psychosis that was different from

other childhood disorders, although each was similar

to childhood schizophrenia. He described the

characteristics of the early infantile syndrome as:

- Extreme autistic aloneness
- Language abnormalities
- Obsessive desire for the maintenance of
  sameness
- Good cognitive potential
- Normal physical development
- Highly intelligent, obsessive, and cold
  parents

Further investigation (2) reduced these symptoms to

four criteria: onset within 30 months of birth,

poor social development, late language development,

and a preference for regular, stereotyped activity.

Autism's characteristics have been identified (3):

    1. Qualitative impairment in reciprocal social
       interaction

    2. Impairment in communication and imaginative
       activity

    3. Markedly restricted repertoire of
       activities and interests

      In the United States, autism affects one out

of 2,500 children, and is not usually diagnosed

until the child is between two and five years of

age (4). Typically, the child is diagnosed

Cite a number immediately after the name of the source.

Autism 2

around the age of 4 years (5). The remarkable story of one father's ordeal with an autistic child has been recorded (6).

In recent years, studies have focussed on infantile and preschool characteristics of autism in order to detect children with autism earlier. Many children with autism, if detected early enough and if enrolled in intensive early intervention programs, may be admitted into the mainstream of regular education without any special services (7, 8). Early intervention seems to be the preferred action, especially since the "facilitated communication" technique was condemned with vitriolic criticism in 1994 (9). Facilitated communication requires a person guiding the autistic's hand over a computer keyboard, but the person doing the guiding may have more input than the autistic person.

Accordingly, special qualifying characteristics have been devised in order to successfully identify infants with autism. A public policy directive (PL99-457) has provided money to fund the design of programs geared especially for the infant or toddler with disabilities and their families (8).

Cause

Rutter (10) listed three possible causes: behavioral syndrome, organic brain disorder, or a range of biological and psychosocial factors. In 1994, it was acknowledged (11, p. 311) that the "organic basis of autism" was generally agreed upon.

Refer to several sources in one citation by citing more than one number.

Separate two sources by a comma.

Add a page number if you quote the source.

Note: Omitted pages of this essay can be found in the full essay in APA style in Chapter 10, pages 319–332.

Autism 12

Social and joint attention behaviors show a
marked difference between normal and autistic
children. Communicative behaviors show a
difference but are not as statistically viable
as the first two behaviors. Also the autistic
children showed more autistic symptoms than the
normal children. The study showed that there are
identifiable traits associated with infant autism.

Discussion

Early intervention has proved beneficial (22)
in educating and assisting children with autism,
especially if the home environment is not adequate
to provide social, physical, cognitive, or
emotional development. Many times, a child that is
not diagnosed until school age will not respond as
well to treatment; their defects may have caused
further delay in their normal progress. Therefore,
every effort should be made to identify infants and
preschoolers at risk for autism.

There is hope in the future that both the
cause and the cure for autism will be found. For
the present, early identification and intervention
offers some hope for the children at risk for
autism and their families. Since autism is
sometimes outgrown, childhood treatment offers the
best hope for the autistic person who must try to
survive in an alien environment.

References

The reference list is numbered by appearance of the source in the text, not by alphabetic order.

The citations on this page conform to the style of JAMA and other medical journals.

1. Kanner, L. Autistic disturbances of affective contact. Nervous Child. 1943;2:217-250.

2. Rutter, M. Diagnosis and definition of childhood autism. Journal of Autism and Childhood Schizophrenia. 1978;8:139-161.

3. American Psychiatric Association. Diagnostic and statistical manual of mental disorders. 3rd ed., rev. Washington, DC: Author; 1987.

4. Koegel, R., & Schreibman, L. Teaching autistic and other severely handicapped children. Austin: Pro-ed; 1981.

5. Siegel, B., Pliner, C., Eschler, J., & Elliott, G. R. How children with autism are diagnosed: Difficulties in identification of children with multiple developmental delays. Developmental and Behavioral Pediatrics. 1988;9(4):199-204.

6. Martin, R. Out of silence: A journey into language. New York: Holt; 1994.

7. Lovaas, O. I. Behavioral treatment and normal educational and intellectual functioning in young autistic children. Journal of Consulting and Clinical Psychology. 1987;55:3-9.

8. Powers, M. Early intervention for children with autism. In D. Berkell, Autism: Identification, education, and treatment. Hillsdale, NJ: Erlbaum; 1992, pp. 225-252.

9. Berger, J. Shattering the silence. New York Times 1994 Feb. 12;Sect L:21.

10. Rutter, M. Cognitive deficits in the pathogenesis of autism. Journal of Child Psychology and Psychiatry. 1983;26:513-531.

11. Rutter, M., Bailey, A. Bolton, P., & Le Couteur, A. Autism and known medical conditions: Myth and substance. Journal of Child Psychology and Psychiatry. 1994;35,vol.2:311-322.

12. Gallagher, B., Jones, B., & Byrne, M. A national survey of mental health professionals concerning the causes of early infantile autism. Journal of Clinical Psychology. 1990;46:934-939.

Autism 14

13. Fay, M. Child of silence. Life 1986 Sept:84-89.

14. Happé, G. Annotation: Current psychological theories of autism: The "theory of mind" account and rival theories. Journal of Child Psychology and Psychiatry. 1994;35(2):215-229.

15. Osterling, J., & Dawson, G. Early recognition of children with autism: A study of first birthday home videotapes. Journal of Autism and Developmental Disorders. 1994;24:247-257.

16. Rimland, B. Infantile autism. New York: Appleton-Century-Crofts; 1984.

17. Vandershaf, S. Autism: A chemical excess? Psychology Today 1987 Mar:15-16.

18. Dahlgren, S., & Gillberg, C. Symptoms in the first two years of life: A preliminary population study of infantile autism. European Archives of Psychiatry and Neurological Sciences. 1989;238:169-174.

19. Ornitz, E., Guthrie, D., & Farley, A. The early development of autistic children. Journal of Autism and Childhood Schizophrenia. 1977;7:207-229.

20. Adrien, J., Faure, M., Perrot, A., Hameury, L., Garreau, B., Barthelemy, C., & Sauvage, D. Autism and family home movies: Preliminary findings. Journal of Autism and Developmental Disorders. 1991;21:43-49.

21. Adrien, J., Perrot, A., Sauvage, D., Leddet, I., Larmande, C., Hameury, L., & Barthelemy, C. Early symptoms in autism from family home movies. Acta Paedopsychiatrica. 1992;55:71-75.

22. Berkson, G. Children with handicaps: A review of behavioral research. Hillsdale, NJ: Erlbaum, 1993.

11c USING THE FOOTNOTE SYSTEM

The fine arts and some fields in the humanities (not literature) employ traditional footnotes, which should conform to standards set by the *The Chicago Manual of Style,* 14th ed., 1993. With this system, you must employ superscript numerals within the text, (like this[15]) and place documentary footnotes on corresponding pages. Although no Works Cited page is usually necessary, some instructors may ask for one at the end of the paper; if so, see page 364. The discussion in this section assumes that notes will appear as footnotes. However, some instructors accept endnotes, that is, the grouping of all notes together at the end of the paper, not at the bottom of individual pages (see pages 360–61 and also 219–222).

If available on your software, use the footnote or endnote feature. It will not only insert the raised superscript numbers but also keep your footnotes arranged properly at the bottom of each page. In most instances, the software will first insert the superscript numeral in the text and then skip to the bottom of the page so that you can write the footnote. However, it will not write the note automatically; you must type in the essential data in the correct style.

In-Text Citation: Superscript Numerals   Use arabic numerals typed slightly above the line (like this[12]). Place this superscript numeral at the end of quotations or paraphrases, with the number following immediately without a space after the final word or mark of punctuation, as in this sample:

> Colonel Warner soon rejoined his troops despite severe pain. He wrote in September of 1864: "I was obliged to ride at all times on a walk and to mount my horse from some steps or be helped on. My cains [<u>sic</u>] with which I walked when on foot were strapped to my saddle."[6] Such heroic dedication did not go unnoticed, for the <u>Washington Chronicle</u> cited Warner as "an example worthy of imitation."[7] At Gettysburg Warner's troops did not engage in heavy fighting and suffered only limited casualties of two dead and five wounded.[8]

The use of "[*sic*]" indicates an error, such as a misspelling, in the original quotation. Avoid placing one superscript numeral at the end of a long paragraph because readers will not know whether it refers to the final sentence only or to the entire paragraph. A better strategy is to introduce borrowed materials with an authority's name and then place a superscript numeral at the end. By doing this, you direct the reader to the full extent of the borrowed material.

Footnotes   Place footnotes at the bottom of pages to correspond with superscript numerals. Some papers require footnotes on almost every page. Follow these conventions:

1. *Spacing.* Single-space each footnote, but double-space between footnotes.

2. *Indentation.* Indent the first line 5 spaces.

3. *Numbering.* Number the footnotes consecutively throughout the entire paper.

4. *Placement.* Collect at the bottom of each page all the footnotes to citations made on that page.

5. *Distinguish footnotes from text.* Separate footnotes from the text by triple spacing or, if you prefer, by a 12-space bar line beginning at the left margin.

6. *Footnote form.* Basic forms of footnotes should conform to the following:

For a Book.

    1. James K. Greer, <u>Texas Ranger: Jacks Hays in the
Frontier Southwest</u> (Bryan: Texas A & M University Press,
1994), 28.

For a Journal Article.

    2. Peter Hedstrom, "Contagious Collectivities: On
the Spatial Diffusion of Swedish Trade Unions, 1890-
1940," <u>American Journal of Sociology</u> 99 (1994): 1157-79.

For a Collection.

    3. Lonne Elder, "Ceremonies in Dark Old Men," in
<u>New Black Playwrights: An Anthology</u>, ed. William Couch,
Jr. (Baton Rouge: Louisiana State University Press,
1968), 62-63.

For an Edition with More than Three Authors.

    4. Albert C. Baugh et al., <u>A Literary History of
England</u>. 2d ed. (New York: Appleton, 1967), 602-11.

For a Magazine Article.

    5. Ken Auletta, "Free Speech," <u>The New Yorker</u>, 12
September 1994, 40-43.

For a Newspaper Article.

    6. Karen Grassmuck, "More Small Colleges Merge with
Larger Ones, but Some Find the Process Can Be Painful,"
<u>The Chronicle of Higher Education</u>, 18 September 1991,
sec. A, pp. A37-A39.

For a Review Article.

> 7. Michael Rogers, review of <u>Keats the Poet</u>, by
> Stuart Sperry, <u>Library Journal</u>, 15 March 1994, 105.

7.   *Subsequent footnote references* after a first full reference should be shortened to the name of the author(s) and the page number. When an author has two works mentioned, employ a shortened version of the title (e.g., [3]Jones, *Paine,* 25). In general, avoid Latinate abbreviations such as *loc. cit.* or *op. cit.;* however, whenever a note refers to the source in the immediately preceding note, you may use "Ibid." with a page number as shown below. (Note especially the difference between footnotes 4 and 6.)

> 3. Jerrold Ladd, <u>Out of the Madness: From the</u>
> <u>Projects to a Life of Hope</u> (New York: Warner, 1994), 24.
> 4. Ibid., 27.
> 5. Michael Schulman and Eva Meckler, <u>Bringing Up a</u>
> <u>Moral Child</u>, rev. ed. (New York: Doubleday, 1994), 221.
> 6. Ladd, <u>Out of the Madness</u>, 24.
> 7. Ibid., 27.

8.   *Endnotes.* With permission of your instructor, put all your notes together as a single group of endnotes to make keyboarding your paper easier. Most computer software programs help you with this task by inserting the superscript numerals in the text and by allowing you to keyboard the endnotes consecutively at the end of the text, not at the bottom of each page. Follow these conventions:

a. Begin notes on a new page at the end of the text.
b. Entitle the page "Notes," centered, and placed 2 inches from the top of the page.
c. Indent the first line of each note 5 spaces, number the note followed by a period, begin the note, and use the left margin for succeeding lines.
d. Double-space the notes, and double-space between the notes.
e. Triple-space between the heading and the first note.

Conform to the following sample:

Notes

> 1. Jerrold Ladd, <u>Out of the Madness: From the</u>
> <u>Projects to a Life of Hope</u> (New York: Warner, 1994), 24.
> 2. Ibid., 27.
> 3. Michael Schulman and Eva Meckler, <u>Bringing Up a</u>
> <u>Moral Child</u>, rev. ed. (New York: Doubleday, 1994), 221.

4. W. V. Quine, <u>Word and Object</u> (Cambridge, Mass.: MIT Press, 1966), 8.

5. Schulman and Meckler, 217.

6. Abraham J. Heschel, <u>Man Is Not Alone: A Philosophy of Religion</u> (New York: Farrar, Straus, and Young, 1951), 221.

7. Ladd, <u>Out of the Madness</u>, 24.

8. Ibid., 27.

9. Quine, <u>Word and Object</u>, 9-10.

10. Ladd, <u>Out of Madness</u>, 28.

Using the Footnote System for Papers in the Humanities

History   Philosophy   Religion   Theology

In-Text Citation   Use the form of raised superscript numerals as explained on pages 358–59.

List of References   Place the references at the bottom of each page on which a citation occurs. See explanation above, pages 358–59, and duplicate the form and style of the following footnotes:

Footnotes for a Paper on Religion

1. Stephanie Dowrick, <u>Intimacy and Solitude</u> (New York: Norton, 1994), 23-27.

2. Jo Ann Hackett, "Can a Sexist Model Liberate Us? Ancient New Eastern 'Fertility' Goddesses," <u>Journal of Feminist Studies in Religion</u>, 5 (1989): 457-58.

3. Claude Levi-Strauss, <u>The Savage Mind</u> (Chicago: University of Chicago Press, 1966), 312.

4. Ibid., 314.

5. Edward Evans Evans-Pritchard, <u>Theories of Primitive Religion</u> (Oxford: Clarendon Press, 1965), 45.

6. Evans-Pritchard, <u>Nuer Religion</u>, (Oxford: Clarendon Press, 1956), 84.

7. Evans-Pritchard, <u>Primitive Religion</u>, 46.

8. Patrick T. Humphries, "Salvation Today, Not Tomorrow," Sermon (Bowling Green, KY: First Methodist Church, 1994).

9. Rom. 6:2.

10. 1 Cor. 13:1-3.

11. Report of a Commission Appointed by the
Archbishops of Canterbury and York in 1949, <u>The Church
and the Law of Nullity of Marriage</u>, (London: Society for
Promoting Christian Knowledge, 1955), 12-16.

Footnotes for a History Paper

1. Richard Zacks, <u>History Laid Bare: Love, Sex,
and Perversity from the Ancient Etruscans to Warren G.
Harding</u> (New York: HarperCollins, 1994), 34.

2. Thomas Jefferson, <u>Notes on the State of
Virginia</u> (1784), ed. William Peden (Chapel Hill:
University of North Carolina Press, 1955), 59.

3. Ralph Lerner, <u>Revolutions Revisited: Two Faces
of the Politics of Enlightenment</u> (Chapel Hill:
University of North Carolina Press, 1994), 56-60.

4. <u>Encyclopedia Britannica: Macropaedia</u>, 1974 ed.,
s.v. "Heidegger, Martin."

Note: The abbreviation *s.v.* stands for *sub verbo,* which means "under
the word."

5. Henry Steele Commager, <u>The Nature and Study of
History</u>, Social Science Seminar Series (Columbus, Ohio:
Merrill, 1965), 10.

6. Department of the Treasury, "Financial Opera-
tions of Government Agencies and Funds," <u>Treasury
Bulletin</u> (Washington, D.C.: GPO, June 1974), 134-41.

7. U. S. Constitution, art. 1, sec. 4.

8. United Kingdom, <u>Coroner's Act, 1954</u>, 2 & 3
Eliz. 2, ch. 31.

9. <u>State v. Lane</u>, Minnesota 263 N. W. 608 (1935).

10. Papers of Gen. A. J. Warner (P-973, Service
Record and Short Autobiography), Western Reserve
Historical Society.

11. Ibid., clipping from the <u>Washington Chronicle</u>.

12. Gregory Claeys, "The Origins of the Rights of
Labor: Republicanism, Commerce, and the Construction of
Modern Social Theory in Britain, 1796-1805," <u>The Journal
of Modern History</u> 66 (1994): 249-90.

13. Lerner, 54-55.

Using the Footnote System for Papers in the Fine Arts

Art   **Dance**   **Music**   **Theater**

Documentation for a research paper in the fine arts uses superscript numerals in the text (see pages 358–59).

Endnotes for a Paper in the Fine Arts

Notes

1. Natasha Staller, "Melies's 'Fantastic' Cinema and the Origins of Cubism," <u>Art History</u> 12 (1989): 202-39.

2. There are three copies of the papal brief in the archives of the German College, now situated on Via S. Nicola da Tolentino. The document is printed in Thomas D. Culley, <u>Jesuits and Music</u> (Chicago: Jesuit Historical Institute Press, 1970), I, 358-59.

3. Staller, "Cubism," 214.

4. Denys Hay, ed., <u>The Age of the Renaissance</u>, 2nd ed. (London: Guild, 1986), 286.

5. Aristophanes, <u>The Birds</u>, in <u>Five Comedies of Aristophanes</u>, trans. Benjamin B. Rogers (Garden City, N.Y.: Doubleday, 1955), 1.2.12-14.

6. Jean Bouret, <u>The Life and Work of Toulouse Lautrec</u>, trans. Daphne Woodward (New York: Abrams, n.d.), 5.

7. Cyrus Hoy, "Fathers and Daughters in Shakespeare's Romances," in <u>Shakespeare's Romances Reconsidered</u>, ed. Carol McGinnis Kay and Henry E. Jacobs (Lincoln: University of Nebraska Press, 1978), 77-78.

8. Lionello Venturi, <u>Botticelli</u> (Greenwich, Conn.: Fawcett, n.d.), p. 214, plate 32.

Note: Add "p." for page only if needed for clarity.

9. Cotton Vitellius MSS, A., 15. British Museum.

10. <u>Hamlet</u>, 2.3.2.

11. George Henry Lewes, review of "Letters on Christian Art," by Friedrich von Schlegel, <u>Athenaeum</u> 1117 (1849): 296.

12. Ron Stoppelmann, "Letters," <u>New York</u>, 23 August 1982, 8.

13. The World Book Encyclopedia, 1976 ed., s.v. "Raphael."

14. The Last Tango in Paris, United Artists, 1972.

15. Wolfgang A. Mozart, Jupiter, Symphony No. 41.

16. William Blake, Comus, photographic reproduction in Irene Taylor, "Blake's Comus Designs," Blake Studies 4 (spring 1972): 61, plate 4.

17. Lawrence Topp, The Artistry of Van Gogh (New York: Matson, 1983), transparency 21.

18. Eric Sevareid, CBS News (New York: CBS-TV, 11 March 1975); Media Services Videotape 1975-142 (Nashville: Vanderbilt University, 1975).

19. Daniel Zipperer, "The Alexander Technique as a Supplement to Voice Production," Journal of Research in Singing 14 (June 1991): 1-40.

Writing a Bibliography for a Paper That Uses Footnotes

In addition to footnotes or endnotes, you may need to supply a separate bibliography that lists sources used in developing the paper. Use a heading that represents its contents, such as "Selected Bibliography," "Sources Consulted," or "Works Cited."

If you write completely documented footnotes, the bibliography is redundant. Check with your instructor before preparing one because it may not be required. Separate the title from the first entry with a triple space. Keyboard the first line of each entry flush left; indent the second line and other succeeding lines 5 spaces. Alphabetize the list by last names of authors. List alphabetically by title two or more works by one author. The basic forms are shown here.

For a Book.

Mapp, Alf J., Jr. Thomas Jefferson: A Strange Case of
    Mistaken Identity. New York: Madison, 1987.

For a Journal Article.

Aueston, John C. "Altering the Course of the Constitu-
    tional Convention." Yale Law Journal 100 (1990):
    765-783.

For a Newspaper.

Stephenson, D. Grier, Jr. "Is the Bill of Rights in
    Danger?" USA Today, 12 May 1991, sec. 3, p. 83.

See also the bibliographies that accompany the sample papers, pages 356–57 and 262–63.

Appendix*
Reference Sources

Index to List of Reference Sources, by Discipline

African-American Literature, 383
African-American Studies (see Ethnic Studies, 374)
American Fiction (see Novel, the, 386, and Short Story, 387)
American Literature, 384
Art, 366
Asian-American Studies (see Ethnic Studies, 373
Biological Sciences, 367
British Fiction (see Novel, the, 386, and Short Story, 387)
British Literature, 384
Business, 368 (see also Economics, 371)
Chemistry and Chemical Engineering, 369
Computer Science, 369
Drama and Theater, 385
Ecology, 370
Economics, 371 (see also Business, 368)
Education, 371
Electronics, 372
English Language Studies (see Literature and Language, 383)
Environmental Studies (see Ecology, 370)
Ethnic Studies, 373
Feminist Literature (see Women's Studies, 396)

Folklore (see Mythology and Folklore, 385)
French Language Studies, 375
Geography, 377
Geology, 378
German Language Studies, 375
Government (see Political Science, 391–92)
Health and Physical Education, 379
Hispanic-American Studies (see Ethnic Studies, 374)
History, 380
Journalism and Mass Communications, 381
Latin Language Studies, 375
Law, 382
Literature and Language Studies, 383
Mass Communications (see Journalism and Mass Communications, 381)
Mathematics, 387
Medical Studies, 388
Music, 389
Mythology and Folklore, 385
Native American Studies (See Ethnic Studies, 373)
Novel, the, 386
Nursing (see Medical Studies, 388)
Philosophy, 390
Physics, 391
Physical Education (see Health and Physical Education, 379–80)
Political Science, 391
Psychology, 393
Religion, 394
Russian Language Studies, 375

*Revised and annotated by Anne May Berwind, head of Library Information Services, Austin Peay State University.

Short Story, 387
Social Work (*see* Sociology and Social Work, 395–96)
Sociology and Social Work, 395
Spanish Language Studies, 376
Sports (*see* Health and Physical Education, 379)
Theater (*see* Drama and Theater, 385)
Women's Studies, 396
World Literature, 387

List of Reference Sources, by Discipline

The double asterisk(**) before an entry signals a particularly important source within a discipline. A brief annotation explains the nature of these special reference works.

Art

Basic Sources and Guides to Art Literature

American Art Directory. New York: Bowker, 1952–present.

American Graphic Design, A Guide to the Literature. Westport, CT: Greenwood, 1992.

Art Research Methods and Resources: A Guide to Finding Art Information. Ed. L. S. Jones. Dubuque, IA: Kendall/Hunt, 1985.

A Biographical Dictionary of Women Artists in Europe and America Since 1850 . Ed. P. Dunford. Philadelphia: U of Pennsylvania P, 1990.

Britannica Encyclopedia of American Art. Ed. M. Rugoff. Chicago: Encyclopaedia Britannica, 1973.

Contemporary Architects. 2nd ed. Chicago: St. James, 1987.

Contemporary Artists. 3rd ed. New York: St. James, 1989.

Contemporary Designers. 2nd ed. Chicago: St. James, 1990.

Contemporary Photographers. 2nd ed. Chicago: St. James, 1988.

Dictionary of American Painters, Sculptors, and Engravers. Ed. M. Fielding. Poughkeepsie, NY: Apollo, 1986.

Dictionary of Contemporary American Artists. 5th ed. New York: St. Martin's, 1988.

Encyclopedia of Architecture: Design, Engineering, and Construction. Ed. S. A. Wilkes and R. T. Packard. 5 vols. New York: Wiley, 1988–1990.

**Encyclopedia of World Art.* 15 vols. New York: McGraw, 1959–1968. Supplements, 1983 and 1987.
An international, scholarly encyclopedia covering all aspects of art. Articles are historical (e.g, baroque art), conceptual (e.g., biblical subjects), and geographic (e.g., Americas), so it's best to use the index volume to locate information on a particular subject or artist.

Fletcher, B. *A History of Architecture.* 18th ed. New York: Scribner's, 1975.
Lists vital information on every important building.

Focal Encyclopedia of Photography. 3rd ed. Ed. L. Stroebel and R. Zakia. Stoneham, MA: Focal P, 1993.

A Glossary of Art, Architecture, and Design Since 1945. 3rd ed. Ed. J. A. Walker. Boston: Hall, 1992.

A Guide to Art. Ed. S. Sproccati. Bergenfield, NJ: Abrams, 1992.

***Guide to the Literature of Art History.* Ed. E. Arntzen and R. Rainwater. Chicago: ALA, 1980.
A comprehensive listing of sources in art history worldwide. A section on general reference sources is followed by sections on individual arts (e.g., sculpture), which are organized by time period and by country. Has a subject index.

Historical Art Index A.D. 400–1650: People, Places, and Events Depicted. Jefferson City, NC: McFarland, 1989.

International Dictionary of Art and Artists. 2 vols. Ed. J. Vinson. Detroit, MI: St. James, 1990.

Larousse Dictionary of Painters. New York: Larousse, 1981.

Macmillan Encyclopedia of Architects. 4 vols. New York: Free P, 1982.

Mayer, R. *HarperCollins Dictionary of Art Terms and Techniques.* 2nd ed. New York: Harper Perennial, 1991.

Oxford Companion to Twentieth Century Art. Oxford: Oxford UP, 1981.

Oxford Illustrated Encyclopedia of the Arts. New York: Oxford UP, 1990.

Pelican History of Art. 50 vols. Baltimore: Penguin, 1953–present (in progress).

Print Index: A Guide to Reproductions. Comp. P. J. Parry and K. Chipman. Westport, CT: Greenwood, 1983.

Random House Library of Painting and Sculpture. 4 vols. New York: Beazley, 1981.

Research Guide to the History of Western Art. Chicago: ALA, 1982.

Who's Who in American Art. New York: Bowker, 1935–present. Annually.

Bibliographies to Art Books and Other Sources

Annotated Bibliography of Fine Art. 1897; rpt. Boston: Longwood, 1976.

Applied and Decorative Arts: A Bibliographic Guide. ed. D. L. Ehresmann. 3rd ed. Littleton, CO: Libraries Unlimited, 1993.

Art Books. 1876–1949. New York: Bowker, 1981. Supplements, 1950–1979 and 1980–1984.

Arts in America: A Bibliography. Ed. B. Karpel. 4 vols. Washington, DC: Smithsonian, 1979–1980.

Bibliographic Guide to Art and Architecture. Boston: Hall, 1977–1985.

Fine Arts: A Bibliographic Guide. Ed. D. L. Ehresmann. 2nd ed. Littleton, CO: Libraries Unlimited, 1979.

Electronic Sources to Art Literature

ACADEMIC INDEX
ARCHITECTURE DATABASE (RILA)
ARTBIBLIOGRAPHIES MODERN
ART LITERATURE INTERNATIONAL (RILA)
ARTS & HUMANITIES SEARCH
WILSONDISC: ART INDEX

Indexes to Articles in Art Journals

ARTbibliographies Modern. Santa Barbara, CA: ABC Clio, 1969–present.

**Art Index.* New York: Bowker, 1929–present
Indexes most art journals, such as *American Art Journal, Art Bulletin, Artforum, Design, Sculpture Review,* and many others.

RILA. Repetoire international de le littérature de l'art. Williamstown, MA: RILA, 1975–date.

Biological Sciences

Basic Sources and Guides to Biological Sciences Literature

Agriculture: Illustrated Search Strategy and Sources. Ann Arbor, MI: Pierian P, 1992.

Biolexicon: A Guide to the Language of Biology. Springfield, IL: Thomas, 1990.

Biology Data Book. Ed. P. L. Altman and D. S. Dittmer. 2nd ed. 3 vols. Madison, WI: FASEB, 1972–1974.

Dictionary of Biology. 6th ed. Baltimore: Penguin, 1978.

Encyclopedia of Bioethics. 2 vols. New York: Macmillan, 1982.

Encyclopedia of the Biological Sciences. Ed. P. Gray. 2nd ed. New York: Reinhold, 1970.

Encyclopedia of Human Biology. 8 vols. Ed. R. Dulbecco. New York: Academic P, 1991.

Grzimek's Encyclopedia of Mammals. 5 vols. New York: McGraw, 1990.

Guide to the Literature of the Life Sciences. Ed. R. C. Smith and W. M. Reid. 9th ed. Minneapolis, MN: Burgess, 1980.

Guide to Sources for Agricultural and Biological Research. Berkeley: U of California P, 1981.

Henderson's Dictionary of Biological Terms. Ed. E. Lawrence. 10th ed. New York: Wiley, 1987.

**Information Sources in the Life Sciences.* Ed. H. V. Wyatt. 4th ed. London: Bowker-Saur, 1994.
Consists of in-depth bibliographic essays on the literature of biology. Includes chapters focusing on subspecialties such as microbiology.

Magill's Survey of Science: Life Science Series. Ed. F. Magill. 6 vols. Englewood Cliffs, NJ: Salem, 1991.

Bibliographies to Biological Sciences Books and Other Sources

Bibliography of Bioethics. Detroit, MI: Gale, 1975–present.

Biological Abstracts. Philadelphia: Biological Abstracts, 1926–date.

Electronic Sources to Biological Sciences Literature

ACRICOLA
AGRIS INTERNATIONAL
AQUACULTURE
BIOSIS PREVIEWS
LIFE SCIENCES COLLECTION
SCISEARCH
WILSONDISC: BIOLOGICAL & AGRICULTURAL INDEX
ZOOLOGICAL RECORD

Indexes to Articles in Biological Sciences Journals

**Biological Abstracts.* Philadelphia: Biological Abstracts, 1926–present.
Indexes and gives brief descriptions of books and journal articles, especially to journals such as *American Journal of Anatomy, American Zoologist, Biochemistry, Journal of Animal Behavior, Quarterly Review of Biology, Social Biology,* and many others.

**Biological and Agricultural Index.* New York: Wilson, 1964–date.

Indexes about 275 periodicals, including *American Journal of Physiology, Field Crops Research, Human Biology, Journal of Bacteriology,* and *Quarterly Review of Biology.*

General Science Index. New York: Wilson, 1978–present.

Covers about 100 science periodicals, including *American Naturalist, Biological Bulletin,* and *Human Biology.*

Business

See also Economics, page 371.

Basic Sources and Guides to Business Literature

Basic Business Library: Core Resources. Ed. B. S. Schlessinger. 2nd ed. Phoenix, AZ: Oryx, 1989.

Business Information Desk Reference. New York: Macmillan, 1991.

***Business Information Sources.* Ed. L. M. Daniells. 3rd ed. Berkeley: U of California P, 1993.

A selective guide to business sources, arranged by subject area (e.g., insurance). Within each subject area are listed several recommended reference sources by type (e.g., handbooks).

Businesss Rankings Annual. Detroit: Gale, 1994–present. Annually.

Dictionary for Business and Finance. 2nd ed. Fayetteville: U of Arkansas P, 1990.

Dictionary of Business and Management. New York: Wiley, 1992.

Dow Jones-Irwin Business and Investment Almanac. New York: Dow Jones-Irwin. 1977–Annually.

Encyclopedia of American Business History and Biography. 9 vols. Ed. W. H. Baker. New York: Facts on File, 1987–1994.

Encyclopedia of Banking and Finance. 9th ed. Chicago: Probus, 1993.

Encyclopedia of Business Information Sources. 10th ed. Ed. J. Woy. Detroit, MI: Gale, 1994.

Handbook of Business Information. Englewood, CO: Libraries Unlimited, 1988.

Hoover's Handbook of American Business. Austin, TX: Reference P. Annually.

International Directory of Company Histories. Detroit, MI: St. James, 1990–present (in progress).

Portable MBA Desk Reference. New York: Wiley, 1993.

Small Business Sourcebook. 7th ed. Detroit, MI: Gale, 1994.

Bibliographies to Business Books and Other Sources

Bibliographic Guide to Business and Economics. 3 vols. Boston: Hall, 1975–present. Annually.

Business Publications Index and Abstracts. Detroit: Gale, 1983–present. Annually.

Core Collection. Cambridge, MA: Harvard UP, 1971–present. Annually.

Historical Bibliography of Administration, Business, and Management. Ed. D. D. Van Fleet. Monticello, IL: Vance Biblios., 1978.

Electronic Sources to Business Literature

ABI/INFORM
ACADEMIC INDEX
AGRIBUSINESS U.S.A.
BUSINESSWIRE
CENDATA
D&B DUN's FINANCIAL RECORDS
D&B ELECTRONIC YELLOW PAGES
DISCLOSURE
ECONOMIC LITERATURE INDEX
FINIS (Financial Industry National Information Service)
LABORLAW
MANAGEMENT CONTENTS
MOODY's CORPORATE NEWS
PTS F&S INDEXES
PTS PROMPT
STANDARD & POOR's NEWS
TRADE AND INDUSTRY INDEX
WILSONDISC: BUSINESSS PERIODICALS INDEX

Indexes to Articles in Business Journals

***Accountants' Index* (1921–1991) and *Accounting and Tax Index* (1992–present). New York: AICPA.

Indexes accounting and tax subjects in journals such as *Accountants' Digest, Accounting Review, Banker's Magazine, CA Magazine, Journal of Finance, Tax Adviser,* and many others.

***Business Periodicals Index.* New York: Wilson, 1958–date.

Indexes journals such as *Business Quarterly, Business Week, Fortune, Journal of Business, Journal of Marketing, Personnel Journal,* and many others.

Personnel Literature. Washington, DC: OPM Library, 1942–present.

Indexes articles on personnel management.

The Wall Street Journal Index. New York: Dow Jones, 1958–present. Annually.

Indexes the *Wall Street Journal* and *Barron's.*

Chemistry and Chemical Engineering

Basic Sources and Guides to Chemistry and Chemical Engineering Literature

ACS Style Guide: A Manual for Authors & Editors. Ed. J. S. Dodd. Washington, DC: ACS, 1985.
Chemical Engineers' Handbook. 6th ed. New York: McGraw, 1984.
Chemical Publications, Their Nature and Use. New York: McGraw, 1982.
CRC Handbook of Chemistry and Physics. Boca Raton, FL: CRC. Annually.
Dictionary of Chemistry. 2 vols. New York: International, 1969.
Encyclopedia of Chemical Technology. 4th ed. 27 vols. Ed. J. I. Kroschwitz and M. Howe-Grant New York: Wiley, 1991–present (in progress).
Guide to Basic Information Sources in Chemistry. Ed. A. Antony. New York: Wiley, 1979.
Hawley's Condensed Chemical Dictionary. 12th ed. New York: Reinhold, 1992.
**How to Find Chemical Information: A Guide for Practicing Chemists, Teachers, and Students.* Ed. R. E. Maizell. 2nd ed. New York: Wiley, 1987.
A detailed overview of selected sources in chemistry. Good explanations of how to use major sources (e.g., *Chemical Abstracts*). Also covers online searching and patents.
Lange's Handbook of Chemistry. 14th ed. Ed. J. A. Dean. New York: McGraw, 1992.
Noether, D. *Encyclopedic Dictionary of Chemical Technology.* New York: VCH, 1993.
Riegel's Handbook of Industrial Chemistry. 9th ed. New York: Reinhold, 1992.

Bibliographies to Chemistry and Chemical Engineering Books and Other Sources

Chemical Abstracts. Easton, PA: ACS, 1907–present. Weekly.
Chemical Titles. Easton, PA: ACS, 1960. Biweekly.
Selected Titles in Chemistry. 4th ed. Washington, DC: ACS, 1977.

Electronic Sources to Chemistry and Chemical Engineering Literature

BEILSTEIN ONLINE
CA SEARCH
CHEMICAL INDUSTRY NOTES
CHEMNAME
CHEMSIS
Claims/U.S. PATENTS ABSTRACTS
COMPENDEX
HEILBRON
INSPEC
NTIS
SCISEARCH
WILSONDISC: GENERAL SCIENCE INDEX

Indexes to Articles in Chemistry and Chemical Engineering Journals

***Chemical Abstracts: Key to the World's Chemical Literature.* Easton, PA: American Chemical Society, 1907–present. Weekly.
Indexes such journals as *Applied Chemical News, American Chemical Society Journal, Chemical Bulletin, Chemist, Journal of the Chemical Society,* and many more. Provides a good abstract even if your library does not house the journal.
General Science Index. New York: Wilson, 1978–present.
Covers about 100 science periodicals, including *Analytical Chemistry, Inorganic Chemistry,* and *Journal of Organic Chemistry.*

Computer Science

Basic Sources and Guides to Computer Science Literature

Computer Glossary. 6th ed. New York: AMACOM, 1993.
Computer Sciences Resources: A Guide to Professional Literature. Ed. D. Myers. White Plains, NY: Knowledge Industries, 1981.
Dictionary of Computing. 3rd ed. New York: Oxford, UP 1990.
Encyclopedia of Computer Science. 3rd ed. New York: Reinhold, 1992.
Encyclopedia of Computer Science and Technology. Ed. J. Belzer. 22 vols. New York: Dekker, 1975–1991.
IBM Dictionary of Computing. Ed. G. McDaniel. New York: McGraw, 1994.
McGraw-Hill Personal Computer Programming Encyclopedia. 2nd ed. New York: McGraw, 1989.
Macmillan Encyclopedia of Computers. 2 vols. Ed. G. G. Biter. New York: Macmillan, 1992.
***Scientific and Technical Information Sources.* Ed. C. Chen. 2nd ed. Cambridge, MA: MIT P, 1988.

A useful, up-to-date resource for identifying sources to consult in this field. Includes computer science as a section within each chapter on types of sources (e.g., bibliographies, handbooks).

Software Encyclopedia 1993: A Guide for Personal, Professional, and Business Users. 2 vols. New Providence, NJ: Bowker, 1993.

Bibliographies to Computer Science Books and Other Sources

ACM Guide to Computing Literature. 1978–present. Annually.

Bibliographic Guide to the History of Computing, Computers, and the Information Processing Industry. Westport, CT: Greenwood, 1990.

Computer-Readable Bibliographic Data Bases: A Directory and Data Sourcebook. Washington, DC: ASIS, 1976–present.

Electronic Sources to Computer Science Literature

BUSINESS SOFTWARE DATABASE
COMPENDEX PLUS
COMPUTER DATABASE
COMPUTER-READABLE DATABASES
INSPEC
MICROCOMPUTER INDEX
WILSONDISC: APPLIED SCIENCE AND TECHNOLOGY

Indexes to Articles in Computer Science Journals

**Applied Science and Technology Index.* New York: Wilson, 1958–date.
Indexes articles in *Byte, Computer Design, Computers in Industry, The Computer Journal, Computer Methods, Computer, Data Processing,* and *Microcomputing.*

Computer Abstracts. West Yorks, UK: Technical Information, 1957–date.

Computer Literature Index. Phoenix, AZ: ACR, 1971–present.

Ecology

Basic Sources and Guides to Ecology Literature

Atlas of United States Environmental Issues. New York: Macmillan, 1991.

Earth Care Annual. Emmaus, PA: Rodale, 1990.

Encyclopedia of Environmental Studies. New York: Facts on File, 1991.

Energy Information Guide. Ed. D. R. Weber. Rev. ed. 3 vols. San Carlos, CA: Energy Info P, 1994.

Environment Information Access. New York: EIC, 1971–present.

The Green Encyclopedia. New York: Prentice-Hall, 1992.

The Last Rain Forest: A World Conservation Atlas. New York: Oxford UP, 1990.

Recycling in America: A Reference Handbook. Santa Barbara, CA: ABC-Clio, 1992.

Toxics A to Z: A Guide to Everyday Pollution Hazards. Berkeley: U of California P, 1991.

***World Resources.* Oxford: Oxford UP, 1986–present. Annually.
Contains chapters on conditions and trends in the environment worldwide (e.g., energy). Also provides statistical tables (e.g., Net Additions to the Greenhouse Heating Effect).

Bibliographies to Ecology Books and Other Sources

Energy Abstracts for Policy Analysis. Oak Ridge, TN: TIC, 1975–1989.

Environment Abstracts. New York: EIC, 1971–present.

Pollution Abstracts. Washington, DC: Cambridge Scientific Abstracts, 1970–present.

Selected Water Resources Abstracts. Springfield, VA: NTIS, 1968–present.

Electronic Sources to Ecology Literature

ACADEMIC INDEX
BIOSIS PREVIEWS
COMPENDEX
ENVIRONLINE
ENVIRONMENTAL BIBLIOGRAPHY
GEOBASE
POLLUTION ABSTRACTS
TOXLINE
WATER RESOURCES ABSTRACTS
WILSONDISC: APPLIED SCIENCE AND TECHNOLOGY
WILSONDISC: BIOLOGICAL AND AGRICULTURAL INDEXES

Indexes to Articles in Ecology Journals

***Biological Abstracts.* Philadelphia: Biological Abstracts, 1926–present.
Indexes articles on environmental issues in journals such as *American Forests, The Conservationist, Florida Naturalist,*

Journal of Soil and Water Conservation, The Living Wilderness, Sierra, Ambio, Ecology, Environmental Pollution, and others.

**Biological and Agricultural Index.* New York: Wilson, 1964–present.
Includes coverage of *Ecology, Environmental Pollution, Forest Ecology and Management,* and *Journal of Environmental Biology,* as well as others.

Ecological Abstracts. Norwich, UK: Geo Abstracts, 1974–present.

Environment Abstracts Annual. New York: Bowker, 1970–present.

**The Environmental Index.* Ann Arbor, MI: UMI, 1992–present.
Gives additional indexing of other journals, such as *Environment, Environmental Ethics, Journal of Applied Ecology, Solar Age,* and others.

**General Science Index.* New York: Wilson, 1978–present.
Covers about 100 science periodicals, including *Ecologist, Ecology,* and *Environmental Science and Technology.*

Economics

See also Business, pages 368.

Basic Sources and Guides to Economics Literature

American Dictionary of Economics. Ed. D. Auld et al. New York: Facts on File, 1983.

Basic Statistics of the European Communities. New York: Unipub. Annually.

Bibliographic Guide to Business and Economics, 1991. 3 vols. Boston: Hall, 1992.

Dictionary of Banking and Financial Services. Ed. J. M. Rosenberg. New York: Wiley, 1985.

Emory, C. W. *Business Research Methods.* 4th ed. Homewood, IL: Irwin, 1990.

Encyclopedia of Economics. New York: McGraw, 1982.

**Information Sources in Economics.* Ed. J. Fletcher. 2nd ed. London: Saur, 1984.
Covers research sources by type (e.g., databases) and also by subject areas (e.g., macroeconomics). Describes and evaluates the sources listed.

**The New Palgrave: A Dictionary of Economics.* Ed. J. Fletcher. 3 vols. New York: Stockton, 1992.
A scholarly, thoroughly documented work that covers all aspects of econom-

ic theory and thought. The bibliographies following each article are very helpful.

Rutherford, D. *Dictionary of Economics.* New York: Routledge, 1992.

Survey of Social Science: Economics Series. 5 vols. Ed. F. Magill. Englewood Cliffs, NJ: Salem, 1991.

Who's Who in Finance and Industry. New Providence, NJ: Marquis. Biennially.

Bibliographies to Economics Books and Other Sources

Bibliographic Guide to Business and Economics. Boston: Hall, 1975–present. Annually.

Brealey, R., and H. Edwards. *A Bibliography of Finance.* Cambridge, MA: MIT, 1991.

Business and Economics Book Guide. 2 vols. Boston: Hall, 1974. Supplements.

Business and Economics Books, 1876–1983. 5 vols. New Providence, NJ: Bowker, 1985.

Economics Books. Clifton, NJ: Kelley, 1974–present. Annually.

Electronic Sources to Economics Literature

ACADEMIC INDEX
ECONBASE: TIME SERIES AND FORECASTS
ECONOMIC LITERATURE INDEX
FOREIGN TRADE AND ECONOMIC ABSTRACTS
PTS INTERNATIONAL FORECASTS
PTS U.S. FORECASTS

Indexes to Articles in Economics Journals

Index of Economic Articles. Homewood, IL: Irwin, 1961–present.

**Journal of Economic Literature.* Nashville, TN: American Economics Assn., 1964–present.
Indexes such journals as *American Economist, Applied Economics, Business Economics, Economic History Review, Economic Journal, Federal Reserve Bulletin, Journal of Economic Issues,* and many more.

The Wall Street Journal Index. New York: Dow Jones, 1958–present.

Education

Basic Sources and Guides to Education Literature

American Educators' Encyclopedia. Westport, CT: Greenwood, 1991.

**Education: A Guide to Reference and Information Sources.* Englewood, CO: Libraries Unlimited, 1989.
Lists a variety of reference sources in education and sources in other related fields (e.g., social work). Each source is described and evaluated.

Education Journals and Serials. Ed. M. E. Collins. Metuchen, NJ: Scarecrow, 1988.

Educator's Desk Reference. New York: Macmillan, 1989.

Encyclopedia of Early Childhood Education. Ed. L. R. Williams et al. New York: Garland, 1992.

The Encyclopedia of Education. Ed. L. C. Deighton. 10 vols. New York: Macmillan, 1971.

Encyclopedia of Educational Research. Ed. M. C. Alkin. 6th ed. 4 vols. New York: Free P, 1992.

A Guide to Sources of Educational Information. Ed. M. L. Woodbury. 2nd ed. Arlington, VA: Information Resources, 1982.

Handbook of Research on Teaching. Ed. M. C. Wittrock. 3rd ed. New York: Macmillan, 1986.

Handbook of World Education. Houston, TX: American Collegiate Service, 1991.

International Encyclopedia of Education. Ed. T. Husen and T. N. Postlethwaite. 10 vols. Elmsford, NY: Pergamon, 1985. Supplements 1988 and 1990.

International Yearbook of Education. Paris: UNESCO, 1948–present.

Library Research Guide to Education. Ed. J. R. Kennedy. Ann Arbor, MI: Pierian P, 1979.

Multicultural Education: A Source Book. New York: Garland, 1989.

World Education Encyclopedia. 3 vols.. New York: Facts on File, 1988.

Bibliographies to Education Books and Other Sources

Bibliographic Guide to Education. Boston: Hall, 1978–date.

Bibliographic Guide to Educational Research. Ed. D. M. Berry. 3rd ed. Metuchen, NJ: Scarecrow, 1990.

Resources in Education (formerly *Research in Education*). Washington, DC: ERIC, 1956–present.

Subject Bibliography of the History of American Higher Education. Westport, CT: Greenwood, 1984.

Electronic Sources to Education Literature

ACADEMIC INDEX
A-V ONLINE (nonprint educational materials)
ERIC
EXCEPTIONAL CHILD EDUCATION RESOURCES
WILSONDISC: EDUCATION INDEX

Indexes to Articles in Education Journals

Current Index to Journals in Education. Phoenix, AZ: Oryx, 1969–present.

**Education Index.* New York: Wilson, 1929–date.
Both preceding titles index articles in such journals as *Childhood Education, Comparative Education, Eduation Digest, Educational Forum, Educational Review, Educational Studies, Journal of Educational Psychology, Review of Education,* and many more.

Exceptional Child Education Resources. Reston, VA: CEC, 1968–present.

State Education Journal Index. Westminster, CO: SEJI, 1963–present.

Electronics

Basic Sources and Guides to Electronics Literature

Advances in Electronics and Electron Physics. New York: Academic P, 1948–present (continuous).

Buchsbaum's Complete Handbook of Practical Electronics Reference Data. 2nd ed. Englewood Cliffs, NJ: Prentice-Hall, 1987.

Dictionary of Electronics. Ed. S. W. Amos. 2nd ed. Woburn, MA: Butterworth, 1987.

Electronic Properties Research Literature Retrieval Guide. 4 vols. New York: Plenum, 1979.

Electronics Style Manual. Ed. J. Markus. New York: McGraw, 1978.

Encyclopedia of Computer Science and Technology. Ed. J. Belzer. 21 vols. New York: Dekker, 1975–1989.

Encyclopedia of Electronics. 2nd ed. Ed. E. S. Gibilisco and N. Sclater. Blue Ridge Summit, PA: TAB Books, 1990.

**A Guide to the Literature of Electrical and Electronics Engineering.* Ed. S. B. Ardis. Littleton, CO: Libraries Unlimited, 1987.
Lists research sources in engineering and is useful for choosing where to start looking for information.

Handbook of Modern Electronics and Electrical Engineering. New York: Wiley, 1986.

International Encyclopedia of Robotics: Applications and Automation. 3 vols. New York: Wiley, 1988.

Modern Dictionary of Electronics. Ed. R. Graf. 6th ed. Indianapolis, IN: Sams, 1984.

Scientific and Technical Information Sources. Ed. C. Chen. 2nd ed. Boston: MIT P, 1987.

Bibliographies to Electronics Books and Other Sources

Bibliography of the History of Electronics. Ed. G. Shiers. Metuchen, NJ: Scarecrow, 1972.

Electronics: A Bibliographical Guide. Ed. C. K. Moore and K. J. Spencer. 3 vols. New York: Plenum, 1961–1973.

Electronic Sources to Electronics Literature

COMPENDEX
INSPEC
SCISEARCH
SUPERTECH
WILSONDISC: APPLIED SCIENCE AND TECHNOLOGY

Indexes to Articles in Electronics Journals

**Applied Science and Technology Index*. New York: Wilson, 1958–date.
Indexes electronics articles in journals such as *Bell System Technical Journal, Electrial Communication, Electrical Engineer, Electrical Review, Electronic News, Electronics, Electronics Letters,* and many more.

Engineering Index. New York: Engineering Information, 1906–present.

Ethnic Studies

Basic Sources and Guides to Ethnic Studies Literature

Allen, J., and E. Turner. *We the People: An Atlas of America's Ethnic Diversity.* New York: Macmillan, 1988.

Dictionary of American Immigration History. Ed. F. Cordasco. Metuchen, NJ: Scarecrow, 1990.

Ethnic Periodicals in Contemporary America: An Annotated Guide. Ed. S. Ireland. Westport, CT: Greenwood, 1990.

Ethnic Theatre in the United States. Ed. M. Seller. Westport, CT: Greenwood, 1983.

Guide to Multicultural Resources, 1993/1994. Ed. C. A. Taylor. Ft. Atkinson, WI: Highsmith, 1993.

Harvard Encyclopedia of American Ethnic Groups. Ed. S. Thernstrom. Cambridge, MA: Belknap/Harvard UP, 1980.

Kinloch, G. *Race and Ethnic Relations: An Annotated Bibliography*. New York: Garland, 1984.

Minority Organizations: A National Directory. 4th ed. Garrett Park, MD: Garrett Park P, 1992.

Multiculturalism in the United States: A Comparative Guide. Westport, CT: Greenwood, 1992.

Peck, D. R. *American Ethnic Literatures: Native American, African American, Chicano/Latino, and Asian American Writers and Their Backgrounds, An Annotated Bibliography*. Englewood Cliffs, NJ: Salem, 1992.

Stevens, G. I. *Videos for Understanding Diversity: A Core Selection and Evaluative Guide*. Chicago: ALA, 1993.

Guides and Bibliographies to Native American Studies

American Indian Novelists: An Annotated Critical Bibliography. New York: Garland, 1982.

**Guide to Research on North American Indians*. Ed. A. Hirschfelder. Chicago: ALA, 1983.
Lists basic sources of information for researching Native Americans. Chapters cover a variety of aspects, including history, economics, society, religion, the arts, and literature.

Handbook of North American Indians. 20 vols. Washington, DC: Smithsonian, 1978–present (in progress).

Indians of North America. Methods and Sources for Library Research. New Haven, CT: Library Professional Pubs., 1983.

Native American Women: A Biographical Dictionary. Ed. G. Bataille. New York: Garland, 1993.

Native Americans: An Annotated Bibliography. Englewood Cliffs, NJ: Salem, 1991.

Reference Encyclopedia of the American Indian. Ed. B. Klein. 6th ed. West Nyack, NY: Todd, 1993.

Ruoff, L. *American Indian Literatures: An Introduction, Bibliographic Review, and Selected Bibliography*. New York: MLA, 1990.

Statistical Record of Native North Americans. Ed. M. A. Reddy. Detroit, MI: Gale, 1993.

Studies in American Indian Literature: Critical Essays and Course Designs. New York: MLA, 1983.

Guides to Asian-American Studies

**Asian American Studies*. Ed. H. Kim. Westport, CT: Greenwood, 1989.

A bibliography of books and articles about Asian Americans. Includes historical and cultural and sociological studies as well. Most items listed have brief descriptions.

Chen, J. *The Chinese of America.* New York: Harper & Row, 1982.

Cheung, K. *Asian American Literature.* New York: MLA, 1988.

Japanese-American History: An A to Z Reference from 1868 to the Present. Ed. B. Niiya. New York: Facts on File, 1993.

Melendy, H. B. *Asians in America: Filipinos, Koreans, and East Indians.* New York: Hippocrene, 1981.

Montero, D. *Vietnamese Americans: Patterns of Resettlement and Socioeconomic Adaptation in the United States.* Boulder, CO: Westview, 1979.

Statistical Record of Asian Americans. Detroit, MI: Gale, 1993.

Wilson, R. A., and B. Hosokawa. *East to America: A History of the Japanese in the United States.* New York: Quill, 1980.

Guides and Bibliographies to Afro-American Studies

See also Afro-American Literature, page 383.

The African American Almanac. 6th ed. Detroit, MI: Gale, 1994.

African American Biographies: Profiles of 558 Current Men and Women. Jefferson, NC: McFarland, 1992.

**African American Encyclopedia.* 6 vols. North Bellmore, NY: Marshall Cavendish, 1993.

A thorough alphabetic listing of Afro-American issues, personalities, and events.

**Afro-American Reference.* Ed. N. Davis. Westport, CT: Greenwood, 1985.

A selective listing of sources on all aspects of the Afro-American experience. Lists other reference sources as well as recommends individual books on particular subjects (e.g., Afro-Americans in motion pictures).

Bibliographic Guide to Black Studies. Boston: Hall, 1975–present.

Black Index: Afro-Americans in Selected Periodicals 1907–1949. New York: Garland, 1981.

Black Women in America: An Historical Encyclopedia. 2 vols. Ed. D. C. Hine. Brooklyn, NY: Carlson, 1993.

Blacks in the Humanities, 1750–1984. Ed. D. F. Joyce. Westport, CT: Greenwood, 1986.

Blacks in Science and Medicine. Ed. V. O. Sammons. New York: Hemisphere, 1989.

Contemporary Black Biography. Ed. M. L. LaBlanc. Detroit, MI: Gale, 1992–present (in progress).

Contributions of Black Women to America. 2 vols. Ed. M. W. Davis. Columbia, SC: Kenday, 1982.

Dictionary of American Negro Biography. Ed. R. W. Logan and M. R. Winton. New York: Norton, 1982.

Encyclopedia of African-American Civil Rights. Westport, CT: Greenwood, 1992.

Encyclopedia of Black America. Ed. W. A. Low. New York: McGraw, 1981.

**Glover, D. M. *Voices of the Spirit: Sources for Interpreting the African American Experience.* Chicago: ALA, 1994.

A good starting point for the beginning researcher. Glover points you in the right direction for a multitude of scholarly projects.

Hughes, L., et al. *A Pictorial History of Black Americans.* 5th rev. ed. New York: Crown, 1983.

***In Black and White.* Ed. M. M. Spradling. 4th ed. Detroit, MI: Gale, 1994.

A bibliography of magazine and newspaper articles and books on 15,000 Afro-American individuals and organizations, past and present.

Index to Periodical Articles by and About Blacks. Boston: Hall, 1973–present. Annually.

The Kaiser Index to Black Resources, 1948–1986. 5 vols. Brooklyn, NY: Carlson, 1992.

Notable Black American Women. Ed. J. C. Smith. Detroit, MI: Gale, 1992.

Statistical Record of Black America. Detroit: Gale, 1990.

Who's Who Among Black Americans. Northbrook, IL: WWABA, 1976–present.

Guides and Bibliographies to Hispanic-American Studies

Chicano Literature: A Reference Guide. Ed. J. A. Martinez and F. A. Lomeli. Westport, CT: Greenwood, 1985.

Handbook of Hispanic Culture of the U.S. Houston, TX: Arte Publico, 1993.

Hispanic-American Almanac. Ed. N. Kanellos. Detroit, MI: Gale, 1993.

Hispanic American Periodicals Index. Los Angeles: UCLA Latin American Center, 1974–present.

Hispanic Americans Information Directory. Detroit, MI: Gale, 1989.

The Hispanic Presence in North America.
New York: Facts on File, 1991.
Hispanics in the United States: A New Social Agenda. Ed. P. S. J. Cafferty and W. McCready. New Brunswick, NJ: Transaction, 1984.
Literature Chicana. Comp R. G. Trujillo. Encino, CA: Floricanto P, 1985.
Manual of Hispanic Bibliography. 2nd ed. Ed. D. W. Foster and V. R. Foster. New York: Garland, 1976.
Notable Hispanic American Women. Ed. D. Telgen and J. Kamp. Detroit, MI: Gale, 1993.
¿Quien Sabe?: A Preliminary List of Chicano Reference Materials. Los Angeles: U of California Chicano Studies Research Center, 1981.
***Sourcebook of Hispanic Culture in the United States.* Chicago: ALA, 1982. Essays surveying Mexican-American, Puerto Rican-American, Cuban-American, and Hispanic-American literature, education, sociolinguistics, and music. Each essay concludes with lengthy, evaluative bibliographies of recommended books and periodical articles, many in English.
Spanish-American Women Writers: A Bibliographical Research Checklist. Ed. L. E. R. Cortina. New York: Garland, 1982.
Statistical Record of Hispanic Americans. Ed. M. A. Reddy. Detroit, MI: Gale, 1993.
Who's Who Among Hispanic Americans. Detroit, MI: Gale, 1991.
Zimmerman, M. *U.S. Latino Literature: An Essay and Annotated Bibliography.* Chicago: March Abrazo, 1992.

Electronic Sources to Ethnic Studies Literature

ACADEMIC INDEX
AMERICA: HISTORY AND LIFE
POPULATION BIBLIOGRAPHY
SOCIAL SCISEARCH
SOCIOLOGICAL ABSTRACTS
WILSONDISC: SOCIAL SCIENCES AND HUMANITIES INDEXES

Indexes to Articles in Ethnic Studies Journals

MLA International Bibliography. New York: MLA, 1921–present.
Indexes ethnic languages and literatures.
Sage Race Relations Abstracts. London and Beverly Hills, CA: 1976–present.
***Social Sciences Index.* New York: Wilson, 1974–present.

Indexes articles on many minority topics in journals such as *American Journal of Physical Anthropology, Aztlan, Black Scholar, Ethnic Groups, Ethnic and Racial Studies, Ethnohistory, Ethnology, Journal of Black Studies, Journal of Ethnic Studies, Japan Quarterly, Modern Asian Studies,* and others.
Sociological Abstracts. La Jolla, CA: Sociological Abstracts, 1952–present.

Foreign Language Studies

Basic Sources and Guide to Foreign Language Studies Literature

French
Coleman, K. *Guide to French Poetry Explication.* Boston: Hall, 1993.
Concise Oxford Dictionary of French Literature. Ed. J. Reid. Oxford: Clarendon, 1976.
Critical Bibliography of French Literature. Syracuse, NY: Syracuse UP, 1947–1985 (in progress).
Dictionnaire étymologique de la langue française. New York: French and European, 1975.
Dictionnaire de la littérature française contemporaine. New York: French and European, 1977.
***French Language and Literature: An Annotated Bibliography.* Ed. F. Bassan et al. 2nd ed. New York: Garland, 1989. A listing of reference books, periodicals, and other books to consult when researching French. Includes historical and cultural aspects of French language and literature in France and other French-speaking countries.
French Literature: An Annotated Guide to Selected Bibliographies. Ed. R. Kempton. New York: MLA, 1981.
French Twenty Bibliography: Critical and Biographical References for the Study of French Literature Since 1885. Ed. D. W. Alden. New York: French Institute, 1969–present. Annually.
Grand larousse encyclopedique. 12 vols. Elmsford, NY: Maxwell, 1964. Supplements.
Levi, A. *Guide to French Literature.* Volume 1: *1789 to the Present;* Volume 2: *Beginnings to 1789.* Detroit, MI: St. James, 1992 and 1994.
New History of French Literature. 2 vols. Cambridge: Harvard UP, 1989.

German

Collins German-English, English-German Dictionary, Unabridged. 2nd ed. New York: HarperCollins, 1993.

Critical Bibliography of German Literature in English Translation: 1481–1927. 2nd ed. Metuchen, NJ: Scarecrow, 1965. Supplements.

Der Grosse Duden. Ed. R. Duden. 10 vols. New York: Adler's, 1971.

Deutsches Woerterbuch. Ed. J. Grimm and W. Grimm. 32 vols. New York: Adler's, 1973.

**Introduction to Library Research in German Studies.* Ed. L. Richardson. Boulder, CO: Westview, 1984.
A listing of reference sources for research on German language, literature, art, and civilization (history, folklore, philosophy and religion, music, and cinema). Includes descriptive and evaluative comments.

Oxford Companion to German Literature. Ed. H. Garland. 2nd ed. New York: Oxford UP, 1986.

Reallexikon der deutschen Literaturgeschichte. Ed. W. Kohlschmidt and W. Mohr. 3 vols. New York: DeGruyter, 1958–1977.

Selected Bibliography of German Literature in English Translation: 1956–1960. Ed. M. F. Smith. Metuchen, NJ: Scarecrow, 1972.

Wer Ist Wer. 20th ed. New York: IPS, 1973. Supplements.

Latin

**Ancient Writers: Greece and Rome.* Ed. T. J. Luce. 2 vols. New York: Scribner's, 1982.
Detailed information on 47 classical authors and their works. Each article is followed by a selective listing of recommended reading.

Cambridge History of Classical Literature. New York: Cambridge UP, 1982–present (in progress).

Classical Greek and Roman Drama, An Annotated Bibliography. Englewood Cliffs, NJ: Salem, 1989.

The Classical World Bibliography of Roman Drama and Poetry and Ancient Fiction. New York: Garland, 1978.

Grant, M. *Greek and Latin Authors, 800 BC–1000 AD, A Biographical Dictionary.* New York: Wilson, 1980.

McGuire, M. R., and H. Dressler. *Introduction to Medieval Latin Studies: A Syllabus and Bibliographical Guide.* 2nd ed. Washington, DC: Catholic UP, 1977.

Oxford Companion to Classical Literature. 2nd ed. Ed. M. C. Howatson. New York: Oxford UP, 1989.

Oxford Latin Dictionary. Ed. P. G. Glare. New York: Oxford UP, 1982.

Repertoire des index et lexiques d'auteurs latins. Ed. P. Faider. 1926; rpt. New York: Burt Franklin, 1971.

Wagenvoort, H. *Studies in Roman Literature, Culture and Religion.* New York: Garland, 1978.

Russian

Basic Russian Publications: A Bibliographic Guide to Western-Language Publications. Ed. P. L. Horecky. Chicago: U of Chicago P, 1965.

Basic Russian Publications: A Selected and Annotated Bibliography on Russia and the Soviet Union. Ed. P. L. Horecky. Chicago: U of Chicago P, 1962.

Bibliography of Russian Literature in English Translation to 1945. Ed. M. B. Line. 1963; rpt. Totowa, NJ: Rowman, 1972.

Bibliography of Russian Word Formation. Ed. D. S. Worth. Columbus, OH: Slavica, 1977.

Corten, I. H. *Vocabulary of Soviet Society & Culture: A Selected Guide to Russian Words, Idioms, and Expressions of the Post-Stalin Era, 1953–1991.* Durham, NC: Duke UP, 1992.

Dictionary of Russian Literature. Ed. W. E. Harkins. 1956; rpt. Westport, CT: Greenwood, 1971.

Dictionary of Russian Literature Since 1917. New York: Columbia UP, 1988.

Elsevier's Dictionary of Science and Technology: Russian-English. Comp. G. Chakalov. New York: Elsevier, 1993.

Elsevier's Russian-English Dictionary. 4 vols. New York: Elsevier, 1990.

Guide to Bibliographies of Russian Literature. Ed. S. A. Zenkovsky and D. L. Armbruster. Nashville, TN: Vanderbilt UP, 1970.

Guide to Russian Reference Books. Ed. K. Maichel. 5 vols. Stanford, CA: Hoover, 1962–1967.

Handbook of Russian Literature. Ed. V. Terras. New Haven, CT: Yale UP, 1985.

**Introduction to Russian Language and Literature.* Ed. R. Auty and D. Obolensky. New York: Cambridge UP, 1977.
A survey of the history of Russian, with chapters on linguistics, printing, prose, poetry, and theater. Each chapter presents a chronological overview and includes selective bibliographies of resources, many of them in Russian.

Literature of the Soviet Peoples: A Historical and Biographical Survey. Ed. H. Junger. New York: Ungar, 1971.

Modern Encyclopedia of Russian and Soviet Literature. Gulf Breeze, FL: Academic International, 1971–present (in progress).

Russia, the USSR, and Eastern Europe: A Bibliographic Guide to English Language Publications, 1975–1980. Littleton, CO: Libraries Unlimited, 1982. Supplements, 1981–1985, 1987.

Who Was Who in the U.S.S.R. Metuchen, NJ: Scarecrow, 1972.

Spanish

Bibliography of Old Spanish Texts. 3rd ed. Ed. A. Cardenas et al. Madison, WI: Hispanic Seminary, 1984.

Biographical Dictionary of Hispanic Literature in the United States. Westport, CT: Greenwood, 1989.

**Bleznick, D. W. *A Sourcebook for Hispanic Literature and Language.* 2nd ed. Metuchen, NJ: Scarecrow, 1983.
Lists a selection of reference sources and other recommended reading on the literatures of Spain and Spanish America. Includes some sources written in English.

Chandler, R. E., and K. Schwartz. *New History of Spanish Literature.* Baton Rouge, LA: LSU, 1991.

Collins Spanish-English, English Spanish Dictionary. 3rd ed. New York: HarperCollins, 1992.

Contemporary Spanish American Poets. A Bibliography of Primary and Secondary Sources. Ed. J. Sefami. Westport, CT: Greenwood, 1992.

Diccionario de la literatura latinoamerica. Washington, DC: OAS, 1950.

Dissertations in Hispanic Languages and Literatures: An Index of Dissertations Completed in the United States and Canada. Ed. J. R. Chatham and C. C. McClendon. Lexington: UP of Kentucky, 1981.

Flores, A. *Spanish American Authors, The Twentieth Century.* New York: Wilson, 1992.

Handbook of Latin American Literature. Comp. D. W. Foster. New York: Garland, 1987.

Handbook of Latin American Studies. Gainesville: UP of Florida, 1935–date.

Historia de la literature espanola and hispanoamerica. Spain: Aguilar, 1983.

The Latin American Short Story: An Annotated Guide to Anthologies and Criticism. Ed. D. Balderston. Westport, CT: Greenwood, 1992.

Latin American Writers. Ed. C. A. Solé. 3 vols. New York: Scribner's, 1989.

The Literature of Spain in English Translation: A Bibliography. Comp. Robert S. Rudder. New York: Ungar, 1975.

Modern Spanish and Portuguese Literatures. Ed. M. J. Schneider and I. Stern. New York: Ungar, 1988.

Oxford Companion to Spanish Literature. Ed. F. Ward. Oxford: Clarendon, 1978.

Spanish American Women Writers. Ed. D. Marting. Westport, CT: Greenwood, 1990.

Spanish and Spanish-American Literature: An Annotated Guide to Selected Bibliographies. Ed. H. C. Woodbridge. New York: MLA, 1983.

Electronic Sources to Foreign Language Studies Literature

ACADEMIC INDEX
ARTS AND HUMANITIES SEARCH
LLBA (Linguistics and Language Behavior Abstracts)
MLA BIBLIOGRAPHY
WILSONDISC: HUMANITIES INDEX

Indexes to Articles in Foreign Language Studies Journals

Humanities Index. New York: Wilson, 1974–present.

**MLA International Bibliography.* New York: MLA, 1921–present.
Indexes articles in journals such as *Yale French Studies, German Quarterly, Philological Quarterly, Journal of Spanish Studies,* and many others. It features special indexes to foreign language studies in the literature of the foreign country.

Geography

Basic Sources and Guides to Geography Literature

Encyclopedia of the Peoples of the World. Ed. A. Gonen. New York: Holt, 1993.

Encyclopedia of the Third World. 4th ed. 3 vols. New York: Facts on File, 1990.

Encyclopedia of World Cultures. Boston: Hall, 1991–present (in progress).

Facts About the Cities. New York: Wilson, 1992.

Goode's World Atlas. Ed. B. Rodner. 18th ed. Chicago: Rand McNally, 1990.

Guide to Information Sources in the Geographical Sciences. London: Croom Helm, 1983.

Guide to the Republics of the Former Soviet Union. Westport, CT: Greenwood, 1993.

**Illustrated Encyclopedia of Mankind.* 22 vols. Freeport, NY: Marshall Cavendish, 1989.
Good starting place for background information on the cultures of 500 different peoples of the world. Also includes articles giving cross-cultural overviews on various topics (e.g., marriage).

**The Literature of Geography: A Guide to Its Organization and Use*. 2nd ed. New Haven, CT: Shoe String, 1978.
An introductory overview of geographic research methods and materials. Includes chapters on specific areas of geography (e.g., regional) with lists of sources for research.
Modern Geography: An Encyclopedic Survey. Ed. G. S. Dunbar. New York: Garland, 1991.
Research Catalogue of the American Geographical Society. 15 vols. Boston: Hall, 1962. Supplements, 1962–1976.
Source Book in Geography. Ed. G. Kish. Cambridge: Harvard UP, 1978.
The Times Atlas of the World. 9th ed. London: Times Books, 1992.
Weather Almanac. 6th ed. Detroit, MI: Gale, 1992.

Bibliographies to Geography Books and Other Sources

Geographers: Bio-Bibliographical Studies. Ed. T. W. Freeman et al. London: Mansell, 1977–present. Annually.
Geographical Bibliography for American Libraries. Ed. C. D. Harris. Washington, DC: Assn. of American Geographers, 1985.
Geography and Local Administration: A Bibliography. Ed. K. Hoggart. Monticello, IL: Vancy, 1980.
International List of Geographical Serials. 3rd ed. Chicago: U of Chicago P, 1980.

Electronic Sources to Geography Literature

ACADEMIC INDEX
GEOBASE
SOCIAL SCISEARCH
WILSONDISC: SOCIAL SCIENCES INDEX

Indexes to Articles in Geography Journals

Geo Abstracts. Norwich, UK: Geo Abstracts, 1966–present.
**Social Sciences Index*. New York: Wilson, 1974–present.
Indexes articles in journals such as *American Cartographer, Cartographic Journals, Cartography, Economic Geography, Geographical Analysis, Geographical Journal, Geographical Magazine, Geographical Review, Geography, Journal of Geography, Journal of Historical Geography,* and others.

Geology

Basic Sources and Guides to Geology Literature

Challinor's Dictionary of Geology. 6th ed. New York: Oxford UP, 1986.
**Encyclopedia of Field and General Geology*. Ed. C. W. Finkle. New York: Reinhold, 1982.
One volume of the *Encyclopedia of Earth Sciences* series. Gives technical, documented information and references to other sources.
The Encyclopedia of the Solid Earth Sciences. Ed. P. Kearey et al. London: Blackwell, 1993.
Geologic Reference Sources: A Subject and Regional Bibliography. Ed. D. C. Ward, M. Wheeler, and R. Bier. 2nd ed. Metuchen, NJ: Scarecrow, 1981.
Glossary of Geology. Ed. R. L. Bates and J. A. Jackson. 3rd ed. Falls Church, VA: AGI, 1987.
Guide to Information Sources in Mining, Minerals, and Geosciences. Ed. S. R. Kaplan. New York: McGraw, 1978.
Information Sources in the Earth Sciences. Ed. J. Hardy et al. 2nd ed. New Providence, NJ: Bowker-Saur, 1990.
McGraw-Hill Encyclopedia of the Geological Sciences. 2nd ed. New York: McGraw, 1988.
Magill's Survey of Science: Earth Science Series. 5 vols. Englewood Cliffs, NJ: Salem, 1990.
**Use of Earth Sciences Literature*. Ed. D. N. Wood. New York: Archon, 1973.
Discusses types of information sources (e.g., maps and review publications) and then provides extensive bibliographies in specific areas of geology (e.g., stratigraphy).

Bibliographies to Geology Books and Other Sources

Bibliography and Index of Geology. Alexandria, VA. Monthly with annual indexes, 1969–present.
Bibliography of North American Geology. 49 vols. Washington, DC: Geological Survey, 1923–1971.
Catalog of the U.S. Geological Survey Library. Boston: Hall, 1964. Supplements.
Geological Reference Sources: A Subject and Regional Bibliography. Ed. D. Ward, M. Wheeler, and R. Bier. Metuchen, NJ: Scarecrow, 1981.

Publications of the Geological Survey.
Washington, DC: GPO, 1979.
An annual listing of USGS publication,
updated by their monthly *New Publications of the Geological Survey.*
Strategic Minerals: A Bibliography. Waterloo, ON: U of Waterloo P, 1987.

Electronic Sources to Geology Literature

APILIT (American Petroleum Institute)
COMPENDEX
GEOARCHIVE
GEOBASE
GEOREF
INSPEC
WILSONDISC: APPLIED SCIENCE AND
TECHNOLOGY and GENERAL SCIENCE

Indexes to Articles in Geology Journals

**Bibliography and Index of Geology.* Boul-
der, CO: AGA, 1933–present.
Indexes geology journals, such as
*American Journal of Science, American
Mineralogist, Chemical Geology, Earth
Science, Geological Magazine, Geologi-
cal Society of America Bulletin, Geology,
Journal of Geology,* and others.
Bibliography and Index of Geology. Boul-
der, CO: GSA. Monthly with annual in-
dexes.
**General Science Index.* New York: Wil-
son, 1978–present.
Covers about 100 science periodicals,
including *Earth Science, Geological
Society of America Bulletin,* and *Miner
alogical Record.*

Health and Physical Education

See also Education, page 371, and Medical
Studies, pages 388.

Basic Sources and Guides to Health and Physical Education Literature

*Author's Guide to Journals in the Health
Field.* New York: Haworth, 1980.
**Biographical Dictionary of American
Sports.* Westport, CT: Greenwood,
1987–1989. Supplement, 1992.
Features four separate volumes on base-
ball, basketball, football, and other out-
door sports.
Columbia Encyclopedia of Nutrition. New
York: Putnam, 1988.

Consumer Health Information Source Book.
4th ed. Phoenix, AZ: Oryx, 1994.
Dictionary of American Food and Drink.
New York: Hearst, 1994.
*Dictionary of the Sport and Exercise Sci-
ences.* Champaign, IL: Human Kinetics,
1991.
*Encyclopedia of Health Information
Sources.* 2nd ed. Ed. P. Wasserman.
Detroit, MI: Gale, 1993.
Encyclopedia of Sports. New York: Barnes
and Noble, 1978. Supplements.
Food and Nutrition Information Guide.
Englewood, CO: Libraries Unlimited,
1988.
*Foundations of Physical Education and
Sport.* C. A. Bucher. St. Louis, MO:
Mosby, 1986.
***Introduction to Reference Sources in
Health Sciences.* Ed. F. Roper and J.
Boorkman. 2nd ed. Metuchen, NJ:
Scarecrow, 1984.
Discusses and lists health science refer-
ence materials, bibliographic sources,
and other specialized sources (e.g., sta-
tistical). Explains how to use many of
the sources described.
*Kirby's Guide to Fitness and Motor Perfor-
mance Tests.* Cape Girardeau, MO:
BenOak, 1991.
Research Processes in Physical Education.
2nd ed. Englewood Cliffs, NJ: Prentice-
Hall, 1984.
***Sports and Physical Education: A Guide to
the Reference Resources.* Ed. B. Gratcher
et al. Westport, CT: Greenwood, 1983.
Lists biographical, statistical, and other
sources on physical education and many
individual sports. Briefly describes each
source.
Vitamin and Health Encyclopedia. Pleasant
Grove, UT: Woodland, 1986.

Bibliographies to Health and Physical Education Books and Other Sources

*Annotated Bibliography of Health Econom-
ics.* Ed. A. J. Culyer et al. New York: St.
Martin's, 1977.

Electronic Sources to Health and Physical Education Literature

ACADEMIC INDEX
ERIC
MEDLINE
SOCIAL SCISEARCH
SPORT
WILSONDISC: EDUCATION and GENERAL
SCIENCE INDEXES

Indexes to Articles in Health and Physical Education Journals

See also Education, page 383, and Medical Studies, pages 388.

Current Index to Journals in Education. Phoenix, AZ: Oryx, 1969–present.

**Education Index.* New York: Wilson, 1929–present.

Both preceding titles index articles on physical education and health education in such journals as *Journal of Physical Education and Recreation, Journal of School Health, Physical Educator, Research Quarterly for Exercise and Sport,* plus many others.

**General Science Index.* New York: Wilson, 1978–present.

Indexes 100 science journals including *American Journal of Public Health, Health, JAMA, The Physician,* and *Sportsmedicine.*

Physical Education Index. Cape Giradeau, MO: BenOak, 1978–present.

Physical Fitness and Sports Medicine. Washington, DC: GPO, 1978–present.

History

Basic Sources and Guides to History Literature

Barzun, J., and H. Graff. *The Modern Researcher.* 5th ed. New York: Harcourt, 1992.

Britannica Book of the Year. Chicago: Encyclopaedia Britannica, 1938–present.

**Dictionary of American History.* 8 vols. New York: Scribner's, 1976.

Although dated, this encyclopedia is a well-documented, scholarly source for background information on the people, places, and events in U.S. history. Most of the articles include brief bibliographies of recommended sources.

Dictionary of the Middle Ages. Ed. J. R. Strayer. 13 vols. New York: Scribner's, 1982–1989.

Encyclopedia of American History. Ed. R. Morris. 6th ed. New York: Harper, 1982.

Encyclopedia of American Social History. 3 vols. Ed. Cayton, Gorn, and Williams. New York: Scribner's, 1993.

Encyclopedia of Asian History. 4 vols. New York: Scribner's, 1988.

Encyclopedia of Colonial and Revolutionary America. New York: Facts on File, 1989.

Encyclopedia of the Renaissance. New York: Facts on File, 1987.

Explorers and Discoverers of the World. Ed. D. B. Baker. Detroit, MI: Gale, 1993.

Facts on File Yearbook. New York: Facts on File, 1946–present.

Grum, B. *Timetables of History.* 3rd ed. New York: Simon & Schuster, 1991.

Harper Encyclopedia of Military History: From 3500 BC to Present. 4th ed. New York: HarperCollins, 1993.

**Library Research Guide to History.* Ed. E. Frick. Ann Arbor, MI: Pierian P, 1980.

Step-by-step guide to using reference sources in American history. Does not list many sources but thoroughly explains and analyzes all of the major tools in history. Good source for the beginning researcher.

**Prucha, F. P. *Handbook for Research in American History.* Lincoln: U of Nebraska P, 1987.

Lists sources of information, arranged by type of material and then by subject. A good resource for comprehensive research in American history when the basic sources are exhausted.

Pulton, H. J., and M. S. Howland. *The Historian's Handbook.* Norman: U of Oklahoma P, 1986.

Research in Archives: The Use of Unpublished Primary Sources. Ed. P. C. Brooks. Chicago: U of Chicago P, 1968.

Times Atlas of World History. Ed. G. Parker. 4th ed. Maplewood, NJ: Hammond, 1993.

Bibliographies to History Books and Other Sources

Bibliographer's Manual of American History. 5 vols. Philadelphia: Henkels, 1907–1910.

Bibliography of British History. Oxford: Clarendon, 1928–1977.

Combined Retrospective Indexes to Journals in History: 1838–1974. 11 vols. Arlington, VA: Carrollton, 1977.

The English Historical Review. Harlow, Essex, England: Longman, 1886–present. This journal regularly features valuable bibliographies.

Goldentree Bibliographies in History. A series of books published in different years by different publishers.

Historical Abstracts. Santa Barbara, CA: ABC-Clio, 1955–present.

International Bibliography of Historical Sciences. New York: Wilson, 1930–present.

Wars of the United States. New York: Garland, 1984–present.

A series of annotated bibliographies.

Writings on American History. Washington, DC: AHA, 1902–present.

Electronic Sources to History Literature
ACADEMIC INDEX
AMERICA: HISTORY AND LIFE
HISTORICAL ABSTRACTS
WILSONDISC: HUMANITIES INDEX

Indexes to Articles in History Journals

**America: History and Life.* Santa Barbara,
CA: ABC-Clio, 1964–present.
    Well indexed and provides both articles
    and bibliographies.

**American Historical Association. *Recently
Published Articles.* 1976–present.
    Indexes articles on American history in
    journals such as *American Historical Re-
    view, Civil War History, Journal of
    American History, Journal of the West,
    Reviews in American History,* and many
    others.

Historical Abstracts. Santa Barbara, CA:
ABC-Clio, 1955–present.
    Provides international coverage of Euro-
    pean and world history.

**Humanities Index.* New York: Wilson,
1974–present.
    Indexes world history and American his-
    tory in *Canadian Journal of History,
    English Historical Review, European His-
    torical Quarterly, Journal of Modern
    History,* and many others.

Journalism and Mass Communications

*Basic Sources and Guides to Journal-
ism and Mass Communications
Literature*

*The Associated Press Stylebook and Libel
Manual.* Rev. ed. New York: AP, 1992.

Black, E. S., and J. K. Bracken. *Communication and the Mass Media, A Guide to
the Reference Literature.* Englewood,
CO: Libraries Unlimited, 1991.

Broadcast Communications Dictionary.
Ed. L. Diamant. Westport, CT: Greenwood, 1989.

Broadcasting Cablecasting Yearbook.
Washington, DC: Broadcasting Publications, 1982–present. Annually.

**Cates, J. A. *Journalism: A Guide to the
Reference Literature.* Englewood, CO:
Libraries Unlimited, 1990.
    An extensive listing of sources of use in
    researching print and other mass media.
    Provides evaluative, descriptive comments
    on each of the 700 sources included.

Encyclopedia of American Journalism. Ed.
D. Paneth. New York: Facts on File,
1983.

*Encyclopedia of Twentieth-Century Journal-
ists.* Ed. W. H. Taft. New York: Garland, 1984.

Galvin, K. *Media Law: A Legal Handbook
for the Working Journalist.* Berkeley,
CA: Nolo Press, 1984.

Halliwell's Film Guide. New York: Harper,
1993.

*Information Sources in the Press and
Broadcast Media.* Ed. S. Eagle.
New Providence, NJ: Bowker-Saur, 1991.

**International Encyclopedia of Communi-
cations.* Ed. E. Barnouw et al. 4 vol.
New York: Oxford UP, 1989.
    A very scholarly, thorough treatment of
    a great variety of subjects. Includes arti-
    cles on key people in mass communica-
    tions (e.g., Charlie Chaplin) as well as
    concepts and issues (e.g., copyright, cy-
    bernetics).

Les Brown's Encyclopedia of Television. 3rd
ed. Detroit, MI: Gale, 1992.

Nelson, H. L., D. L. Teeter, Jr, and R. D.
LeDuc. *Law of Mass Communications.*
7th ed. Mineola, NY: Foundation,
1992.

Pruett, B. *Popular Entertainment Research:
How to Do It and How to Use It.*
Metuchen, NJ: Scarecrow, 1992.

The Reporter's Handbook. New York: St.
Martin's, 1990.

**Rubin, R. B., et al. *Communication Re-
search.* 3rd ed. Belmont, CA:
Wadsworth, 1993.
    Along with chapters providing guidance
    in library research plans and the sources
    needed for them, also contains useful
    information on conducting formal re-
    search studies.

**Variety's Film Reviews.* New Providence,
NJ: Bowker, 1983–present.
    Already comprising more than 20 vol-
    umes, this set reprints all film reviews
    that have appeared in *Variety* since
    1907.

*Bibliographies to Journalism and Mass
Communications Books and Other
Sources*

American Journalism History. Ed. W. D.
Sloan. Westport, CT: Greenwood, 1989.

Annotated Media Bibliography. Ed. B. Con-
gdon. Washington, DC: ACC, 1985.

Black Media in America: A Resource Guide.
Ed. G. H. Hill. Boston: Hall, 1984.

*Broadcasting Bibliography: A Guide to the
Literature of Radio and Television.* Rev.
ed. Washington, DC: National Association of Broadcasters, 1989.

Journalism Biographies: Master Index. Detroit, MI: Gale, 1979. Supplements.

The Journalist's Bookshelf. Ed. R. F. Wolseley and I. Wolseley. 8th ed. Atlanta, GA: Berg, 1986.

Law of Mass Communications: Freedom and Control of Print and Broadcast Media. Mineola, NY: Foundation, 1989.

The Literature of Journalism: An Annotated Bibliography. Ed. W. C. Price. Minneapolis: U of Minnesota P, 1959.

Manchel, F. *Film Study: An Analytical Bibliography.* 4 vols. Madison, NJ: Farleigh Dickinson, 1990.

Mass Media Bibliography. Ed. E. Blum et al. Champaign: U of Illinois P, 1990.

Mass Media and the Constitution: An Encyclopedia of Supreme Court Decisions. Ed. R. F. Hixson. New York: Garland, 1989.

News Media and Public Policy: An Annotated Bibliography. Ed. J. P. McKerns. 2 vols. New York: Garland, 1985.

Radio and Television: A Selected, Annotated Bibliography. Metuchen, NJ: Scarecrow, 1978. Supplements to 1982.

Violence and Terror in the Mass Media: An Annotated Bibliography. Westport, CT: Greenwood, 1988.

Electronic Sources to Journalism and Mass Communications Literature

ACADEMIC INDEX
AP NEWS
ARTS AND HUMANITIES SEARCH
COURIER PLUS
MAGAZINE INDEX
NATIONAL NEWSPAPER INDEX
NEWSEARCH
REUTERS
SOCSCI SEARCH
UPI NEWS
WILSONDISC: BUSINESS, HUMANITIES, and the READERS' GUIDE INDEXES

Indexes to Articles in Journalism and Mass Communications Journals

**Business Periodicals Index.* New York: Wilson, 1958–present.
Indexes such industry periodicals as *Broadcasting, Communications News, Television/Radio Age,* and *Telecommunications.*

Communications Abstracts. Beverly Hills, CA: Sage, 1978–present.
Indexes approximately 100 journals and selected books.

**Humanities Index.* New York: Wilson, 1974–present.
Indexes journalism articles in such journals as *Journalism History, Journalism Quarterly, Columbia Journalism Review,*

Commentary, Quill, Encounter, Communications Quarterly, Journal of Broadcasting, and others.

**Readers' Guide to Periodical Literature.* New York: Wilson, 1900–date.
Indexes news and general interest magazines, such as *Nation, Newsweek, New York Review of Books, New Republic, Saturday Review, U.S. News and World Report,* and others.

Law

See also Political Science, pages 391–393

Basic Sources and Guides to Law Literature

American Jurisprudence. 2nd ed. Rochester, NY: Lawyers Cooperative, 1962–present (continuously revised and supplemented).

The American Law Dictionary. Santa Barbara, CA: ABC-Clio, 1991.

Black's Law Dictionary. 6th ed. St. Paul, MN: West, 1990.

Cohen, M., and K. C. Olson. *Legal Research in a Nutshell.* 5th ed. Minneapolis, MN: West, 1992.

Corpus Juris Secundum. New York: American Law Book, 1936–present (continuously revised and supplemented).

Dictionary of Modern Legal Usage. New York: Oxford UP, 1987.

Encyclopedia of Legal Information Sources. 2nd ed. Ed. P. Wasserman et al. Detroit, MI: Gale, 1992.

Fox, J. R. *Dictionary of International and Comparative Law.* Dobbs Ferry, NY: Oceana, 1992.

**Guide to American Law.* 12 vols. and annual yearbooks. St. Paul, MN: West, 1985.
An encyclopedia of law written for the nonspecialist. Provides background and explanations of legal topics and issues (e.g., abortion, civil rights).

Guide to the Supreme Court. 2nd ed. Washington, DC: Congressional Quarterly, 1990.

Historic U.S. Court Cases, 1690–1990: An Encyclopedia. Ed. J. W. Johnson. New York: Garland, 1992.

How to Research the Supreme Court. Washington, DC: Congressional Quarterly, 1992.

Legal Research in a Nutshell. 5th ed. St. Paul, MN: West, 1992.

Legal Research and Writing. 4th ed. St. Paul, MN: West, 1992.

Modern Dictionary for the Legal Profession. Buffalo, NY: Hein, 1993.

National Survey of State Laws. Detroit, MI: Gale, 1993.

Bibliographies to Law Books and Other Sources

Index to Legal Books. 6 vols. New York: Bowker, 1989.

The U.S. Supreme Court: A Bibliography. Washington, DC: Congressional Quarterly, 1990.

United States Supreme Court Decisions. 2nd ed. Metuchen, NJ: Scarecrow, 1983.

Electronic Sources to Law Literature

CRIMINAL JUSTICE PERIODICALS INDEX
LABORLAW
LEGAL RESOURCE INDEX
LEXIS
NCJRS (National Criminal Justice Reference Service)
WILSONDISC: INDEX TO LEGAL PERIODICALS

Indexes to Articles in Law Journals

**Index to Legal Periodicals.* New York: Wilson, 1909–present.
Indexes such journals as the *American Bar Association Journal, Harvard Law Review,* and *Trial.*

**PAIS International in Print* (formerly *PAIS Bulletin*). New York: PAIS, 1915–present.
Indexes government publications and other books, as well as such journals as *High Technology Law Journal, Labor Law Journal, Law and Contemporary Problems,* and *Real Estate Law Journal.*

Literature and Language Studies

Basic Sources, Guides, and Bibliographies to Literature

Abrams, M. H. *A Glossary of Literary Terms.* 6th ed. New York: Harcourt, 1993.

Bracken, J. K. *Reference Works in British and American Literature.* Vol. 1: *Literature;* Vol. 2: *Writers.* Englewood, CO: Libraries Unlimited, 1990–1991.

Cambridge Guide to Literature in English. New York: Cambridge UP, 1993.

Contemporary Authors. Detroit, MI: Gale, 1962–present.

Contemporary Literary Criticism. Detroit, MI: Gale, 1973–present.

The Critical Temper: A Survey of Modern Criticism on English and American Literature. New York: Ungar, 1969. Supplements, 1981 and 1989.

**Dictionary of Literary Biography.* Series. Detroit, MI: Gale, 1978–present (in progress).
Already comprising more than 130 volumes, this excellent, well-documented encyclopedia is the best source for finding background information and selected bibliographies on individual authors.

Essay and General Literature Index. New York: Wilson, 1900–present.

**Harner, J. L. *Literary Research Guide.* 2nd ed. New York: MLA, 1993.
A comprehensive guide to major literary reference tools and other sources for literature worldwide.

Hawthorn, J. *A Glossary of Contemporary Literary Theory.* New York: Routledge, 1992.

**Holman, C. H., and W. Harmon. *Handbook to Literature.* 6th ed. New York: Macmillan, 1992.
An excellent dictionary of the words and phrases used in the study of English and American literature. Uses many literary examples for each major term.

**Literary Criticism Index.* 2nd ed. Ed. A. R. Weiner and S. Means. Metuchen, NJ: Scarecrow, 1993.
Indexes about 85 standard bibliographies of literary criticism. For each writer, there are listings of criticisms and places to find his or her specific works.

**Magill's Bibliography of Literary Criticism.* Ed. F. Magill. 4 vols. Englewood Cliffs, NJ: Salem, 1979.
An index to selected critical articles, books, or chapters in books that deal with specific works of western literature. Includes listings for 2,500 works of literature by 600 different authors.

Reference Guide for English Studies. Ed. M. J. Marcuse. Berkeley: U of California P, 1990.

Research Guide for Undergraduate Students: English and American Literature. New York: MLA, 1985.

Afro-American Literature

See also Ethnic Studies, page 373.

Bibliographic Guide to Black Studies. New York: Hall, 1980. Supplements.

A Bibliographical Guide to African-American Women Writers. Ed. C. L. Jordan. Westport, CT: Greenwood, 1993.

Black American Fiction: A Bibliography. Ed. C. Fairbanks and E. A. Engeldinger. Metuchen, NJ: Scarecrow, 1978.

Black American Writers: Bibliographic Essays. 2 vols. New York: St. Martin's, 1978.

Black American Writers Past and Present: A Biographical and Bibliographical Dictionary. Ed. T. G. Rush et al. 2 vols. Metuchen, NJ: Scarecrow, 1975.

Black Americans in Autobiography: An Annotated Bibliography of Autobiographies and Autobiographical Books Written Since the Civil War. Durham, NC: Duke UP, 1984.

Conjuring: Black Women, Fiction, and Literary Tradition. Bloomington: Indiana UP, 1985.

Davis, A. *From the Dark Tower: Afro-American Writers from 1900 to 1960.* Washington, DC: Howard UP, 1974.

Gilkin, R. *Black American Women in Literature.* Jefferson, NC: McFarland, 1989.

Poetry of the Negro: 1746–1970. Ed. L. Hughes and A. Bontempts. New York: Doubleday, 1970.

Werner, C. *Black American Women Novelists.* Englewood Cliffs, NJ: Salem, 1989.

Whitlow, R. *Black American Literature: A Critical History.* Totowa, NJ: Littlefield, 1974.

American Literature

American Bibliography. Ed. C. Evans. 14 vols. Magnolia, MA: Smith, 1967.

American Literary Scholarship. Durham, NC: Duke UP, 1963–present. Annually.

American Novel: 1789 to 1968. Ed. D. Gerstenberger and G. Hendrick. Chicago: Swallow, 1961 and 1970.

American Writers. 4 vols. New York: Scribner's, 1961–1981. Supplements.

Articles on American Literature. (Separate titles covering 1900–1950, 1950–1967, and 1968–75). Durham, NC: Duke UP, 1954, 1970, and 1979.

Bibliographical Guide to the Study of Literature of the USA. Ed. C. Gohdes. 5th ed. Durham, NC: Duke UP, 1984.

A Bibliographical Guide to the Study of Western American Literature. Ed. R. W. Etulain. Lincoln: U of Nebraska P, 1982.

Bibliography of American Literature. New Haven; Yale UP, 1955–present.

Bibliography of Bibliographies in American Literature. Ed. C. H. Nilon. New York: Bowker, 1970.

Cambridge Handbook of American Literature. Ed. J. Salzman. New York: Cambridge UP, 1986.

Literary History of the United States. Ed. R. E. Spiller et al. 4th ed. 2 vols. New York: Macmillan, 1974.

Mathiessen, F. O. *American Renaissance: Art and Expression in the Age of Emerson and Whitman.* London: Oxford UP, 1968.

Modern American Literature. Ed. D. Nyren. 4th ed. New York: Unger, 1969–1976. Supplements.

Oxford Companion to American Literature. Ed. J. D. Hart. 5th ed. New York: Oxford UP, 1983.

The Transcendentalists: A Review of Research and Criticism. Ed. J. Myerson. New York: MLA, 1984.

British Literature

Anglo-Irish Literature: A Review of Research. Ed. R. J. Finneran. New York: MLA, 1976. Supplement, 1983.

Baker, E. A. *History of the English Novel.* 11 vols. New York: Barnes and Noble, 1975 (reprint of 1924–1967 ed.).

Bibliographical Resources for the Study of Nineteenth Century English Fiction. Ed. G. N. Ray. Folcroft, PA: Folcroft, 1964.

British Writers. Ed. I. Scott-Kilvert. 8 vols. New York: Scribner's, 1979–1983. Supplements, 1987 and 1992.

British Writers and Their Works. 10 vols. Lincoln: U of Nebraska P, 1964–1970.

Cambridge Bibliography of English Literature. Ed. G. Wilson. 5 vols. New York: Cambridge UP, 1965.

Cambridge Guide to English Literature. Ed. M. Stapleton. New York: Cambridge UP, 1983.

Cambridge History of the English Literature. 15 vols. Cambridge: Cambridge UP, 1961 and 1992.

A Descriptive Catalogue of the Bibliographies of Twentieth Century British Poets, Novelists, and Dramatists. Ed. E. W. Mellown. 2nd ed. Troy, NY: Whitston, 1978.

Encyclopedia of Victorian Britain. Ed. S. Mitchell. New York: Garland, 1987.

The English Romantic Poets: A Review of Research and Criticism. 4th ed. New York: MLA, 1985.

Evans, G. L., and B. Evans. *The Shakespeare Companion.* New York: Scribner's, 1978.

McGraw-Hill Guide to English Literature. 2 vols. Ed. K. Lawrence, B. Seifter, and L. Ratner. New York: McGraw, 1985.

Modern British Literature. 4 vols. Literary Criticism Series. New York: Ungar, 1966–1975. Supplements, 1885–present.

New Cambridge Bibliography of English Literature. 5 vols. New York: Cambridge UP, 1969–1977.

Oxford Companion to English Literature. Ed. M. Drabble. 5th ed. Oxford: Clarendon, 1985.

Oxford History of English Literature. Oxford: Clarendon, 1945–present.

Romantic Movement: A Selective and Critical Bibliography. New York: Garland, 1980–present.

Drama and Theater

American Drama Criticism: Interpretations, 1890–1977. Ed. F. E. Eddleman. New Haven, CT: Shoe String, 1979. Supplements 1984, 1989, and 1992.

Bailey. J. *A Guide to Reference and Bibliography for Theatre Research.* 2nd ed. Columbus: Ohio State U, 1983.

British Theatre, A Bibliography from the Beginning to 1985. Romsey, UK: Motley, 1989.

Cambridge Guide to American Theatre. Ed. D. B. Wilmeth and T. L. Miller. New York: Cambridge UP, 1993.

Cambridge Guide to Theatre. Ed. E. Banham. New York: Cambridge UP, 1992.

Catalog of the Theatre and Drama Collections. Boston: Hall, 1967. Supplements.

Chicorel Index Series. Ed. M. Chicorel. 27 vols. New York: Chicorel Library, 1970–1978.

Contemporary Dramatists. Ed. J. Vinson. 4th ed. New York: St. Martin's, 1987.

Critical Survey of Drama. Ed. F. N. Magill. 8 vols. Englewood Cliffs, NJ: Salem, 1994.

Drama Criticism. 3 vols. Detroit, MI: Gale, 1991–1993.

Drury's Guide to Best Plays. 4th ed. Metuchen, NJ: Scarecrow, 1987.

Index to Full Length Plays: 1895–1964. 3 vols. Westwood: Faxon, 1956–1965.

Index to Plays in Periodicals. Metuchen, NJ: Scarecrow, 1979 and 1977–1987. Supplement, 1990.

McGraw-Hill Encyclopedia of World Drama. 2nd ed. 5 vols. New York: McGraw, 1983.

Oxford Companion to the Theatre. 4th ed. Fair Lawn, NJ: Oxford UP, 1984.

Play Index. New York: Wilson, 1953–present.

Silvester, R. *United States Theatre, A Bibliography from the Beginning to 1990.* Boston: Hall, 1993.

A Survey and Bibliography of Renaissance Drama. 4 vols. Lincoln: U of Nebraska P, 1975–1978.

Language Studies

American Literature and Language: A Guide to Information Sources. Detroit, MI: Gale, 1982.

Cambridge Encyclopedia of Language. Ed. D. Crystal. New York: Cambridge UP: 1988.

Campbell, G. L. *Compendium of the World's Languages.* 2 vols. New York: Routledge, 1991.

Crystal, D. *An Encyclopedic Dictionary of Language and Languages.* Oxford: Blackwell, 1993.

A Dictionary of American English on Historical Principals. Ed. W. Craigie and J. R. Hulbert. 4 vols. Chicago. U of Chicago P, 1938–1944.

Dictionary of American Regional English. Ed. F. Cassidy. Cambridge: Harvard UP, 1985–present (in progress).

International Encyclopedia of Linguistics. 4 vols. New York: Oxford UP, 1991.

Linguistics: A Guide to Reference Literature. Englewood, CO: Libraries Unlimited, 1991.

The Oxford Companion to the English Language. Ed. T. McArthur. New York: Oxford UP, 1992.

Oxford English Dictionary. 2nd ed. Ed. J. A. Simpson et al. 20 vols. New York: Oxford UP, 1989.

The World's Major Languages. Ed. B. Comrie. New York: Oxford UP, 1987.

Mythology and Folklore

American Folklore: A Bibliography. Metuchen, NJ: Scarecrow, 1977.

The Arthurian Encyclopedia. Ed. N. J. Lacy. New York: Bedrick, 1987.

Arthurian Legend and Literature: An Annotated Bibliography. 2 vols. New York: Garland, 1983.

Ashlimar, D. L. *Guide to Folktales in the English Language.* Westport, CT: Greenwood, 1987.

Bibliography of Greek Myth in English Poetry. Ed. H. H. Law. Folcroft, PA: Folcroft, 1955.

Bullfinch's Mythology. New York: Avenel, 1978.

Campbell, J. *Historical Atlas of World Mythology.* San Francisco: Harper, 1983–present (in progress).

Dictionary of Celtic Myth and Legend. Ed. M. J. Green. London: Thames & Hudson, 1992.

Dictionary of Classical Mythology Ed. R. S. Bell. Santa Barbara, CA: ABC-Clio, 1982.

Dictionary of Native American Mythology. Santa Barbara, CA: ABC-Clio, 1992.

Fable Scholarship: An Annotated Bibliography. Ed. P. Carnes. New York: Garland, 1982.

Facts on File Encyclopedia of World Mythology and Legend. Ed. A. S. Mercatante. New York: Facts on File, 1988.

Folklore of American Holidays. Detroit, MI: Gale, 1987.

Folklore and Literature in the United States: An Annotated Bibliography. Ed. S. S. Jones. New York: Garland, 1984.

Folklore of World Holidays. Detroit, MI: Gale, 1992.

Frazer, J. *The Golden Bough.* New York: St. Martin's, 1955.

Grimal, P. *Dictionary of Classical Mythology.* New York: Blackwell, 1986.

Index to Fairy Tales, 1949–1972. Ed. N. O. Ireland. Metuchen, NJ: Scarecrow, 1973. Supplements.

Mythological and Fabulous Creatures: A Source Book and Research Guide. Westport, CT: Greenwood, 1987.

Oxford Guide to Classical Mythology in the Arts, 1300–1990s. Ed. J. D. Reid. New York: Oxford UP, 1993.

Steinfirst, S. *Folklore and Folklife: A Guide to English-Language Reference Sources.* New York: Garland, 1992.

Storyteller's Sourcebook. Detroit, MI: Gale, 1982.

Tale Type—and Motif—Indexes: An Annotated Bibliography. Ed. D. S. Azzolina. New York: Garland, 1987.

Novel, The

American Fiction: A Contribution Toward a Bibliography. 3 vols. Ed. L. H. Wright. San Marino, CA: Huntington Library, 1969 and 1979.

American Fiction 1900–1950: A Guide to Information Sources. Ed. J. Woodress. Detroit, MI: Gale, 1974.

The American Novel: A Checklist. Vol. 2: *Criticism Written 1960–68.* Ed. D. Gerstenberger and G. Hendrick. Chicago: Swallow, 1970.

The American Novel 1789–1959: A Checklist of Twentieth Century Criticism. Denver: Swallow, 1961.

The Contemporary English Novel: An Annotated Bibliography of Secondary Sources. Ed. H. W. Drescher and B. Kahrmann. New York: IPS, 1973.

The Contemporary Novel: A Checklist of Critical Literature on the British and American Novel Since 1945. Ed. I. Adelman and R. Dworkin. Metuchen, NJ: Scarecrow, 1972.

The Continental Novel: A Checklist of Criticism in English, 1900–1960. Metuchen, NJ: Scarecrow, 1967–1980. Supplement, 1983.

Critical Survey of Long Fiction. Ed. F. N. Magill. 8 vols. Englewood Cliffs, NJ: Salem, 1991.

English Language Criticism on the Foreign Novel. Athens, OH: Swallow, 1989.

English Novel: 1578–1956: A Checklist of Twentieth Century Criticism. Ed. J. F. Bell and D. Baird. Denver: Swallow, 1958.

English Novel Explication: Criticism to 1972. Ed. H. Palmer and J. Dyson. New Haven, CT: Shoe String, 1973. Supplements, 1976–present.

Facts on File Bibliography of American Fiction, 1588–1865. New York: Facts on File, 1994.

Facts on File Bibliography of American Fiction, 1866–1918. 2 vols. New York: Facts on File, 1993.

Facts on File Bibliography of American Fiction, 1919–1988. 2 vols. New York: Facts on File, 1991.

Kellman, S. G. *The Modern American Novel: An Annotated Bibliography.* Englewood Cliffs, NJ: Salem, 1991.

Poetry

American and British Poetry: A Guide to the Criticism, 1925–1978. Athens, OH: Swallow, 1984.

Columbia Granger's Index to Poetry. Ed. W. J. Smith. 10th ed. New York: Columbia UP, 1994.

Critical Survey of Poetry. Ed. F. N. Magill. 8 vols. Englewood Cliffs, NJ: Salem, 1982.

English Poetry: Select Bibliographical Guides. Ed. A. E. Dyson. New York: Oxford UP, 1971.

Guide to American Poetry Explication. 2 vols. Boston: Hall, 1989.

Martinez, N. C. *Guide to British Poetry Explication. Volume 1: Old English-Medieval.* Boston: Hall, 1991.

New Princeton Encyclopedia of Poetry and Poetics. 3rd ed. Princeton, NJ: Princeton UP, 1993.

Pearce, R. H. *The Continuity of American Poetry.* Middletown, CT: Wesleyan, 1987.

Poetry Explication: A Checklist of Interpretations Since 1925 of British and American Poems Past and Present. Boston: Hall, 1980.

Subject Index to Poetry for Children and Young People. Ed. D. B. Frizzell-Smith and E. L. Andrews. Chicago: ALA, 1977.

Waggoner, H. H. *American Poetry: From the Puritans to the Present.* Boston: Houghton, 1968.

Short Story

American Short-Fiction Criticism and Scholarship, 1959–1977: A Checklist. Ed. J. Weixlmann. Athens: Ohio UP, 1982.

Critical Survey of Short Fiction. Ed. F. N. Magill. 7 vols. Englewood Cliffs, NJ: Salem, 1993.

Short Story Index. Ed. D. E. Cook and I. S. Monro. New York: Wilson, 1953. Supplements.

Twentieth-Century Short Story Explication. Ed. W. S. Walker. 3rd ed. Hamden, CT: Shoe String, 1977. Supplements. Also, new series began in 1993.

World Literature

See also Foreign Language Studies, pages 375.

Benet's Reader's Encyclopedia. 3rd ed. New York: Harper & Row, 1987.

Columbia Dictionary of Modern European Literature. 2nd ed. Ed. J.-A. Bede and W. Edgerton. Columbia UP, 1980.

Dictionary of World Literary Terms. Ed. J. T. Shipley. Boston: Writer, 1970.

Encyclopedia of World Literature in the 20th Century. New York: Ungar, 1967 and 1981.

Reader's Companion to World Literature. Rev. ed. Ed. L. H. Horstein. New York: NAL, 1956.

Electronic Sources to Literature and Language Studies

ACADEMIC INDEX
ARTS AND HUMANITIES SEARCH
BOOK REVIEW INDEX
LLBA (Linguistics and Language Behavior Abstracts)
MLA BIBLIOGRAPHY
WILSONDISC: HUMANITIES INDEX

Indexes to Articles in Literature and Language Studies Journals

***Abstracts of English Studies.* Urbana, IL: NCTE, 1958–date.

Provides abstracts to monographs and journal articles. Tenth issue each year features a subject index.

Abstracts of Folklore Studies. Austin: U of Texas P, 1962–1975. (Ceased publication.)

Indexes folklore journals, such as *Dovetail, Kentucky Folklore Record, Relics,* and others.

Book Review Digest. New York: Wilson, 1905–present.

Book Review Index. Detroit, MI: Gale, 1965–present.

***Humanities Index.* New York: Wilson, 1974–present.

Provides general indexing to literary and language topics in several key journals.

Index to Book Reviews in the Humanities. Detroit, MI: Thompson, 1960–present.

***MLA International Bibliography of Books and Articles on the Modern Language and Literatures.* New York: MLA, 1921–present. Annually.

The best overall index to major literary figures and language topics.

Mathematics

Basic Sources and Guides to Mathematics Literature

Biographical Dictionary of Mathematicians. 4 vols. New York: Scribner's, 1991.

CRC Handbook of Mathematical Sciences. Ed. W. Beyer. 6th ed. West Palm Beach, FL: CRC, 1987.

Encyclopaedia of Mathematics. 10 vols. Norwell, MA: Reidel/Kluwer, 1988–present (in progress).

***Encyclopedic Dictionary of Mathematics.* Ed. K. Ito. 2nd ed. 4 vols. Cambridge: MIT P, 1987.

Provides thorough but concise coverage of 450 different concepts and phenomena of mathematics (e.g., algebraic groups). Also includes bibliographies listing important sources of research.

Hoggar, S. G. *Mathematics for Computer Graphics.* New York: Cambridge UP, 1993.

This work draws on many areas of pure math, applying them to computer graphics.

***How to Find Out in Mathematics.* Ed. J. E. Pemberton. 2nd ed. Elmsford, NY: Pergamon, 1970.

A description of the resources available for research, including reference books, periodicals, and monographs. Also includes sections on careers, education, and the history of math.

International Catalogue of Scientific Literature: 1901–1914. Section A: "Mathematics." Metuchen, NJ: Scarecrow, 1974.

Mathematical Journals: An Annotated Guide. Comp. D. F. Liang. Metuchen, NJ: Scarecrow, 1992.

The Mathematics Dictionary. 5th ed. New York: Reinhold, 1992.

Mathematics Encyclopedia: A Made Simple Book. Garden City, NY: Doubleday, 1977.

Motz, L., and J. H. Weaver. *The Story of Mathematics.* New York: Plenum, 1993. This work provides an excellent history of mathematics.

Use of Mathematics Literature. Ed. A. R. Darling. Boston: Butterworth, 1977.

Using the Mathematical Literature: A Practical Guide. Ed. B. K. Schaefer. New York: Dekker, 1979.

The VNR Concise Encyclopedia of Mathematics. 2nd ed. Ed. W. Gellert et al. New York: Reinhold, 1989.

Bibliographies to Mathematics Books and Other Sources

Annotated Bibliography of Expository Writing in the Mathematical Sciences. Ed. M. P. Gaffney and L. A. Steen. Washington, DC: Mathematics Assn., 1976.

Bibliography and Research Manual of the History of Mathematics. Ed. K. L. May. Toronto: U of Toronto P, 1973.

Current Information Sources in Mathematics: An Annotated Guide to Books and Periodicals: 1960–72. Ed. E. M. Dick. Littleton, OH: Libraries Unlimited, 1973.

Omega Bibliography of Mathematical Logic. Ed. G. H. Muller and W. Lenski. 6 vols. New York: Springer-Verlag, 1987.

Schaaf, W. I. *A Bibliography of Recreational Mathematics.* 4 vols. Washington, DC: NCTM, 1970.

Schaaf, W. I. *The High School Math Library.* 8th ed. Reston, VA: NCTM, 1987.

Vestpocket Bibliographies. Ed. W. I. Schaaf. See miscellaneous issues of the *Journal of Recreational Mathematics,* 1983–present.

Electronic Sources to Mathematics Literature

MATHSCI
WILSONDISC: GENERAL SCIENCE INDEX

Indexes to Articles in Mathematics Journals

***General Science Index.* New York: Wilson, 1978–present.

Covers about 100 science periodicals, including *American Mathematical Monthly, Journal of Recreational Mathematics,* and *Mathematics Magazine.*

Mathematical Reviews. Providence, RI: AMS, 1940–present.

Medical Studies

Basic Sources and Guides to Medical Studies Literature

American Medical Association Encyclopedia of Medicine. New York: Random, 1989.

Author's Guide to Journals in the Health Field. Ed. D. Ardell and J. James. New York: Haworth, 1980.

Black's Medical Dictionary. 37th ed. Lanham, MD: Barnes and Noble, 1992.

Cambridge World History of Human Disease. Ed. K. F. Kipple. New York: Cambridge UP, 1993.

Core Collections in Nursing and Allied Health Sciences. Phoenix, AZ: Oryx, 1990.

Information Sources in the Medical Sciences. Ed. L. T. Morton and S. Godbolt. 4th ed. London: Butterworth, 1992.

International Dictionary of Medicine and Biology. 3 vols. New York: Wiley, 1986.

***Introduction to Reference Sources in Health Sciences.* 2nd ed. Ed. F. Roper and J. Boorkman. Chicago: MLA, 1984. Discusses and lists health science reference materials, bibliographic sources, and other specialized sources (e.g., statistical). Explains how to use many of the sources described.

Logan, C., and M. K. Rice. *Logan's Medical and Scientific Abbreviations.* Philadelphia: Lippincott, 1987.

Polit, D., and B. Hungler. *Nursing Research: Principles and Methods.* 4th ed. Philadelphia: Lippincott, 1991.

**Stauch, K., et al. *Nursing: Illustrated Search Strategy and Sources.* 2nd ed. Ann Arbor, MI: Pierian P, 1993. Provides guidance in formulating a research plan, as well as information on finding and using specific research tools. Also has a listing of recent sources in major areas of nursing (e.g., community health issues).

Bibliographies to Medical Studies Books and Other Sources

AIDS Information Sourcebook. 3rd ed. Phoenix, AZ: Oryx, 1991.

An Annotated Bibliography of Health Economics. Ed. A. J. Culyer at al. New York: St. Martin's, 1977.

Medical Reference Works, 1679–1966. Ed. J. Blake and C. Roos. Chicago: Medical Library Association, 1967. Supplements.

Nursing Studies Index. Ed. V. Henderson. 4 vols. Philadelphia: Lippincott, 1957–1972.

Resources for Third World Health Planners: A Selected Subject Bibliography. Buffalo, NY: Conch, 1980.

Electronic Sources to Medical Studies Literature

ACADEMIC INDEX
AIDSLINE
BIOSIS PREVIEWS
EMBASE
MEDLINE
NURSING AND ALLIED HEALTH
SCISEARCH
WILSONDISC: GENERAL SCIENCE INDEX

Indexes to Articles in Medical Studies Journals

***Cumulated Index Medicus.* Bethesda, MD: U.S. Department of Health and Human Services, 1959–present.
Provides indexing to most medical journals published worldwide.

***Cumulative Index to Nursing and Allied Health Literature.* Glendale, CA: CINAHL, 1956–present.
Indexes nursing literature in journals such as *Cancer Nurse, Current Reviews for Recovery Room Nurses, Journal of Practical Nursing, Journal of Nursing Education,* and many more.

International Nursing Index. New York: AJN, 1970–present.

Music

Basic Sources and Guides to Music Literaure

Baker's Biographical Dictionary of Musicians. 8th ed. New York: Schirmer, 1992.

Dictionary of Music. Ed. A. Isaacs and E. Martin. New York: Facts on File, 1983.

Dictionary of Music Technology. Ed. C. Tristam. Westport, CT: Greenwood, 1992.

***Druesdow, J. Library Research Guide to Music.* Ann Arbor: Pierian P, 1982.
An easy-to-follow guide to starting, planning, and carrying out library research in music. Explains how to use the sources, as well as provides a listing of periodical indexes, bibliographies, and other reference tools.

Encyclopedia of Pop, Rock, and Soul. Ed. I. Stambler. New York: St. Martin's, 1989.

Information on Music: A Handbook of Reference Sources in European Languages. 3 vols. Englewood, CO: Libraries Unlimited, 1975–1984.

International Cyclopedia of Music and Musicians. Ed. B. Bahle. 11th ed. New York: Dodd, 1985.

International Encyclopedia of Women Composers. Ed. A. Cohen. 2nd ed. New York: Books and Music USA, 1988.

Music Analyses, An Annotated Guide to the Literature. H. J. Diamond. New York: Schirmer, 1991.

***Music Reference and Research Materials.* Ed. V. Duckles and M. Keller. 4th ed. New York: Schirmer, 1988.
A comprehensive and thorough bibliography of sources for research in music, including recordings and music history. Provides brief comments on many of the 3,200 sources listed.

New College Encyclopedia of Music. New York: Norton, 1981.

New Grove Dictionary of American Music. Ed. H. Hitchcock and S. Sadie. 4 vols. New York: Grove, 1986.

***New Grove Dictionary of Music and Musicians.* Ed. S. Sadie. 20 vols. New York: Macmillan, 1980.
A very scholarly, comprehensive, and international encyclopedia for music and music history. Includes bibliographies of important resources for each major topic.

New Harvard Dictionary of Music. Ed. W. Apel. Cambridge: Harvard UP, 1986.

New Oxford Companion to Music. New York: Oxford UP, 1983.

New Oxford History of Music. 10 vols. London: Oxford, 1957–1974.

Slonimsky, N. *Music Since 1900.* 5th ed. New York: Schirmer, 1992.

Bibliographies to Music Books and Other Sources

Bibliographic Guide to Music. Boston: Hall, 1976–present. Annually.

General Bibliography for Music Research. Ed. K. E. Mixter. 2nd ed. Detroit, MI: Information Coordinators, 1975.

General Index to Modern Musical Literature in the English Language Including Periodicals for the Years 1915–1926. 1927; rpt. New York: DaCapo, 1970.

*Popular Music: An Annotated Index of
American Popular Songs.* Detroit, MI:
Gale, 1963–present (continuing).
Source Readings in Music History. Ed. O.
Strunk. 5 vols. New York: Norton, 1950.

Electronic Sources to Music Literature
ACADEMIC INDEX
ARTS & HUMANITIES SEARCH
RILM ABSTRACTS (Repertoire Interna-
tionale de Littérature Musicale)
WILSONDISC: HUMANITIES INDEX

Indexes to Articles in Music Journals
**Humanities Index.* New York: Wilson,
1974–present.
    Indexes topics in music in such journals
    as *American Music, Early Music, Jour-
    nal of Musicology,* and *Musical Quarter-
    ly.*
**Music Article Guide.* Philadelphia: Infor-
mation Services, 1966–present.
    Indexes music education and instrumen-
    tation in such journals as *Brass and
    Wind News, Keyboard, Flute Journal, Pi-
    ano Quarterly,* and many more.
**Music Index.* Warren, MI: Information Co-
ordinations, 1949–present.
    Indexes music journals such as *Ameri-
    can Music Teacher, Choral Journal,
    Journal of Band Research, Journal of
    Music Therapy, Music Journal, Musical
    Quarterly,* and many others.
*RILM (Repertoire Internationale de Littéra-
ture Musicale).* New York: City U of
New York, 1967–present.
    Indexes international music information.

Philosophy

Basic Sources and Guides to
Philosophy Literature
A Companion to Aesthetics. Ed. D. E. Coop-
er. Cambridge, MA: Blackwell, 1993.
Dictionary of the History of Ideas. Ed. P.
Winer. 5 vols. New York: Scribner's,
1974.
Dictionary of Philosophy. Ed. A. R. Lacey.
New York: Paul/Methuen, 1987.
Dictionary of Philosophy. Ed. D. D. Runes.
Rev. ed. New York: Philosophical Li-
brary, 1984.
Encyclopedia of Ethics. 2 vols. Ed. L. C.
Becker and C. B. Becker. New York:
Garland, 1992.
**Encyclopedia of Philosophy.* Ed. P. Ed-
wards. 8 vols. New York: Macmillan,
1967–1968.

Although dated, this is still an excellent
source for background information on
concepts (e.g., analytic and synthetic
statements), movements (e.g., Darwin-
ism), issues (e.g., certainty), and
philosophers. Includes brief bibliographies of important works for each major
article.
Fifty Major Philosophers: A Reference Guide.
Ed. D. Collinson. New York: Routledge,
1987.
Great Thinkers of the Western World. Ed. I.
P. McGreal. New York: HarperCollins,
1992.
Handbook of Western Philosophy. Ed. G. H.
R. Parkinson et al. New York: Macmillan, 1988.
The Philosopher's Guide. Ed. R. T. DeGe-
orge. Lawrence, KS: Regents, 1980.
*Philosophy: A Guide to the Reference Litera-
ture.* Ed. H. E. Bynago. Littleton, CO:
Libraries Unlimited, 1986.
**Research Guide to Philosophy.* Ed. T. N.
Tice and T. P. Slavens. Chicago: ALA,
1983.
    Consists of 30 bibliographical essays on
    sources in the history of philosophy
    (e.g., seventeenth century) and various
    areas of philosophy (e.g., logic). Con-
    cludes with a bibliography of reference
    works.
Who's Who in Philosophy. 1942; rpt. West-
port, CT: Greenwood, n.d.
*World Philosophy: Essay Reviews of 225 Ma-
jor Works.* Ed. F. Magill. 5 vols. Engle-
wood Cliffs, NJ: Salem, 1982.

Bibliographies to Philosophy Books
and Other Sources
Burr, J. R. *World Philosophy: A Contemporary Bibliography.* Westport, CT: Greenwood, 1993.
*The Classical World Bibliography of Philoso-
phy, Religion, and Rhetoric.* New York:
Garland, 1978.
Philosophers Index: A Retrospective Index
[1940–1966]. Bowling Green, OH:
Bowling Green U, 1978.
Roth, J. K. *Ethics: An Annotated Bibliography.* Englewood Cliffs, NJ: Salem,
1991.

Electronic Sources to Philosophy
Literature
ACADEMIC INDEX
ARTS & HUMANITIES SEARCH
PHILOSOPHER's INDEX
WILSONDISC: HUMANITIES INDEX

*Indexes to Articles in Philosophy
Journals*

**Humanities Index.* New York: Wilson,
1974–present.
Provides a general index to philosophical topics in journals such as *British
Journal of Philosophy, Environmental
Ethics, International Philosophy Quarter, Journal of the History of Ideas, Journal of Philosophy,* and many others.

**Philosopher's Index.* Bowling Green, OH:
Bowling Green U, 1967–present.
Indexes philosophy articles in journals
such as *American Philosophical Quarterly, Humanist, Journal of the History
of Ideas, Journal of Philosophy, Philosophical Revew, Philosophy Today,* and
many more.

Physics

*Basic Sources and Guides to Physics
Literature*

American Institute of Physics Handbook. Ed.
D. E. Gray. New York: McGraw, 1972.

*Annual Review of Nuclear and Particle Sci-
ence.* Annual Reviews, Inc.: Palo Alto,
CA: 1952–date.

*The Astronomy and Astrophysics Encyclope-
dia.* Ed. S. P. Maran. New York: Reinhold, 1992.

*Dictionary of Effects and Phenomena in
Physics.* Ed. J. Schubert. New York:
VCH, 1987.

Encyclopedia of Physics. 2nd ed. New
York: VCH, 1991.

Encyclopedia of Physics. 3rd ed. New
York: Van Nostrand Reinhold, 1990.

Encyclopedia of Physics. 54 vols. New
York: Springer-Verlag, 1956–date.

A Guide to the Literature of Astronomy. Ed.
R. A. Seal. Englewood, CO: Libraries
Unlimited, 1977.

How to Find Out About Physics. Ed. B.
Yates. New York: Pergamon, 1965.

*An Introductory Guide to Information
Sources in Physics.* Ed. L. R. A. Melton.
Bristol, England: Inst. of Physics, 1978.

*Magill's Survey of Science: Physical Science
Series.* 6 vols. Ed. F. N. Magill. Englewood Cliffs, NJ: Salem, 1992.

Space Almanac. 2nd ed. New York: Arc-
soft, 1992.

*Bibliographies to Physics Books and
Other Sources*

**Physics Abstracts.* London: IEE, 1898–present. Bimonthly.

A guide to the most recent work in
physics worldwide. It provides an abstract that you can use in your research
even though the journal itself might be
unavailable.

Solid State Physics Literature Guides. New
York: Plenum, 1972–1981.

Sources of History of Quantum Physics.
Ed. T. S. Kuhn et al. Philadelphia: APS,
1967.

*Electronic Sources to Physics
Literature*

INSPEC
SCISEARCH
SPIN (Searchable Physics Information No-
tices)
WILSONDISC: GENERAL SCIENCE INDEX

*Indexes to Articles in Physics
Journals*

**Applied Science and Technology Index.*
New York: Wilson, 1958–present.
Indexes general physics topics in *Laser
Focus, Monthly Weather Review, Physics
Today,* and others.

Current Papers in Physics. London: IEE,
1966–date. Bimonthly.

**Current Physics Index.* New York: American Institute of Physics, 1975–date.
Consult this work for indexing to
most articles in physics journals
such as *Applied Physics, Journal of
Chemical Physics, Nuclear Physics,
Physical Review, Physics Letters,* and
many more.

Political Science

*Basic Sources and Guides to Political
Science Literature*

*Blackwell Encyclopedia of Political Institu-
tions.* Ed. V. Boddanor. Oxford: Blackwell, 1987.

Communism in the World Since 1945. Ed.
S. K. Kimmel. Santa Barbara, CA: ABC-
Clio, 1987.

Congress A to Z. 2nd ed. Washington, DC:
Congressional Quarterly, 1993.

*Congress and Lawmaking: Researching the
Legislative Process.* 2nd ed. Santa Barbara, CA: ABC-Clio, 1989.

Diller, D. C. *Russia and the Independent
States.* Washington, DC: Congressional
Quarterly, 1993.

*Dorsey Dictionary of American Government
and Politics.* Belmont, CA: Dorsey,
1988.

Encyclopedia of the American Presidency.
4 vols. Ed. L. W. Levy and L. Fisher.
New York: Simon & Schuster, 1994.
Encyclopedia of Arms Control and Disar-
mament. 3 vols. Ed. R. D. Burns. New
York: Scribner's, 1993.
Encyclopedia of Government and Politics. 2
vols. Ed. M. Hawkesworth and M. Ko-
gan. New York: Routledge, 1992.
Encyclopedia of Public Affairs Information
Sources. Ed. P. Wasserman et al. De-
troit, MI: Gale, 1988.
Encyclopedia of the United Nations and In-
ternational Relations. 2nd ed. New
York: Taylor and Francis, 1990.
A Guide to Library Sources in Political Sci-
ence: American Government. Ed. C. E.
Vose. Washington, DC: APSA, 1975.
Guide to Official Publications of Foreign
Countries. Chicago: ALA, 1990.
Information Sources of Political Science.
Ed. F. L. Holler. 4th ed. Santa Barbara,
CA: ABC-Clio, 1986.
Lowery, R. C. *Political Science: Illustrated*
Search Strategy and Sources. Ann Ar-
bor, MI: Pierian P, 1993.
**Morehead, J. *Introduction to United States*
Information Sources. 4th ed. Littleton,
CO: Libraries Unlimited, 1992.
Covers all forms of information sources
(books, periodicals, databases) for re-
search on American politics and govern-
ment, international relations, and the
study of foreign governments.
Political Handbook of the World. Ed. A. S.
Banks. New York: McGraw. Annually.
Political Science: A Guide to Reference and
Information Sources. Ed. H. York. En-
glewood, CO: Libraries Unlimited, 1990.
Safire, W. *Definitive Guide to the New Lan-*
guage of Politics. 4th ed. New York:
Random, 1993.
Sources of Information in the Social Sci-
ences. Ed. W. H. Webb. 3rd ed. Chica-
go: ALA, 1986.
State Yellow Book: A Directory. New York:
Monitor, 1989–present. Semiannually.
The Statesman's Yearbook. New York: St.
Martin's, 1964–date. Annually.
Wars and Peace Treaties 1816–1991. New
York: Routledge, 1992.
Yearbook of the United Nations. Lake Suc-
cess, NY: United Nations, 1947–present.
Annually.

Bibliographies to Political Science Books and Other Sources

Bibliography on the American Left. Comp. L.
M. Wilcox. Kansas City, MO: ERS, 1980.
Edelheit, A. J. *The Rise and Fall of the Sovi-*
et Union: A Selected Bibliography of
Sources in English. Westport, CT:
Greenwood, 1992.
Free-thought in the United States: A Descrip-
tive Bibliography. Westport, CT: Green-
wood, 1978.
International Bibliography of Political Sci-
ence. New York: IPS, 1979. Supple-
ments.
The Literature of Political Science: A Guide
for Students, Librarians, and Teachers.
New York: Bowker, 1969.
Monthly Catalog of U.S. Government Publi-
cations. Washington, DC: GPO,
1895–present.
Political Science: A Bibliographical Guide to
the Literature. Metuchen, NJ: Scarecrow, 1965. Supplements, 1966–present.
Russia and Eastern Europe, 1789–1985: A
Bibliographical Guide. Manchester, UK:
Manchester UP, 1989.
Skidmore, C., and T. J. Spahn. *From Radi-*
cal Left to Extreme Right: A Bibliography.
3rd ed. Metuchen, NJ: Scarecrow, 1987.

Electronic Sources to Political Science Literature

ACADEMIC INDEX
ASI
CIS
CONGRESSIONAL RECORD ABSTRACTS
FEDERAL REGISTER ABSTRACTS
GPO MONTHLY CATALOG
NATIONAL NEWSPAPER INDEX
PAIS
UNITED STATES POLITICAL SCIENCE
    DOCUMENTS
WASHINGTON PRESSTEXT
WILSONDISC: SOCIAL SCIENCES INDEX
WORLD AFFAIRS REPORT

Indexes to Articles in Political Science Journals

**ABC: Pol Sci.* Santa Barbara, CA: ABC-
Clio, 1969–present.
Indexes the tables of contents of about
300 international journals in the original
language.
**International Political Science Abstracts.*
Olso: International Political Science
Assn., 1951–present.
Comprehensive, worldwide coverage of
more than 600 periodicals; also provides
abstracts in English.
**PAIS International in Print* (formerly *PAIS*
Bulletin). New York: PAIS, 1915–pre-
sent.
Indexes government publications and
books, as well as such journals as *An-*
nals of the American Academy of Politi-
cal and Social Science and
International Studies Quarterly.

**Social Sciences Index.* New York: Wilson, 1974–present.

Indexes articles in such journals as *American Journal of Political Science, American Political Science Review, British Journal of Political Science, Political Quarterly, Political Science Quarterly,* and many others.

Psychology

Basic Sources and Guides to Psychology Literature

American Handbook of Psychiatry. Ed. S. Arieti. 2nd ed. 8 vols. New York: Basic, 1974–1981.

Bachrach, A. J. *Psychological Research: An Introduction.* 4th ed. New York: Random, 1981.

Borchardt, D. H. *How to Find Out in Psychology.* Elmsford, NY: Pergamon, 1986.

Diagnostic and Statistical Manual of Mental Disorders. 4th ed. Washington, DC: American Psychiatric Assn., 1994.

Dictionary of Behavioral Science. 2nd ed. New York: Academic P, 1989.

**Encyclopedia of Psychology.* Ed. R. J. Corsini. 2nd ed. 4 vols. New York: Wiley, 1984.

A scholarly, thorough introduction to all aspects of psychology including its major theorists. Most of the articles include references to other sources, all of which are listed in the extensive bibliography in the index volume.

Encyclopedia of Psychology. 3 vols. New York: Seaburg, 1979.

Encyclopedia of Sleep and Dreaming. Ed. M. A. Carskadon. New York: Macmillan, 1993.

Encyclopedic Dictionary of Psychology. Ed. G. Harre and R. Lamb. Cambridge: MIT P, 1983.

International Handbook of Psychology. Westport, CT: Greenwood, 1987.

Library Research Guide to Psychology. Ann Arbor, MI: Pierian P, 1984.

**Library Use: A Handbook for Psychology.* Ed. J. C. Reed and R. M. Baxter. 2nd ed. Washington, DC: APA, 1992.

A thorough overview of the research process in psychology. Provides guidance in choosing and narrowing topics as well as suggesting research sources to consult in psychology and such related fields as education and management. Also explains how to use sources such as *Psychological Abstracts.*

Oxford Companion to the Mind. Ed. R. Gregory. New York: Oxford UP, 1987.

Research Guide for Psychology. Ed. R. G. McInnis. Westport, CT: Greenwood, 1982.

Survey of Social Science: Psychology Series. 6 vols. Ed. F. Magill. Englewood Cliffs, NJ: Salem, 1993.

Bibliographies to Psychology Books and Other Sources

Annual Reviews of Psychology. Palo Alto, CA: Annual Reviews, 1950–date.

Bibliographical Guide to Psychology. Boston: Hall, 1982–present. Annually.

Bibliography of Aggressive Behavior: A Reader's Guide to the Research Literature. Ed. J. M. Crabtree and K. E. Mayer. New York: Liss, 1977.

The Index of Psychoanalytic Writings. Ed. A. Grinstein. 14 vols. New York: International Universities, 1956–1971.

Psychoanalysis, Psychology, and Literature: A Bibliography. Ed. N. Kiell. 2nd ed. 2 vols. Metuchen, NJ: Scarecrow, 1982. Supplement, 1990.

Psychological Abstracts. Washington, DC: APA, 1927–present.

Psychological Index. 42 vols. Princeton, NJ: Psychological Review, 1895–1936. Superseded by *Psychological Abstracts.*

Electronic Sources to Psychology Literature

ACADEMIC INDEX
CHILD ABUSE AND NEGLECT
ERIC
MENTAL HEALTH ABSTRACTS
PSYCINFO
SOCIAL SCISEARCH
SOCIOLOGICAL ABSTRACTS
WILSONDISC: SOCIAL SCIENCES INDEX

Indexes to Articles in Psychology Journals

Child Development Abstracts and Bibliography. Chicago: U of Chicago P, 1927–present.

**Psychological Abstracts.* Washington, DC: APA, 1927–present.

Indexes and provides brief abstracts to psychology journals such as *American Journal of Psychology, Behavioral Science, Journal of Abnormal and Social Psychology, Psychological Review,* and many more.

**Sociological Index.* New York: International Sociological Assn., 1952–present.

Indexes such journals as *American Journal of Community Psychology, Journal of Drug Issues, Sex Roles,* and many others.

Religion

Basic Sources and Guides to Religion Literature

The Anchor Bible Dictionary. 6 vols. Ed. D. N. Freedman et al. New York: Doubleday, 1992.

Churches and Church Membership in the U.S. 1990. Ed. M. B. Bradley et al. Atlanta, GA: Glenmary Research Center, 1992.

Concise Encyclopedia of Islam. Ed. C. Glasse. San Francisco: Harper, 1989.

Eliade, M., et al. *Eliade Guide to World Religions*. San Francisco: Harper, 1991.

Encyclopedia of African American Religions. Ed. L. G. Murphy, J. G. Melton, and G. L. Ward. New York: Garland, 1993.

Encyclopedia of American Religions. Ed. G. J. Melton. 4th ed. Detroit: Gale, 1992.

Encyclopedia of the American Religious Experience. 3 vols. Ed. C. Lippy and P. Williams. New York: Scribner's, 1987.

Encyclopedia Judaica. 16 vols. Ed. C. Roth. New York: Macmillan, 1972. (Annual yearbooks serve to supplement.)

Encyclopedia of Native American Religions. New York: Facts on File, 1992.

***Encyclopedia of Religion*. 16 vols. Ed. M. Eliade. New York: Macmillan, 1987. A scholarly, thorough treatment of worldwide religions, religious thinkers, and religious issues (e.g., the afterlife). Useful bibliographies follow nearly all articles.

Guide to Hindu Religion. Ed. D. J. Dell. Boston: Hall, 1981.

Harper Atlas of the Bible. Ed. J. Pritchard. New York: Harper, 1987.

The International Standard Bible Encyclopedia. Ed. G. W. Bromley. 4 vols. Grand Rapids, MI: Eerdmans, 1979–1988.

Introduction to Theological Research. Ed. C. J. Barber. Moody, 1982.

***Library Research Guide to Religion and Theology*. Ed. J. Kennedy. 2nd ed. Ann Arbor, MI: Pierian P, 1984. A good, step-by-step introduction to the basic sources in religious studies. Also includes a bibliography of sources in specific areas (e.g., the Bible, comparative religion).

Melton, J. G., and M. A. Koszegi. *Religious Information Sources: A Worldwide Guide*. New York: Garland, 1992.

Nelson's Complete Concordance to the Revised Standard Version of the Bible. Ed. J. W. Ellison. New York: Nelson, 1978.

New Catholic Encyclopedia. 17 vols. New York: McGraw, 1977–1979. Supplement, 1989.

New Dictionary of Theology. Ed. J. Komonchak et al. Wilmington, DE: Glazier, 1987.

The New Standard Jewish Encyclopedia. Ed. G. Wigoder. New York: Facts on File, 1992.

Oxford Dictionary of the Christian Church. New York: Oxford UP, 1974.

Research Guide to Religious Studies. Ed. J. F. Wilson and T. Slavens. Chicago: ALA, 1982.

Who's Who in Religion. Chicago: Marquis, 1975/1976–present.

Yearbook of American and Canadian Churches. New York: Abingdon. Annually.

Bibliographies to Religion Books and Other Sources

A Critical Bibliography of Writings on Judaism. Lewiston, NY: Mellen, 1989.

Index Islamicus. Vols. covering 1665–1905 (Millersville, PA: Adiyok, 1989); 1906–1950 (Cambridge: 1958); and five-year cumulations since 1971 (London: Bawker-Saur, 1972–present).

Reference Works for Theological Research: An Annotated Selective Bibliographical Guide. Ed. R. Kepple. 2nd ed. UP of America, 1981.

Religion and Society in North America; An Annotated Bibliography. Ed. R. Brunkow. Santa Barbara, CA: ABC-Clio, 1983.

Religious Books and Serials in Print. New York: Bowker, 1987.

Warden, J. *Classical Approaches to the Study of Religion: Aims, Methods, and Theories of Research*. Part 2: "Bibliography." Hawthorne, NY: Mouton, 1974.

Wiersbe, W. W. *A Basic Library for Bible Students*. Grand Rapids, MI: Baker, 1981.

Electronic Sources for Religion Literature

ACADEMIC INDEX
RELIGION INDEX
WILSONDISC: HUMANITIES INDEX

Indexes to Articles in Religion Journals

The Catholic Periodical and Literature Index. New York: Catholic Library Assn., 1934–present.
Indexes 170 Catholic periodicals.

**Humanities Index. New York: Wilson, 1974–present.

Indexes religious journals such as *Church History, Harvard Theological Review,* and *Muslim World.*

***Index of Articles on Jewish Studies.* Jerusalem: Jewish National & Univ. Library P, 1969–present.

Indexes 10,000 periodicals for all phases of Jewish religion and studies.

***Religion: Index One: Periodicals, Religion and Theological Abstracts.* (Formerly *Index to Religious Periodicals Literature*). Chicago: ATLA, 1949–present.

Indexes religious articles in journals such as *Biblical Research, Christian Scholar, Commonweal, Harvard Theological Review, Journal of Biblical Literature,* and many others.

Sociology and Social Work

Basic Sources and Guides to Sociology and Social Work Literature

American Families: A Research Guide and Historical Handbook. Ed. J. M. Hawes and E. I. Nybakken. Westport, CT: Greenwood, 1991.

Child Abuse and Neglect: An Information and Research Guide. New York: Garland, 1992.

Crime Dictionary. Rev. ed. Ed. R. DeSola. New York: Facts on File, 1988.

Encyclopedia of Adolescence. 2 vols. New York: Garland, 1991.

Encyclopedia of Child Abuse. New York: Facts on File, 1989.

Encyclopedia of Homelessness. New York: Facts on File, 1994.

Encyclopedia of Homosexuality. 2 vols. Ed. W. R. Dynes. New York: Garland, 1990.

Encyclopedia of Marriage, Divorce, and the Family. New York: Facts on File, 1989.

Encyclopedia of Social Work. 18th ed. Ed. A. Minahan. 3 vols. New York: NASW, 1988. Supplement, 1990.

***Encyclopedia of Sociology.* 4 vols. Ed. E. F. Borgatta and M. L. Borgatta. New York: Macmillan, 1992.

The first authoritative, scholarly encyclopedia devoted to sociology. Articles cover concepts, theories, and research and provide good lists of references for further research.

Handbook of Sociology. Ed. N. Smelser. Newbury Park, CA: Sage, 1988.

Library Research Guide to Sociology. Ed. P. McMillan and J. R. Kennedy. Ann Arbor, MI: Pierian P, 1981.

Social Work Almanac. Silver Spring, MD: NASW, 1992.

The Social Work Dictionary. 2nd ed. Silver Springs, MD: NASW, 1991.

***Sociology, A Guide to Reference and Information Sources.* Ed. S. Aby. Littleton, CO: Libraries Unlimited, 1987.

Good starting place when trying to find which indexes, bibliographies, and other reference books might be relevant. Covers 600 major resources in sociology and related fields, giving descriptive and evaluative information for each.

Statistical Record of Older Americans. Detroit, MI: Gale, 1994.

Statistical Handbook on the American Family. Phoenix, AZ: Oryx, 1992.

***Student Sociologist's Handbook.* Ed. P. B. Bart and L. Frankel. 4th ed. New York: McGraw, 1986.

Along with listing recommended sources for researching sociological topics, also includes sections on trends in the field and on writing different types of sociology papers.

Bibliographies to Sociology and Social Work Books and Other Sources

Families in Transition. Ed. J. Sadler. New Haven, CT: Anchor, 1988.

Henslin, J. M. *Homelessness: An Annotated Bibliography.* New York: Garland, 1993.

Reference Sources in Social Work: An Annotated Bibliography. Ed. J. H. Conrad. Metuchen, NJ: Scarecrow, 1982.

Sociological Aspects of Poverty: A Bibliography. Ed. H. P. Chalfant. Monticello, IL: Vance Biblios., 1980.

Electronic Sources to Sociology and Social Work Literature

ACADEMIC INDEX
CHILD ABUSE AND NEGLECT
FAMILY RESOURCES
NCJRS (National Criminal Justice Reference Service)
SOCIAL SCISEARCH
SOCIOLOGICAL ABSTRACTS
WILSONDISC: SOCIAL SCIENCES INDEX

Indexes to Articles in Sociology and Social Work Journals

Popular Periodical Index. Roslyn, PA: PPI, 1973–present.

Indexes contemporary and regional issues in magazines such as *GEO, Life, Ohio Magazine, Playboy, Rolling Stone, Texas Monthly,* and others.

**Social Sciences Index.* New York: Wilson, 1974–present.
Indexes articles in such journals as *Child Welfare, Families in Society,* and *Social Problems.*

**Sociological Abstracts.* New York: Sociological Abstracts, 1952–present.
Indexes and provides brief descriptions of articles in journals such as *American Journal of Sociology, Environment and Behavior, Journal of Applied Social Psychology, Journal of Marriage and the Family, Social Education, Social Research, Sociological Inquiry, Sociology,* and many others.

Social Work Research and Abstracts. New York: NASW, 1964–present.

Speech

See also Drama and Theater, page 385, and Journalism and Mass Communications, pages 381.

Basic Sources and Guides to Speech Literature

American Orators of the 20th Century: Critical Studies and Sources. Westport, CT: Greenwood, 1987.

Index to Speech, Language, and Hearing: Journal Titles, 1954–78. San Diego, CA: College Hill, n.d.

Lanham, R. A. *Handlist of Rhetorical Terms.* Berkeley: U of California P, 1991.

Lend Me Your Ears: Great Speeches in History. New York: Norton, 1992.

***Research Guide in Speech.* Ed. G. Tandberg. Morristown, NJ: General Learning P, 1974.
Dated, but nevertheless a very useful source for guidance on all stages of preparing oral presentations. Also includes a brief history of oratory and a selective listing of recommended sources for research in various subject areas as well as the field of speech.

Sprague, J., and D. Stuart. *The Speaker's Handbook.* 3rd ed. New York: Harcourt, 1991.

Bibliographies to Speech Books and Other Sources

American Orators Before 1900: Critical Studies and Sources. Westport, CT: Greenwood, 1987.

Bibliography of Speech and Allied Areas, 1950–1960. Westport, CT: Greenwood, 1972.

Radio and Television: A Selected Annotated Bibliography. Metuchen, NJ: Scarecrow, 1978. Supplements, 1982 and 1989.

Rhetoric and Public Address: A Bibliography: 1947–1961. Madison: U of Wisconsin P, 1964. (Continued annually in *Speech Monographs.*)

Table of Contents of the Quarterly Journal of Speech, Speech Monographs, and Speech Teacher. Ed. J. McPhee. New York: Farrar (in association with the Speech Association of America), 1985.

Electronic Sources to Speech Literature

ACADEMIC INDEX
COMMUNICATIONS INDEX
ERIC
LLBA (Language and Language Behavior Abstracts)
MLA BIBLIOGRAPHIES
SOCIAL SCISEARCH
WILSONDISC: HUMANITIES INDEX

Indexes to Articles in Speech Journals

***Humanities Index.* New York: Wilson, 1974–present.
Indexes such speech journals as *Communication, Journal of Communication, Quarterly Journal of Speech, Speech Monographs,* and *Studies in Public Communication.*

MLA International Bibliography. New York: MLA, 1921–present.
Indexes rhetorical subjects.

Women's Studies

Basic Sources and Guides to Women's Studies Literature

Bloomsbury Guide to Women's Literature. Ed. C. Buck. New York: Prentice-Hall, 1992.

Encyclopedia of Child Bearing: Critical Perspectives. Ed. B. K. Rothman. Phoenix, AZ: Oryx, 1993.

Fishburn, K. *Women in Popular Culture. A Reference Guide.* Westport, CT: Greenwood, 1982.

Guide to Social Science Resources in Women's Studies. Ed. E. H. Oakes and K. E. Sheldon. Santa Barbara, CA: ABC-Clio, 1978.

Handbook of American Women's History. Ed. A. H. Zophy. New York: Garland, 1990.

Index-Directory of Women's Media. Washington, DC: Women's Institute for Freedom of the Press, 1975–present.

Index to Women of the World from Ancient to Modern Times: Biographies and Portraits. Westwood, CA: Faxon, 1970. Supplement, 1988.

Primer on Sexual Harassment. Lanham, MD: BNA, 1992.

**Searing, S. *Introduction to Library Research in Women's Studies.* Boulder, CO: Westview, 1985.
A multidisciplinary listing of sources for researching women's issues and problems in the social sciences.

Snyder, P. *European Women's Almanac.* New York: Columbia UP, 1992.

Statistical Handbook on Women in America. Phoenix, AZ: Oryx, 1991.

Statistical Record of Women Worldwide. Ed. L. Schmittroth. Detroit, MI: Gale, 1991.

Who's Who of American Women. Chicago: Marquis, 1958–present.

Womanhood Media: Current Resources About Women. Metuchen, NJ: Scarecrow, 1972. Supplement, 1975.

Women Today: A Multidisciplinary Approach to Women's Studies. Ed. M. A. Baker et al. Monterey, CA: Brooks/Cole, 1979.

Women's Action Almanac: A Complete Resource Guide. Ed. J. Williamson et al. New York: Morrow, 1979.

** *Women's Studies Encyclopedia.* 3 vols. Westport, CT: Greenwood, 1989–present (in progress).
A multidisciplinary reference source on all issues relating to women. Vol. 1 covers views from the sciences (1989); vol. 2 deals with literature, arts, and learning (1990).

Bibliographies to Women's Studies Books and Other Sources

American Women and Politics: A Selected Bibliography and Research Guide. New York: Garland, 1984.

American Women Writers: An Annotated Bibliography. Ed. B. A. White. New York: Garland, 1976.

American Women Writers: A Critical Reference Guide. 4 vols. Ed. L. Mainiero and L. L. Faust. New York: Continuum, 1982. Supplement, 1993.

Annotated Bibliography of Feminist Criticism. Ed. M. Humm. Boston: Hall, 1987.

Annotated Bibliography of Twentieth Century Critical Studies of Women and Literature; 1660–1800. New York: Garland, 1977.

Bibliographic Guide to Studies on the Status of Women: Development and Population Trends. Paris: UNESCO, 1983.

Bibliography on Women Workers: 1961–1965. 2nd ed. Washington, DC: International Labor Office, 1974.

Biographies of American Women. Santa Barbara, CA: ABC-Clio, 1990.

Feminist Companion to Literature in English. Ed. V. Blain et al. New Haven: Yale UP, 1990.

Feminist Resources for Schools and Colleges: A Guide. Ed. A. Chapman. Feminist P, 1986.

Fischer, G. V. *Journal of Women's History Guide to Periodical Literature (1980–1990).* Bloomington: U of Indiana P, 1992.

New Feminist Scholarship: A Guide to Bibliographies. Ed. J. Williamson. Westbury, NY: Feminist P, 1979.

Older Women in 20th-Century America: A Selected Annotated Bibliography. New York: Garland, 1982.

The Status of Women: A Selected Bibliography. New York: United Nations, n.d.

Women and Work: Paid and Unpaid: A Selected Annotated Bibliography. Ed. M. A. Ferber. New York: Garland, 1987.

Women in America: A Guide to Information Sources. Ed. V. R. Terris. Detroit, MI: Gale, 1980.

Women's Studies: A Recommended Core Bibliography. Ed. E. Stineman and C. Loeb. Littleton, OH: Libraries Unlimited, 1979.

Electronic Sources to Women's Studies Literature

ACADEMIC INDEX
ERIC
SOCIAL SCISEARCH
SOCIOLOGICAL ABSTRACTS
WILSONDISC: SOCIAL SCIENCES INDEX and HUMANITIES INDEX

Indexes to Articles on Women's Studies Journals

** *Social Sciences Index.* New York: Wilson, 1974–present.
Indexes such journals as *Feminist Studies, Ms., Signs, Womanpower, Woman Activist, Woman's Journal, Women and Literature, Women's Studies, and Women's World.*

Women Studies Abstracts. Rush, NY: Rush, 1972–present.

** *Women's Studies Index (1989–present).* Boston: Hall, 1992–present. Annually. Currently, the best source for immediate information on women's issues.

Index

Note: **Bold** page numbers indicate main discussions.

Abbreviations, 177, **206–213**
  biblical works, 210–211
  days and months, 208
  literary works, 211–213
  publishers' names, 208–209, 273
  state names, 208
abr., 206
Abstracts
  of APA style paper, 318, 320
  bibliography form for, 294–295, 300–301,
    316–317
  CD-ROM, 294–295
  defined, 133
  to evaluate articles, 104–106
  in final manuscript, 203–204
  in on-line databases, 13, 14–15, 38
  searching, 14–15, 54–56
  using précis to write, 133
  writing, 133
Accent marks, 213
Acknowledgments, 214, 222
ACS style, 347–348
AD, 206
Addresses
  published, bibliography form for, 284
  unpublished, 304
Advertisements, bibliography form for, 298–299
Afro-American literature, reference sources,
    383–384
Afro-American studies, reference sources, 374–375
Afterword, bibliography form for, 278–279
Agriculture
  name and year system, 333, 339
  periodical index for, 53
AIP style, 350–351
Alphabetized works, bibliography form for, 266, 275
AMA style, 351–352
American literature, reference sources, 384
American Psychological Association. *See* APA style
Ampersands, 214, 311

AMS style, 348–349
Analogues, 291
Analysis, as writing strategy, 19–20, 167
Analytical categories, 25
Annotated bibliographies, **112–114**, 131–132, 214
Announcements, bibliography form for, 302–303
anon., 206
Anonymous authors, bibliography form for, 274,
    284
Anthologies
  APA style for, 311, 314–315
  MLA style for, 187–189, 269, 276–277
Anthropology
  name and year system, 333, 339–340
  periodical index for, 53
APA style, **307–332**
  abstracts in, 318, 320
  ampersands, 214
  capitalization, 218
  for headers, 236
  hyphenation, 234
  in-text citations, 309–312
  numeral use, 214–215
  reference form, 313–318, 329–331
  running heads, 236
  sample paper in, 318–332
  spacing, 236–237
  tense in, 155, **307–309**
  working drafts in, 312–313, 319
Apostrophes, 214
Appendixes, book, 106
Appendixes, research paper
  APA style, 332
  MLA style, 205, 261
Applied Science and Technology Index, 53
Applied sciences, number system, 348–351
Arabic numerals, **214–217**
  for book edition, 271
  for citations, 195
  for content endnotes, 219

for footnote system, 358
for illustrations and tables, 226–227
superscripts, 219–220, 237–238, 358
Archaeology
name and year system, 333, 339–340
reference sources, 53
Archives
library, 31
national, 75
Argumentative papers, 20
Art
bibliography form for, 299
footnote system, 333, 363–364
paradigm for analysis of, 88
reference sources, 111, 366–367
art., arts., 206
Arts and Humanities Citation Index (AHCI), 102
Asian-American studies, reference sources,
373–374
assn., 206
assoc., 206
Assumptions, challenging, 161
Asterisks, 217
Astronomy, name and year system, 333, 341
Audience
adapting language for, 155
meeting needs of, 20–21
for persuasive paper, 20–21
remembering while writing, 155
Audiovisual materials, bibliography form, 73, 299,
301, 306
Author cards, 67
Authors
anonymous, 274, 284
in APA style, 309–312, 314
on bibliography cards, 33
bibliography form for books, 268–269,
273–275
bibliography form for newspapers, 288
bibliography form for periodicals, 283, 284
corporate, 185, 274–275, 312, 315
listed by initial, 274
in literature study conclusion, 170
in MLA style, 182–184, 266
more than one work by, 268–269, 274, 311
multiple, 190, 268, 274, 311
not listed, 184–185, 288
pseudonymous, 274
reliability of, 99
voice of, 21

Background information, 158, 159–161
BC, 206
*Bell and Howell's Index to the Christian Science
Monitor*, 59
Bias
in persuasive papers, 20
sexist language, 177–179
in source materials, 99
Bible
abbreviations, 210–211
bibliography form for, 275–276
in-text citation for, 217
Bibliographic Index, 18, 45–46, 51
Bibliographies. *See also* Reference form; Works
Cited (MLA style)
annotated, **112–114**, 131–132, 214

defined, 31
to determine relevance, 112–114
general, 45–46
specialized, 48–51
trade, 46–48
Bibliography cards
with computer search systems, 12–13
index cards for, 31–33
information on, 31
from preliminary reading, 28
sample, 32–35, 44–46, 52, 57
working, 32–39
writing basic, 31–35
Bibliography form for abstracts, 294–295, 300–301,
316–317
Bibliography form for books
APA style, 313–315
MLA style, 187–188, 268–282
sample entries, 273–282
Bibliography form for government documents,
289–291
Bibliography form for newspapers
APA style, 316
MLA style, 287–289
Bibliography form for periodicals
APA style, 316–318
MLA style, 282–287, 289
sample entries, 284–287
Bibliography page, 265
Biographical dictionaries, bibliography form for,
275
Biographies, indexes to, 56–59
Biological and Agricultural Index, 53
Biological sciences
CBE system, 341–342
name and year system, 333
reference sources, 53, 367–368
Bio-medical science, number system, 333,
351–352
BITNET (Because It's Time Network), **44**, 291
bk., bks., 206
Blanket citation, 220
Body of the paper
APA style, 321–328
MLA style, 251–259
revision of, 172–174
writing, 163–169
Booklist, The, 102
Book reviews, 102–103, 114–118
Books
APA style for, 313–315
bibliography card for, 33–34
bibliography form for, 268–282, 293–294,
313–315
CD-ROM, 293–294
computerized card catalog for, **12–13**, 27, 28,
29, 36
evaluation of, 106
headings in, 18
indexes, 16–17
indexes within, 56–59
MLA style for, 187–188, 268–282
reliability of, 98–99
republished, 280
table of contents, 15–16, 106
Books in Print, 47
Borders, 217

Botany
    CBE system, 341–342
    name and year system, 333
    periodical index for, 53
Braces, 200
Brackets, 198–200, **234**
British literature, reference sources, 384–385
Bulletins, bibliography form for, 300
Bullets, 217
Business
    decimal outline, 91
    name and year system, 333, **344–345**
    reference sources, 111, 368
Business Periodicals Index, 27, 53

ca., c., 206
Call numbers, **67–71**
    on bibliography cards, 33
    Dewey Decimal, 68
    Library of Congress, 68
Capitalization, **217–219**
    of foreign titles, 224, 281
    in quotations, 141, 195–196
Captions, 227–228
Card catalogs, 29
    author card, 67
    computerized, **12–13**, 27, 28, 29, 36
    for government documents, 61–62
    recording call numbers at, 65–71
    subject cards, 66
    title cards, 68
CARL UNCOVER (Internet navigator), 42–43
Cartoons, bibliography form for, 300
Casebooks
    APA style for, 311, 314–315
    MLA style for, 281
Case studies
    bibliography card for, 78
    as resource material, 78
Catalog of National Archives Microfilm Publications, 75
Cause and effect
    for topic discovery, 11
    as writing strategy, 164–165
CBE style, 217, 341–342
CD-ROM facilities, **13–15**, 27, 28, 30, 36, 37–38
    abstracts, 294–295, 317
    bibliography form for sources on, 292–295
    defined, 291
    using, **13–15**
cf., 206
ch., chs., chap., chaps., 206
Chapters, bibliography form for, 269–270
Character sets, computer, 213, 219
Charts, bibliography form for, 305
Chaucer, abbreviations for, 212–213
Chemical engineering, reference sources, 369
Chemistry
    number system, 333, **347–348**
    reference sources, 369
Chicago Manual of Style, 358
Chronology, **163–164**, 173
Circulation desk, 29
Citation indexes, 102
Citations
    footnote. *See* Footnote system
    in-text. *See* In-text citations

reference. *See* Reference form; Works Cited (MLA style)
Citation searching, 99–102
Citing evidence, as writing strategy, 166–167
Classical studies
    bibliography form for, 276, 279
    periodical index for, 53
Classification
    as outlining method, 84
    for topic discovery, 11
    as writing strategy, 167
Clip art, 219
Closed stacks, 30
Closing paragraphs, to determine relevance, 104
Clustering, 10
Coherence, in writing, 157–158
col., cols., 206
Collaborative learning, 8
Collections, bibliography form for, 276–277
Colons, **233**
    capitalization after, 218
    with quotations, 192, 196
    with volume number, 189–190
Commas, **233**
    with numbers, 215
    with quotations, 191–192, 196
Comments, bibliography form for, 285
Committee reports, bibliography form for, 274–275, 276
Common knowledge, 141
comp., 206
Comparative study, paradigm for, 89–90
Comparisons
    in conclusion, 170–171
    for topic development, 83
    for topic discovery, 11, 24
    as writing strategy, 164
Compilers, bibliography form for, 269, 270
Computers
    accent marks and, 213
    in bibliography development, 35–45
    bibliography form for electronic sources, 43, 291–298, 317–318
    borders with, 217
    card catalogs on, **12–13**, 27, 28, 29, 36
    CD-ROM facilities. *See* CD-ROM facilities
    character sets, 213, 219
    clip art, 219
    DIALOG access, 36, **39–41**, 296
    E-mail (electronic mail), **44**, 291, 298
    fonts, 223, 230
    grammar checkers, 175
    graphics, 219, 224
    Internet access, 28, 36, **42–43**, 292, 297–298
    note-taking with, 121–122, 152–153
    Public Access Catalog (PAC), **12–13**, 27, 28, 29, 36
    in revision process, 174–177
    spelling checkers, 176
    in topic discovery, 11–15
    writing on, **150–153**
Computer science
    number system, 333, **348–349**
    reference sources, 53, 369–370
Computer software, bibliography form for, 300
Conclusions, **169–172**
    avoiding mistakes in, 171–172

revision of, 173
techniques for, 169–172
Conference proceedings, bibliography form for, 300
Congressional papers, bibliography form for, 290
Congressional Record, 63
Consequences, as outlining method, 84
Contemporary Authors, 57, 99
Content endnotes, **219–222**
for acknowledgments, 214, 222
examples, 220–222, 260
notes page for, 205
for sources not quoted, 265
Contractions, 176
Contrast
as outlining method, 84
for topic development, 84
as writing strategy, 164
Copyright law, 222. *See also* Plagiarism
Corporate authors
bibliography form for, 274–275, 315
in-text citation of, 185, 312
Corrections, 222–223
Council of Biology Editors style. *See* CBE style
County government documents, 75
Researcher, 60–61
Criteria of judgment, as writing strategy, 167
Critical response, as writing strategy, 167
Critical views, challenging, 161
Cross references, in bibliography, **277**
APA style, 314–15
Cumulative Book Index, 48
Current Biography Yearbook, 57
Current Book Review Citations, 102
Cutter Three-Figure Author Table, 68

Dance, footnote system, 333, 363–364
Dashes, **233**
Data
gathering, 27–79
in introduction, 162
in the library, 27–71
outside the library, 71–79
Databases
abstracts in, 13, 14–15, 38
bibliography form for, 295–296
DIALOG, 36, **39–41**, 296
library facilities, 30
Dates
abbreviating, 208
in citations, 283–284
Decimal outlines, 91
Definition
of key words, 162, 165
as outlining method, 84
quotation marks with, 223
for topic development, 83–84
for topic discovery, 11
as writing strategy, 165
Descriptors, database, 40
Dewey Decimal system, 68–69
DIALOG, 36
bibliography form for sources on, 296
using, **39–41**
Dictionary of American Negro Biography, 99
Dictionary of Literary Biography, 57–59
Directive, in conclusion, 171
Direct quotation, **173–93**

and plagiarism, 192
of primary sources, 124–125
of secondary sources, 125–128
Discriminating language, avoiding, 177–179
Diskettes, computer
bibliography form for sources on, 295
defined, 291
diss., 206
Dissertations
bibliography form for, **300–301**
indexes to, **54–56**, 296, 300–301
rules for submission, 238
doc., 206
Drafting the paper, **154–158**
APA style, 312–313, 319
Drama
footnote system, 334, **363–364**
paradigm for analysis of, 88
reference sources, 53, 385, 394–395

Ecology, reference sources, 53, 370–371
Economics
name and year system, 333, **344–345**
reference form, 344–345
reference sources, 53, 371
ed., eds., 206
Editing the paper, **174–179**
Edition
bibliography form for books, 271, 278
bibliography form for newspapers, 288
and printing, 272
Editors, bibliography form for, 269, 270, 278
Education
name and year system, 333, 335–336
reference sources, 53, 111, 371–372
Educational Film & Video Locator, 73
Education Index, 53
e.g., 206
Electronic addresses, 297–298
Electronics
periodical index for, 53
reference sources, 372–373
Electronic sources, bibliography form for, 43,
291–298, 317–318
Ellipsis points, 196–198
E-mail (electronic mail), **44**, 291, 298
Emphasis, 240
Empirical research
bibliography card for, 79
content endnotes describing, 221–222
as resource material, 78–79
sample paper in APA style, 318–332
Encyclopaedia Britannica, 17
Encyclopedia of Psychology, 49, 51
Encyclopedias
in bibliography development, 49
bibliography form for, 275, 278, 315
reliability of, 98–99
for topic discovery, 17
Endnotes
content. *See* Content endnotes
in footnote system, 223, 360–361, 363–364
spacing, 236
Engineering
name and year system, 333
number system, 349
reference sources, 53, 369

enl., 206
Environmental science, reference sources, 53,
    370–371
Equations, 237
    fractions in, 200
esp., 206
Essay and General Literature Index, 64–65
Essays
    bibliography card for, 35
    indexes to, 64–65
    sample paper, 240–246
et al., 206, 311
etc., 206, 223
Ethnic studies, reference sources, 373–375
et pas., 206
et seq., 206
Exclamation marks, **233**
    with quotation marks, 192–193
Executive branch documents, bibliography form
    for, 290
Experiments. *See* Empirical research
Explanatory purpose, 19

f., ff., 206
Facsimile (FAX) machines, 45
Fiction, paradigm for analysis of, 88
fig., 207
Film, bibliography form for, 301
Film File, 73
Final manuscript, format, 201–205
Final thesis sentence, 146–148
Fine arts
    bibliography form for, 299
    footnote system, 333, 363–364
    paradigm for analysis of, 88
    reference sources, 111, 366–367
First person, 156–157
fl., 207
Folklore
    periodical index for, 53
    reference sources, 385–386
Fonts, computer, 223, 230
Footers, running, 224
Footnote system, 333, 334, **358–364**
    endnotes, 223, 360–361, 363–364
    footnotes, 359–364
    in-text citation, 358
Foreign cities, 223
Foreign languages, 223–224
    reference sources, 375–377, 385
Foreign newspapers, bibliography form for, 288
Foreign titles, 224, 281, 287
Foreword, bibliography form for, 278–279
Fractions, 200
Freewriting, 9
French
    reference sources, 375
    titles, 224
FTP (File Transfer Protocol), 291

Gender, avoiding discriminating language with,
    177–179
General bibliographies, 45–46
General indexes, 51–61
General reference books, 45–46
Geography
    name and year system, 333, 336
    reference sources, 53, 377–378

Geology
    name and year system, 333, **342–344⁻**
    reference sources, 53, 378–379
German
    reference sources, 376
    titles, 224
GOPHER (Internet navigator), 42
Government documents, 111
    bibliography cards for, 62, 76
    bibliography form for, 289–291
    index to, 61–64
    outside the library, 75–76
    searching, 61–64
Grammar checkers, 175
Graphics, 219, 224
Guide to Reference Books, 46
Guide to the National Archives of the United States,
    75

Headers, running, 224, 236
Headings, 224–225
    reference book, 18
    rough outline, 10, 82–83
Health
    number system, 333, **351–352**
    reference sources, 379–380
Hispanic-American studies, reference sources,
    374–375
History
    footnote system, 333, 362
    paradigm for analysis of events in, 89
    reference sources, 53, 111, 380–381
Home economics, name and year system, 333,
    336
Humanities, footnote system, 333, 361–362
Humanities Index, 18, 36
Hypertext links, 225
Hyphenation, 225, **234**

ibid., 207
i.e., 207
illus., 207
Illustration, as outlining method, 84
Illustrations, 225–229
    in appendix, 205
    bibliography form for, 305
Imagination for topic discovery, 9–11
Indentation, **229**
    of long poetry quotation, 194
    of long prose quotation, 193–194, 310–311
    outline, 90–91
    on References page, 313
    on Works Cited page, 266
Independent matter, parentheses for, 235
Index cards
    for bibliography cards, 32–35
    for note-taking, 122–123
Indexes
    to biographies, 56–59
    citation, 102
    defined, 51–52
    to determine relevance, 106
    to dissertations, 54–56
    to essays, 64–65
    general, 51–61
    to microfilm holdings, 65
    to newspapers, 59–60
    to pamphlets, 60

to periodicals, 18, 52–53
specialized, 53
for topic discovery, 16–17
Index to Book Reviews in the Humanities, 102
Index to Book Reviews in the Social Sciences, 102
InfoTrac, 13–14, 38
Infra, 207
Interlibrary loans, 30
International Index, 53
International Index to Recorded Poetry, 73
Internet, 28, 36, 292
bibliography form for sources on, 297–298
using, **42–43**
Interviews
bibliography card for, 72
broadcast, bibliography form for, 299
published, bibliography form for, 284
as source material, 71–72, 317
for topic discovery, 8
unpublished, bibliography form for, 301, 317
In-text citations
APA style, 309–312
for the Bible, 217
CBE style, 341
endnote for frequent, 221
footnote system, 358
MLA style, 181–200
name and year system, 334–345
number system, 345–352, 353–355
numeral use, 216–217
parentheses for, 235
Intro., introd., 207
Introduction, book, bibliography form for, 278–279
Introduction, research paper, **158–163**
avoiding mistakes in, 162–163
revision of, 173
thesis statement in, 158–159
Issue number, bibliography form for periodicals, 283
Issues
in comparison topics, 24
outlining for topic discovery, 10
as writing strategy, 167
Italian titles, 224
Italics, **177**, 199, 230, **238–239**
underscoring for, 312, 313

Journalism, reference sources, 381–382
Journals
APA style for, 316
bibliography card for, 34, 37
evaluation of articles from, 104–105
indexes to, 53
MLA style for, 282–287
reliability of, 98
title capitalization, 217

Key words
in computer search for topic, 11–15
in database searches, 40
in introduction, 162, 165
listing for topic discovery, 9
for note-taking, 82
in rough outlines, 10, 82–83

Language (discipline)
MLA style, 333

periodical index for, 53
Language studies. *See also specific languages*
foreign, 223–224
name and year system, 333, 336–337
quotation marks and underlining in, 235, 240
quoting slang in, 236
reference sources, 385
Latin, reference sources, 376
Law and criminology, reference sources, 53, 382–383
Leaflets, bibliography form for, 302–303
Lectures, 74
bibliography form for, 304
Legal citations, bibliography form for, 290–291
Length, of papers, 230
Letters (of alphabet)
plural form, 214
superscript, 229
Letters (documents)
APA style for, 317
bibliography card for, 73
MLA style for, 285, 301–302
as source materials, 72–73, 317
Librarian, 29
Libraries, **27–71**
archives, 31
call numbers, 65–71
card catalog, 29, 65–71
CD-ROM facilities, **13–15**, 27, 28, 30, 36, 37–38
circulation desk, 29
computerized card catalog, **12–13**, 27, 28, 29, 36
computer search systems in, 11–15
database facilities, 30, 36, **39–41**, 296
gathering data in, 27–71
interlibrary loans, 30
librarians, 29
microforms, **31**, 35, 65, 75, 302
nonprint materials in, 31
organization, 29–31
photocopiers, 30
preliminary reading in, 28
Public Access Catalog (PAC), **12–13**, 27, 28, 29, 36
reference room, 29
reserve desk, 30
special collections, 31
stacks, 30
Library of Congress system, 48, 68, 69–71
Linguistics. *See* Language studies
Literature
abbreviations for, 211–213
conclusion of paper in, 170
MLA system, 333
paradigm for analysis of, 88
reference sources, 53, 111, 383–387
reviewing in introduction, 160
specialized indexes for, 64–65
Literature review paper, 102–103, 114–118
loc. cit., 207
Location, as writing strategy, 167
Loose-leaf collections, bibliography form for, 302
LSA style, 336

Magill's Bibliography of Literary Criticism, 48–49
Magazines
APA style for, 316

evaluation of articles from, 104–105
index to general, 52
in-text citation of, 184
MLA style for, 184, 282–287
reliability of, 98
title capitalization, 217
Magnetic tape, 292
Manuscript, final
APA style, 312–313, 319
bibliography form for, 279, 302
MLA style, 201–205
Maps, bibliography form for, 302
Margins, 230
Mass communications, reference sources, 381–382
Mathematics, 237
appendix for proofs, 205
number system, 333, 334, **349–350**
reference sources, 53, 387–388
Medical sciences
number system, 333, 334, **351–352**
reference sources, 53, 388–389
Microforms, **31**, 35, 65
bibliography form for, 302
government documents on, 75
Mimeographed material, bibliography form for, 302
MLA International Bibliography, 49–50
MLA style, **181–306**
Arabic numerals, 214–217
bibliography cards in, 33–35, 42, 44
disciplines using, 333
hyphenation, 234
in-text citation, 181–200
reference form, 184–193, 205, 265–306
sample papers in, 240–263
tense in, 155, 307–309
Works Cited, 184–193, 205, 265–306
Modern Language Association style. *See* MLA style
Monetary units, 230–231
Monographs, bibliography form for, 285, 303
Monthly Catalog of United States Government Publications, 61–62, 75
ms., mss. (Ms., Mss.), 207
Music
bibliography form for composition, 303
footnote system, 334, 363–364
reference sources, 389–390
Mythology, reference sources, 385–386

n., nn., 207
Name and year system, 333, **334–345**
Names
author. *See* Authors
capitalization of, 218
first and subsequent mentions, 231
foreign, 224
in one source quoting another, 185–186
narr., 207
Narration, as outlining method, 84
National Archives, 75
National Union Catalog: A Cumulative Author List, 48
Native Americans, reference sources, 383–384
n.d., 207, 273
Newspapers
bibliography form for, 287–289, 316
foreign, 288

indexes to, 59–60
on microfilm, 65
title capitalization, 217
New York Times, The, editions and sections, 288
New York Times Guide to Reference Materials, 46
New York Times Index, 59
no., nos., 207
Nonprint sources. *See also* Computers
APA style for, 317–318
citation omitted for, 185
in the library, 31
microforms, **31**, 35, 65, 75, 302
MLA style for, 43, 291–298
in Sources Cited, 265
Note cards, **119–44**
in drafting the paper, 154
paraphrased, 134–136
personal, 136–138
plot summary, 132–133
precis, 119, 128, **129–133**
quotation, 119, **123–128**, 134–135
summary, 119, **128–129**
technique for using, 120–123
Notes in a periodical, bibliography form for, 285
Note-taking, 81–96
avoiding plagiarism, 138–144
with computers, 121–122, 152–153
idea selection for, 107
methods, 119–144
note card techniques, 120–123
paradigms to stimulate, 87–90
with preliminary outline, 81–90
source material evaluation, 97–103
Novels, reference sources, 386
n.p., 207, 273
ns., 207
Numbered series, bibliography form for, 280–281
Numbers. *See also* Arabic numerals; Roman numerals
bullets with, 217
fractions, 200
plural form, 214
superscript, 219–220, 237–238, 358
Number systems, **345–357**
disciplines using, 333, 334, **345–347**
sample paper, 352–357
Nursing, number system, 334, **351–352**

Objective writing, 150
Official Index (to *The London Times*), 59
Online, defined, 292. *See also* Computers
Online posting, 298
op. cit., 207
Opening, of the paper. *See* Introduction, research paper
Opening page. *See* Title page
Outlines, **90–96**
decimal, 91
disciplinary approaches to, 85
dynamic order in, 94–96
in final manuscript, 203
formal, 90–96
indentation, 90–91
key words in, 10, 82–83
and paradigms, 87
preliminary, 10, 81–90
question method, 83

revision during research, 86
of sample paper, 248–250
sentence, **92–93**, 248–250
of source material, 108
standard symbols, 90–91
and thesis sentence, 96
topic, 91–92
for topic discovery, 10
using methods of development for, 84

p., pp., 207
Page numbers
APA style for, 310
bibliography form for books, 269–270, 273
bibliography form for newspapers, 287
bibliography form for periodicals, 283–284
for content endnotes page, 205
frequent, in same work, 187
nonprint sources and, 185
for outline pages, 203
with quotations, 191
for text of paper, 205, 224, 231–232
with volume number, 189–190
Works Cited page, 205
Pamphlets
bibliography form for, 303
indexes to, 60
Paper, for final draft, 232
Paperbound Books in Print, 47
Paradigms, 87–90
to advance a theory, 87
for analysis of historical events, 88–89
for a comparative study, 89–90
defined, 81, 87
for empirical research report, 318
and outlines, 87
for position papers, 88
Paragraphs
in body of paper, 168–169
revision of, 173
Paraphrases
citation for, 186
note cards, 119, 134–136
and plagiarism, 140–144
Parentheses, **235**
with year in APA style, 310–312
Past tense, 155–156, 307–309
Percentages, 232
Performing arts. *See also specific performing arts*
bibliography form for, 303–304
periodical index for, 53
Periodicals
bibliography form for, 282–287, 289, 293,
316–318
CD-ROM, 293
indexes to, 18, 52–53
InfoTrac indexing system, 13–14, 38
in-text citation of, 184
Periods, **234**
with quotation marks, 191–192
Person, first and third, 156–157
Personal experience, for topic discovery, 7
Personal note cards, 119, 136–138
Personal papers, 76. *See also* Letters (documents)
bibliography card for, 77
Persuasive purpose, 20–21
Philosophy

footnote system, 334, 361
paradigm for position papers in, 88
reference sources, 53, 390 391
Photocopiers, 30, 108
Photographs, bibliography form for, 305
Photography, periodical index for, 53
Physical education
name and year system, 334, 337–338
reference sources, 379–380
Physics
number system, 334, **350–351**
reference sources, 53, 391
Plagiarism, avoiding, 138–144
Plays, bibliography form for, 279
Plot summary, in body of research paper,
163–164
Plot summary note cards, 132–133
Poetry
bibliography form for, 279–280
paradigm for analysis of, 88
quotation of, 194–195
reference sources, 386–387
title capitalization, 217
turnover indication, 195
Poetry Explication, 49
Point of view, of author, 21
Political science
name and year system, 334, 338
paradigm for analysis of events, 89
paradigm for position papers in, 88
reference sources, 53, 111, 391–393
Position papers, paradigm for, 88
Possessive, apostrophe with, 214
Posters, bibliography form for, 302–303
Précis, defined, 110
Précis note cards, 119, 128, **129–133**
Preface
bibliography form for, 278–279
to evaluate source, 106
Preliminary outline, 81–90
Preliminary reading, 28
Preliminary thesis, 21–24
Present tense, 155, 307–309
Primary sources, 110–111
quotation from, 124–125
proc., 207
Proceedings, bibliography form for, 300
Process
as outlining method, 84
for topic development, 83–84
for topic discovery, 11
as writing strategy, 165
Programs, bibliography form for, 302–303
Pronouns, 176–177, 178–179
Proofreaders' marks, 232, inside back cover
Proofreading, 179–180
corrections and, 222–223
defined, 172
final printout, 179–180
ProQuest, 13, 38
pseud., 207
Pseudonyms, 231, 274
Psychological Abstracts, 13, 27
Psychology
APA style. *See* APA style
in-text citation, 309–312
reference form, 313–318

reference sources, 54–55, 393
pt., pts., 207
Public Access Catalog (PAC), **12–13**, 27, 28, 29, 36
Public addresses, bibliography form for, 304
Public Affairs Information Service Bulletin, 63
Publication information
    on bibliography cards, 33
    bibliography form for, 272–273
    not provided, 272–273
    in trade bibliographies, 46–48
Public Papers of the Presidents of the United States, 63
Public statutes, bibliography form for, 290–291
Published form (APA style), 312–313, 319
Publishers
    abbreviations for, 208–209, 273
    bibliography form for, 272–273
    in-text citation of, 185
Publisher's Trade List Annual, 47
Publishers Weekly, 47
Punctuation, 232–235. *See also individual punctuation marks*
    checking, 177
    of quotations, 191–193
    space after, 237
Purpose of research paper, 19–20, 149–150, 155

Queries, bibliography form for, 285
Question marks, 192–193
Questionnaires, 77–78
    bibliography card for, 77
    results in appendix, 205
Questions
    to outline ideas, 83
    for topic discovery, 10–11
    as writing strategy, 166
Quotation marks, **234–235**
    brackets with, 198–200, 234
    ellipses points with, 196–198
    for English translation, 235
    omitted with long quotation, 193–194
    with other punctuation, 191–193, 234–235
    page citations with, 191
    and plagiarism, 140–144
    with poetry, 194–195
    single, for quote within quote, 193
    single, with definition, 223, 235
    for slang, 236
    with titles, 238–239, 287
Quotation note cards, 119, **123–128**, 134–135
Quotations
    within article titles, 287
    brackets with, 234
    citation, double reference, 185–186
    in conclusions, 170
    direct, 123–128, 140–144, 186, 192
    foreign language, 223–224
    initial capital in, 141, 195–196
    long, 193–195, 229, 310–311
    of primary sources, 124–125
    punctuation of, 191–193
    of secondary sources, 125–128
    undocumented, 140

Radio program
    bibliography form for, 305–306
    as source material, 74

Readers' Guide to Periodical Literature, 13, 18, 36, 52
Reading, preliminary, 28
Read only memory (ROM), 13
Recently Published Articles, 53
Recording, record or tape, bibliography form for, 304
Reference books, bibliographies in, 45–46
Reference form. *See also individual disciplines*
    APA. *See* APA style
    CBE system, 341–342
    footnote system, 258–364
    MLA. *See* MLA style
    name and year system, 334–345
    number system, **345–352**, 356–357
Reference room, 29
Religion
    footnote system, 334, 361–362
    paradigm for position papers in, 88
    reference sources, 53, 394–395
Reports
    bibliography form for, 230, 274–275, 276, 285, 293, 305, 317
    CD-ROM, 293
    in-text citation of, 185
Reprints, of journal article, bibliography form for, 286
Reproductions, bibliography form for, 305
Republished book, bibliography form for, 280
Research journals, **8–9**, 94
Research proposals, to guide note-taking, 81–82
Reserve desk, 30
rev., 207
Review of the literature, 102–103, 114–118
Reviews, bibliography form for, 286, 317
Revision, 172, 174–177
Rhetorical modes
    for topic development, 83
    for topic discovery, 11
    in writing the paper, 163–168
Roman numerals, **235–236**
    listed, 236
    for outline pages, 203
    page numbers, 232
    for titles of persons, 235
rpt., 207
Running heads, 224, 236
Russian, reference sources, 376–377

Sample annotated bibliography, 112–114
Sample bibliography cards, 32–35, 44–46, 52, 57
Sample papers
    in APA style, 318–332
    in MLA style, 240–263
    review of the literature, 114–118
    using number system, 352–357
Scholarly books, 98
Science Citation Index (SCI), 102
Sciences. *See also individual disciplines*
    decimal outline, 91
    primary and secondary sources, 111

sec(s)., 207
Secondary sources, 110–111
    quotation from, 125–128
Select List of Publications of the National Archives and Record Service, 75

Semicolons, **233**
    with quotation marks, 192
Sentence outlines, **92–93**, 248–250
ser., 207
Series, bibliography form for, 231, 271, 280–281,
    286–287, 289
Series headings, parentheses for, 235
sess., 207
Setting, as writing strategy, 167
Sexist language, avoiding, 177–179
Shakespeare, abbreviations for, 211–212
sic, 199, 207
SilverPlatter, 13
Single quotation marks
    with definitions, 223, 235
    for quote within quote, 193
Slang, 236
Social Issues Resources Series (SIRS), 60
Social sciences. *See also individual disciplines*
    name and year system, 335–338
    primary and secondary sources, 111
Social Sciences and Humanities Index, 53
Social Sciences Citation Index (SSCI), 102
Social Sciences Index, 27, 36, 52–53
Social work
    name and year system, 334, 338
    reference sources, 395–396
Sociology
    name and year system, 334, 338
    reference sources, 53, 395–396
Solutions, in conclusion, 171
Sourcebooks, bibliography form for, 281
Source materials
    blending into writing, 181–200
    in drafting the paper, 154–155
    evaluation of, 97–103
    and narrowing the topic, 25
    nonprint. *See* Nonprint sources
    orderly search of, 28
    plagiarism, 138–144
    primary, 110–111, 124–125
    recent, 98
    reliability of, 98–99
    research journals as, 94
    responding to, 106–110
    secondary, 110–111, 125–128
    for topic discovery, 11–18
Sources Cited. *See* Works Cited (MLA style)
Spacing, 236–237, 266
Spanish
    reference sources, 377
    titles, 224
Specialized bibliographies, 48–51
Speeches, reference sources, 396
Spelling, 237
Spelling checkers, 176
st. sts., 207
St., Sts., 207
Stacks, 30
State government documents, 75, 290
States, abbreviations for, 208
Statistics, 237
    in appendix, 205
    in content endnote, 222
    in introduction, 162
Statutes, bibliography form for, 290–291
Strategies of writing, 167

Structure, as writing strategy, 167
Subject. *See* Topic
Subject cards, 66
Subject Guide to Books, 46–47
Subject Index to Psychological Abstracts, 54–55
Subjective writing, 150
Summary
    defined, 110
    in introduction, 162
    of source material information, 110
Summary note cards, 119, **128–129**
sup., 207
Superscript letters, 229
Superscript numerals, 237–238
    for content endnotes, 219–220
    in footnote system, 358
suppl., 207
Surveys, with questionnaires, 77–78
s.v., s.vv., 207

Table of contents
    book, 15–16, 106
    research paper, 238
Tables, 225–229
    in appendix, 205
    bibliography form for, 305
Tape recording, bibliography form for, 304
Television programs
    bibliography card for, 74
    bibliography form for, 299, 305–306
    as source material, 74
Telnet, 292
Tense, 155–156
    in APA style, 155, **307–309**
    in MLA style, 155, 307–309
Terminology
    key words, 10, 162
    in narrowing the topic, 25
Tests
    content endnotes describing, 221–222
    as resource material, 78–79
    results, in conclusion, 171
Textbooks
    APA style for, 311, 314–315
    MLA style for, 187–189
Theater
    footnote system, 334, 363–364
    reference sources, 53, 385, 394–395
Theology
    footnote system, 334, 361–362
    paradigms for position papers in, 88
    reference sources, 53, 394–395
Thesaurus of ERIC Descriptors, 40
Thesaurus of Psychological Index Terms, 40
Theses. *See* Dissertations
Thesis statement
    to determine relevance, 104
    final, 146–148
    in introduction, 158–159
    and outlines, 96
    preliminary, 21–24
    and preliminary outline, 85–86
    restatement of, in conclusion, 169–170
Third person, 156–157
Title cards, 68
Title of research paper, 148–149
Title of sources

on bibliography cards, 33
bibliography form for books, 270
bibliography form for newspapers, 287
bibliography form for periodicals, 283, 287
capitalization of, 217–218, 224, 281
to determine relevance, 106
foreign, 224, 281, 287
omitted, in periodical, 287
quotation marks with, 238–239
quotation within, 287
shortened in the text, 236
titles within, 287
underlined, 238–240
Title page, of research paper
in APA style, 319
in MLA style, 201–203, 247
Titles of persons, 231
foreign, 224
Roman numerals for, 235
Topic, **5–25**
comparison, 24
disciplinary, 25
discovery, 6–18
in introduction to paper, 158
narrowing, 24–25, 28
Topic outlines, 91–92
Trade bibliographies, 46–48
Trade books, 98
trans., tr., 207
Translation
of foreign titles, 281
of foreign words, 235
Translator, bibliography form for, 269, 270,
281–282
Transparency, bibliography form for, 306
ts., tss., 207
Turnover indication, 195
Twentieth Century Short Story Explicator, 49
Typescripts, bibliography form for, 302

Ulrich's International Periodicals Directory, 48
Underscoring, **238–240**
in APA style, 312, 313
book title in bibliography, 270
for emphasis, 240
of linguistic forms, 235
special words, 240
titles, 238–239
*Union List of Serials in Libraries of the United
States and Canada,* 48
Unity, in writing, 157–158
Unnumbered series, bibliography form for,
280–281
Unpublished papers
abstracts from, 316
bibliography form for, 306

VERONICA (Internet navigator), 42
Vertical File Index, 60

Video Source Book, 73
Videotapes, bibliography form for, 299, 301, 306
viz., 207
Voice, of author, 21
Voice mail, bibliography form for, 306
Vol., vols., 208
Volume number, 271–272, 282
bibliography form for books, 270, 282
bibliography form for periodicals, 283, 285
in citation, 189–190
vs., v., 208

Wall Street Journal Index, 59
*Where to Find What: A Handbook to Reference
Service,* 46
Who's Who in Philosophy, 99
Women's studies, reference sources, 396–397
Word division, 240
Word processors. *See* Computers
Words discussed, quotation marks for, 235
Working draft (APA style), 312–313, 319
Works Cited (MLA style), 184–193, 205, **265–306.**
See also Bibliographies; Bibliography form;
Reference form
alphabetization, 266
Arabic numerals with, 216–217
bibliography cards for, 31–33
book form, 268–282
endnote documentation, 220
format, 266–267
government documents, 289–291
indentation, 229
newspaper form, 287–289
in paper format, 205
periodical form, 282–287
sample format, 267
of sample papers, 246, 262–263
World Bibliography of Bibliographies, A, 46
World literature, reference sources, 387
Writing the paper, **145–180**
blending in reference materials, **181–200**
body, 163–169
with a computer, 150–153
conclusion, 169–172
drafting, 154–158
editing, 174–179
final thesis sentence, 146–148
freewriting, 9
introduction, 158–163
proofreading, 179–180
purpose in, 149–150
revision, 172–174
strategies, 167
title, 148–149

Zoology
CBE system, 341–342
footnote system, 334
periodical index for, 53